Graph Transformation for Software Engineers

Reiko Heckel • Gabriele Taentzer

Graph Transformation for Software Engineers

With Applications to Model-Based
Development and Domain-Specific
Language Engineering

 Springer

Reiko Heckel
University of Leicester
Leicester, UK

Gabriele Taentzer
Philipps-Universität Marburg
Marburg, Germany

ISBN 978-3-030-43918-7   ISBN 978-3-030-43916-3   (eBook)
https://doi.org/10.1007/978-3-030-43916-3

This Springer imprint is published by the registered company Springer Nature Switzerland AG
The registered company address is: Gewerbestrasse 11, 6330 Cham, Switzerland

Forewords

Abstraction and modelling are two fundamental conceptual cornerstones of informatics. They are absolutely key to software engineering. Engineers need abstraction to dominate complexity of software design, implementation, deployment and operation. They need precise models to formalise abstractions and reason about them. Graphs are a powerful and general notation that can formally model software structures. They can express snapshots of complex relations among entities of different kinds. Through graph rewriting rules, one can formalise how complex structures evolve over time. By formally analysing models, both statically and dynamically, engineers can verify that the system under design behaves as expected, prior to implementing it and perhaps discovering later that it does not, thus wasting huge investments.

This book fills a much needed gap in the literature. It is the first comprehensive and systematic presentation of graph-based modelling and applications to the practice of software engineering. It can be of use in teaching, to present the foundations of software modelling and verification. It is also a reference book for researchers who are active in software modelling. I have personally often founded my research on graph transformation: in my early years, to formalise data structures and formally analyse them through parsing; more recently, to formalise and analyse spatio-temporal systems (like smart buildings) and their dynamics. I fully share the authors' point that graph transformations are an extremely powerful and tremendously useful tool that can empower software engineers and help them to develop better and higher quality software. This book is a decisive step in this direction.

Carlo Ghezzi

Modern software development is a complex and messy business. Requirements are often incomplete. New development uses complex existing libraries, tools and components that can fail. Multiple development teams proceed on different schedules, making it difficult to assure that their artefacts will "talk to each other" as intended.

I believe that keys to building quality software systems are abstraction and automation. A graph-based approach is a universally applicable and very powerful approach to modelling software at the level of abstraction where its key properties can be represented. Graph rewriting approaches can then support a variety of formal analyses, from requirements completion via property verification to the analysis of product lines. They also support "what if" analysis, allowing developers to determine the impact of their proposed change before investing in fully implementing it. Therefore, it comes as little surprise that graph-based approaches form a basis for many model-driven modelling and development techniques.

I strongly recommend this book to researchers who want to learn about software modelling, and to any senior undergraduate and graduate students who want to be equipped with foundational knowledge and tools to be able to build high-quality, safe software systems.

Marsha Chechik

This book is a pleasant and big surprise. The software engineering community needed such a book, but so far missed experts dedicating their effort to writing it. Graphs and graph transformations play a key role in conceiving, designing, and implementing complex software systems, but they work behind the scenes, so their importance and that of their theoretical foundations is often underestimated. Software engineering is full of models and graphical notations that help experts to tackle very diverse problems, but oftentimes they are defined only informally and lack rigour and precision. Most of these models (can) have a graph-based (abstract) syntax and semantics: this is where the foundations of graphs and graph transformations enter the scene, and this is where a book like this is key.

While methodologies for software architecture design, configuration and version management, and deployment employ diverse graph-based notations, practitioners tend to underestimate the importance of formally defining these models in order to manipulate and transform them in a systematic and sound way. Practitioners and experts in foundations risk ignoring each other; however they represent two sides of the same coin: sound engineering benefits hugely from formal theories, and formal approaches find concrete applications in software engineering. For example, the termination and confluence of a graph transformation system can avoid some tedious problems, while conflicting rules can lead to non-deterministic transformations. These problems can be understood and addressed based on formal foundations. There is a big gap between problems and available theoretical solutions and this book provides an excellent reference guide to help researchers, educators, students, and practitioners to address and solve a large diversity of relevant problems.

Many different software engineering artefacts, including design models, deployment topologies, and development processes, that can be rendered as graphs and manipulated through graph transformations, could benefit from the mature theory developed over the last thirty years. Many solutions have been presented at conferences and workshops, but the necessary coherent collection of their applications to software engineering problems was missing. In the era of systematic literature reviews, this book moves a relevant step ahead, and provides a unique entry point to the main theories and their applications in the context of software engineering, written by two key members of the graph transformation community. Gabi and Reiko did a great job in collecting, harmonising, and presenting all the different findings and solutions in this book. We particularly appreciate the mix of rigour and formality along with proper context and concrete examples.

We are sure that this book will quickly become an essential reference for those interested in the formal underpinnings of graph-based software engineering notations and artefacts, including those interested in exploiting the results presented here to develop original solutions. This book also gives a good overview of the body of work Gabi and Reiko have carried out over recent decades, and we are happy they have decided to present it in this form.

Gregor Engels, Luciano Baresi and Mauro Pezzé

I believe it was in 2010, during the International Conference on Graph Transformation held at the University of Twente, that I expressed the view that the field had matured enough to create both the need to consolidate the state of affairs and the means to fulfil that need. The need, because so many insights had been gained over the years, both about the modelling power of graph transformation and how this can be used in software engineering; insights, however, that were scattered over many papers and in danger of being lost for being insufficiently visible. The means to fulfil the need existed, because the body of knowledge was, by then, sufficiently extensive to merit a monograph where all this could be written up in a unified way.

This is not to suggest that the step of consolidation had not been taken before, successfully. In 1997, the "Handbook of Graph Grammars and Computing by Graph Transformation" appeared, in three volumes, collecting the views and achievements of a large cross-section of the research at the time, doing full justice to its diversity. In 2006, the "Fundamentals of Algebraic Graph Transformation" saw the light, presenting a thorough, unified overview of the theoretical underpinnings, taking into account the (then) most recent advances. Neither of these, however, attempted to convey the message to the software engineering community at large, that solution approaches for some of the pervading problems can be found in graph transformation, while also exposing enough of that field to give newcomers an entrance.

To my delight, I was approached immediately after ICGT 2010 by Gabriele Taentzer and Reiko Heckel, who told me they had concrete plans for just such a monograph as I had imagined. Now these are two scientists thoroughly embedded in the field, who like hardly any others have both an excellent grasp of the theory and an unsurpassed knack for applications in software engineering. In other words, they were the perfect people for the job.

Time has passed since then. For scientists, it is really very hard to find time to write a monograph with sufficient scope, when the day-to-day pressure to also keep contributing to smaller, shorter-term, more urgent activities almost always takes priority. I was very happy to be invited to the project, yet eventually realised that I was unable to find the time to do my bit, and so had to drop out as a co-author. As we all know, however, urgency does not equal importance. I think it is supremely important that a book such as this one has eventually been finished, and I applaud Reiko's and Gabi's perseverance.

The book that lies before you is everything one could wish it to be. Part I presents the necessary background on a sufficiently formal level to be accessible to anyone with a moderate knowledge of discrete mathematics, while at the same time illustrating all presented concepts using recurring, small-scale examples. More importantly still, Part II presents example after example of how all this can indeed be used across the board in all phases of software engineering, from requirements gathering through analysis, design and specification to testing. Not surprisingly, given the close proximity of graphs to (UML-style) models, special attention is paid to concepts of model-driven engineering.

It is a sign of the broad experience of the authors that each and every chapter of Part II is actually based on published research, and ends with extensive pointers to the research literature. Though the book is not meant as a survey, and makes no claims to completeness, it does provide a very good entrance.

Given these many qualities, the potential target audience of the book is diverse. It can be used in academic teaching as the basis for any of a number of courses, complemented with projects to be carried out in any of the topics of Part II; it can act as a great source of reference; but most importantly, it can serve as a means by which researchers and (research-minded) practitioners in software engineering can get to know graph transformation. You can read the book either way: from the more theoretical end, by working your way through Part I and then browsing Part II, or from the more practical side, delving into one of the topics in Part II and where necessary looking up the formal details in Part I. All in all, there is little doubt in my mind that in years to come, this book will be seen to stand out as an authoritative, go-to source of information, indispensable on any (physical or digital) bookshelf.

Arend Rensink

Preface

The digital transformation of society affects all aspects of human life, offering new opportunities but also creating challenges and risks. More tasks will be automated using software. Workflows and business processes are becoming increasingly data driven. Engineering such systems correctly, efficiently and fairly is one of the most critical problems facing us today.

Graphs are of great help when coping with the complexity of software systems. They make explicit the designs of component architectures, process flows and data structures, and provide visual and yet formal representations to analyse them. In order to remain useful and relevant, many real-world software systems are continuously adapted and improved. Their graph-based models need to be transformed to plan or reflect this evolution.

In the Internet of Things, for example, mobile and embedded devices are networked to enable new kinds of applications. We use terms such as "smart home", "smart grid", or "smart city" to describe the highly complex, heterogeneous and adaptive application networks that interact with both human users and their physical environment. The topologies of such networks can be represented by graphs consisting of nodes and edges, where each node represents a device or an application component and each edge models a logical or physical network link. Smart applications are able to adapt their network's topology according to changing needs or context. *Graph transformation systems* are uniquely suited to modelling such adaptations in a direct and visual way. Based on a formal and executable semantics we can validate their operation through simulations and formally analyse their properties.

Today's real-world software systems, built using a variety of languages and technologies and being often distributed, need to be able to evolve in order to remain relevant while allowing integration with other systems. To deal with the resulting heterogeneity and longevity, *model-based software development* lifts essential software engineering tasks to a higher level of abstraction, where we use models to represent the functionality and architecture of applications in a technology-independent, domain-oriented way. This requires concepts and tools that can bridge the gap between models and implementations through code generation, reverse engineering and automated testing.

At the same time, software is becoming more and more data centric, relying on and manipulating structured and unstructured data from a variety of sources. Graphs provide a simple and flexible model for integrating and linking data across formats and applications. They are at the heart of high-level and scalable data representations, such as graph databases designed to store large heterogeneous data sets, using graph-based technologies for efficient querying and transformation.

Model-based engineering employs a variety of modelling languages and techniques targeting application domains, such as Web or mobile applications and cyber-physical or embedded systems. Such *domain-specific modelling languages* require tool support for editing, simulation, compilation, analysis, and version management, which, in order to be produced efficiently and correctly, should be based on definitions of the languages' syntax and semantics. Graphs and graph transformations provide a general mechanism to define and represent models and to specify their manipulation through editing operations, model refactoring, simulation, translation, consistency checking, and synchronisation across languages. They provide a technical (solution) space for domain-specific language engineering, to support the definition and implementation of modelling languages.

Purpose of This Book

Research on graph transformation dates back over 50 years. Yet there is a lack of accessible texts suitable for explaining the most commonly used concepts, notations, techniques and applications without focusing on one particular mathematical representation or implementation approach. To provide a general, widely accessible introduction, the first part of this book will present the foundations of the area in a precise but largely informal way, providing an overview of popular graph transformation concepts, notations and techniques. In the second part, a range of applications of both model-based software engineering and domain-specific language engineering are presented. The variety of applications presented demonstrates how broadly graphs and graph transformations can be used to model, analyse and implement complex systems and languages.

Readers of This Book

We expect this book to be useful and accessible to both current and potential users of graph transformation in the area of software engineering. If you are interested in the use of graph-based modelling and transformation in applications to your own field, this should be the book for you whether you are in academia or industry, had prior exposure to the area or are a complete novice.

While we hope to contribute to the standardisation of notation and presentation, the book is not intended to cover the current state of research. Rather than being comprehensive, we aim to cover work that is both established and stable, inevitably omitting important original results for the sake of presentation.

Although not written as a course book, most parts are suitable for students undertaking postgraduate study at either advanced MSc or PhD level.

Web Site

Further resources, including exercises (with solutions on request) and slides of lectures based on the book, are available at

> `www.graph-transformation-for-software-engineers.org`

with related links and information about updates and corrections.

Acknowledgements

The idea of writing this book was first raised in 2001 by Mauro Pezzé. A first meeting in the afternoon sun during the second workshop on "Graph Transformation and Visual Modelling Techniques" in Crete confirmed our interest in the general concept, but produced little more than an outline before we all went back to our daily business.

Several years went past before the plan was revived by a group including Luciano Baresi, Gregor Engels, Hartmut Ehrig, Mauro Pezzé and the authors of this book, leading to a first collection of draft chapters at various degrees of completion, somewhat heterogeneous in content and style. Unfortunately, activities fizzled out again: probably a case of too many cooks.

When, after several more years, the current authors revisited the concept, Arend Rensink expressed an interest in a book that could provide a comprehensive introduction to graph transformation, and agreed to join the project. With his involvement, we were able to develop most of Part I. Our different backgrounds allowed us to view the same concepts from different points of view and, in fruitful and passionate discussions, to develop a broader, more balanced view of the material now presented in Part I. When, due to changing priorities, Arend was no longer able to contribute, we continued to develop Part II in the same spirit.

We are especially grateful to Ronan Nugent at Springer for his encouragement and exceptional patience. At annual meetings during ETAPS throughout the long years of this project, he provided us with invaluable guidance, helping us to shape and position the book in the best possible way.

The entire book was proofread by Jens Kosiol and, in parts, by Anthony Anjorin, Berthold Hoffmann and Steffen Vaupel, as well as students attending the module "Formal Methods in Software Engineering" in 2018/19 at the University of Marburg, Germany.

We would like to thank our friends and colleagues who inspired, helped, and motivated us to complete this project. Foremost among them, our friends and mentors Hartmut Ehrig and Michael Löwe are sadly no longer with us. Hartmut was the unstoppable driving force behind the double-pushout approach to graph transformation and a keen promoter of its application to software engineering. Michael was instrumental in restarting the software-engineering-related research during our formative years in Berlin based on his single-pushout approach to graph transformation, which played a big part in directing our own interests.

This book is important to us and, we believe, to the wider graph transformation community in giving access to the wealth of ideas and concepts developed in over 50 years of research on graph transformation and its application to software engineering. As such, it is the first systematic and comprehensive presentation of this range of material directed at an audience beyond the core graph transformation community. This would not have been possible without Arend's contributions and critical feedback, for which we are especially grateful.

Reiko Heckel and Gabriele Taentzer

Contents

Part II Graph Transformation in Software Engineering

Part I

Foundations of Graph Transformation

Graphs represent a wide variety of structures in computer science and beyond. In software engineering, it is common to use graphs to model system structures such as software architectures, class and object structures, and control or process flow. As software systems evolve over time, these graphs may also change. If graphs are used to present object or data structures at run time, for example, graph changes model system behaviour. Graph transformation specifies graph changes in a rule-based way, using graph pattern matching to determine where rules can be applied and then replacing the matched part of the graph as specified by the rule.

This part gives a broad overview of the basic and advanced concepts for modelling with graphs and graph transformations. We analyse the commonalities and differences between these concepts and distill the results into feature-based taxonomies providing a high-level orientation. These taxonomies are not meant to be normative, but should establish an overview of available concepts and explain how they are related. In the selection of the concepts considered we lean towards the gluing approach to graph transformation. This approach is defined comprehensively in [85] and supported by tools such as AGG [98, 12], Groove [107], Henshin [139], eMoflon [18, 93] and ViaTra [285]. The presentation of graph transformation concepts in this book is largely informal, sometimes semi-formal, incorporating examples for illustration. Part I of the book is organised as follows:

- Chapter 1 surveys different notions of graphs as they are used throughout software engineering. While all graphs consist of vertices and edges, there are many variations, such as simple graphs and multigraphs, with directed or undirected edges, binary edges or hyper-edges, using vertex and edge labels, types, or additional attributes at graph elements.
- Chapter 2 first introduces the basic ideas of graph transformation, contrasting the gluing and embedding approaches. Then, the gluing approach is explained in more detail. An atomic graph change is specified by a transformation rule in *if–then* form. Such a rule is applied to a graph by finding an occurrence of its left-hand side and replacing that occurrence by a new copy of its right-hand side. To control rule applications, application conditions are presented. The chapter concludes by presenting advanced features of graph transformation required by applications in software engineering.
- Chapter 3 considers graph transformations beyond individual rules. After identifying three main use cases, explicit control mechanisms for rule applications are presented, leading to transactional graph transformation units.
- Chapter 4 gives an overview of useful analysis techniques for graph transformation systems. Starting with the properties of interest, we map them to the techniques and constructions available to check these properties. Then, the most popular techniques are presented in detail and illustrated with examples from applications in software engineering.

All chapters finish with a summary and pointers to further reading.

1

Graphs for Modelling and Specification

Graphs are used to model entities and their relations in domains as diverse as chemistry, biology, physics, the social sciences, linguistics and, in particular, computer science. For example, communication networks, data structures, control and data flows of computations are represented by graphs. In software engineering, graphs are used as notations and formal models supporting systematic approaches to key activities such as requirements capture, software design, the modelling and analysis of software architectures, and the definition and implementation of domain-specific languages.

For example, software architectures can be represented by graphs whose nodes and edges model components and their dependencies. Such graphs are useful for performing analysis and optimisation tasks, for example by investigating graph properties such as connectedness to determine if each component is reachable from every other one. Optimising an architecture modelled as a graph, for example to remove redundant connections, involves changing the graph. A systematic approach to changing graphs is their rule-based manipulation. This is the subject of the field of graph transformation.

Below, we will discuss examples of graphs representing different kinds of information. We start with a broad range of such examples before considering structures in software engineering. This will help us to establish an intuitive understanding of graphs and their use for modelling. In the rest of this chapter, we introduce basic and advanced features of graphs and discuss them in the context of these examples.

Example 1.1 (Euler walks). The first graph ever considered is shown in Fig. 1.1. It was created by the mathematician Leonhard Euler as an abstraction of the map of the city of Königsberg [42]. The graph shows as vertices the main landmasses of the city and as edges the bridges spanning the arms of the river running through it. The problem Euler was trying to solve was, whether or not it was possible to walk through the city using each of the bridges exactly once, arriving back at the origin of the walk.

© Springer Nature Switzerland AG 2020
R. Heckel, G. Taentzer, *Graph Transformation for Software Engineers*,
https://doi.org/10.1007/978-3-030-43916-3_1

It turns out that such an Euler walk does not exist in this case, and Euler's theorem states that such a walk is possible if and only if every vertex in the graph has an even number of edges attached to it.

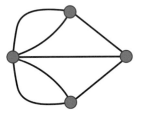

Fig. 1.1. The seven bridges of Königsberg[1]

□

Example 1.2 (chemical valence graphs). Another well-known example of graphs comes from chemistry. Fig. 1.2 shows a *valence* graph of the dichlorine heptoxide molecule. The vertices stand for atoms of a certain chemical element, in this example seven labelled "O" for oxygen and two labelled "Cl" for chlorine. The edges represent bonding between atoms: essentially, each edge models a single bond induced by a saturated valency.

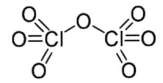

Fig. 1.2. Valence graph of the dichlorine heptoxide molecule[2]

□

Example 1.3 (food web). A mouse eats plants and is a delicacy for a snake, which has to hide so as not to be caught by a kite. Such food chains occur in all ecosystems. Since they are highly interconnected, they actually form a food web. A sample food web graph is depicted in Fig. 1.3. It contains several food chains, all starting with green plants and ending with some carnivore.

□

Example 1.4 (London Tube map). When travelling by underground in London, a Tube map helps us with finding out which line to take and where to change lines. A section of the London Tube map is shown in Fig. 1.4. It can be interpreted as a graph in which each station forms a vertex, and each connection by each line forms an edge. As we see in the map, two stations may

---

[1] From en.wikipedia.org/wiki/Eulerianpath.
[2] From en.wikipedia.org/wiki/Valence_(chemistry).

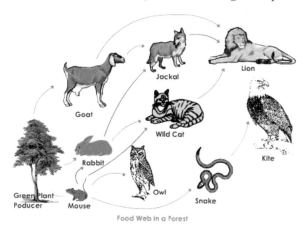

Fig. 1.3. A food web graph[3]

be connected by several lines: for instance, Earl's Court and South Kensington (bottom left) are connected by two lines, coloured blue and green. In the graph of stations and connections, Earl's Court and South Kensington would be vertices and the connections would become two parallel edges labelled by different colours. Once we have represented the Tube map as a graph structure, it can be used to find the path with the least number of stops between two given stations, maybe combined with the minimum number of changes. Hence, it can be used to provide travel suggestions.

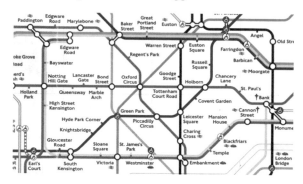

Fig. 1.4. Section of the London Tube map[4]

□

Example 1.5 (Voice-over-IP network). To model a peer-to-peer architecture, we can use graphs with peers represented by vertices and connections between peers represented by edges. Originally, the Skype IP telephony application stored user and connectivity information in decentralised form [117], i.e. without

---

[3] See the food web graph at `biology.tutorvista.com/ecology/food-web.html`.
[4] See the London Tube map at `https://tfl.gov.uk/maps/track/tube`.

the use of a central infrastructure. Skype allows registered users to make voice-over-IP (VoIP) calls and send messages to other users. A small example of a VoIP network is shown in Fig. 1.5. User activities cause frequent changes in VoIP networks. Hence, this example deals with highly dynamic graphs that are transformed to reflect ongoing network reconfiguration.

Fig. 1.5. A small voice-over-IP network

☐

Example 1.6 (visualisation of software package dependencies). Graphs are often used to represent dependency structures of software modules. The graph in Fig. 1.6 shows dependencies between software packages of a Web application written in Java. Vertices represent packages and edges show package dependencies; each edge is labelled by a number which stands for the number of references causing a dependency. The shading of a vertex also conveys information: internal, application-specific packages are shown in black, whereas the grey boxes correspond to external packages that are referenced by the internal ones.

To better understand the information illustrated, we shall explain the graph in Fig. 1.6 in more detail. A dependency graph can be used to calculate each package's resilience to change by computing its instability metric I. This is calculated as $I = Ce/(Ce + Ca)$, with Ce and Ca being the efferent and afferent couplings of the package. The afferent coupling of a package denotes the number of classes in other packages that depend upon classes within this package, while the efferent coupling is the number of classes in other packages that the classes in this package depend upon. The instability metric I ranges from 0 to 1, with $I = 0$ indicating a completely stable package and $I = 1$ indicating a completely unstable package. For instance, the dependency graph in Fig. 1.6 has two unstable packages, `application` and `test`, with $I = 1$, and two rather stable packages, `daos` ($I = 0.3$) and `entities` ($I = 0.2$). ☐

Example 1.7 (visualisation of data structures). During the development of a software system, the design of its data structures is a crucial task. The visualisation of sample structures can help to get a clear idea of what to develop. Fig. 1.7 (top) shows a list of tasks as a doubly linked list. Each list entry contains two links: one to the previous and one to the next entry. If an entry is

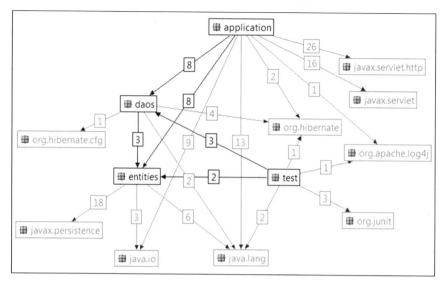

Fig. 1.6. Software package dependency graph

the first or last one, its predecessor or successor, respectively, is a specifically designated entry not holding data and links, to terminate traversal. While the adding and removing of list entries requires more change actions than in singly linked lists, these actions can be realised in a more uniform way, since the first and last entries do not have to be handled differently.

The bottom half of Fig. 1.7 shows a corresponding graph with type information. List entries are Tasks, storing task names in the attribute details. Links are represented as edges, distinguished by types. The list itself is represented by a List vertex pointing to its first and last entries by specifically typed outgoing first and last edges. The list entries point to the next and previous elements using next and prev edges, except for the first and the last entry. To complete this structure, the doubly linked list could be made circular by inserting next and prev edges between the first and the last list entry as well.

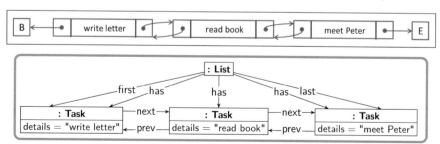

Fig. 1.7. Schema (top) and graph representation (bottom) of a doubly linked list

Another graph representation of this sample list annotates edges with numbers to order tasks. Hence, edges are annotated by the indices of their adjacent list elements. The corresponding graph representation of the sample list is shown in Fig. 1.8. When changing such a list representation, we have to ensure that the edge annotations remain consistent, i.e. their numbers still represent indices of list elements. □

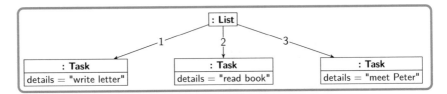

Fig. 1.8. Graph representation of list using edge labels

Having considered a variety of examples, we will see that their graph representations can also differ considerably. Graph transformations have been proposed for a range of graph models to cater for the requirements of different applications. In the following, we give an overview of the core features of graphs and how they are related to each other. Thereafter, these features are explained in detail.

1.1 Feature Model for Graphs

Following work on model transformation approaches by Czarnecki and Helsen in [68], we present the results of a domain analysis [66] of the variabilities and commonalities of graph models used in graph transformation. Figure 1.9 shows a feature diagram defining a taxonomy of the relevant notions of graphs. Each vertex of the feature model shows a point of variation. The legend in Fig. 1.9 explains which combinations of features are possible and which are mandatory.

All graph variants have a basic graph structure, in which there are three independent variation points. First of all, there is a choice between simple graphs, which allow at most one edge between any pair of vertices, and multigraphs, which support any number of such edges. Furthermore, rather than sticking to binary edges with source and target vertices only, one may opt for hypergraphs, in which the edges have arbitrary (though fixed) numbers of attachments. Finally, edges may also be undirected.

As the next feature group, graphs may be decorated. We distinguish three levels of decoration. In the most basic case, one may use unstructured labels, which are just atoms associated with vertices or edges that provide additional information and may arbitrarily assigned. Types can be considered as more elaborate forms of labels. Graph elements that are assigned types are expected to keep them throughout their lifetime. Following the object-oriented paradigm, types may be abstract, may have subtypes, may have multiplicities or

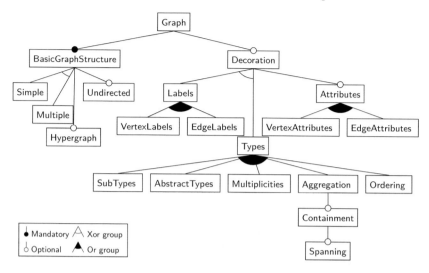

Fig. 1.9. Feature model for graphs

may include aggregations, more specifically containments, often forming spanning trees for given graphs. Moreover, collection types may be ordered. Finally, attributes can be used to equip vertices and edges with additional data values, for instance integers or strings. Types and attributes play much the same role as they do in object-oriented modelling.

In the rest of this chapter, the graph features mentioned are presented in more detail and illustrated by examples in combination with selected variants.

1.2 Basic Graph Structures

In this section, we recall and discuss several different basic graph models as they occur in the literature (e.g. [252, 204]). In all variants, a graph G is defined by a pair $G = (V, E)$ consisting of vertex set V and an edge set E. We use variables v, w to denote typical elements of V. One difference between the variants lies in how the edges in E are represented.

For a uniform representation, we need to introduce some notation:

- $\mathcal{P}(X) = \{Y | Y \subseteq X\}$ stands for the powerset of X, i.e. the set of all subsets of X. So, if $X = \{1, 2\}$ then $\mathcal{P}(X)$ consists of $\emptyset$, $\{1\}$, $\{2\}$ and $\{1, 2\}$. Furthermore, $\mathcal{P}_2(X)$ denotes the subset of $\mathcal{P}(X)$ containing only sets of size 2.
- $\mathcal{M}(X)$ stands for the set of *multisets* over X. A multiset (sometimes called a *bag*) is a subset of X in which every element may occur an arbitrary number of times. It can be considered as a function $X \to \mathbb{N}$. So, for $X = \{1, 2\}$ as above, $\mathcal{M}(X)$ is an infinite set containing, for instance,

[], [1], [1, 1], [1, 1, 1], [1, 2], [1, 2, 2], ... Furthermore $\mathcal{M}_2(X)$ denotes the subset of $\mathcal{M}(X)$ containing only multisets of size 2.

1.2.1 Simple Graphs

In a simple directed graph, the edge set E consists of pairs of vertices denoting their start and end points. Considering, for example, the food web graph in Fig. 1.3, each vertex represents an animal or a green plant producer, while an edge (v, w) from v to w means that v is eaten by w. A food chain is represented by a sequence of adjacent edges $(v_0, v_1), (v_1, v_2), \ldots$ or, more succinctly, by the induced sequence of vertices $v_0, v_1, v_2, \ldots$; for example, GreenPlantProducer, Rabbit, Jackal, Lion.

This kind of graph is often used for analysing graph-theoretic properties, such as connectedness or shortest paths. It does not allow multiple edges in the same direction between the same two vertices, since edges do not have their own identities but are represented by pairs of vertices.

In undirected graphs, on the other hand, we do not designate one end point of an edge as its source and the other as its target; instead, the two end points are symmetric. Rather than pairs, we may use two-element multisets $[v, w] = [w, v]$ to represent edges of this kind. (Note that we need multisets rather than ordinary sets to account for loops, i.e. edges that lead from a vertex to itself. In graph theory [73], loops are very often disregarded, in which case two-element sets $\{v, w\}$ with $v \neq w$ are sufficient.) Alternatively, an undirected edge may be equated to a pair of oppositely directed edges (hence, $[v, w] = \{(v, w), (w, v)\}$); again, loops are special because they are their own opposites.

An example of a simple undirected graph was given in the voice-over-IP telephony net in Fig. 1.5: here, edges represent connection lines between peers. Considering the undirected edges as bidirected ones is also meaningful if edges are thought of as bidirectional communication channels; for example, Gabi can talk to Reiko and vice versa.

1.2.2 Multigraphs

In contrast to simple graphs, multigraphs allow parallel edges between the same vertices. They also come in undirected and directed variants. An example of a directed multigraph was given in Fig. 1.6, where every edge stands for a separate dependency of its source package on its target package. (In the graph as shown, the parallel edges have been combined for the sake of simplicity; the numbers on the combined edges represent how many parallel edges have been wrapped into them.) Examples of undirected multigraphs include the map of Königsberg in Fig. 1.1 (which may alternatively be thought of as a bidirected graph, where once more each undirected edge stands for two oppositely directed ones), the valence graph in Fig. 1.2 and the London Tube map in Fig. 1.4.

Formally, the edge set E of a directed multigraph does not consist of pairs of vertices; rather, it is a set of (otherwise unspecified) objects with two functions $src, tgt : E \to V$ that connect them to their source and target vertices. Alternatively, as shown by the package dependency graph in Fig. 1.6, we may interpret E as a multiset in $\mathcal{M}(V \times V)$, rather than a set in $\mathcal{P}(V \times V)$ as for simple graphs. For the undirected variant, rather than two distinct functions src, tgt one can use a single *attachment function* $att : E \to \mathcal{M}_2(V)$ (again simplifying the codomain to $\mathcal{P}_2(V)$ if the graph has no loops).

Example 1.8 (VoIP net as multigraph). Every simple graph can also be considered as a multigraph but not vice versa, as parallel edges are possible in multigraphs but not in simple graphs. The peer-to-peer net in Fig. 1.5 can be represented as a directed multigraph with vertex and edge sets as follows: $V = \{\text{Peter}, \text{Gabi}, \text{Reiko}\}$ and $E = \{\text{ag}, \text{gr}\}$ with $src(\text{ag}) = \text{Peter}, tgt(\text{ag}) = \text{Gabi}, src(\text{gr}) = \text{Gabi}$ and $tgt(\text{gr}) = \text{Reiko}$.   □

1.2.3 Summary

To summarise our discussion of simple graphs and multigraphs, we present Table 1.1 that shows the basic graph structure in two dimensions. The idea is that graphs become more expressive (i.e. have more structure) as one goes to the right and down in this table.

Table 1.1. Edge structure of graphs ($\mathcal{M}$ denotes a multiset, $\mathcal{P}$ denotes a powerset)

	Undirected, no loops	Undirected, with loops	Directed
Simple graphs	$E \subseteq \mathcal{P}_2(V)$	$E \subseteq \mathcal{M}_2(V)$	$E \subseteq V \times V$
Alternatively	$E \in \mathcal{P}(\mathcal{P}_2(V))$	$E \in \mathcal{P}(\mathcal{M}_2(V))$	$E \in \mathcal{P}(V \times V)$
Multigraphs	$att : E \to \mathcal{P}_2(V)$	$att : E \to \mathcal{M}_2(V)$	$src, tar : E \to V$
Alternatively	$E \in \mathcal{M}(\mathcal{P}_2(V))$	$E \in \mathcal{M}(\mathcal{M}_2(V))$	$E \in \mathcal{M}(V \times V)$

The previous examples of formally defined graphs show that vertices and edges have to be identified to formally refer to them. This is often done by names. Some of the example names may suggest that they can be used to store additional information. However, these names are not formally part of the graph; they are just used to refer to its structure. The following note states how vertex and edge identifiers should be understood throughout the book.

> **Note 1.1: Vertex and edge identifiers.** It is essential to realise that, whatever the graph model, for the purposes of graph transformation the choice of vertex and edge sets V and E is considered to be irrelevant. It is the *structure* of the graph (possibly supplemented with additional information) that is important: whether graph elements are represented by numbers, coordinates in a grid, database keys or any other encoding

does not make any difference. Technically, we will always consider graphs with the same structure and additional information to be equivalent. In example graphs, it is often convenient to use strings as vertex and edge identifiers so as to be able to refer to them. Such an identifier should *not* be understood as the *identity* of a graph element. In other words, vertex and edge identifiers are not actually parts of the graph: they are just there for readability and ease of reference.

1.3 Decorations: Labels, Types and Attributes

Using graphs for modelling often requires their vertices and edges to be annotated with additional information such as names, colours, numbers or truth values. As pointed out above, vertex and edge identifiers are not the right place to store additional information. Instead, such data can be represented in the form of *decorations*. We recognise three kinds of decoration: simple labels, types and attributes. Below, we introduce them and illustrate their differences using the example graphs seen earlier in this chapter.

1.3.1 Labelled Graphs

The simplest way of equipping a graph with additional information is labelling. In their basic form, labels are just elements of a given set, which are associated with the vertices and edges. Labels may change during the lifetime of a graph, but no computations can be carried out over simple labels as they come without any further structure or operations.

An example of a labelled graph is the food web graph in Fig. 1.3, where vertices are labelled by species names and pictures. The London Tube map can also be considered as a labelled graph, where vertices are labelled by station names and other symbols, and edges are labelled by colours (representing metro lines). The diagram in Fig. 1.6 can be formalised in two different ways: Edge annotations describe how many dependencies exist between two software packages. Hence, the chosen representation can be considered as a compact form for a directed multigraph, and the edge annotations show numbers of parallel edges. Edge labels are not really adequate here, however, since changes in the graph could require computations, for example when increasing the number of dependencies represented by a given edge by one.

Example 1.9 (VoIP network as labelled graph). We can see the VoIP network shown in Fig. 1.5 as a labelled graph whose vertices are labelled while its edges are not. Each network node is equipped with the name of its user. The resulting labelled graph is shown in Fig. 1.10.   □

Fig. 1.10. VoIP network as labelled graph

Vertex and edge labels are typically taken from different domains, as they model different kinds of information. Essentially, labelling is added to the graph model through (possibly partial) functions $lab_V : V \to L_V$ and $lab_E : E \to L_E$, where L_V and L_E are the sets of vertex and edge labels, respectively. For some of the basic graph variants discussed above, this representation may be simplified: for instance, if the edge-labelling function is total, then directed simple graph edges may instead be taken directly from $V \times V \times L_E$ (rather than from $V \times V$ as before), in which case lab_E is implicitly given by projection to the third component.

Labelling works best if there is no more than a single piece of information per graph element. In principle, this can always be "faked" by letting the elements of L_V or L_E be records or sequences rather than single values; however, such representations quickly become cumbersome to handle.

1.3.2 Typed Graphs

Types are useful for classifying individual elements. Typed graphs distinguish different kinds of vertices and edges by associating them with predefined types. In contrast to labels, the types of graph elements do not change throughout their lifetime.

For example, if we want to use graphs as snapshots of a dynamic system, all snapshot graphs should be typed over the same set of types. Similarly, a number of graphs may show individual instances of a general concept, such as different VoIP network graphs, all made up of peer nodes and connection edges. Hence, we assume that the typing information can be encapsulated in a separate graph, the so-called *type graph*, where each type is represented exactly once. In the following, we consider VoIP nets as typed instance graphs. Type and instance graphs form a pattern that is shared with many other domains, such as classes and objects, database schemata and states, and XML schemata and documents.

Compared with simple labels, the difference is twofold: (1) the vertex and edge labels L_V and L_E (now called vertex and edge types) are combined into a type graph, which imposes additional constraints on their usage, as we will see below; and (2) in contrast to simple labels, the types of graph elements are immutable. As will be shown below, an instance graph conforms to a type graph if there is a mapping of the instance graph to the type graph that preserves the graph structure.

In order to model the VoIP net in Fig. 1.5 as a typed graph, a simple choice would be to consider a single vertex type for peers and a single edge type for connections. However, from the study of VoIP networks in [117] we know that peers are distinguished into client and super nodes. This is in response to the fact that computers connected to the network provide different levels of resources such as computational power, storage capabilities and connection bandwidth. Peers equipped with sufficient resources can be super nodes, thus assuming management functions, while simultaneously continuing to serve as clients. Super nodes form an *overlay network* among themselves, while clients can only connect to super nodes acting as their servers. The conceptual abstraction introduced by this description, classifying individual objects into Client and Super nodes, can be captured in the type graph. Moreover, we can distinguish the users from the application components (client or server nodes) they are interacting with.

Instead, at the object level, we could represent aspects of concrete network states such as illustrated in Fig. 1.5. We indicate three nodes, serving users Peter, Gabi and Reiko. Gabi's application, running on a desktop, is modelled as a Super node and is connected to both Peter's and Reiko's Client nodes, running on laptops.

Example 1.10 (VoIP network as typed graph). The graph G in Fig. 1.11 (top) represents our running example of a VoIP system as a typed graph. In this graph, vertices s: Super, c1, c2: Client and peter, gabi, reiko: User represent participants. Each vertex is represented by a name followed by the vertex type.

Note that such "user names" are used only to refer to User vertices in diagrammatic representations and textual explanations; they do not represent user names in the context of the VoIP application (see also Note 1.1). We will represent application-level user names using attributes later.

Edges represent connections between network nodes and their relationships with users: they are typed as link and usr edges, respectively. Hence, vertex and edge types in this example represent the corresponding real-world concepts. They are arranged in the type graph shown in the bottom of Fig. 1.11.   □

Summarising, the relation between concepts and their occurrences in snapshots is formally captured by the notion of *typed graphs*: a fixed *type graph TG* represents the type (concept) level and its *instance graphs* represent individual snapshots. In Section 1.5, we consider further typing concepts that stem from object-oriented modelling; for example, subtyping and multiplicities.

1.3.3 Graphs with Attributes

Attributes can be used to decorate graph elements with further information, typically from data sets with algebraic operations, for which values can be computed by evaluating expressions. Attributes can have integer, string or

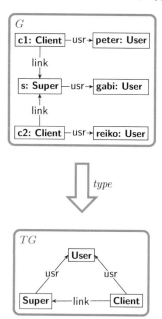

Fig. 1.11. Type and instance graph of the VoIP network

Boolean values, for example, with all the usual operations such as addition (for numbers), concatenation (for strings) or Boolean connectors. As the diagram in Fig. 1.9 shows, attributes are an optional feature that can be used independently of label or type decorations; however, the combination of types and attributes is by far the most common one, and the one mainly used in the remainder of the book.

To allow more than one attribute per graph element, attributes are equipped with names. In a typed setting, the type graph also specifies the attribute names and value domains; i.e. each vertex type may be further specified by a list of its attributes. This means that all instances of a given type are attributed in the same way. A Super node in a VoIP net, for example, may be further specified by a name, computational power, storage capabilities and connection bandwidth. In some cases, attributes are used to uniquely define vertices, essentially acting like database keys, such as in the case of user IDs or registration numbers.

Example 1.11 (VoIP network as typed attributed graph). In Fig. 1.10, we used simple labels to encode user names; in Example 1.9, user names only served the presentation but where not formally part of the graph. The simple-label solution means that every possible name has to be in the set of labels, and that name changes, such as those which may happen in the case of marriage, cannot be computed by concatenating two existing names. Instead, it is better to keep names as separate from the graph structure; i.e. using attributes. We also use an attribute at Super nodes to count the number of clients attached.

While the instance graph G holds concrete attribute values, the type graph TG just specifies attribute names and types such as Integer and String. Edges are not attributed at all.   □

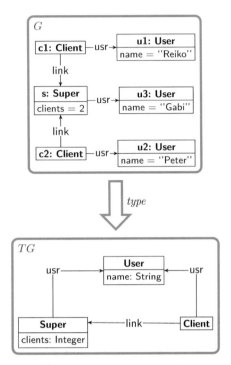

Fig. 1.12. Type and instance graphs of the attributed VoIP model

Example 1.12 (data structures as typed attributed graphs). Figure 1.7 shows a graph representing a doubly linked list. It can be considered as a typed attributed graph. The type graph, depicted in Fig. 1.13, can be easily deduced from the visual notation. It shows two vertex types List and Task, which are connected by edge types first, last, next and prev. (Note that next and prev are two edge types although only one arrow is shown in Fig. 1.7.) In addition, the graph is attributed, meaning that a Task vertex has an attribute details of type String. Edges are not attributed.   □

A straightforward way to encode attributes is to equip graphs with a set of functions, one for each attribute name, assigning to every graph element of the corresponding type a value from the appropriate data domain. (Compare, for example, the definition of attributed graphs in [292].) To allow attribute values to be undefined (which is sometimes useful), attribute functions may be chosen to be partial. For VoIP networks, attribution functions clients : $V \rightarrow$ Integer and name : $V \rightarrow$ String would be needed. However, these functions should only be defined on vertices of the correct type (Super and User, respectively).

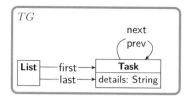

Fig. 1.13. Type graph for doubly linked lists

Another approach to graph attribution, which supports typed graphs more naturally, is to represent all data values from a required data domain D as vertices of a special kind, so-called *data vertices*. Graph vertices are linked to data vertices by *attribute edges* i.e. edges running from graph vertices to data vertices. They come in addition to the "normal" graph edges running between graph vertices. A graph element can change its attribute value by redirecting the corresponding attribute edge accordingly (or replacing it by a new one pointing to the new value). Note that, in contrast to the first attribution concept, this representation allows several values for one and the same attribute name at a chosen graph element. (See [136, 85] for more details of this attribution concept.)

A consequence of the second approach is that instance graphs conceptually have an infinite number of data vertices, in order to reflect the values of data domains such as natural numbers and strings: each value becomes a separate data vertex. But since the data domains remain static throughout graph transformations, there is no need to explicitly represent all data vertices: it suffices to include only those that are used as targets of data edges. [5]

Example 1.13 (VoIP network as typed attributed graph with data vertices). Following the second encoding discussed above, Fig. 1.14 shows an example of an attributed graph with a detailed representation of the attribute edges and the attribute values used. The typed attributed graph G in Fig. 1.12 is shown in detail. Attribute edges of types clients and name are represented explicitly and point to concrete data vertices (shown as ellipses). The (infinitely many) unused attribute vertices of the data domains Integer and String are not shown. □

1.3.4 Summary

We have considered graph decorations that may be pure labels, types or attributes. Table 1.2 shows the different forms of decoration that graph elements can carry, and their properties. The multiplicity * of attributes refers to the number of attributes a graph element can carry, normally distinguished by

---

[5] To represent edge attributes in the same way, we would need another type of data edge, running *from normal edges* to data vertices. Though this is conceptually unproblematic, we will not use edge attributes in this book.

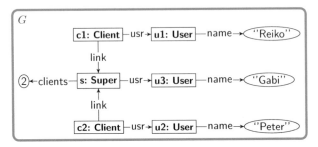

Fig. 1.14. Instance graph of the VoIP model with attributes as data vertices

names, and also refers to the fact that in some approaches a single attribute can have multiple values.

Table 1.2. Decorations on graphs

	Multiplicity	Modifiable?	Representation
Labels	0..1	Yes	Functions $V \to L_V$ and $E \to L_E$
Types	1	No	Mapping from instance graph G to type graph TG
Attributes	* (named)	Yes	Functions $V \to D$
Alternatively			Named edges from graph vertices of V to data vertices of D

1.4 Hypergraphs

The edge sets of simple graphs define binary relations over vertices. Though this is sufficient for most applications, there are cases which require n-ary relations for any $n \geq 0$. Interesting examples are visual diagram specifications [214], where visual objects may be strongly interconnected by spatial relationships, and term rewriting, where operations with n parameters can be considered as $n + 1$-ary relations [147]. This generalisation gives rise to so-called *hypergraphs*.

Example 1.14 (Nassi–Shneiderman diagrams as hypergraphs). Diagrams may be considered as assemblies of visual objects with spatial relationships such as *above* and *contains* between them. This structure can be described by a graph. Figure 1.15 shows an example of a so-called Nassi–Shneiderman diagram. This kind of diagram was introduced to visually represent structured programs. Since visual objects in Nassi–Shneiderman diagrams may have more than two attachment points, with the actual number dependent on their type, hypergraphs are well suited to representing their spatial relationships.

Each visual object is represented by a hyperedge of type *text, while* or *cond*, corresponding to, respectively, textual statements, while loops and if–then–else conditions. Dependent on its type, each hyperedge may have four or even six attachment points represented by untyped vertices. For instance, the left-hand side of Fig. 1.15 shows a Nassi–Shneiderman diagram; the corresponding hypergraph (without attributes) is shown to its right.   □

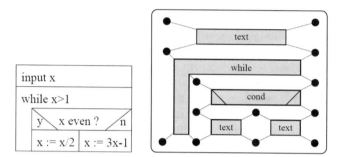

Fig. 1.15. Nassi–Shneiderman diagram with its hypergraph representation[6]

Thus, *hyperedges* can be used to model *n*-ary relations over vertices. Instead of pairs $E \subseteq V \times V$ as for simple graphs, hyperedges can be modelled as lists of vertices, i.e. $E \subseteq V^*$. The vertices in the list are called *tentacles* or *attachment points*, based on the visual notation for hyperedges as illustrated in Fig. 1.15. Regarding the possible range of attachments, hyperedges can be defined with any number of attachment points, which may be zero, one, two or more. Since the attachment points form a list, they are ordered and can be distinguished, just like the source and target of (directed) binary edges. Moreover, similarly to binary loops, hyperedges may be attached to the same vertex more than once. However, there is also a variant where all attachments points of a hyperedge are mutually distinct [74]. Like simple graphs or multigraphs, hypergraphs may be typed and attributed. Hyperedges of the same type are assumed to have the same number of attachment points. The hypergraph in Fig. 1.15 is well typed: for instance, all *text* hyperedges have four tentacles.

In the explanation above, hypergraphs were defined as an extension of directed simple graphs. They may equally well be defined as an extension of undirected graphs, or of multigraphs. Table 1.3 presents all the possible edge structures for hypergraphs, where $\mathcal{P}_f(V)$ denotes the set of all finite subsets V, and $\mathcal{M}_f(V)$ the set of all finite multisets over V. This is entirely analogous to (but more general than) Table 1.1 for binary edges, except that we have left out the case of hyperedges without loop.

Yet another possible representation of multi-hypergraphs is obtained by representing the hyperedges themselves as "relational" vertices, and the ten-

---

[6] Figures taken from [11].

Table 1.3. Edge structure of hypergraphs ($\mathcal{M}$ denotes a multiset, $\mathcal{P}$ denotes a powerset)

	Undirected	Directed
Simple hypergraphs	$E \subseteq \mathcal{M}_f(V)$	$E \subseteq V^*$
Alternatively	$E \in \mathcal{P}(\mathcal{M}_f(V))$	$E \in \mathcal{P}_f(V^*)$
Multi-hypergraphs	$att : E \to \mathcal{M}_f(V)$	$att : E \to V^*$
Alternatively	$E \in \mathcal{M}(\mathcal{M}_f(V))$	$E \in \mathcal{M}(V^*)$

tacles as directed binary edges from those new, relational vertices to the pre-existing, ordinary vertices. This gives rise to a directed (binary) simple graph, of a kind that is called *bipartite*, meaning that it has two classes of vertices and all edges go from one class to the other. For the example in Fig. 1.15, for instance, the grey labelled areas can be regarded as relational vertices, and the black circles as ordinary vertices. Though this has the advantage of a simpler, more regular structure, the typing discipline is weaker in this representation: for instance, the type of a (relational) vertex no longer fixes its number of attachment points.

Many of the concepts and constructions in this book are applicable across a wide range of different graph models. We restrict ourselves to binary edges, because they are the model most widely used.

1.5 Advanced Graph Features

Our considerations so far have made it clear that graphs are a general data structure that can be used in many different ways. Looking more closely at software engineering, graphs have been used especially to formally underpin object-oriented artefacts. For this purpose, plain type graphs as seen so far are often not enough. Therefore, we discuss here several kinds of advanced features: type inheritance, multiplicities, whole–part relationships and collections.

1.5.1 Inheritance and Multiplicities

Attributed type graphs form a basis to define object-oriented structures but lack certain features, such as inheritance and multiplicities. To start with the former, in object-oriented modelling, class inheritance is introduced to allow a form of reuse of model parts. Similarly, vertex types may inherit edge and attribute types from supertypes, leading to more compact type graphs and the possibility of reuse (which will be exploited in the next chapter). Moreover, if vertex types are introduced just to define a meaningful inheritance relation, it could make sense to make some or all supertypes *abstract*, meaning that they are not allowed to be instantiated.

If an edge types in a given type graph specifies a specific form of relationship between, such as "has a" or "consists of", it is worthwhile to consider additional concepts for type graphs to formulate further constraints on instance graphs. Object-oriented concepts such as inheritance and multiplicities can be integrated straightforwardly: inheritance can be modelled by additional edges of a certain type, and multiplicities can decorate the source and target ends of edges. A multiplicity 0..1 at an edge type expresses that there is at most one edge of that type, while a multiplicity 1..* demands a non-empty set of edges. A multiplicity * is no actual constraint but clarifies the fact that any number of instances is allowed. The following example shows the use of inheritance, abstract vertex types and multiplicities.

Example 1.15 (advanced type graph for VoIP nets with instance graph). The attributed type graph shown before in Fig. 1.12 can be further refined (as in Fig. 1.16) by introducing an abstract supertype of Super and Client nodes, called *Node*. As this node is abstract, its type name is depicted in italics. Inheritance edges are depicted with hollow arrowheads. Both subtypes have an outgoing usr edge to User which can be lifted to *Node*. Moreover, instance graphs must not have vertices of type *Node*, so this type should be abstract. Multiplicities determine that a *Node* always belongs to a User, who, vice versa, does not need to be connected to some *Node*. While Super nodes may have arbitrary many Clients, a Client always has to have a connection to one such Super node. Moreover, Super nodes may be connected by overlay edges, labelled ovl.   □

It should be noted that multiplicities can alternatively be expressed by so-called *graph constraints* (introduced in the next chapter). We will see in addition that whole–part relationships, which are introduced next, can also be expressed by graph constraints.

1.5.2 Whole–Part Relationships and Spanning Trees

The feature model in Fig. 1.9 shows three levels of "whole–part relationships": *aggregation*, *composition* and *spanning trees*. While an aggregation merely ensures that elements are not in a cyclic relationship, compositions are more restrictive and require in addition that each element has to be in exactly one container.

The strongest form of whole–part relationship is a *spanning tree*, which is a designated subgraph in the form of a tree (an acyclic structure without vertex sharing and with a single root) connecting all its vertices. A slightly weaker form is a *spanning forest*, which is not restricted to a single root element. In the following, we consider object-oriented models as used in the Eclipse Modeling Framework (EMF) [92] more closely, as EMF is a widely used technology for defining software models. An EMF model has a distinct containment structure defining a spanning tree (or sometimes a spanning forest) of the underlying graph structure. Two conditions have to be true for containment structures: each node has to be contained in some other node, except for root nodes,

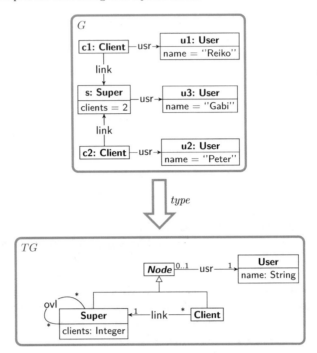

Fig. 1.16. VoIP network with subtypes and multiplicities

and a node must not (transitively) contain itself. In [41], it was shown that typed attributed graphs with inheritance and containment are able to formally underpin EMF models.

Example 1.16 (graph structure of EMF models). The EMF model in Fig. 1.17 specifies a simplified variant of a *statechart*, a particular kind of model of system behaviour based on hierarchical automata. A StateMachine consists of state vertices which may be PseudoStates used to indicate initial states and States that may be further refined to FinalStates. Since the behaviour of a State may be specified by an automaton, it may contain vertices and Transitions. Containment edges are indicated by black diamonds in Fig. 1.17. Together with the requirement that a model must always contain a single StateMachine vertex, this definition of containment relations allows and enforces spanning trees with StateMachine instances as roots.

Figure 1.18 shows a simple statechart as an instance model in three different views. While the diagrammatic view on the right shows the statechart in its concrete syntax, its containment structure is shown on the left in a tree-like representation. This view shows that StateMachine contains a State "Phone", which contains some states and transitions. State "Active" is further refined and contains again states and transitions. At the bottom right, a so-called

---
[7] Figure taken from [41].

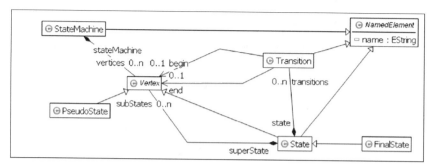

Fig. 1.17. EMF model for defining simplified statecharts[7]

properties view is shown, depicting the details of the transition running from State "DialTone" to State "Idle". A section of the underlying graph structure is shown in Fig. 1.19. This shows States "Active" and "Idle" contained in an overall "StateMachine" container, as well as State "Dial Tone", a substate of "Active", and a Transition "caller hangs up" running from "Dial Tone" to "Idle". Note that the complete underlying graph structure can be deduced from the different EMF views.   □

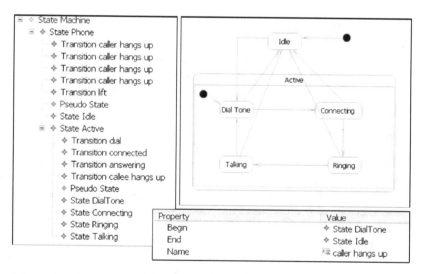

Fig. 1.18. EMF instance model of a statechart modelling a simple phone[8]

Another example with a prominent spanning-tree structure are XML documents represented as graphs. In this case, XML elements are represented as vertices and child elements are connected by containment edges forming a spanning tree. In addition, cross-references (called IDREFs) are common in XML: in a graph-based view, those correspond to additional edges. This graph

---

[8] Figure taken from [41].

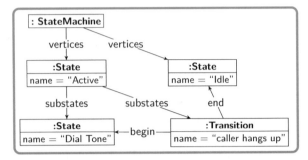

Fig. 1.19. Partial graph structure of the statechart in Fig. 1.18

representation can simplify the navigation of XML structures in XSLT (used to transform XML documents) or XQUERY (which supports querying XML documents). In [272], a graph-based approach to transform XML documents is presented, discussing the differences between XSLT and graph transformation.

Equipping a graph with a spanning tree enables the efficient implementation and traversal of vertices. Hence, the spanning tree can be used as a kind of backbone for complex graph operations (see e.g. [288, 27]). But we also have to take into account the fact that there is an additional structure to be managed. In particular, when the graph is modified, we have to ensure that the spanning tree is not destroyed. While the containment relation in the statechart example above defines a very natural spanning tree, there is not always such a natural candidate. In class diagrams, for example, the containment of classes in packages has to compete with other class relations, such as all kinds of associations that are usually considered as more relevant.

Summary of whole–part relationships

Table 1.4 shows the different forms of whole–part relationships and their defining properties. The *multiplicity* refers to the number of containers elements can be related to, for example, they can be aggregated into any number of containers, but must be composed into exactly one. Considering the *structure*, both kinds of relationships are locally acyclic, i.e. for a specific aggregation or composition relation in the type graph, such as Vertices in the state machine metamodel, the edges of this type in any instance graph form an acyclic graph. A spanning tree uses composition, so is subject to the same constraints, but requires the union of all composition edges to be acyclic and demands that all vertices (except the root) have a container.

As already pointed out for multiplicities, structure constraints can also be specified by graph constraints (which are introduced in the next chapter). When graphs are modified, any constraints imposed on the graph structure have to be preserved (by imposing restrictions on the transformations that are allowed) or enforced (by manipulating the graph after the transformation). As an example of the latter, composition relationships imply a dependency

Table 1.4. Whole–part relationships in type graphs

	Multiplicity	Structure
Aggregation	*	Acyclic
Composition	1	Acyclic, no sharing
Spanning tree	1	Acyclic, no sharing, single root

between the container and the contained element: if the container is removed, the contained element is deleted as well.

1.5.3 Ordering and Collections

Although graphs are a very flexible data structure, they are not particularly well suited to representing ordered structures such as lists. In a direct graph representation, list elements could be represented by vertices that are sequenced by connecting edges. Although quite flexible with respect to adding and removing elements, this solution does not support elements being shared among lists. To circumvent this problem, "slot" vertices have to be introduced defining available slots in lists that can be filled by elements. Besides yielding a rather complex graph structure, this solution also requires additional conditions to be checked as, for example, that slots are filled in a sensible way. Another possibility is to attribute edges with indices. This solution is good in the sense that it supports the sharing of elements between lists. But indices require updating whenever list elements are added or removed. Therefore, so-called *list edges* were proposed in [216]. A list edge generalises a simple edge by allowing a sequence of vertices as a target.

Example 1.17 (representation of lists). Figure 1.20 shows a graph that represents three lists for sports events, more precisely, skating events (taken from [216]). While the left two *Event* lists share three *Participants*, the third list is empty. The order in a list corresponds to the starting order at the event. All three *Event* vertices are sources of a list edge each named *parts*. The 1500 m event has four participants, shown in order from top to bottom, while the 5 km event has three participants, namely Kramer, Tuitert and Davis (in that order).   □

Ordering (of list elements) can also be seen in the context of *collections*. Collections are ad hoc groups of elements; in graphs they are modelled by outgoing edges of a given type, with multiplicity * or 1..*, from one and the same vertex. The collection then consists of all vertices that the edges point to. In the popular modelling languages UML and EMF, collections can vary in two dimensions: they can, on the one hand, be *singular* or *multiple*, meaning that the same element may occur just once or multiple times in the same collection and, on the other hand, they can be *ordered* or *unordered*. All four

---

[9] Figure taken from [216].

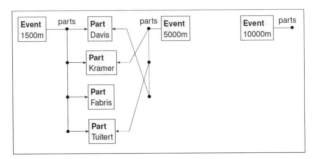

Fig. 1.20. Representation of three lists using list edges[9]

combinations give rise to meaningful kinds of collections. Table 1.5 lists them, as well as the graph features necessary to support them conveniently.

Table 1.5. Kinds of collection and their representation

	Singular	Multiple
Unordered	Sets	Bags (= multisets)
Graph structure	Simple edges	Multi-edges
Ordered	Ordered sets	Sequences (= lists)
Graph structure	Simple list edges	List multi-edges

1.6 Summary and Further Reading

In this chapter, we have given an overview of some basic and advanced features of graphs, illustrated them by examples and pointed out the advantages of the different variants. In most of the remainder of this book, we will concentrate on a single variant only, which supports a combination of features.

> **Note 1.2: Graph choice.** To represent and transform structures as they occur in software engineering, we use *typed attributed multigraphs with inheritance, abstract types and multiplicities* throughout this book.

1.6.1 Formal Definitions of Graphs

While we have considered the various kinds of graphs in a semi-formal way, their formal definitions can be found in the literature. Simple graphs as they are typically used to formulate graph algorithms, are defined in, for example, [204, 73]. In [252], the main approaches to graph transformation are presented, each coming with its definition of a graph. Node replacement grammars, for example, are based on simple graphs with node labels. In hypergraph replacement, hyperedges are labelled but nodes are not. The algebraic approaches to graph transformation commonly use multigraphs as transformation of multigraphs can be well defined in an algebraic way. Since multiple edges between two nodes are allowed, the union of two graphs, for example, which is one of the basic constructions, can be computed by the componentwise unions of their sets of nodes and edges.

1.6.2 Formal Considerations of Graph Attribution

Attribute functions are especially suitable for untyped graphs, such as in the graph optimisation problems considered in [292], including graph clustering. In the context of graph transformation, attribution functions were used in [234] in combination with graph labelling: essentially, vertex labels are semi-structured entities that may be used to contain attribute values.

Note that, in contrast to attribute functions, attribute edges ending at data vertices allow several values for one and the same attribute name at a chosen graph element. This attribution concept is well suited to algebraic graph transformation approaches. As with multigraphs, attributed graphs following this attribution concept allow the componentwise union of attribute edges. See [136, 85] for more details of this attribution concept. Although we restrict ourselves to node attributes throughout this book, this attribution concept supports edge attributes as well.

Orejas [227] proposed symbolic graphs whose labels are variables which come with a set of logical formulas that constrain their possible values.

2

Graph Transformation Concepts

When software systems evolve, their model-level representations have to evolve with them to maintain consistency. A program change, for example, may induce a change to its control flow graph. The application of a design pattern may result in a change to the class structure of a software component. A new requirement may introduce a change to the associated analysis model. Since these models are based on graphs, this raises the need for a systematic specification, implementation and analysis of graph manipulations.

Graph changes in software engineering are mostly *local*, i.e. a small part of the graph is changed while the rest remains the same. However, these changes often extend beyond individual nodes or edges to involve more complex graph patterns. The refactoring of a class structure, for example, may require several classes, attributes, methods and references to be modified. This means that, considering a class model before and after refactoring, a potentially complex pattern may have been replaced. Hence, for specifying graph manipulations we need the ability to specify the replacement of *graph patterns*.

The range of notations and techniques supporting the systematic manipulation of graphs using pattern-based rules is collectively referred to as *graph transformation* [252]. A change in a graph is achieved by the creation and deletion (addition and removal) of graph elements. A *graph transformation rule* specifies these changes with the context required to relate them to the remainder of the graph and any additional conditions for the application. To understand the basic ideas of rule-based graph transformation, let us start with a simple example.

Example 2.1 (transformation, gluing approach). Figure 2.1 gives an example of graph manipulation in the context of dynamic VoIP networks: the state displayed at the bottom left changes as a result of Reiko shutting down his laptop, thus disconnecting his client from Gabi's super node. This change is described more generally by the rule consisting of the connected graphs at the top of the figure, which shows a generic super node and client disconnecting.

© Springer Nature Switzerland AG 2020
R. Heckel, G. Taentzer, *Graph Transformation for Software Engineers*,
https://doi.org/10.1007/978-3-030-43916-3_2

The difference between the rule and the transformation is twofold. First, the rule does not mention unnecessary context, but only those nodes that are needed for the change to take place. In our case, Peter's node was deemed irrelevant to the disconnection of Reiko's from Gabi's node. Second, the rule also abstracts from the concrete identity of the objects in the states. For example, the same rule could now be used to disconnect Peter's node. This exemplifies the second basic idea of graph transformation: the use of rules to specify state transformations. □

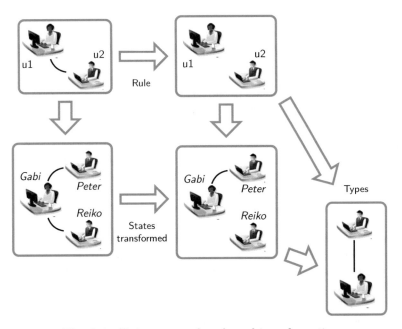

Fig. 2.1. Gluing approach, rule and transformation

This example demonstrates the principles that hold true in all graph transformation approaches:

- A graph rule specifies the conditions under which a graph transformation can take place and the actions that should be performed in that transformation. In the above example, only an edge was deleted; it is assumed that this edge runs between two network nodes that exist and are preserved.
- Each such rule consists of a left-hand side, specifying the situation before the change, and a right-hand side, corresponding to the situation after the change. Applying the rule, the context outside the area matched by the rule's left-hand side is not changed. In our example, Peter's node and its connection to Gabi's node are not effected.

We distinguish two fundamentally different approaches to graph transformation, which we will refer to as *gluing* and *embedding*. They differ in the mechanism used to combine the right-hand side of the rule with the context left over from the given graph after deletion of the matched left-hand side. In the gluing approach, the new graph is formed by gluing the right-hand side to the context along a common subgraph. This principle was illustrated in Example 2.1 above. In the embedding approach, on the other hand, the new graph is formed by a disjoint union, with new edges created to connect the right-hand side with the rest of the graph. This is illustrated by the following example.

Example 2.2 (example transformation, embedding approach). Figure 2.2 shows an example transformation in the embedding approach. The rule in question creates a new server node; it has an associated embedding relation which states that this new server should be connected to all existing servers. Note that the left-hand side of the rule is empty, meaning that this rule is always applicable (there is nothing to be matched).   □

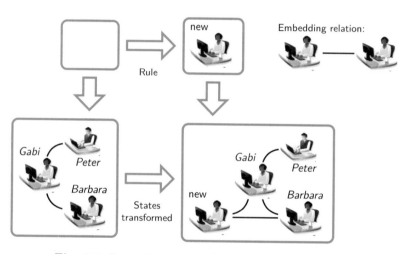

Fig. 2.2. Embedding approach, rule and transformation

More abstractly, in the embedding approach, the transformation starts by finding a match of the left-hand side L in the graph, as indicated by the left graph in the bottom row of Fig. 2.3. The matched part is deleted from the graph; adjacent edges of deleted vertices are deleted as well. This leaves the so-called context graph (depicted by a grey ring), which is unchanged. Subsequently, a copy of the right-hand side R is added to that context graph. At this point, the question is how to connect R with the context graph. Just putting them side by side without any connections, in other words taking their disjoint union, is usually not the intention of the developer. Therefore, the embedding approach supports the definition of an *embedding relation* between vertices of R and of the context graph. This relation is defined in the form "If a context vertex with label x is present and connected by an e-edge to vertex y, then delete the *e*-edge and replace it by an *f*-edge to vertex z in R." Hence, the application of this relation results in additional edges connecting the two graphs, as illustrated at the bottom right of Fig. 2.3. While a rule in the embedding

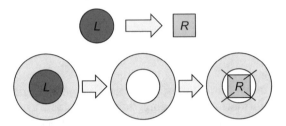

Fig. 2.3. Schematic view of the embedding approach to graph transformation

approach consists of two graphs L and R plus the embedding relation, the gluing approach does not require an embedding relation but instead relies on a so-called *gluing graph* shared between the left- and right-hand sides of a rule. Figure 2.4 gives a schematic view of the gluing approach. Once more, the red part (of the left-hand side) denotes the graph elements to be deleted while the green part (at the right-hand side) denotes new graph elements to be inserted. This time, however, the left- and right-hand sides contain a common gluing graph, so that the developer can use it to specify exactly how the deleted and created elements are connected to the context graph. After a match of the left-hand side (including the gluing graph) has been found, all graph parts matched by the left-hand side, but not by the gluing graph, are deleted, while graph elements in the match of the gluing graph are preserved. They form the required graph part that is needed to insert new graph elements as specified by R. No additional embedding relation is needed here. An example was given in Fig. 2.1. With this basic understanding of graph transformation at hand, we

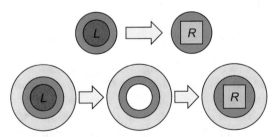

Fig. 2.4. Schematic view of the gluing approach to graph transformation

now consider the relevant graph transformation concepts. We present another feature model to get an overview of the core features of graph transformations and to understand how they are related. Then the gluing approach to graph transformation is explained in detail.

2.1 Feature Model for Graph Transformation Concepts

As we did for the features of graphs, we analyse the domain of graph transformation approaches according to the commonalities and variabilities of concepts. Figure 2.5 shows a feature diagram defining a taxonomy for graph transformation concepts. As before in Fig. 1.9, this feature model is not meant to be normative but is intended to establish an overview of the available graph transformation concepts and explain how they are interrelated.

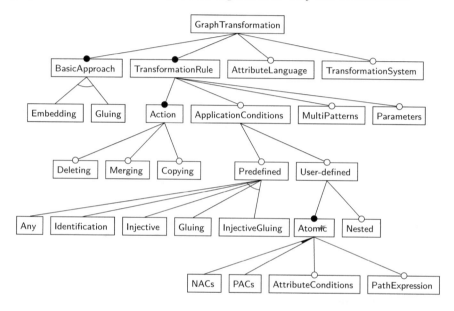

Fig. 2.5. Feature model for graph transformation concepts

As stated at the beginning of this chapter, we understand graph transformation to be rule-based. Given a basic approach, i.e. gluing or embedding (see above), the main point of variability is the concept of a transformation rule. The structure of transformation rules and the way they are applied to graphs can vary greatly. All rules have in common that they are able to check the availability of certain patterns during the process of matching.

Note 2.1: Pattern-based rewriting. Graph transformation is pattern-based: a rule is applied by checking for the existence (and non-existence, in the case of negative conditions) of graph patterns specified in its left-hand side, and replacing an occurrence of this pattern by a copy of the right-hand side.

Replacing the left-hand side pattern by the right-hand side pattern can be broken down into basic actions.

Note 2.2: Basic actions. Two basic actions are used to change graphs: the *create* action is able to add new graph elements; the *delete* action can be seen as the inverse of creation. A combination of deletion and creation can be used to specify *replacement*. In the case of attributed graphs, attribute values can also be deleted, added and changed, just like graph elements.

Creation is the one basic action that is shared by all graph transformation approaches; therefore it is not a point of variability, and so does not occur in Fig. 2.5. Deleting rules, however, are not always possible. Hence, this feature occurs in this feature model. More advanced rule actions include **merging** and **copying** of graph elements. These operations could be seen as inverse to each other, but this is not entirely so: merging two vertices automatically unifies their sets of adjacent edges, while copying a vertex copies all adjacent edges, hence first merging and then copying will generally result in more edges.

In addition, rules can have **parameters** to exchange references to graph elements and attribute values with each other and the environment. This is analogous to the parameter lists of functions and procedures in programming languages.

An important aspect of a rule are its **application conditions**, which determine exactly when and where the rule may be applied in a given host graph. Some application conditions are **predefined**, meaning that they can be selected from a set of standard conditions to hold for single rules or for the whole transformation system; others are **user-defined**, meaning that they have to be specified by the user on a rule-by-rule basis.

Predefined application conditions typically represent generic restrictions on the way in which rules may be matched. A well-known restriction is **injectivity**, meaning that the rule pattern must be structurally equal to the matched subgraph. In contrast, non-injective matches can map distinct rule elements to one and the same graph element. This can help to keep the rule set more concise: if a rule performs an action involving two graph elements that may be the same, in the case of injective matching we need two rules to cover both cases, whereas with non-injective matching, they can be condensed into one rule. For a more extensive discussion of injectivity and the other global application conditions, see Section 2.3.

User-defined application conditions can be positive or negative (**PACs** and **NACs** for short); these conditions test for the existence and non-existence, respectively, of specific graph patterns. In addition, dedicated **attribute conditions** may be used to further constrain attribute values in the matched part of the graph. Furthermore, application conditions may contain path expressions requiring or forbidding not only single edges but also paths of edges. These so-called atomic conditions may be generalised into **nested conditions**, allowing one to equip a condition with a condition again.

Rules may include **multipatterns** that may be matched arbitrarily often, including not at all. Multipatterns allow one to specify concisely the manipulation of repetitive and/or optional graph structures.

Another point of variability is the way in which the manipulation of attributes is integrated into the transformation rules. In Fig. 2.5 this is called the **attribute language**. In the simplest case, the graphs being transformed have no attributes at all; however, as seen in Section 1.3, it is common for a graph formalism to offer at least basic data types as attributes. In that case, the attribute language determines which attribute operations may be performed and what attribute constraints can be formulated within rules.

Finally, the application of transformation rules may be restricted by external control structures defined in **transformation systems**. These are discussed in more detail in Chapter 3.

In the remainder of this chapter, we discuss most of the features of Fig. 2.5 in more detail. With respect to the basic transformation approaches (embedding versus gluing), we concentrate on the gluing approach. Though we recognise the advantages of embedding, our choice is motivated by the simplicity of gluing. We will show how we can emulate the embedding approach using multipatterns.

2.2 Rules and Transformations

Focussing on the gluing approach to graph transformation, we will describe in detail how a rule is specified and how it is applied to a given graph. We will investigate simple rule applications first before progressing to more advanced graph transformation concepts.

Following the idea that a rule generalises transformations, a rule's left-hand side has two roles. Firstly, it has to describe the graph elements directly affected by the transformation with their immediate context such as, for example, the source and target nodes of edges to be deleted. This means that the left-hand-side is part of the rule's specification of the effect of a transformation. Secondly, the left hand side has to restrict the rule's applicability to situations in which we want a transformation to happen, i.e. it is acting as a precondition.

The difference between the left-hand side and the right-hand side of a rule specifies the actions to be performed. All elements which occur in the left-hand side only are deleted while elements that occur in the right-hand side only have their copy added to the graph. The elements which are in both sides of a rule have to be present in the given graph and are preserved. Differences between the left- and right-hand sides in the values of corresponding attributes indicate changes to these values. They are usually described by assignments to the right-hand side occurrences of these attributes using attribute expressions evaluated at the time of the application.

Example 2.3 (introductory example of a graph transformation). Figure 2.6 shows a detailed graph representation of the transformation shown in Fig. 2.1. The additional details concern the clients count in the Super node and the name attributes in the User nodes. Note that all graphs, both in the rule and in the concrete transformation, conform to the type graph of Fig. 1.16.

In the rule, generalisation is achieved by focusing on the relevant subgraph of the given graph IN and observing its changes in the derived graph OUT. The context graph (in terms of Fig. 2.4) is not shown explicitly but can be deduced from the rule by identifying all elements that occur both in the left- and the right-hand side. Since this particular rule does not add graph elements, its gluing graph is equal to the right-hand side without the assignment to the clients attribute whose update is realised by the deletion of the link to the old value and the creation of a link to the new value. We abstract from concrete attribute values, replacing, for example, clients = 2 in graph IN by clients = n, and clients = 1 in OUT by clients = n-1.   □

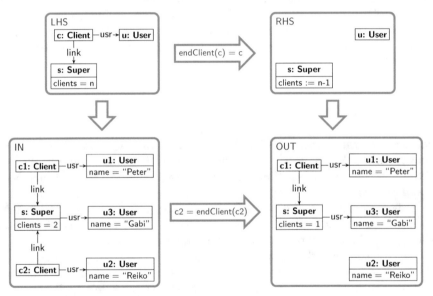

Fig. 2.6. From state transformations to rules: graph representation (LHS: left-hand side, RHS: right-hand side

2.2.1 Elementary Rules

A rule combines a number of checks and actions that should be executed together. In this sense it is similar to an operation or a method in programming. To be able to refer to these checks and actions abstractly, a rule has a signature consisting of a rule name and a list of formal parameters. A formal parameter name corresponds to either a node identity or an attribute value which is used in the left- or right-hand side. For instance, the parameter nm of endClient in Fig. 2.6 corresponds to the value of the name attribute of the User node to which the rule is applied. All input parameters are listed in the parentheses following the rule name, in turn possibly followed by an output parameter. If a parameter is both input and output parameter, it occurs twice. The rule signature endClient(c2) = c2 defines c2 as input and output parameter. Note that the types of parameters are usually not shown in rule signatures, as they can be unambiguously deduced from the overall rule specification and/or the type graph. Otherwise parameters are shown with their types.

We will now give a more precise definition of a rule in the setting of typed graphs. We choose a type graph TG and assume all graphs and rules to be typed by that graph.

An *elementary graph transformation rule* $r(par) : L \to R$ consists of a name r, a list par of (formal) parameters (which may be input or output parameters), a pair of instance graphs typed over TG and a partial mapping from L to R. This mapping ensures that there exists a subgraph of L that maps to a structurally identical subgraph of R. These subgraphs of L and R form the gluing graph, intuitively given by the intersection $L \cap R$ and schematically shown as a blue ring in Fig. 2.4. This gluing graph represents all graph elements that have to exist to apply the rule and are preserved (rather than deleted) by the application. The left-hand side L represents the preconditions of the rule, while the right-hand side R describes the postconditions. The left-hand side L may be the empty graph, in which case the precondition is always satisfied, or R may equal L, in which case the application of the rule is without effect. A rule without effect is useful to just check a condition on a graph without modifying it.

Each parameter in par has a (distinct) name and a type; the latter may be a data type or a node type from TG, and it may be omitted if it can be deduced from the rule itself. A data type parameter can be used inside a rule as part of an attribute expression or condition (see above); a node type parameter can appear as a symbolic node name.

2.2.2 Attribute Handling

The rule in Fig. 2.6 shows a fragment of the attribute language we will use throughout this book, for example, for updating the value of the clients counter of the Super node. The update is specified through the assignment in the right-hand side of the rule. Note that the Pascal-type assignment symbol := is used to distinguish it from the equality sign used elsewhere in the rule, in particular in the left-hand side. An expression such as clients = n in the left-hand side specifies that, when a match is found, the variable n will be bound to the value of the clients attribute, whereas an assignment such as clients := n-1 specifies that, when the rule is applied, clients is set to the value of the expression n-1.

The attribute language is also used in attribute conditions. These are Boolean expressions in the left-hand side of a rule delimited by { }. An example is the expression {clients < max} in rule linkClient of Fig. 2.7. Here max is a constant that is globally defined for a set of rules. Such an expression constrains the possible matches of the rule to those where it evaluates to true. Apart from the assignment symbol, we will use Java-like syntax for expressions.

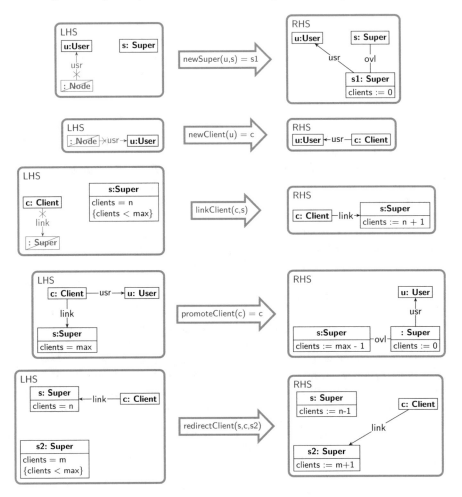

Fig. 2.7. Rules for joining the network and making connections

2.2.3 Example Rules

In our running example of a dynamic VoIP network, rules are used to model basic service operations. Some of these operations are local, taking place on only one network node, while others require the cooperation between several nodes. Common to all service operations is that they behave as transactions, i.e. they are atomic. Such atomic behaviour is also in the nature of a rule application. Hence a rule is at the right level of granularity to specify a service operation. We will continue this discussion at the end of Section 2.4. Modelling a service-oriented system with graph transformation can help in reasoning about the software architecture, especially when evaluating its quality-of-service properties. We will consider this question in detail in Chapter 9.

Operations of the VoIP service are specified by the rules shown in Figs. 2.7 and 2.8. We first discuss the rules in Fig. 2.7:

- When a User requires the services of the network and is not already connected to it, a Client or a Super node is created by newClient or newSuper, respectively. In the latter case, the clients attribute of the new Super node is set to 0, indicating that the node is not yet connected to a Client. The new Super node is always connected to an existing node via an overlay link ovl. Conceptually a bidirectional connection, this is visualised by a line without an arrowhead and formalised by a symmetric pair of edges. The fact that the user is not (yet) connected to the network is expressed by a negative condition, shown in red. Negative conditions will be presented in more detail in Section 2.4.2.
- Connections are made by rule linkClient in Fig. 2.7, provided that the number of clients has not reached the maximum number and the Client node is not yet connected to a Super node. As a result of the rule's application, a new link edge is created and the value of the clients attribute is increased by one.
- The rule promoteClient has the effect that one of a Super node's clients can be promoted if the number of clients connected to that Super node has reached its maximum. This reduces the number of clients by one, while the new Super node does not have any client connections yet, but is related to its former Super node via an overlay link.
- The rule redirectClient changes the topology of the network by changing the Super node to which a Client connects. Note that this can happen only if the new Super node has not yet reached its maximum number of clients.

Figure 2.8 shows another batch of rules, dealing with the dual case where clients and servers leave the network:

- The rule endSuper shows that Super nodes terminate in a selfish manner, without notifying clients or other Super nodes of their departure. When a node is deleted, all edges connected to it are deleted as well. Thus, if a Super node is deleted, all its incident overlay edges with other Super nodes and all links with Client nodes are implicitly deleted. We will consider different deletion behaviours later in Section 2.3.
- The rule disconnectSuper just deletes the overlay link between two Super nodes.
- The rule endClient specifies that when a linked Client is removed, its Super node link is deleted and the corresponding counter is decreased by one.

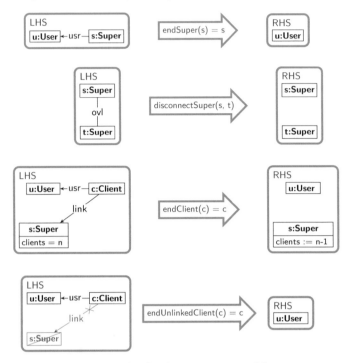

Fig. 2.8. Rules for disconnecting and leaving

- The rule endUnlinkedClient deals with the removal of unlinked clients, in which case no counter needs to be decreased. The restriction to unlinked clients is ensured via another negative application condition; if this condition were omitted, then (as with endSuper) the rule would also be applicable to clients that actually have a link edge, resulting in the incorrect behaviour of removing a Client without decreasing the clients counter.

These example rules illustrate how a single rule can express a precondition and effect of a complex process in a single, atomic step. Any implementation of rule promoteClient in a real distributed system would require a collaborative effort between the Super node s, which recognised that another Super node was needed, and the Client selected for promotion. The fact that we can describe this process by a single step raises significantly the level of abstraction of the model. This means that the model is easier to understand and analyse. The abstraction becomes possible by ignoring certain aspects of the implementation, such as the detailed interaction between the Super and Client nodes.

2.2.4 Rule-Based Graph Transformation

A rule is applied to a given graph G by replacing in G an occurrence of the left-hand side with a new copy of the right-hand side. Every rule is invoked with a sequence of actual parameters that is consistent with the rule signature.

- An input parameter is bound to a value before the rule is applied. This value is passed into the left-hand side or right-hand side by substituting it for the formal parameter name. For instance, in Fig. 2.6, the formal parameter c is instantiated with ihe actual parameter c2. This constrains the application of the rule to that part of the graph which actually contains a Client node with the identifier c2. An input parameter can also represent data used in assigning or computing new attribute values, in which case it will occur in the right-hand side of the rule. For example, a rule newUser(nm: String) could be defined to create a new user and assign its name attribute the actual value inserted for nm, so newUser("Gabi") would create a new User node with name = "Gabi".
- An output parameter provides a value after the rule has been applied. For instance, we can interpret the parameter of rule endClient in Fig. 2.6 as an (input and) output parameter. The rule can match two different subgraphs, corresponding to values c1 and c2 for c. Whichever way the rule is applied, the corresponding value is provided as output. Considering c: Client as an input and output parameter, the rule signature is endClient(c) = c, while a *rule invocation* returning c2 would be written as c2 = endClient(c2). If input or output parameters do not play a role in the context in which a rule signature is mentioned, they may be omitted. If a parameter can be set arbitrarily, this is indicated by an underscore "_" in an invocation. For example, c = endClient(_) represents an invocation where we do not specify the client to be terminated, but which returns the client selected by the match via the output parameter c.

A graph transformation step is constructed in three substeps:

1. *Find* a match m of the left-hand side L in the given graph G. The parameter assignment may already be partially given before the matching takes place. In that case, this assignment must be respected by m and will steer (and thereby simplify) the search for the match. The match determines images in G for all elements in L, as well as values for all attribute variables in L and all remaining (i.e. output) parameters that occur in L. For convenience, when presenting examples, the rule's object identifiers are often named like the ones in the host graph, so that the parameter assignment is an identical mapping. The same rule may also be shown with different identifiers to distinguish different matches.
2. *Delete* from G all vertices and edges matched by $L \setminus R$ as well as all edges in the resulting structure $G \setminus m(L \setminus R)$ that have lost a source or target node and would be left dangling otherwise.[1] Note that the deletion also extends to attribute edges in $m(L \setminus R)$. Let us refer to the graph obtained by deleting from G as D.

---

[1] The implicit removal of dangling edges is one possible behaviour, which we refer to as *radical* in Section 2.3. See there for a discussion of the different variants.

3. *Paste* a *new copy* of $R \setminus L$ into D at the match of $L \cap R$, yielding the derived graph H. For each modified attribute, the new value is computed by evaluating the corresponding expression in R. Then a new attribute edge is added, pointing to that value. As a consequence of this process, the remaining parameters, namely those that occur only in R, are also assigned a value.

Transformations that do not delete dangling edges are invertible by a kind of undo step. In such an inverse transformation we apply the rule from right to left, exchanging the roles of its left- and right-hand sides and considering the derived graph as the given host graph. In that case, the co-match would become the match and vice versa.

A *transformation* from a graph G to a graph H, also called *rule application*, is denoted by

$$G \xrightarrow{r(arg),m,f} H,$$

where r is the name of the rule, arg is a list of actual parameter values (in one-to-one correspondence with the formal parameter list par), m is a match of r and f is a partial function, called *tracking function*, mapping all vertices and edges of G preserved by the transformation to their counterparts in H. A rule name r together with a list arg of actual parameters is called a *rule invocation* or *call*, written $r(arg)$. The tracking function f and the target graph H are determined (up to renaming their nodes and edges) by the other parts of the transformation $(G, r, arg$ and $m)$. The tracking function f allows us to reason about the evolution of graphs in graph transformation sequences.[2]

In many cases, knowing the match m and the tracking function is not relevant; if this is the case, we may neglect them in the transformation label and just write $G \xrightarrow{r(arg)} H$. If, moreover, the rule has no parameters or the argument values are not important, we may just write $G \xrightarrow{r} H$.

Example 2.4 (transformation step, detailed form). Figure 2.9 demonstrates an application of promoteClient shown in Fig. 2.7. The match m of the rule's left-hand side in the host graph G is shown by listing explicitly the mapping of L's vertices to those of G. In the context of this application, the constant max is taken to equal 2.

Node c1: Client in G and its two connecting edges are deleted because they are matched by node c: Client and its edges in L, neither of which occur in R. The clients attribute of node s1 is also deleted. Into the graph obtained after deletion, we paste a new copy of node sn with new usr and ovl edges as specified in R; the node copy is given a fresh identity, symbolically represented here by the identifier s2. The match m tells us where the new edges of types usr and ovl must point, i.e. to u1 and s1, respectively, in the resulting graph H. At the same time, the value of max-1 = 1 is computed and assigned to the clients attribute of node s1. The (partial) tracking function maps c2 in G to c2 in H,

---

[2] We will use f in Chapter 3 to semantically interpret graph transformations.

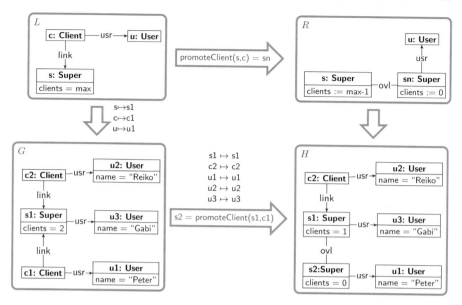

Fig. 2.9. Transformation step using rule promoteClient

s1 to s1, u2 to u2, u3 to u3 and u1 to u1, but is undefined for node c1 in G, reflecting the fact that this is deleted by the transformation. □

Generally, a rule can be applied in more than one way to a given graph. For instance, in the example above, another option would be to map c to c2, promoting the other client instead. Also, we could have chosen to apply the endClient rule instead of promoteClient. Hence, there are two causes of non-determinism in each rule-based graph transformation step.

Note 2.3: Non-determinism in graph transformation. There are two causes of non-determinism in each rule-based graph transformation step: choosing one out of a number of available rules, and choosing one of several possible matches of its left-hand side when applying it.

Given a set R of rules, a *graph transformation (sequence)* $G \overset{R}{\Longrightarrow}_* H$ is a sequence of zero to many graph transformation steps $G = G_0 \overset{r_1}{\Longrightarrow} G_1 \dots \overset{r_n}{\Longrightarrow} G_n = H$ for $n \geq 0$ and $r_i \in R$. A *graph transformation system* $GTS = (TG, R)$ consists of a typegraph TG and a set R of rules. Its semantics is the set of all graph transformations starting at some graph that is typed over TG and applying rules of R.

A consequence of the way graph transformations have been defined is that a single rule can affect only a relatively small part of a graph: in principle, the effects are restricted to the image of L under the match m, with the proviso that incident edges of deleted nodes are also affected (viz., they are implicitly deleted) despite not necessarily being in $m(L)$. Moreover, attribute computations may yield values which are not explicitly in the match, but are determined by the evaluation of attribute expressions. Even with this proviso, the following principle holds, and helps in making graph transformation tractable.

Note 2.4: Principle of locality. The application of a graph transformation rule replaces a match of the left-hand side by a new copy of the right-hand side and affects attribute values only within its match or co-match. This means that a rule application has only local effects on the given graph.

2.3 Global Application Conditions: Injectivity and Gluing

The high-level description of the application of a rule given above (find a match, delete the image of $L \setminus R$ and paste a new copy of $R \setminus L$) ignores some important choices in how the first and second of these steps are carried out precisely. It is on these choices that a lot of the research on graph transformation has concentrated. To be precise, within the gluing approach, there are certain conditions one can impose that restrict the allowed rule applications. The more restrictions, the "better behaved" the allowed transformations are, in the sense that one can predict their combined effect better and guarantee the absence of some unexpected, and presumably unwanted, phenomena.

2.3.1 Mapping Distinct Rule Nodes to the Same Graph Node

The first of the restricting conditions is the so-called *identification condition*:

Identification condition: A node or edge that is deleted by a rule may not be identified with (i.e. have the same image as) other nodes/edges of the left-hand side.

The identification condition serves to avoid conflicts in the application of a rule and to help guarantee invertibility of rule applications. To see this, first consider the transformation shown in Fig. 2.10. This rule allows one to identify its nodes by a match, i.e. the identification condition does not have to hold as indicated by the supplement NIdC (No Identification Condition) in the left-hand side. The rule specifies that ar2 should be deleted whereas ar1 should not, yet the two are identified by the match, i.e. both are mapped to ag in the host graph. This is an example of a conflict: should ag be deleted from the host graph or not? As the figure shows, the typical choice is to delete

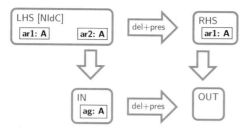

Fig. 2.10. Violation of the identification condition, leading to conflict (resolved by deleting the conflicted node)

host graph nodes for which a conflict of this type occurs; but another choice is to avoid conflict altogether, by imposing the identification condition.

Another example where the identification condition is violated is shown in Fig. 2.11. In this case, both ar1 and ar2 are deleted. Again they are identified

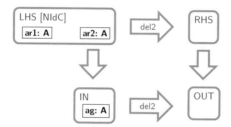

Fig. 2.11. Violation of the identification condition, leading to lack of invertibility

by the match. Note that there is now no conflict: it is clear that ag should be deleted from the host graph. In this case there is another, more subtle objection. Sometimes it is desirable to be able to *invert* a rule, by swapping its left- and right-hand sides and applying the inverted rule to the target graph, and so reconstruct the original host graph. However, in Fig. 2.11 this is clearly not going to work out: the application of the inverted rule, applied to the (empty) target graph, would result in a graph with *two* distinct A-typed nodes. Imposing the identification condition saves the day by forbidding this particular match.

Where the identification condition forbids only particular elements of the left-hand side from being matched by the same host graph elements, *injectivity* is a more restrictive condition:

Injectivity condition: No two distinct nodes or edges of the left-hand side may be identified.

Non-injective rule matching can be a useful feature, as it allows one to combine several different cases into a single rule. An example is given in Fig. 2.12: this shows an association between a B and an A node that swings around to another A node. If the two A nodes are matched by one and the same node in the graph, however, no change ensues. If matching were required to be injective, this special case would have to be modelled by a dedicated rule.

The fact that non-injective matches are allowed is indicated by the NInjC (No Injectivity Condition) annotation in the left-hand side. In such a case, the identification condition is still required by default.

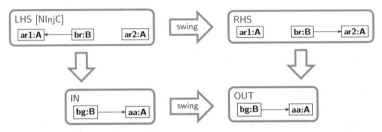

Fig. 2.12. Non-injective rule matching, avoiding the need for a rule for a special case

On the other hand, there are cases where injectivity is required. For instance, the rule in Fig. 2.13 builds the transitive closure of the overlay relation between Super nodes. If nodes s2 and s3 are mapped to the same node of the host graph, then that node receives an ovl loop instead, which is not intended. To avoid such problems, we consider injective matching the default, indicated by the absence of any annotation.

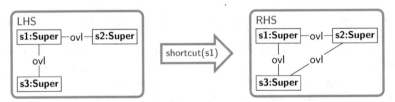

Fig. 2.13. Transitive closure of ovl: injective matching is required

Another example showing the usefulness of injectively matched rules is if one wants to guarantee the existence of a minimum number of nodes of a particular kind; in other words, if one wants to *count* occurrences of a node. The natural way to encode this is to put that many nodes in the left-hand side; but if those nodes may be matched non-injectively, then no conclusion can be drawn about the number of nodes in the host graph (except that there must be at least one).

2.3.2 Gluing Conditions

Invertibility of rules can also be hampered by another effect, namely that in which a node is deleted – naturally resulting in the deletion of all its incident edges as well – but cannot be fully reconstructed by the inverted rule, i.e.

together with all its original edges. This occurs if more edges are deleted from the host graph than the rule explicitly specifies; in other words, if some of the incident edges in the host graph are not in the match of the left-hand side. Such edges are said to be left *dangling* by the rule application (in which case the only reasonable solution is to remove them, as otherwise we would be left with something that is not a graph). The *dangling condition* precisely forbids this situation. In practice, the dangling condition is always combined with the identification condition; the combination is called the *gluing condition*:

Dangling condition: A node that is deleted by a rule must be matched to a node of the host graph such that all its incident edges are in the match as well.

Gluing condition: Both the identification condition and the dangling condition hold.

An example is given in Fig. 2.14: the host graph edge from the A node to the B node must be deleted by the rule application because the A node is, and we cannot have a dangling edge; but this edge is not itself in the match of the left hand side. If we were to invert the rule and apply it to the target graph,

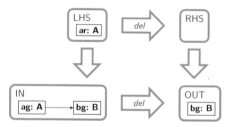

Fig. 2.14. Violation of dangling condition, resolved by deleting the dangling edge

the result would not equal the original host graph, as the edge would not be reconstructed.

Imposing the gluing condition avoids not only this case of non-invertibility but *guarantees full invertibility of rules*. This is a very important advantage if one wants to precisely analyse and predict the outcome of a graph transformation.

The strongest of the restrictions we will discuss here is the combination of injectivity and the dangling condition:

Injective gluing condition: Both the injectivity and the dangling condition hold.

Because injectivity implies the identification condition, injective gluing implies the gluing condition.

2.3.3 Summary: From Conservative to Radical

Altogether, we have five different global application conditions, some of which are strictly stronger than others. Fig. 2.15 shows them in relation to one another. Transformations satisfying the source condition also satisfy the target condition. The conditions shown in Fig. 2.15 can be described as follows:

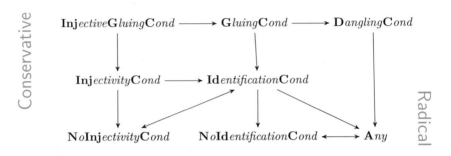

Fig. 2.15. Global application conditions, from conservative to radical

- **A**ny: does not impose restrictions.
- **Id**$entification$**C**ond: no element in $L \setminus R$ is identified by m with any other element from L, i.e., for $x \in L \setminus R, y \in L, m(x) = m(y)$ implies $x = y$.
- **Inj**$ectivity$**C**ond: no two elements in L are identified by m with each other, i.e., for $x, y \in L, m(x) = m(y)$ implies $x = y$.
- **D**$angling$**C**ond: no edge in the context is attached to deleted nodes, i.e. for node $x \in m(L \setminus R)$ and edge $y \in G, s(y) = x$ or $t(y) = x$ implies $y \in m(L \setminus R)$.
- **G**$luing$**C**ond: Both **Id**$entification$**C**ond and **D**$angling$**C**ond are satisfied.
- **Inj**$ectiveGluing$**C**ond: Both **Inj**$ectivity$**C**ond and **D**$angling$**C**ond are satisfied.
- **N**o**Inj**$ectivity$**C**ond: **Inj**$ectivity$**C**ond may not be satisfied, but **Id**$entification$Condition is satisfied.
- **N**o**Id**$entification$**C**ond: **Id**$entification$**C**ond may not be satisfied.

The fewer restrictions one imposes, the more radical the effects of a rule application can be; conversely, the stronger the restrictions, the more conservative their effects. As explained above, conservatism is beneficial for analysability; on the other hand, a more radical approach results in a more compact set of rules, since each rule may combine cases that under a conservative global application condition require distinct rules.

We consider injectivity of matches as the default condition in the rest of this book because developers tend to specify patterns as they occur in practice. Considering the dangling condition, it depends on the application whether or not the deletion of nodes should be allowed in unknown contexts. We indicate the presence of the dangling condition by an annotation DC on the left-hand side, while the gluing condition is indicated by GC or, equivalently NInjC, DC, since the default for matches that are not necessarily injective is the identification condition.

2.4 Advanced Graph Transformation Features

In this section we introduce a number of features that extend the basic rule-based approach, by

- more precise specification of the class of instance graphs by means of constraints and
- more expressive rules, allowing additional application conditions, universally quantified operations and the merging of graph elements.

2.4.1 Graph Constraints

When specifying transformations, it is desirable to have a precise understanding of the class of graphs that may be encountered or are generated by the rules. Type graphs, even with subtyping and multiplicities, are not expressive enough to define more complex constraints on the structure of instance graphs, especially when conditions on attributes are involved. For example, in the peer-to-peer model above we use the attribute clients in Super nodes as a counter for the number of clients attached. To make sure that, for example, the rule in Fig. 2.20 in Section 2.4.4 is applicable if and only if no client is linked to Super node s, we could add a constraint on Super such as

```
self.clients=0 iff self.link->isEmpty()
```

The same constraint can be expressed graphically, as shown in Fig. 2.16, where it is broken down into two forbidden patterns, a Super node with clients $= 0$, but linked to a client, and one with clients > 0 but no client linked.

Fig. 2.16. Two variants of a visual graph constraint

Constraints restrict the set of admissible instance graphs. Usually, the start graph G_0 is required to satisfy them and, for each rule r, we have to guarantee that, if $G \stackrel{r}{\Longrightarrow} H$ is a transformation and G satisfies the constraints, the same is true for H. In that case it follows that all reachable graphs satisfy the constraints. In our case, this means that we have to guarantee that whenever a client link is created or deleted, the clients attribute is updated.

In an alternative operational interpretation, constraints can be used to control the transformation process by ruling out transformations leading to non-admissible graphs. This is comparable to the integrity mechanism in a database management system, which checks the validity of constraints after each update, but before the new state is committed. In this case, constraints become part of the operational specification of the system.

In addition to the simple forbidden patterns covered here, we will consider required patterns and more complex constraints in Chapter 4.

2.4.2 Negative Application Conditions

The phenomenon of "dangling edges" is caused by the fact that a node in a graph may, in general, have an unknown number of connections. This is in contrast with, for example, the rewriting of strings where the linear structure provides information about the connections of any substring. The more complicated situation for graphs has led to extensions of the basic approach by application conditions, which have already been used informally in the VoIP network example in Figs. 2.7 and 2.8.

Generalising the default gluing conditions of the conservative approach, user-defined application conditions specify constraints on the immediate context of the match of the rule's left-hand side.

Example 2.5 (forbidden patterns). Figure 2.17 shows a rule that detects weaknesses in the network's topology. The termination of a Super node s1 may

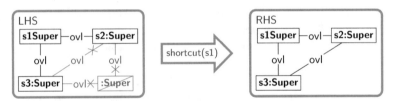

Fig. 2.17. Creating redundant links

increase the distance between two other nodes s2, s3 currently using s1 as an intermediary. Such a situation is detected by checking that s1 is actually connected to s2 and s3, and also that there is neither a direct link between them nor a two-step path via another Super node. These two forbidden patterns are expressed by the red, crossed-out elements in the left-hand side of the rule. □

Forbidden patterns restrict the applicability of a rule. They are interpreted as negative application conditions (NACs), each an extension of the rule's left-hand side L by nodes and edges whose joint presence in the context should prevent the application of the rule. Formally, we define an NAC as a graph N extending L. The elements of $N \setminus L$, drawn in red, constitute the forbidden pattern. A rule with an NAC is applicable to a given graph G if the occurrence of the left-hand side cannot be extended to include any of the forbidden patterns specified by the condition. Note that we map forbidden patterns injectively. In particular, they are not allowed to overlap with occurrences of positive parts of the left-hand side.

A rule may have a number of NACs, which means that each of the specified forbidden patterns must not occur. Putting several forbidden patterns into one NAC would express that at least one forbidden pattern does not occur. We interpret each connected set of elements in $N \setminus L$ as separate forbidden pattern to be put into a separate NAC. Hence, two NACs are integrated into the left-hand side shown in Figure 2.17. Note that this drawing convention does not allow to interpret two separate connected sets of forbidden elements as one forbidden graph part. This represents a limitation with respect to the general concept. If the modeller wants to express a condition like that, the condition has to be drawn separately as done in the following example.

Example 2.6 (negative application conditions). The application conditions of rule shortcut are depicted in Fig. 2.18 in more detail. Fig. 2.18 shows two NACs N_1 and N_2 associated with rule shortcut. We need two NACs, since we have two separate conditions to be checked: (1) there is no direct link (checked by the upper NAC) and (2) there is not a two-step path (checked by the lower NAC). The occurrence shown in the figure satisfies the conditions because

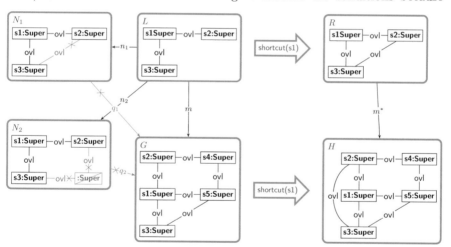

Fig. 2.18. Rule application with negative application condition

there is neither another two-step path between s2 and s3, apart from the one via s1, nor a direct ovl edge. The rule application depicted results in creating such a direct link.   □

2.4.3 Path Expressions

The ability to specify the (non-)existence of certain paths in a graph can support navigation and is generally useful for expressing non-local graph properties. For two nodes n and m of a given graph, a *path* from n to m is a sequence of edges $e_1 e_2 \ldots e_p$ such that the target of edge e_i is the source of edge e_{i+1} for all $1 \leq i \leq p-1$, the source of e_1 is n and the target of e_p is m.

A path expression is a regular expression over edge types. When an edge e in the left-hand side of a rule is labelled by such an expression, this demands the existence of a path $e_1 \ldots e_p$ between the corresponding nodes in G such that the sequence of edge types $t(e_1) \ldots t(e_p)$ satisfies the regular expression, where $t : G \to TG$ maps the elements of G to their types in the type graph TG.

Example 2.7 (path expression). The expression ovl^* specifies a path consisting of a sequence of edges of type ovl. Because it occurs as part of a negative condition, the rule connect in Fig. 2.19 detects situations where two Super nodes are not connected by a path of ovl edges. When it is applied to two such disconnected nodes s1 and s2, a new ovl edge is created between these two nodes.   □

Fig. 2.19. Rule with path expression

In Chapter 4, we will consider further kinds of application conditions requiring, for example, the existence of a certain pattern, so-called *positive application conditions* (PACs), and more complex ones, called *conditional conditions*, which can be seen as nested positive and negative conditions.

2.4.4 Multipatterns

In the basic approach, each element in a rule's left-hand side is matched to exactly one node or edge in a graph the rule is applied to. In many cases, however, we would like to express operations dealing with all elements of a graph satisfying certain structural or attribute conditions. For example, Fig. 2.20 shows the radical version of shutting down a Super node. The Super node is deleted independently of the number of Super nodes still connected.

Fig. 2.20. Super node exit, causing the implicit deletion of all adjacent connections (radical solution)

If we wish to achieve the behaviour modelled by rule shutdownSuper in the conservative approach, we have to be able to delete all ovl edges connected to the Super node in a single step. However, we do not know their number in advance, so no rule with a fixed number of nodes and edges in its left-hand side will be able to achieve this. Instead, for such universally quantified operations, we adopt the concept of *multiobjects* familiar from UML object diagrams.

Fig. 2.21. Super node exit, deleting connections with all other Super nodes (conservative, with multiobjects)

A multiobject such as S in the rule in Fig. 2.21 represents the set of all objects with the specified connections to the fixed objects in the rule. In our case, S would be matched by the set of all Super nodes related to Super node s by an ovl edge. The universal quantification in the match carries over to the action of the rule, i.e. the deletion of the matched ovl edges. Note that, by the identification condition, the image of s cannot be an element of the set matched by S, because the former is deleted while the latter is preserved.

Operationally, a rule $r : L \rightarrow R$ with multiobjects is applied in two stages. First, we find and fix a match $m_0 : L_0 \rightarrow G$ for all "normal" (existentially quantified) elements, making up the *kernel rule* $r_0 : L_0 \rightarrow R_0$. Then, considering all multiobjects as normal elements, all possible extensions $m_i, 1 \geq i \geq n$, of m_0 to $L \supseteq L_0$ are found and a so-called *amalgamated rule* is created by merging n copies of r to duplicate the multiobjects so that one copy exists for each occurrence in the graph. This amalgamated rule is then applied as usual, using the match assembled from m_0 and all the m_i. In our example, this creates a rule with as many copies of Super node S as there are ovl edges outgoing from $m(s)$ in G. Figure 2.22 illustrates the construction of the amalgamated rule *eSM* for a host graph with two matches for the extended rule, leading to two separate copies *eSM1* and *eSM2* that merge into one amalgamated rule, overlapping in the kernel *eSM0*.

Multiobjects allow one to combine the main principles of both the gluing and the embedding approach. While the application of normal rules reflects the gluing approach (recall that $L \cap R$ specifies the overlap of L and R), multiobjects specify the embedding relation inherent in the embedding approach. This relation is generally defined by statements of the following form: *If a context vertex with label x is present and connected by an e-edge to vertex y, then delete the e-edge and replace it by an f-edge to vertex z in R.* When we specify the context vertex as a normal vertex in the kernel rule, it is in the gluing part and therefore preserved. Vertex y is specified as a multivertex in the left-hand side and z as a multivertex in the right-hand side. They are

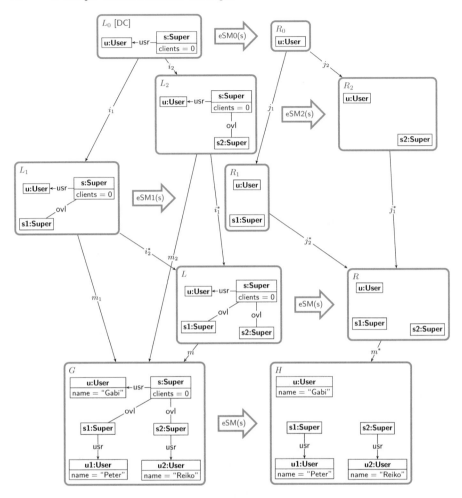

Fig. 2.22. Amalgamated transformation of endSuperMulti (eSM) kernel and extension rules

connected to vertex x by the corresponding edges e and f, respectively.

We introduced multiobjects as means to express universally quantified actions. This concept can be generalised to universal quantification over multipatterns. As with multiobjects, the use of a kernel rule localises the action to one part of the graph. If the kernel rule is empty, the multipattern is applied all over the graph. However, matches of multipatterns may overlap, leading to conflicting transformations. In the following, an example of multipattern use is presented exploring these issues.

Example 2.8 (optimisation of overlay network). To make our VoIP network more resilient against loss of connectivity, we introduced a rule in Fig. 2.17

that detects weaknesses in the network's topology and repairs them by adding redundant connections between Super nodes that are connected neither directly nor via an intermediate Super node. This strengthening of the topology should apply equally across the entire network. One way to achieve this is to apply rule shortcut in Fig. 2.17 for as long as possible in a sequential way. Another way is to define a rule consisting of a multipattern that is applied all over the network. To achieve this, in contrast to the example rule in Fig. 2.21 above, we use a true multipattern here, consisting of more than one multi-object. Furthermore, this rule has an empty kernel rule so the multipattern matches are not restricted.

Consider graph G in Fig. 2.23 (which differs slightly from the graph in Fig. 2.18). Rule parShortcut consists of a multipattern which allows the parallel optimisation of the network. (Note that this rule differs from the one in Fig. 2.17 by having only one negative application condition, here in the multi-pattern.) Intuitively this rule can be applied at four different matches. The first match, for example, maps s1 to n1, s2 to n2 and s3 to n3, etc. If we apply this rule to graph G in Fig. 2.23 at all four matches, the result should be graph H with four new ovl edges, between n2 and n3, n2 and n4, n3 and n4, and n1 and n5.

However, owing to the symmetry between s2 and s3, every one of these four matches has a mirror image. For the first match listed in Fig. 2.23, for example, we can also map s2 to n3 and s3 to n2. Applying the rule to all eight matches would lead to the introduction of parallel edges in H, which is clearly not desirable. More generally, matches may be in conflict in the sense that, when applied, one inserts an edge that another one forbids. For example, match s1,s2,s3 → n1,n2,n3 conflicts with s1,s2,s3 → n1,n3,n2 since they both insert a new ovl edge between n2 and n3. To avoid such conflicting rule applications, we can restrict the application of rule parShortcut to be *safe*, i.e. all parallel steps can be transformed into equivalent sequences of steps that apply the multipattern as a rule (i.e. the rule shortcut) at essentially the same matches. The rule application is safe for all maximal sets of pairwise independent matches. Matches are independent if they overlap in preserved graph elements only. (For more details see Chapter 4.)

Note that the application of rule parShortcut is not equivalent to applying the rule shortcut sequentially for as long as possible. (1) By creating new ovl edges, new matches can be produced which give rise to subsequent applications. By inserting, for example, an ovl edge between nodes n3 and n4, a new match s1,s2,s3 → n4,n3,n5 is created. (2) In the parallel application, application conditions for all matches are checked simultaneously for the given graph G before the rules are applied. In the sequential case, instead, some conditions are checked after some applications have taken place. Thus, later steps are potentially disabled because of the effects of earlier ones. If a parallel rule application is safe, however, this effect does not occur [63].

By applying rule parShortcut to graph H, the network can be further optimised. Match s1,s2,s3 → n4,n2,n5, for example, would lead to a new edge

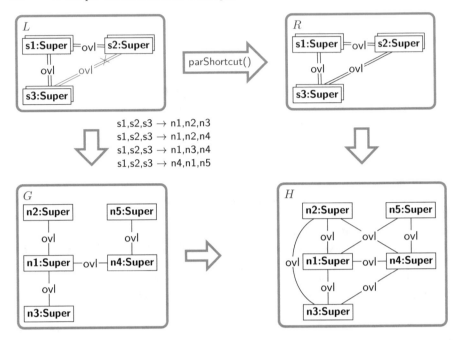

Fig. 2.23. Optimisation of overlay network using a multipattern

between n2 and n5. Assigning s1,s2,s3 → n4,n2,n3, however, would not yield a match, since there is already an edge between n2 and n3 which is not allowed by the NAC.   □

Multipatterns, as introduced so far, represent any number of patterns. If we want to restrict the number of occurrences of a multipattern, multiplicities can be specified. For example, if the application of rule endSuperMulti in Fig. 2.21 should be restricted in order to only delete Super node s if it is connected to at most three other Super nodes, this can be expressed by a multiplicity "0..3" at the multiobject end of the ovl link (Fig. 2.24). This means that the rule is not applicable to a node s with more than three ovl links. If a multipattern multiplicity occurs in an NAC, this rules out the existence of the specified number of matches. For example, consider a rule like endSuperMultiCard but with multiobject S: Super and the ovl multi-edge from s forming a negative condition. In this case, the NAC would be satisfied only if there are more than three ovl edges to Super nodes connected to s.

As discussed in Section 2.3, rule applications that share graph elements to be deleted may lead to conflicts. Although giving priority to deletion can resolve the situation, so that a deterministic result is computed, this solution is not always desirable. The example above shows that the parallel application of rules with negative conditions may not be equivalent to any sequential exe-

Fig. 2.24. Super node exit, deleting connections with up to three Super nodes

cution, even if they do not share any deleted element. Chapter 4 will consider conflicts and dependencies between rule applications in more detail.

2.4.5 Merging

Sometimes it is desirable to merge, for example, two existing nodes into one as part of a rule application. This is useful, for example, if two user accounts are combined into one. When two nodes are merged, we expect that their adjacent edges will be joined.

Example 2.9 (merging). To discuss the merging of graph elements, we consider the type graph in Fig. 1.16, where the multiplicity of *usr* edges is modified to allow more than one *Node* to serve one User, as shown in the type graph in Fig. 2.25. In such a model, it can happen that a user account may be used on several nodes. To merge two User accounts, the rule in Fig. 2.26 combines

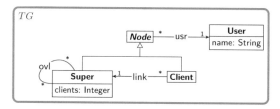

Fig. 2.25. Modified type graph with subtypes and multiplicities

nodes u1 and u2 on the left into one node on the right. The rule takes a user name uid1 as an input parameter to serve as the user name of the merged account, while the other name is discarded. Formally, merging is achieved

Fig. 2.26. Merging two different user accounts

by rules whose left- and right-hand sides are related by non-injective partial mappings, i.e. where two or more elements on the left are mapped to one element on the right.   □

2.4.6 Integrated Notation for Rules

For a more compact representation of rules, their various components $r : L \to R$, potentially equipped with negative conditions, can be combined within a single rule graph, distinguishing rule parts by different colours and styles of elements to representing *readers, erasers, creators* or *embargoes*. As an example, the rules in Fig. 2.27 represent the integrated views of the rules of the same name in Figs. 2.7, 2.8 and 2.21. Readers (in $L \cap R$), represented by thin black solid outlines, are required but not deleted, such as the User node in newClient and the User and Super nodes in endClient. Erasers (in $L \setminus R$), represented by thin dashed blue outlines, are to be deleted by the rule, for example, the Client node in endClient with its two edges. Creators (in $R \setminus L$), represented by slightly wider dotted outlines in green, such as the Client node in newClient, are to be created by the rule. Embargoes (in $N \setminus L$) represented by a red outline and crossed out, such as the node of type Node with its usr edge in newClient, must be absent for the rule to be applicable. Attribute updates are indicated by using :=. The representation of multinodes is just reused in the integrated view.

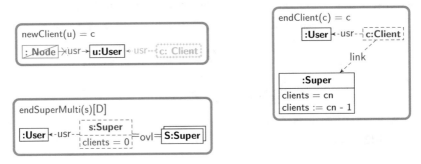

Fig. 2.27. Rules newClient and endClient in integrated notation

This integrated notion for rules is especially helpful if the reader part is large, since it needs to be drawn only once. It can become somewhat confusing if several embargoes are used, attribute values are read and computed, and larger parts are created. If a NAC refers to a node which is already in the left-hand side of the rule forbidding a certain type refinement or attribute value, the integrated notation contains two nodes with the same identifier but with different types. The variant with the forbidden type forms the embargo and thus, drawn in that way. When considering, for example, a variant of the rule endSuper which deletes a node if it is not a Client-node, the type refinement to Client is forbidden by a separate node with the same identifier n as shown in

Fig. 2.28. There is a kind of embargoes where the separate notation of NACs is superior: If one NAC contains more than one connected set of elements

Fig. 2.28. A variant of the rule endSuper in an integrated notation

in $N \setminus LHS$, this fact cannot be expressed as we have the convention each conected part of forbidden elements forms a separate NAC. In that case, the NAC is shown separately, also when using the integrated notation of rules. An example for such a rule notation is given in Example 11.1 below.

2.4.7 Inverting Rules

Basic rules appear to be symmetrical, i.e. exchanging their erasers and creators should result in an inverted rule that undoes the effect of the original one. Embargoes (left-sided negative application conditions) can be translated to the right-hand side to become NACs of the inverse rule. Inverting expressions in assignments or conditions is more challenging. Here we have to assume that all operators used have inverses as well. Moreover, input parameters become output parameters, and vice versa.

The idea is that an inverse rule is applicable to the graphs that could have resulted from applications of the original rule, and that it undoes the effects of such an application. This means that for each application $G \xrightarrow{r,m} H$, there should be an application $H \xrightarrow{r^{-1},m'} G$. This is indeed the case in the conservative gluing approach, because it is free of side-effects, i.e. all changes to the graph are explicitly specified in the original rule and can therefore be undone by the inverse rule.

Example 2.10 (inverse rule). By inverting the rules in Fig. 2.27, we get a rule for deleting a client and a rule for inserting and linking a client. Note that the attribute computation in the Super node is inverted as well. The parameter lists may be adapted, as it is done in rule insertAndLinkClient in Fig. 2.29. □

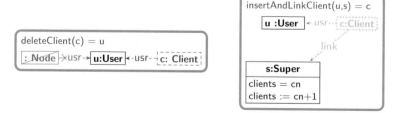

Fig. 2.29. Inverse rules for newClient and endClient in Fig. 2.27

2.4.8 Transactional Behaviour

Throughout this chapter, we have considered a range of actions that can be specified by individual rules, including basic actions such as the creation and deletion of graph elements, but also more advanced actions such as merging and copying graph elements within their specific contexts. All actions specified in one rule are executed within that rule's application.

Note 2.5: Rule application as transactions. A rule can specify a number of actions, and each (attempted) application will either perform all those actions, or none of them. This means that a rule application forms one *atomic* step. Besides combining semantically related actions, this also ensures that the result of the application is again a *consistent* graph; considering, for example, typed graphs, the result has to be well typed again.

If several rules are applied in parallel, they are not allowed to interfere. This means that the parallel step must be serialisable and that the result graph of the parallel step must be the same as the one obtained from any sequential application: the rule applications are *isolated* from each other. In summary, rule applications can be seen as transactions on graphs.

Considering again our running example, it was our design decision to specify within single rules not only local operations but also complex cooperations between network nodes. Instead, we could have designed our rules to be more fine-grained, distinguishing between two kinds of rules: local ones which just change the state of a node, and connection rules that consider exactly two nodes and their relation. An operation such as redirectClient would then be specified by two separate rules, one for deleting the client's link to a Super node and one for creating a link to a Super node. Note that in this case the redirection is performed by two rule applications and might result in linking to the original Super node again. We will detail our discussion of the transactional behaviour of rule applications in Section 3.3.

2.5 Summary and Further Reading

In this chapter, we have presented the main concepts of graph transformation, distinguishing between the embedding and gluing approaches. We focused on the gluing approach and considered graph transformations following simple rules before considering advanced concepts for rules. To establish which of the many approaches in the literature follow the embedding or gluing philosophy, we now give a high-level overview. Then we consider the relation of graph transformation to other rewriting formalisms.

2.5.1 Graph Transformation Approaches in the Literature

Fundamental approaches to graph transformation were surveyed in [252]. They are often introduced from a theoretical point of view and include the algebraic double-pushout (DPO) [80] and single-pushout (SPO) [196] approaches, node-label-controlled (NLC) [151] rewriting, and PROGRES [258, 259], the first graph transformation language designed for applications in software engineering [94]. Further surveys of graph transformation concepts and their possible applications are given in the handbooks [77, 79] and the survey [17].

The basic graph transformation concepts introduced in Section 2.2 are formally based on pushouts over graphs which can be considered as generalised graph gluing. In the single-pushout approach [196], a rule $r : L \rightarrow R$ is represented by a partial graph morphism and its application $G \xRightarrow{r(m)} H$ can be described by a single pushout over partial graph morphisms, with the total morphism $m : L \rightarrow G$ providing the match of its left-hand side into the given graph. When we restrict ourselves to conservative transformations as discussed in Section 2.3, we follow the double-pushout approach over total graph morphisms. Here a rule is given by a span $r : (L \leftarrow I \rightarrow R)$ with the intersection of L and R explicitly represented by I, and a step $G \xRightarrow{r} H$ is described by a pair of pushouts over total morphisms, one in the reverse direction modelling deletion and a forward one modelling addition of graph structure. To ensure that the structure obtained from the first step is again a graph (i.e. no edges are left without source and target nodes), the gluing conditions are imposed as discussed in Section 2.2. (Formally, the satisfaction of the gluing condition is generalized to the existence of a pushout complement.)

In the algebraic approaches, the merging of graph elements is achieved by rule morphisms $I \rightarrow R$ or $L \rightarrow R$ that are non-injective. Cloning or copying of elements is not possible in DPO or SPO, but it can be realised by the sesqui-pushout approach [64]. In particular, all edges adjacent to cloned vertices are copied as well. Limited to rules without cloning, the sesqui-pushout approach is a generalisation of DPO where the dangling condition does not have to be satisfied. This means that its transformations are comparable to SPO transformations satisfying the identification condition.

While both DPO and SPO are gluing approaches, this is not the case for the NLC approach, where a transformation consists in removing the occurrence of the left-hand side, including all edges connecting it to the context, and constructing the new graph by a disjoint union of the remainder with the rule's right-hand side. Then, new edges are created to connect the copy of right-hand side with the remainder based on so-called embedding rules. This powerful answer to the problem of replacing structures in an unknown context is also available in PROGRES. As we have seen, a similar behaviour can be realised by the gluing approach using *set nodes* or *multiobjects*.

Application conditions restricting the applicability of individual rules as well as structural constraints over graphs comparable to invariants or integrity constraints in databases, deal with the (non-)existence of certain patterns.

They are expressed as multiplicities, in terms of first- or higher-order logic, or as graphical conditions. The latter have been introduced for the algebraic approach in [120] and have since been adapted for most other approaches.

2.5.2 Tool Support for Graph Transformations

Graph transformation concepts have been implemented in various tools, some of which focus purely on graph transformation and its implementation, others adapt graph transformation concepts to serve a specific purpose in the context of a wider tool platform. We speak more widely of *graph-transformation-oriented* tools and systems if they incorporate or implement significant graph transformation concepts. The variety of graph-transformation-oriented tools that have been developed includes AGG [98, 270, 12], Atom[3] [189], eMoflon [93], GrGen [105], Groove [107], Henshin [22, 139], PROGRES [259], Verigraph [29] and ViaTra [283, 285]. They are used for editing and executing graph transformation-oriented systems, such as model transformations or behavioural models based on graph transformation, and often also support debugging, testing and analysing such systems. Depending on the purpose and platform, graph-transformation-oriented features are frequently integrated with further concepts such as metamodelling, constraint solving and pattern mining. In the following, we focus on the implementation of graph transformation features in these tools.

Any graph-transformation-oriented tool has to support the creation of a graph transformation system consisting basically of a type graph and a set of rules. Given the ingredients of graph transformation systems, the tool has to support the editing of instance graphs, and potentially type graphs, graph rules and rule control (presented in the next chapter). Although the underlying concepts vary, editing of graphs and editing of rules are basic, universal features. Execution support for graph transformations is typically sequential and often allows some forms of non-determinism with respect to the choice of rule and match. The most time-consuming part of a graph transformation step is rule matching. Tool developers have solved this problem in various ways, such as converting the matching problem into a constraint satisfaction problem to be able to apply fast constraint solvers (AGG), developing elaborate search plans for rules (PROGRES), or implementing incremental pattern matching (eMoflon, ViaTra).

To better understand graph transformation systems and find conceptual flaws, methods analogous to those in programming environments are available, including debugging and testing. Debugging a graph transformation system means stepping through its rule applications. Since graph transformation systems are usually interpreted, there is often little difference between execution and debugging. A central use case for debugging is the setting of breakpoints, which may be specified in several ways: a breakpoint may be, for example, a stop at some rule call potentially in some larger control flow, a condition that is checked on all resulting graphs, the applicability of a selected rule, or a maximum number of rule applications. When stepping through a graph transformation sequence, the developer might want to consider intermediate graphs, rules applied and matches selected, as well as co-matches. Moreover, information about the non-applicability of rules can be interesting.

Another way to detect flaws in graph transformation systems is to formulate test cases for them. A basic form of test case is to specify an input graph, let the transformation system be executed on this graph and check the output graph. The test assertion can be an isomorphism check with some expected output graph or a coarser check where only the size of the result graph, important substructures or attribute values are tested.

Several analysis techniques, to be discussed in Chapter 4, can be applied at specification time. They are concerned with the functional behaviour of graph transformation systems as well as with checking properties of the resulting graphs. Functional behaviour is ensured if a graph transformation system terminates and is strictly confluent. For both properties, sufficient (but not necessary) criteria are available (see Chapter 4). Graph-transformation-oriented tools typically support analysis techniques for specific forms of graph transformation systems, ruling out some advanced features and committing to a given semantic interpretation.

Graph formats include tool-specific ones, such as those ones in AGG and Groove, and standard ones, such as the Eclipse Modeling Framework. They determine the technical space the tool operates in. Purely graph-based tools may support either specific formats or the standard graph exchange language GXL [289, 119].

2.5.3 Relations to Other Transformation Concepts

Graph transformation is only one of a range of approaches to the rewriting of structures such as strings, trees or multisets. Relations to other approaches have been considered in [34]. Here we discuss them from a software engineering perspective.

Context-free Chomsky grammars are used to define the syntax of textual languages, especially programming languages. The notion of *graph grammars* is inspired by Chomsky grammars and actually generalises them [124]: a start graph with a set of graph transformation rules forms a graph grammar which defines a graph language. To find out if an instance graph is member of a the language defined by a graph grammar, a graph parser can be derived from a given graph grammar. (See Section 4.6 for more details.) Graph grammars have been used to define visual modelling languages. (See Chapter 10 for more details.)

Tree transformations are ubiquitous in software engineering, for example, for manipulating or mapping data, and for analysing, interpreting, translating, optimising or refactoring programs. Prominent approaches to tree transformations include XSLT [10] (for transforming XML documents), program transformation languages and term rewriting. XML documents are ordered, node-labelled trees with cross-references represented as attributes. Transformations in XSLT match subtrees using the XPath language and use templates to describe the construction of a new XML document based on the information of the given document.

The underlying structure of a textual program is formed by its abstract syntax tree (AST). Program transformation approaches can rewrite ASTs in a rule-based way. Some approaches to program transformation are based on term rewriting [168] such as Stratego/XT [48], while others are template-based, such as of TXL [62]. Term graph rewriting [261, 233] generalises term rewriting by using directed acyclic graphs. These allow a more efficient implementation of program transformations, since identical subterms can be shared, and so only need to be transformed once.

Petri nets [242] are rewrite systems on sets or multisets. They are commonly used to specify the concurrent behaviour of systems, including software and business processes. Place–transition Petri nets can be simulated by graph transformation systems using typed graphs without edges. In this case, node types represent places and tokens. For each transition, a rule is required that deletes all the nodes representing tokens in the precondition and creates nodes representing tokens in the postcondition.

3

Beyond Individual Rules: Usage Scenarios and Control Structures

We have defined a graph transformation step as the application of a rule, defined over a type graph and a rule signature, to a given instance graph and producing a derived graph in a single, atomic action. In software modelling, individual actions are often combined into processes describing, for example, a business transaction or the implementation of a complex operation. The problem of controlling the application of rules, for example to ensure that certain actions happen in the right order, is the subject of this section.

Just like models in general, a graph-transformation system can describe a system at different levels of detail:

- informally, for illustrating the behaviour of a system;
- as an executable requirements model, to simulate and animate a system;
- as a formal specification, to analyse or verify a system;
- programmatically, to derive an implementation of a system.

For all but the first option, it is important to have a precise understanding of the operational behaviour of a graph transformation model, not just at the level of individual rules and transformations but at the system level. How do rules interact with each other? Can they be applied in any order, or in parallel? Are we interested in every individual step, or only in the overall effect of a complex transformation? What happens when two rules "compete" for application in the same state? Can we express a preference, or control their application to achieve a desired effect?

To answer such questions we present a notion of *graph transformation system* and address both the semantics of such a system, depending on its intended usages, and a range of control mechanisms that allow us to describe which rules can be applied when and where.

One fundamental choice is the local/distributed or global/sequential nature of control. In a distributed system, such as the VoIP network we have modelled, different nodes may be active at the same time and controlling their actions globally may be unrealistic. For example, several nodes deciding to leave the network at the same time could complicate the problem of creating

© Springer Nature Switzerland AG 2020
R. Heckel, G. Taentzer, *Graph Transformation for Software Engineers*,
https://doi.org/10.1007/978-3-030-43916-3_3

a fault-tolerant topology. In contrast, assuming global control, only one node could be allowed to leave at a time, triggering high-priority repair actions to add additional redundant links before the next node can leave.

A distributed scenario could still require control, such as a particular protocol in order to inform neighbouring nodes of the intention to leave, but the impact of such control would be limited to the local context. In this chapter we will encounter both interpretations. It is worth stressing that the main difference is not in the language used, but in our understanding of which control mechanisms are appropriate in a given setting, reflecting the operation of a real system or what is implementable under certain assumptions.

It is important to recognise that graph transformation systems can be used in a variety of contexts and for different purposes. We distinguish three main usage scenarios. Firstly, graph transformation systems can be used to define or characterise a set of graphs, or *graph language*, such as, for instance, the set of abstract syntax graphs of UML state machines. In Chapter 10 we show how the language of well-structured activity diagrams can be described by a graph grammar. Interpreting a graph transformation system as a *graph grammar*, we fix a start graph in addition. All graphs that can be generated from that start graph by grammar rules are considered as members of the graph language. This is in analogy to the formal definition of textual languages by means of string grammars. Graph grammars are often equipped with non-terminals as a means of control. They work by distinguishing, among the derived graphs, those that contain non-terminals (and are therefore seen as intermediate results) from terminal graphs (which are part of the language). Defining a graph grammar without non-terminals is possible as well. In this case, each derived graph is considered to be already an element of the corresponding graph language.

Secondly, graph transformation systems can be used to transform input graphs into output graphs; in other words, to program a *graph relation*. Typical examples are translations between modelling languages, for example, from activity diagrams to Petri nets, and also computations on graphs, such as the transitive closure of edges. Relations can be composed to reflect the sequential composition of computations. The use of graph transformation systems in this scenario often requires the introduction of control structures over rules analogous to those in programming languages, process calculi or flow diagrams. Rule signatures, used like operation signatures in programming, provide an interface between rules and control structures.

Thirdly, graph transformation systems can be used to describe the detailed *dynamic behaviour* of a system. Here, individual rule applications represent actions that can be observed through their parametrised rule names. An example of this scenario is the VoIP network model used as a running example in this book. The semantics is typically captured by a labelled transition system, in which the states are graphs and transitions correspond to transformation steps, labelled by rule calls. Models of this kind are often used to describe the operational semantics of modelling or programming languages, or for verification tasks such as reachability analysis or model checking (as considered in Chapter 4). In the VoIP network model, for example, we may be interested in the question of whether a configuration is reachable in which the network is not connected. Another question is, whether from every disconnected configuration, a connected one is reachable. In this type of scenario, control structures can help to reduce the size of the model, for example, by restricting it to desirable behaviours or by hiding internal states and transitions through procedural and transactional constructs, thus making a model more amenable to analysis.

With this basic understanding of usage scenarios for graph transformation, we first give an overview of control mechanisms for rule application, then present the usage scenarios introduced above in more detail and finally, present some control mechanisms for rule application as they are used for programmed graph transformation.

3.1 Feature Model for Rule Control Mechanisms

The feature diagram in Fig. 3.1 extends the one in Fig. 2.5 by refining the feature TransformationSystem. Depending on the purpose of the transformation system, the right semantic model has to be chosen, as discussed above: graph languages, graph relations or graph transition systems. One special form of transition systems is a stochastic one; stochastic graph transformation systems where each rule is equipped with a number specifying the delay of its application are presented in Chapter 9.

To control which rules are applied and in which order, a variety of control mechanisms are available. A classical form of language definition, already mentioned above, is to use non-terminal symbols to indicate parts that have to be further developed. Some classical forms of control constructs are conditional, choice, sequence and priority and loops applied as long as possible. Combinations of these forms of control expression can be encapsulated into procedures, hence procedural abstraction allows one to encapsulate control expressions. If a control expression is executed in an atomic way, it has to be applicable as a whole, otherwise it is not executed at all, i.e. the atomicity of transactions is required. Finally, rule applications can also be controlled by using integrity constraints to specify allowed input and output graph classes for graph computations. Given an integrity constraint, rules are applied only if the constraint is not violated for the resulting graph. Integrity constraints may also be used to ensure that all rule applications preserve formulated invariants.

3.2 A Matter of Semantics

We continue this chapter with an overview of the semantic models available for graph transformation systems and proceed to discuss control structures and

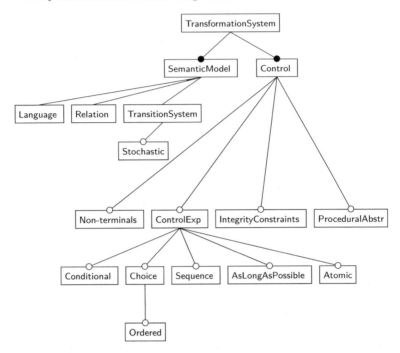

Fig. 3.1. Feature model for rule control mechanisms in graph transformation systems

their possible interpretations based on these models. The semantic interpretation of a graph transformation system $GTS = (TG, R)$ with type graph TG and set of rules R depends on its purpose. Certain control concepts originate from specific interpretations (such as non-terminals increasing the expressiveness of grammars for specifying graph languages) but may also be applied in different contexts. We will therefore defer the discussion of control constructs to Section 3.3 and first elaborate on the three different usage scenarios for graph transformations as introduced above.

The typical interpretation of a system described by a set of graph transformation rules, such as the VoIP network model discussed in the previous chapter, is based on states and non-deterministic transformations between states by means of rules. Recall that a rule call and the tracking function between the elements of the given graph G and the transformed graph H are captured in the notation $G \xrightarrow{r(arg),f} H$. More generally, the set of transformations in a graph transformation system represents a labelled transition system (as, for example, defined in [32]), where each state contains a graph, and the graphs of two successive states are related by a tracking function.

Given a graph transformation system $GTS = (TG, R)$ over a type graph TG and a set of rules R, a *graph transition system*

$$LTS(GTS) = (S, Lab, \rightarrow, I, F)$$

is defined by

- a set of states S representing graphs, i.e. for each state $s \in S$, there is a graph $G_s \in L(TG)$ (with $L(TG)$ being the set of all graphs that conform to the type graph TG);
- a set of labels Lab made up of triples $r(arg), f$ where r is the name of a rule of R, arg is a list of graph elements or data values used as arguments in r and, for any TG-typed graphs G and H, f is a partial tracking function between G and H (for an illustration of the tracking function, see Fig. 2.9 in the previous chapter);
- a labelled transition relation $\_ \Rightarrow \_ \subseteq S \times Lab \times S$;
- a set of *initial* states $I \subseteq S$ (the set I is often a singleton);
- a set of *final* (or accepting) states $F \subseteq S$.

The states in F allow us to distinguish successful from unsuccessful (i.e. incomplete or deadlocked) transformation sequences. A state s without outgoing transitions is called *terminal*. A transformation sequence is *terminal* if it ends in a terminal state. A transformation sequence (whether terminal or not) is *successful* if it ends in a final state $s \in F$. A terminal transformation sequence not ending in a final state is *deadlocked*. (Examples of graph transition systems can be found below; see, for example, Fig. 3.6.) The graphs associated with initial and final states are themselves called *initial* and *final* graphs, respectively.

For a given graph transformation system GTS and a graph G_0, we define an *uncontrolled graph transition system* $LTS(GTS, G_0) = (S, Lab, \rightarrow, I, F)$ as follows:

- $S = L(GTS, G_0)$ is the set of graphs reachable from G_0 along a sequence of transformations (note that in this particular case we equate states and graphs);
- Lab is the set of labels as above;
- $G \xrightarrow{r(arg), f} H$ iff $G \in S$ and $G \xrightarrow{r(arg), f} H$ is a transformation in GTS;
- $I = \{G_0\}$ is the singleton initial graph;
- $F = S$ is the set of all states.

The uncontrolled graph transition system is the most general interpretation of a graph transformation system, unrestricted by additional control structures and without hiding any of the states or transitions. Since the set of final states is defined to contain all states, they do not impose any conditions, i.e. in an uncontrolled graph transition system, all sequences are successful. Note that the level of detail represented can be controlled to a certain extent by choosing rule parameters that expose more or less information about the match.

At this stage, we do not fix a particular way to define the class F of final graphs. However, we will consider different options in the following subsections, where this general notion of a graphical labelled transition system will help us to derive simpler, more restricted semantic models.

3.2.1 Graph Languages

The simplest way of defining a set of graphs, or *graph language L*, is to use a type graph TG such that the language $L = L(TG)$ is formed by TG's instance graphs. For example, all well-structured activity diagrams can be represented as instance graphs over the UML metamodel of activities. However, this language contains many graphs that are not valid activity diagram representations, for instance because they violate constraints such as "every merge node has exactly one outgoing flow edge" or "every activity diagram has a start and an end node". Such additional requirements, which induce a subset of $L(TG)$, can be expressed declaratively by graph constraints, or constructively by graph transformation rules. In this section, we illustrate the constructive technique; the combined usage of both techniques within a language-engineering process is presented in Chapter 10 of this book.

If a graph transformation system GTS is used to define a graph language, it is equipped with a *start graph* G_0 from which all other graphs in the language are derived by graph transformations. Therefore, in the context of graph languages, a graph transformation sequence is also called a *derivation*. GTS and G_0 are referred to jointly as a *graph grammar*. We will use a graph grammar to describe the abstract syntax of activity diagrams in Chapter 10.

If we are not interested in controlling derivations externally, or observing the rules applied in a derivation, no rule names or parameters are required. Therefore, at the most basic level, a graph grammar $GG = (TG, R, G_0)$ consists of a type graph TG, a set of rules R typed over TG, and an instance graph G_0 of TG as the start graph. The semantics of GG is defined by $L(GG) = \{H | G_0 \overset{*}{\Rightarrow} H\}$, the set of all graphs derivable from G_0 using rules of R (which is, by construction, a subset of $L(TG)$): a graph G_n is derivable from G_0 if there is a derivation $G_0 \overset{r_1}{\Longrightarrow} \cdots \overset{r_n}{\Longrightarrow} G_n$ with $n \geq 0$ and $r_i \in R$. The possibility of the empty sequence (of length 0) makes graph G_0 an element of the language.

Example 3.1 (language of VoIP networks). A grammar $GG = (TG, R, G_0)$ describing the set of all VoIP network graphs with at least one Super node is given by

- the type graph TG in Fig. 2.25;
- the set of rules R, consisting of newSuper, newClient and linkClient in Fig. 2.7, together with two additional rules newUser for creating new users and connectToSuper for connecting a user to an existing Super node, as shown in Fig. 3.2;
- a graph consisting of one Super node (without clients) as start graph G_0.

The parameter uid of type String is instantiated non-deterministically from the set of values of the data type, i.e. the set of all strings.   □

Often, not all reachable graphs are desirable members of the language L. In such cases, a specification of final states can be used to restrict L. In

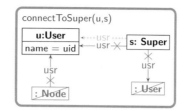

Fig. 3.2. Rules for inserting a new User and connecting to an existing Super node

graph grammars, the most common approach is to identify certain node or edge types as non-terminal types and consider a graph as final if it does not contain instances of such non-terminal types.

3.2.2 Graph Relations

Computations on graphs or mappings from one set of graphs into another can be described by *graph relations*. A binary relation over graphs can be specified or implemented using a graph transformation system. More precisely, a pair of graphs (G, H) is in the graph relation $gr(GTS)$ iff there exists a sequence of transitions $s_0 \xrightarrow{*} s_1$ in the corresponding graph transition system LTS from an initial state $s_0 \in I$ to a final state $s_1 \in F$, such that $G = G_{s_0}$ is the underlying graph of s_0 and $H = G_{s_1}$ is the underlying graph of s_1. More concisely, G is an initial graph and H is a final graph reachable from G. As an example of the use of a graph transformation system to define a graph relation we consider the computation of a spanning tree of Super nodes.

Example 3.2 (identifying a spanning tree of Super nodes). Let us assume that we have an arbitrary VoIP network graph, and the task is to identify the skeleton of the Super nodes in that graph, in the form of a spanning tree of ovl-labelled edges. In other words, we want to define a relation in which the initial graphs are VoIP network graphs, conforming to the type graph in Fig. 2.25, and the final graphs are the same graphs with additional structure showing which ovl edges are part of the spanning tree. To represent that additional structure, we will use TNode vertices and child edges according to the type graph shown in Fig. 3.3. A graph will be final if every Super node is marked by an incoming edge from a TNode.

The relation we are looking for is encoded by the rules in Figs. 3.4 and 3.5. Rule markRoot in Fig. 3.4 takes an arbitrary Super node and marks it as the root by adding a pointer of type TNode, if there is not already a TNode in the graph. The computation is continued by applying rule markChild Fig. 3.5. This rule becomes applicable only after markRoot has been applied; it selects a Super node as the next child if this node has not been included in the spanning tree already. This rule remains applicable as long as there are Super nodes outside the spanning tree (assuming that the input is connected).

The spanning tree computation is non-deterministic: the root and all children are selected non-deterministically by selecting an available match. Thus,

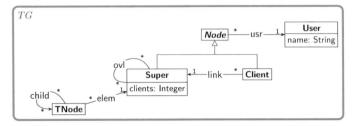

Fig. 3.3. Type graph for spanning-tree computation

Fig. 3.4. Initiating the computation of a spanning tree by marking the root

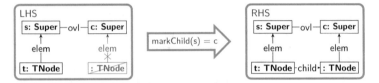

Fig. 3.5. Marking a child non-deterministically

the graph transition system truly defines a relation between any VoIP network graph and *every* corresponding spanning tree. In practice, if one actually wants to compute a spanning tree, probably one that is optimal with respect to some specific characteristic such as balance or cost, some control has to be imposed on the non-deterministic relation to turn it into a deterministic algorithm; for instance, a heuristic function to select the "best" rule application at every junction.   □

3.2.3 Graph Transition Systems and Other Small-Step Models

If we are interested in observing the detailed behaviour of a graph transformation system, which rules are applied where and when, and which can be applied in parallel or sequentially, neither language nor relational semantics are appropriate. So-called *small-step models* of semantics have been proposed to record such information, either in the form of interleaving models relying on a global notion of state or as partial-order models where states are implicit. Graph transition systems (as defined at the start of this section) represent the most common choice of small-step models, making explicit both the state-based nature and the non-determinism of graph transformations, but not their parallelism and concurrency. Before we discuss this aspect in more detail, let us see how normal graph transition systems are used to provide a comprehensive system-level semantics.

Example 3.3 (graph transition system). In order to represent the behaviour reachable from a given graph, we need a graph transition system where that graph is initial. For instance, starting from a VoIP network graph G_0 of two users and one Super node, the transition system is formed by iteratively applying the rules of Figs. 2.7 and 2.8 to G_0 and all successor graphs. Each rule application gives rise to a transition, labelled with the corresponding rule name, arguments and tracking function.

Fig. 3.6 shows a small section of this transition system, starting with the application of rule newSuper to each of the users in the start graph, resulting in state graphs State 1–State 4, shown as vertices of the transition system, with transitions shown as edges labelled by the corresponding rule invocations. The tracking function is implicitly given by the overlapping node identifiers of the source and target vertices. The inverse operation of newSuper is divided into two steps, first disconnecting the Super node using disconnectSuper(s2) and then removing it via endSuper(s2), as illustrated for Super node s2. This gives rise to the additional intermediate State 5.

Although considerably larger than the part shown in Fig. 3.6, the full transition system with State 1 as the start graph is still finite. For instance, an additional state is reached by applying rule shortcut to Super nodes s2 and s3. The new ovl edge gives rise to further states when a Super node is terminated. If, for one or both users, Client nodes are inserted instead of Super nodes, this also results in further states. Altogether, we get 27 possible different states, specifying all possible networks with two users, clients and super nodes in all possible stages of construction and termination.   □

It is easy to see that the representation of the behaviour of a graph transformation system as a labelled transition system expresses branching and termination explicitly: a branching state is one with two or more outgoing transitions; a terminating state does not have any outgoing transitions. Although the level of detail represented can be controlled by choosing rule parameters that expose more or less information about the match, there is no facility for hiding intermediate graphs or steps.

Labelled transition systems are a prerequisite for model checking: given a temporal formula, a graph transformation system can be checked for counterexamples, based on its labelled transition system. Section 4.5 discusses model checking in more detail. By associating a (random, exponentially distributed) application delay with each rule, *stochastic* graph transformation systems can be used for analysing non-functional quantitative properties. This is elaborated on in Chapter 9.

In Section 2.2.3, we discussed the atomicity of individual rule applications and pointed out that this provides a powerful abstraction mechanism allowing us to summarise the precondition and effect of a complex process while hiding their individual actions. In a model representing a distributed system, such as our VoIP network, it is possible for complex processes to interleave their individual actions. If these actions are encapsulated into rules, this is no longer

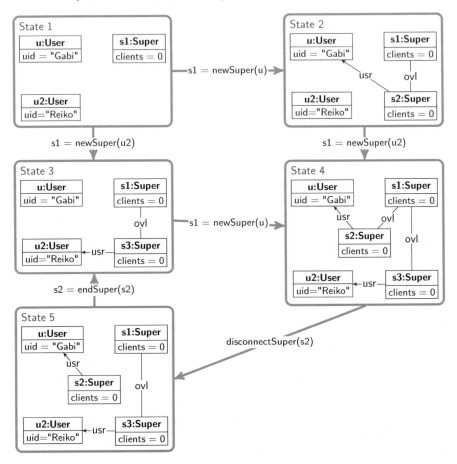

Fig. 3.6. Section of a labelled transition system

possible. This means that, for an implementation to faithfully capture the behaviour of the model, these processes have to be prevented from interfering with each other. In the case of the promoteClient operation, this would mean that Client, Super and User nodes are locked while the promotion is being executed so that no other operations are applicable to these nodes.

This changes when we consider operations specified by control structures as considered in the following section. In this case, it may take several rule applications to perform an operation. Two such complex operations consisting of several steps could be allowed to interleave, which may be appropriate in a distributed system where global control is hard to achieve, while in other cases a non-interleaving, isolated execution may be required. This choice is discussed in more detail in Section 3.3.4 below.

3.3 Taking Control

All the examples shown up to this point have been based on *uncontrolled rule application only*, meaning that the applicability of rules is *implicitly* determined by their preconditions and (mutual) effects. For example, if a rule p creates a vertex, this can enable a subsequent application of a rule q whose precondition requires such a vertex to exist. Analogously, if p deletes a graph element or changes an attribute value, any rule q that has a corresponding negative application condition or attribute constraint may become applicable. We will now discuss a range of constructs by which rule application can be controlled *explicitly*.

3.3.1 Motivating Example

We start with a motivating example, again based on VoIP network graphs conforming to the type graph in Fig. 2.25 and satisfying the constraints in Fig. 2.16. A Super node in a VoIP network graph may have a user, a certain number of clients, and ovl edges to any number of other Super nodes. This variability of context makes the deletion of such a node a potentially complex operation. The solution presented in the previous chapter does not allow for this complexity: the rule endSuper in Fig. 2.8 radically removes, in addition to the Super node itself, all its adjacent edges to other network nodes. This could lead to undesirable effects, such as leaving dependent clients without a connection.

Example 3.4 (regulated shutdown with implicit control). The rules in Fig. 3.7 model a regulated shutdown of a Super node, where clients are handed over to other Super nodes before the Super node leaves the network. We introduce a Boolean attribute shutdown which is set to true to start this process. The shutdown process ends if there is no Super node left with shutdown = true. The sets I and F of initial and final states are defined as those states not containing such Super nodes. Thus, this set of rules defines a relation between instance graphs without Super nodes with shutdown = true.   □

A different solution, using a combination of implicit and explicit control, is shown in Fig. 3.8. This involves a so-called *transformation unit*, which is essentially a named procedure with a control expression as its body specifying in what order and, to some degree, on what graph nodes certain rules should be applied.

Example 3.5 (regulated shutdown with explicit control). Instead of the implicit control encoded by an attribute, we can use explicit control structures, thus avoiding a mix of control and graph structures. *Programmed graph transformation* provides imperative control constructs suitable for rule-based systems, as shown in Fig. 3.8. To execute endSuper(s1) on a given Super node s, we first apply disconnectSuper(s1) of Fig. 2.8 and then redirectClient(s1,c,s2) of Fig. 2.7,

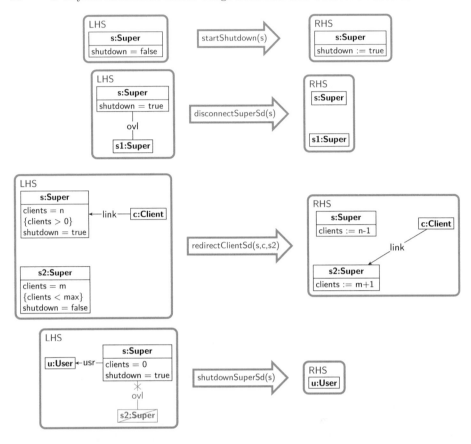

Fig. 3.7. Shutdown of Super node with implicit control

```
1   unit endSuper(s1: Super) {        // definition of transformation unit
2      atomic {                        // all−or−nothing semantics
3         alap {                       // execute for as long as possible
4            disconnectSuper(s1,_)     // invocation of rule by name + args
5         }
6         alap {                       // execute for as long as possible
7            redirectClient (s1,_ ,_) // invocation of rule by name + args
8         }
9         shutdownSuper(s1)            // invocation of rule by name + args
10     }
11  }
```

Fig. 3.8. Transformation unit explicitly shutting down Super node s1

both as long as possible, followed by a single application of shutdownSuper(s1) of Fig. 2.20. Note that we do not rely on an additional attribute here as in the previous example; instead, we use the original rules introduced in Chapter 2. This means that we target the shutdown process at a specific node s rather than all nodes satisfying a certain property such as shutdown = true.

The keyword **atomic** specifies that the effect of these applications is committed only once they have been performed completely, i.e. the Super node s1 is fully disconnected and deleted after executing the transformation unit endSuper(s1). □

3.3.2 Procedural Abstraction and Parameter Passing

Parameterised rules have been used in our VoIP example in order to indicate in the label of a transformation to which elements the rule is applied, such as in disconnectSuper(s2) in Fig. 3.6. As introduced in Section 2.2, rule parameters are declared as part of the rule signature, so that it is statically known that disconnectSuper requires a parameter and that the type of that parameter is known to be a Super node. We have already seen that parameters serve to *observe* part of the match of the transformation in the label and to *determine* part of that match. If, in a rule sequence, some input parameters are instantiated by output parameters of previous steps, we call this a sequence of *rule invocations*. Although some previously free parameters are already bound now, these parameter bindings generally lead to partial matches only. A sequence where all parameters are bound to concrete values is called a *rule call sequence*.

A controlled application of parametrised rules can be abstracted into a *transformation unit*. Each unit has a signature consisting of a name and a list of parameters and contains a control expression over a set of parametrised rules. If a unit parameter is bound, this usually leads to further parameter bindings. For example, if the transformation unit in Fig. 3.8 is invoked in such a way that s1 is bound to some node n in the given graph, this restricts possible applications of disconnectSuper(s1) to those matches that map node s of the rule to n. To understand the use of parameters within a transformation unit, it is important to realise that, apart from the graph currently being transformed, every state also has an associated mapping of the local variables of the transformation unit under execution to concrete values (either node identities of the graph under transformation or attribute values). Moreover, in the case of nested unit invocations, there is such a mapping for every transformation unit in the call stack.

Example 3.6 (parameter passing). In an execution of the transformation unit endSuper(s1) defined in Fig. 3.8, s1 may be bound to a node n of the graph under transformation. This binding partially determines the match of rule disconnectSuper(s1, _) (invoked in line 4 of Fig. 3.8 and defined in Fig. 2.8): Vertex s in that rule must be matched by n, whereas the match of the rule's second parameter t (which is anonymous in the invocation) remains open.

Similarly, in the invocation of redirectClient(s1, _, _) (line 7 of Fig. 3.8, defined in Fig. 2.7), s1 is bound to n, whereas the other parameters are can be bound freely by the chosen match of the rule.

Another example of a transformation unit is given in Fig. 3.9, which computes a spanning tree for a given network graph. In the absence of explicit control, the rules markRoot and markChild (presented in Figs. 3.4 and 3.5) may be applied in any order in which they are applicable. This solution can lead to a large number of unnecessary applicability checks for rules. In this example, the applicability of rule markRoot may be checked again and again, although it is easy to see that it can only be applied at the start. The solution in Fig. 3.9 is therefore more performant.

```
1    unit spanningTree(root: Super) {
2        markRoot(root);
3        markChildren(root)
4    }
5
6    unit markChildren(parent: Super) {
7        alap {
8            child := markChild(parent);
9            markChildren( child )
10       }
11   }
```

Fig. 3.9. Transformation unit marking a spanning tree among Super nodes

When spanningTree is invoked with an argument n, root is bound to n and this is the node to which markRoot is applied, followed by a nested invocation of markChildren where n is also assigned to parent. The rule markChild in Line 3 then non-deterministically selects a neighbour of n to be marked, say m, and assigns it to the node variable child. In the recursive invocation of markChildren(child), parent is bound to m, again restricting its match to ensure that the creation of the spanning tree continues at m.   □

3.3.3 Scheduling Expressions

Scheduling constructs explicitly restrict the order of rule applications; they include sequential composition and as-long-as-possible iterations, denoted by ; and **alap**, respectively, and conditionals, choices and priorities. The form and semantics of rule scheduling constructs may deviate from those in imperative languages in order to account for the non-deterministic and rule-based nature of graph transformation. The as-long-as-possible statement **alap** represents an iteration that uses a test for applicability of its internal action as a guard. In a transactional setting sequential composition ; can be used with an all-or-nothing semantics, only succeeding if both its arguments succeed, otherwise failing without affecting the current state. A **one** statement, arbitrarily selecting one out of several executable actions, represents a form of non-deterministic guarded choice.

Layered graph transformation systems [84] provide a simple control mechanism for rule application, where a given rule set is partitioned into $n > 0$ subsets such that each rule is equipped with a layer number. Layering means that rules are applied for as long as possible in the order of their layers. Only when rules of layer i are no longer applicable does control pass on to layer $i+1$. Using the control constructs introduced above, layering can be expressed by creating an **alap** loop for each layer and composing them in sequence.

As a variant of the common if −then−else statement, try −else combines an if condition and a **then** branch into a single **try** action that performs that branch if its precondition is satisfied. Priorities determine a selection in cases where more than one rule is applicable. Scheduling mechanisms may be nested, allowing more complex programs.

A graphical notation for scheduling rules is provided by UML activity diagrams. In graph transformations, this has been proposed in the form of story diagrams, as presented in [102] and implemented in the Fujaba language and tool [6]. The basic idea is to represent control flow by an activity graph, where each node contains a graph transformation rule describing the action.

If control diagrams are well structured, i.e. they define a hierarchical block structure of nested controls, their use in scheduling transformations is equivalent to the textual representation discussed above. Freely connected control flow diagrams admitting "spaghetti" code correspond to the use of a **goto** construct in a textual language, which can lead to control flow that is hard to understand and maintain. In traditional programming languages, this observation has limited the adoption of graphical control flow specifications that are not well structured, but they are still useful, for example in representing real-life business processes that are not well structured.

Example 3.7 (controlled shutdown of Super nodes continued). Figure 3.10 shows an example diagram of the controlled shutdown of **Super** nodes. Besides start and end nodes, it has three activity nodes containing rules, connected by three kinds of activity edge: those labelled **alap** denote loops that apply the inner rule for as long as possible, **exit** edges represent exits from such loops, taken when the internal rule fails, and unlabelled edges represent sequential application. In the activity diagram in Fig. 3.10 they occur only from and two the start and end nodes.

We see in this example that edges can be defined between arbitrary actions in activity diagrams. This flexibility may be helpful during development, but such "goto" structures can lead to entangled control flow that is hard to understand and maintain. An activity diagram is *well structured* if each activity node (apart from **start** and **end**) has exactly one incoming and one outgoing edge of the unlabelled (sequential) variety. Hence, the diagram in Fig. 3.10 is well structured.   □

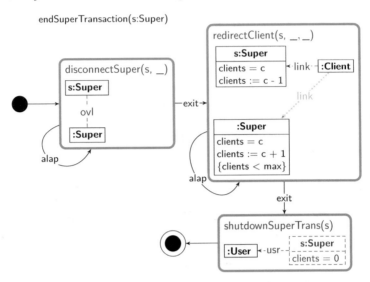

Fig. 3.10. Activity diagram specifying transformation unit endSuperTransaction(s)

3.3.4 Transactional Behaviour

Some features that are well known in database transactions, such as *atomicity, isolation* and *integrity*, are also relevant to controlled graph transformation systems.

Atomicity is the requirement that a complex sequence of operations, combining several internal steps, has an all-or-nothing interpretation. For example, the transformation unit endSuperTransUnit(s) will only succeed in updating the graph if all components are executed successfully. If, for example, the application of the last rule, shutdownSuperTU(s), should fail, the entire unit fails and does not lead to a new state. An additional aspect of atomicity is its reflection in the graph transition system. If atomicity is required at the level of a named transformation unit, we can decide to replace the sequence of internal transitions by a single transition labelled with the name and argument of the transformation unit, thus significantly simplifying the transition system.

Note 3.1: Atomic transformation units as transactions. A transformation unit combines several rule applications into a functional unit. A transformation unit whose body is contained in an **atomic** block represents a transaction. Just as rule applications form transactions over basic actions, transformation units form transactions over rule applications. This means that (1) if a part of a transformation unit cannot be executed, the whole transformation fails, (2) the execution cannot be interleaved with rule applications that create or destroy matches for any of the rules in the

---

unit, and (3) failure of the result graph of a unit to satisfy an integrity constraint leads to the failure of the unit.

Atomicity also affects constructs such as **alap** that are, by themselves, always successful. Units may contain sequences, try−else statements and if−then−else statements which can exhibit partial failure. An **atomic** block turns partial into total failure, so an **alap** block may fail if an internal sequence fails to execute completely.

Consistency requirements can be expressed by graph constraints, introduced in Section 2.4.1 as a means of describing structural properties of graphs. Such constraints can be interpreted in a variety of ways, including as invariants to be satisfied by all reachable graphs, for the declarative specification of graph languages, and as global postconditions for rules or transactions. In the latter interpretation, in analogy to databases, graphs have to be *consistent* meaning that graph constraints allow transformations $G \Rightarrow H$ to succeed only if they are satisfied by the resulting graph H.

Example 3.8 (augmentation of overlay network). In Fig. 2.17, we introduced a "shortcut" rule that adds redundant links to the network in order to improve its tolerance to Super nodes leaving. The rule has negative application conditions which ensure that no new ovl link is added between the Super nodes determined by the match if (1) there already is such a link or (2) there is an alternative two-hop path between the two nodes.

Rather than specifying such conditions as part of the application conditions, they could be given as global integrity constraints. In this case, a variant of the shortcut rule without an application condition could be applied for as long as there are transformations satisfying the global integrity constraint shown in Fig. 3.11 ruling out triangular ovl links as well as parallel two-hop paths. The advantage of such constraints over rule-specific application con-

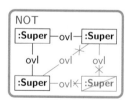

Fig. 3.11. Graph constraint limiting the redundancy in the network

ditions is that global conditions are rule independent, fully declarative and therefore easier to understand and maintain. For example, when rules are added or modified, application conditions have to be adapted, but integrity constraints are usually not directly affected. To ensure that a rule is not tried at the same match over and over again, some bookkeeping of matches may be required.   □

Isolation is relevant if we adopt the distributed interpretation of rule applications as described in the introduction to this chapter. In this case, concurrent execution prevents global control, it is important to understand how complex processes run when different local nodes of a network can interfere. Isolation means that concurrent executions of transformation units should not interfere. This means that any interleaving of the internal transitions of two units should be equivalent to a purely sequential (isolated) execution where each unit is executed as a sequence of consecutive transitions. Syntactically, this property is usually subsumed under the keyword **atomic**, but the following example shows that atomicity (in the sense of all-or-nothing execution) and isolation (in the sense of non-interference) describe different aspects.

Example 3.9 (unwanted interleaving). If the three shutdown rules were applied as part of the overall graph transformation system without further restriction, for example, they could interleave with applications of other rules: new clients could connect to a Super node in the process of being shut down while existing clients are in the process of transfer to other nodes, adding to the list of clients to be handed over before the Super node can eventually be deleted using rule shutdownSuperTrans() in Fig. 3.10. This means that new ovl edges could be added to a Super-node while already existing links are redirected. Isolation should encapsulate the termination process, preventing unwanted interleaving.   □

Durability is concerned with the permanent storage of transaction results. Hence it does not play a significant role at the level of behavioural semantics. Implementing tools should ensure that, once a transaction is performed, all its changes will be stored permanently in the system.

3.4 Summary and Further Reading

Graph transformation has been used in various application scenarios. In this chapter, we have identified applications leading to three different semantic models: (1) graph grammars are used to describe graph languages, (2) graph relations define graph algorithms and, especially, translations, and (3) graph transition systems specify detailed system behaviour. To restrict the behaviour of a rule-based transformation system, we considered a range of control mechanisms. Transformation units implement a form of procedural abstraction with parameter passing. The order of rule applications can be further restricted by control expressions. Atomic transformation units have a transactional behaviour similar to individual rule applications. In the following, we give pointers to relevant literature on the control mechanisms presented.

Transformation units were introduced in [17] as an approach-independent structuring principle for graph transformation systems. In their original form, they consist of specifications for initial and terminal graphs forming pre- and postconditions for transformation units. They are parametric in the underlying graph transformation approaches, such as PROGRES, the double- or single-pushout approaches, and the node- or edge-replacement approaches.

The main composition mechanism of transformation units is the import and use of existing units establishing a hierarchical import relation. Transformation units have been provided with an *interleaving semantics* defining an input–output relation on graphs for each transformation unit, composed of similar relations for imported units and individual rules. A comprehensive theory of transformation units was developed by Kuske in [179].

Habel and Plump [122] have identified a minimal set of control constructs such that a programming language based on graph transformation is computationally complete. This requires the nondeterministic application of a set of transformation rules, sequential composition and loops. Omitting one of these features results in a computationally incomplete language. Computational completeness here means the ability to compute every computable partial function on labelled graphs.

The idea of refining activity diagrams by graph rules and adopting them as a control structure for rule applications goes back to story diagrams and was comprehensively presented by Fischer et al. in [102] and Zündorf in [296]. These authors also introduced the link between rule-based structure transformations and the programmed manipulation of object-oriented structures. In contrast to transformation units, story diagrams do not have a transaction semantics, since they are compiled into Java code.

While by concurrency of transformations we refer to the fact that they can be executed independently, parallel execution means that they are executed simultaneously. We have not thoroughly discussed parallel transformations in this chapter but there are several approaches to parallel graph transformation in the literature. Parallel graph transformation has its origin in *graph L-systems*, a direct generalisation of L-systems describing the context-free parallel replacement of strings. Motivated by the application of L-systems to modelling the development of organisms, graph L-systems have been used to model the evolution of multidimensional structures such as cells [219, 220]. The parallel application of rules has also been exploited for hyperedge replacement, for example, for the generation of collage graphs. The double-pushout approach was extended to the parallel replacement of graphs in [78]. A more general form of parallel graph transformation, allowing non-context-free replacements and more general forms of graph structures, was presented by Taentzer in [268, 269].

4

Analysis and Improvement of Graph Transformation Systems

One motivation for software models is the ability to analyse them, for example to validate requirements and verify the consistency of models with each other or with respect to an implementation. Since we want to use graph transformation systems as software engineering models, we have to provide analysis techniques to answer questions about these systems that arise in their applications to software engineering problems.

Let us assume that we have settled on a semantic interpretation and set of control features as described in Chapter 3 and created a first graph transformation system according to these choices. A common problem at this stage is how to ensure the quality of the graph transformation system, such as its internal well formedness, consistency, or correctness with respect to given requirements. A precise semantics allows us to ask questions that have well-defined, if not always computable, answers. Such questions can be purely analytical, about assessing certain qualities such as if a state property is an invariant of the system, or they may have a constructive aspect, for example, how the rules of the system should be modified such that a state property becomes an invariant. In this section we investigate questions such as these, as well as the answers that have been developed.

We start by introducing a range of questions for each of the different semantic interpretations illustrated with examples, and then give a high-level overview of the popular analysis techniques for graph transformation systems and describe their use for answering the questions identified in Section 4.1. From Section 4.2, onwards we describe these techniques and their application in more detail.

We organise the first part of the discussion in terms of the semantic interpretations identified in Chapter 3 because different questions will arise depending on the interpretation of the graph transformation model, as describing a graph language, a relation between sets of graphs or a graph transition system.

A graph grammar GG is used to generate a *graph language* $L(GG)$. In Chapter 10, we will show how the language of well-structured activity dia-

© Springer Nature Switzerland AG 2020
R. Heckel, G. Taentzer, *Graph Transformation for Software Engineers*,
https://doi.org/10.1007/978-3-030-43916-3_4

grams can be described by a graph grammar. For graph languages, the following properties are relevant:

- *Membership:* Does the graph language $L(GG)$ contain a given graph G?
- *Inclusion:* Does the graph language $L(GG)$ contain another language L', for example, one described by another grammar or a type graph with constraints, or is $L(GG)$ itself a subset of another given graph language?
- *Instance generation:* Can we enumerate the graphs G in $L(GG)$ or sample this set randomly?
- *Non-ambiguity:* Does every graph in $L(GG)$ have a unique derivation up to reordering of independent steps, i.e. for any two derivations from the start graph G_0 to the same graph G, are those derivations equivalent up to reordering?

The last question is relevant in relation to graph parsing, a process by which we search for a derivation of G from the start graph G_0 using the rules in GG, thus solving the membership problem. A typical solution is for the generating rules of the grammar to be turned into *inverse* reduction rules as presented in Chapter 2. If G's derivation is unique, this provides us with information about the syntactic structure of the graph. Efficient parsing also requires reduction rules to be terminating and confluent (i.e. deterministic up to choices that do not affect the end result). Non-ambiguity is not itself a property that can be stated based on the language semantics of sets of derivable graphs. It is actually a property of the transition system, but is included under language properties here because of its relevance to parsing.

The membership problem for the language of well-structured activity diagrams is considered in Chapter 10. It asks if a given graph forms a legal representative of such a diagram. Given a specification of the language of all activity diagrams, the question of whether all *well-structured* diagrams are also in this language is one of language inclusion. Non-ambiguity means that each well-structured diagram can be obtained by a unique sequence of transformations, usually up to reordering of independent steps. This is relevant because the derivation of a well-structured activity diagram reveals its hierarchical block structure. The problem of instance generation is relevant to testing and performance evaluation, for example, of model transformation or analysis tools, where sample diagrams represent individual test cases. A parser for well-structured activity diagrams would produce derivations representing their hierarchical construction.

A typical example of a *graph relation* is a translation between two modelling languages. Chapter 12 presents a translation of class models to relational database schemas. Assuming a transformation unit describing a relation between two sets of graphs, we can consider the following properties:

- *Functional behaviour:* Does the relation describe a function, i.e. does it associate each input graph with at most one output graph?
- *Totality:* Does the relation associate to every input graph at least one output graph?

- *Injectivity:* Does the relation always map different input graphs to different output graphs?
- *Surjectivity:* Does it map an input graph to every graph of the target domain?
- *Correctness:* Is the relation consistent with a given semantic interpretation of graphs? Does it preserve certain properties, in the sense that, when mapping an input graph G to an output graph H, if a property P holds for G, then a property Q holds for H?

For the translation from class models to relational database schemas, functional behaviour and totality ensure that the mapping is well defined as a total function, while injectivity and surjectivity imply that the mapping is one-to-one and reaches all schemas in the target domain. Semantic correctness could mean, for example, that all instances of a given class models, i.e. all object structures over that class model, are matched by concrete tables which conform to the corresponding relational schema. In practice, class models are richer and more flexible than relational schemas since they allow class inheritance. So while a semantically correct mapping may well be a total surjective function, it will not be injective, because different class hierarchies can lead to the same relational schema. This translation is presented in detail in Chapter 12.

In the *graph transition system* interpretation, as represented by the VoIP network model, we can ask questions about (sequences of) transitions and their interrelations. It is worth recalling that a transition in a graph transition system $s_1 \xrightarrow{r} s_2$ is based on a transformation $G_1 \xRightarrow{r} G_2$ between the underlying graphs G_1 and G_2 of states s_1 and s_2 but that not all transformations give rise to transitions, because the graph transition system also captures the restrictions imposed by the control structures introduced in Chapter 3. We will henceforth use the transition notation $s_1 \xrightarrow{r} s_2$ where we do not want to focus on the specifics of the graph transformation step or where control flow is being considered, and continue to use the graph transformation notation $G_1 \xRightarrow{r} G_2$ otherwise. We consider the following properties:

- *Reachability:* Can a given graph, rule or transition be reached from the start graph of the graph transition system? Can they be reached repeatedly?
- *Invariants:* Do all graphs reachable from the start graph satisfy certain constraints or, dually, can we reach graphs that violate such constraints?
- *Deadlocks:* Are there terminal states (i.e. without outgoing transitions) that are non-final?
- *Planning and optimisation:* Can we find a (good or optimal under a certain objective function) path in the graph transition system from a given graph to a graph satisfying certain properties?
- *Temporal properties:* Does the system satisfy certain safety and liveness properties, for example, expressed by temporal logical formulas over paths through the system?

- *Termination:* Does the system only have finite paths from initial states?
- *Confluence:* Can every divergent pair of transition sequences $G_1 \xleftarrow{*} G \xrightarrow{*} G_2$ be joined as $G_1 \xrightarrow{*} H \xleftarrow{*} G_2$? Is this true locally for pairs of transitions $G_1 \leftarrow G \rightarrow G_2$? Is this relation *strict* in the sense that the tracking functions along $G \xrightarrow{*} G_1 \xrightarrow{*} H$ and $G \xrightarrow{*} G_2 \xrightarrow{*} H$ agree? More specifically, can a pair $G_1 \xLeftarrow{r_1} G \xRightarrow{r_2} G_2$ be joined directly as $G_1 \xRightarrow{r_2} H \xLeftarrow{r_1} G_2$? Can we swap the order of steps in a sequence $G \xRightarrow{r_1} G_1 \xRightarrow{r_2} H$ to $G \xRightarrow{r_2} G_2 \xRightarrow{r_1} H$?

In the VoIP network model, invariants such as "Super nodes with clients $= 0$ have no Client nodes attached" need to be maintained for the graphs to be semantically meaningful. Connectivity of the network is a further, more complex example. The transition system in Example 3.3 does not have a deadlock, because all states have outgoing transitions. The question of how, from a disconnected configuration, a connected configuration is reached can be phrased as a planning problem. It becomes an optimisation problem if we ask for the best or nearest such configuration with respect to suitable metrics. This transition system does not terminate, since there is at least one infinite path that applies rules newSuper, disconnectSuper and endSuper, in that order, indefinitely. The system is not confluent. As already shown in Fig. 3.6, applications of newSuper to different User nodes can happen in either order. If the same user connects to different Super nodes, however, this leads to a pair of conflicting transformations that can not be joined.

4.1 Techniques for Analysis and Construction

There are a variety of techniques, including analytical and constructive ones, to ensure the properties listed and illustrated above. They are described in more detail in Sections 4.2–4.5. In particular, we cover the following techniques:

- *CDA:* Conflict and dependency analysis includes static analysis techniques (at rule level rather than involving state graphs and transitions) to determine the possibility of conflicts or dependencies between rules. The transformations $G_1 \xLeftarrow{r_1} G \xRightarrow{r_2} G_2$ are in conflict if the application of r_1 destroys the match for r_2 or vice versa. Otherwise, we consider them to be parallel independent of each other. Starting from just two rules, *critical pair analysis* finds all conflicting pairs of transformations (when these rules are applied) in a minimal context. This is useful for demonstrating confluence. Similarly, *dependency analysis* detects the possibility of situations such as $G_1 \xRightarrow{r_1} G_2 \xRightarrow{r_2} G_3$ where the application of r_2 depends on that of r_1 or where an application of r_2 to G_1 could prevent r_1 from being applied. Otherwise, such a transformation sequence is called sequentially independent.

- *TA:* Termination analysis includes a range of techniques to establish the absence of infinite transformation sequences. Termination is undecidable in general, so these techniques are given in the form of sufficient criteria which, if satisfied, guarantee termination. Under certain conditions, systems can be made to terminate by construction, for example, by adhering to the restrictions of layered systems.
- *CV&E:* Constraint verification and enforcement can be analytical or constructive in nature. Constructive enforcement, given a rule and a graph constraint intended as an invariant, derives the weakest precondition of this constraint as an application condition for the rule. In addition, it may be interesting to check if the weakest precondition constructed is redundant since it is already entailed by existing application conditions or invariants. We call such a check constraint verification; it implements the analytical approach.
- *MC:* Model checking, given a graph transformation system and a start graph, generates the transition system and then analyses it for satisfaction of temporal properties. Owing to its ability to generate counterexamples, model checking can also be used to construct sequences of transformations satisfying certain conditions, for example to generate test cases. For some analyses, such as non-ambiguity, the state space generation, a necessary prerequisite to do model checking, is already enough to get results.
- *GP:* Graph parsing is an attempt to construct a derivation for a graph based on the rules of a given grammar. This can be done in a top-down, speculative way going forwards from the start graph of the grammar, or in a bottom-up way going backwards from the given graph, reversing the rules of the grammar in order to reduce any graph in the language to the start graph. As a result, a derivation is produced which represents the syntactic structure of the graph.

In most cases these techniques provide only incomplete answers to the questions stated earlier, for example, in the form of sufficient criteria for termination. Sometimes combinations of techniques are required to address a single question. For example, to check if a transformation system with a relational semantics implements functional behaviour, we have to establish its confluence. Confluence can be verified based on the computation of critical pairs. If all critical pairs are strictly confluent and the graph transformation system is terminating, its transformation relation is a function. Table 4.1 summarises which technique addresses which questions.

4.1.1 Language Properties

With certain prerequisites (non-ambiguity, functional behaviour of the reversed grammar), *membership* can be solved by graph parsing in an effective way, i.e. without backtracking. An example of parsing for activity diagrams is presented in Chapter 10. Model-checking techniques can provide a partial

Table 4.1. Analysis techniques to address analysis questions

	Conflict and dependency analysis	Termination analysis	Constraint verification	Model checking	Graph parsing
Language					
Membership				X	X
Inclusion			X	X	X
Instance generation	X		X	X	
Non-ambiguity	X	X		X	
Relation					
Functional behaviour	X	X		X	X
Totality		X		X	
Injectivity	X	X		X	X
Surjectivity		X		X	
Correctness	X		X	X	
Transition system					
Reachability				X	X
Invariants			X	X	
Deadlocks				X	
Planning & optimisation				X	
Temporal properties			X	X	
Termination		X		X	
Confluence	X	X		X	

solution, for example, by generating a set of reachable graphs and checking if a given graph is in that set. If the language is finite (and small enough) this can be a complete (if inefficient) solution.

Language *inclusion*, for sets of graphs L, L' with $L \subseteq L'$, can be sampled (tested) by any solution to the respective membership problems. If $L = L(GG)$ is the language generated by a grammar GG and $L' = L(C)$ is the set of graphs satisfying certain constraints C, we can use constraint verification to verify that all graphs generated by GG satisfy C, i.e. $L(GG) \subseteq L(C)$. In Chapter 10, a set of constraints and a graph grammar for activity diagrams are given. We can straightforwardly argue that the grammar fulfils all these constraints.

The *inclusion* question has a constructive version known as the *filter problem* [123]: Given GG and a logical specification of L, how do we derive a grammar GG_L such that $L(GG_L) = L(GG) \cap L$?

Instance generation can be supported by model checking, by generating graphs reachable from the start graph and returning them as counterexamples to properties representing the negation of policies to determine which instances should be returned. For example, in a language of activity diagrams we may want to return graphs representing diagrams with more than one decision node. A temporal formula demanding that the rule to generate decision nodes should be applied at most once would be violated by all paths through the transition system with two or more applications, and such paths would be returned by the model checker as evidence that the formula is not satisfied. Other approaches to sampling "interesting" graphs include CDA and constraint verification, which generate minimal graphs demonstrating conflicts or dependencies or violating constraints. They can be checked for membership using any of the techniques above.

Non-ambiguity can be verified by critical pair analysis on the set of inverse rules: if there are no critical pairs, the grammar is deterministic up to independence of transformations. In this case, all derivations that a parser can return are equivalent. Model checking can test non-ambiguity by trying to establish two different paths to certain graphs.

4.1.2 Relation Properties

As discussed above, *functional behaviour* can be analysed by a combination of critical pair analysis, reachability and termination. Termination guarantees that a transformation relation produces a result, not necessarily unique, for all input graphs. Conversely, if functional behaviour can be established for the reversed system, this can be used to show *injectivity* of the original relation, while totality of this function establishes the surjectivity of the original relation.

We distinguish between syntactic and semantic *correctness*. In the second category, if the semantics is described by operational or semantic mapping rules, *mixed* confluence based on critical pairs between semantic and transformation rules can be used to show correctness. For syntactic correctness, we are interested in showing that all graphs from the input set are mapped to syntactically correct graphs in the output set. This is also part of demonstrating that the function or relation implemented is total, and it can be achieved in part by showing that rules preserve or establish certain graph constraints. If semantic correctness is easy to check for individual pairs of input and output models, a constructive approach to correctness could restrict the transformation relation to exactly such pairs.

In Chapter 12 we consider the translation of class models to relational database schemas and discuss its functional behaviour and correctness in details.

4.1.3 System Properties

Many properties of states, transitions and paths in transition systems can be phrased as model-checking problems. *Invariants* can be verified by checking or enforcing the preservation of graph constraints.

If the state space is described by a suitable grammar, parsing can solve the *reachability* problem. Temporal properties expressing safety conditions, such as the absence of unintended sequences, can be ensured constructively by imposing control structures.

Confluence can be established by critical pair analysis in combination with termination and reachability. Termination and confluence admit both analytical and constructive solutions. Termination by construction can be achieved by control structures such as layered graph grammars. A constructive approach to confluence could reduce non-determinism either by suitable control structures or by completions that add rules to join diverging transformations.

In general, graph languages, relations and transition systems are infinite. Therefore, many questions about them are only semi-decidable. This means that in order to answer them we seek sufficient criteria, or algorithms that over- or under-approximate the relevant properties, such as in the case of critical pairs: their non-existence demonstrates that two rules can never create conflicting transformations, but if a critical pair exists, the corresponding conflict may not be reachable from a given start graph. Reachability itself, like the membership problem, is a semi-decidable property.

4.2 Conflicts and Dependencies

Often, in a graph transformation system, more than one rule is applicable to a given state, or a single rule is applicable at different matches. Then the application of one rule at one match may disable other choices available, creating a *conflict*. Also, one rule application may enable another, leading to a *dependency*. There may be several motivations for developers to understand if and why conflicts or dependencies occur:

1. If graph transformations are used to model the requirements or design of an application, rules define the data flow between actions, which might not be consistent with the control flow expressed, for example, in a process model. Finding potential conflicts and dependencies and comparing them with the control flow can identify such inconsistencies [99]. This interpretation is discussed in detail in Chapter 5.

2. In the optimisation of rule-based computations such as graph parsing [47], conflict and dependency analysis helps to trim the solution space of possible computation paths. When specifying model refactorings as graph transformation rules, their conflicts and dependencies can be analysed. This may help to understand which refactorings have to be applied in which order to reach a desired model structure. Model refactoring by graph transformation is presented in Chapter 11.

3. If a transformation is expected to deliver unique results for all inputs, as illustrated by the optimisation of overlay networks or the termination of Super nodes in Section 2.2.1, we have to demonstrate its functional behaviour. This means that transformation sequences with a common start graph have to end in the same result graph, i.e. they have to be confluent. A sufficient condition for the confluence of a transformation system is the strict confluence of all *critical pairs* [85], provided that the system is terminating. Critical pairs are conflicts and dependencies in minimal contexts.

They are strictly confluent if there exist sequences of transformations leading to a common successor graph, such that the tracking functions of these sequences are commutative, i.e. they are agree on the identities of the nodes and edges.

4.2.1 Conflicting and Dependent Transformations

Two transformations are *parallel independent* if they are applicable to the same graph without invalidating each other's matches. This means that their matches can only share graph elements preserved by both steps. Furthermore, they are not allowed to change the same attribute values, or to create structures forbidden by the other rule's application condition. Otherwise, the transformations are called *conflicting*.

Two transformations are *sequentially independent* if the execution of one transformation is not dependent of the execution on the other one. This means that the match of one rule application does not have to be prepared by applying the other rule in some way.

Given two parallel independent graph transformation steps $H_1 \xLeftarrow{r_1,m_1} G \xRightarrow{r_2,m_2} H_2$, the local Church-Rosser theorem formalises this intuition, stating that there are sequentially independent transformation steps $G \xRightarrow{r_1,m_1} H_1 \xRightarrow{r_2,m_2'} X$ as well as sequentially independent transformation steps $G \xRightarrow{r_2,m_2} H_2 \xRightarrow{r_1,m_1'} X$, both yielding the same result graph X.

There are different *types of conflicts*. If transformations $t_1 : G \xRightarrow{r_1,m_1} H_1$ and $t_2 : G \xRightarrow{r_2,m_2} H_2$ are conflicting, t_1 may disable t_2 or vice versa. Transformation t_1 *disables* transformation t_2 (or t_1 causes a conflict on t_2) if one of the following cases occurs:

- *Delete/use:* Applying r_1 deletes an element used in the application of r_2. A special case is the deletion of a node that should be used as the source or target of a new edge to be inserted with r_2.
- *Produce/forbid:* Applying r_1 produces an element that a NAC of r_2 forbids.
- *Change/use:* Applying r_1 changes an attribute value used in the application of r_2.

In the following, three examples of conflicts are illustrated and discussed.

Example 4.1 (types of conflict). A Super node without clients can be shut down. Obviously, no clients can be linked to it afterwards. Hence, applications of the rules endSuper and linkClient can be in a delete/use conflict. Considering Fig. 4.1, both rules are applicable at the selected matches. We see that if endSuper deletes the Super node used by linkClient, the corresponding rule applications are in a delete/use conflict with respect to Super node s.

For Users not yet part of the network, we can create new Client or Super nodes. In real networks the choice may depend on factors outside the scope of our model, such as the bandwidth of a user's Internet connection. In Fig. 4.2, both rules are applicable creating a conflict because each checks for an existing

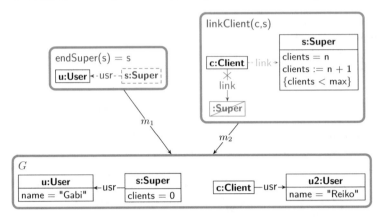

Fig. 4.1. Delete/use conflict between endSuper and linkClient

Node before creating a Client or Super node. Since Node is a supertype of Client and Super, the application of one rule prevents us from applying the other rule to the same User. This is a produce/forbid conflict. In graph G, both rules are applicable to user u. Graph H_1 shows the situation after applying rule newClient; rule newSuper is not applicable to this graph.

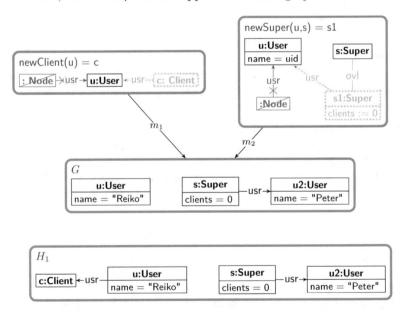

Fig. 4.2. Produce/forbid conflict between newClient and newSuper

Two competing applications of linkClient, linking both to the same Super node, will each increase its clients attribute. Figure 4.3 illustrates how this represents a change/use conflict on the clients attribute. This conflict could be considered less severe, since it does not prevent the application of the second rule altogether. However, the original match does not survive, because it includes the original attribute value 0. Instead, as expected, the deferred second rule application updates clients from 1 to 2.   □

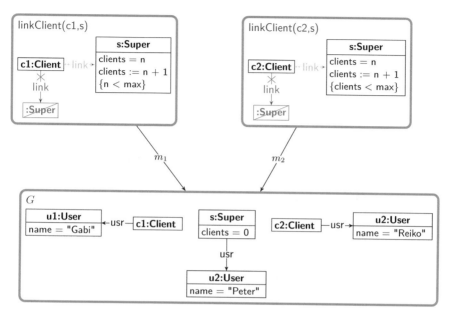

Fig. 4.3. Change/use conflict between linkClient and linkClient

There are different *types of dependencyies*. A sequence of transformations $G \xrightarrow{r_1, m_1} H_1 \xrightarrow{r_2, m_2'} X$ is *dependent* if $G \xrightarrow{r_1, m_1} H_1$ enables $H_1 \xrightarrow{r_2, m_2'} X$. We distinguish the following cases:

- *Produce/use:* Rule r_1 produces an element needed for the match of r_2.
- *Delete/forbid:* Applying r_1 deletes an element that a NAC of r_2 forbids. A special case is the deletion of an edge by r_1 such that the match of r_2 fulfils the dangling condition.
- *Change/use:* Rule r_1 changes an attribute value accessed by the application of r_2.

Example 4.2 (types of dependency). The application of rule linkClient may be dependent on that of newClient if a new Client node c is created before it is linked to a Super node. Figure 4.4 illustrates this dependency using an intermediate graph where Client c has just been created.

After one has ended a client, it is possible to connect the same user to the network by creating a new Super node. In this case, ending the Client node enables the creation of the Super node. Figure 4.5 shows this dependency, with applications overlapping in the User and Super nodes.

To shut down a Super node, all connected clients have to be disconnected first. If the application of rule endClient disconnects the last client, the clients

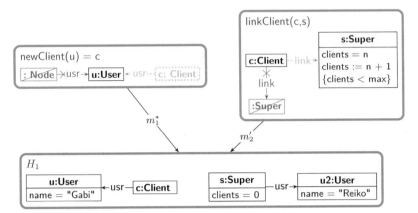

Fig. 4.4. Produce/use dependency of linkClient on newClient

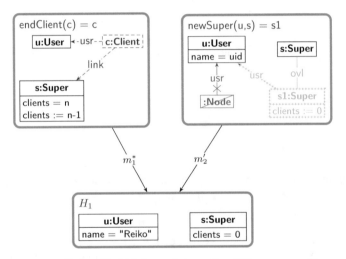

Fig. 4.5. Delete/forbid dependency of endClient on newSuper

attribute is set to 0, which enables the shutdown of the Super node by rule shutdownSuperTrans. This dependency is shown in Fig. 4.6.   □

Given the characterisations above, conflicts and dependencies can be detected dynamically while executing the transformations or constructing the transition system. For designing and reasoning about transformation rules, however, it is also interesting to analyse potential conflicts and dependencies at rule level. This static analysis technique is presented next.

4.2.2 Static Analysis of Conflicts and Dependencies

So far, we have considered conflicts and dependencies between graph transformation steps. However, generating all possible steps to analyse them for

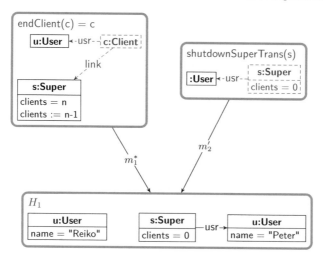

Fig. 4.6. Change/use dependency of shutdownSuperTrans on endClient

dependencies is impossible in general. Hence, in this section we adopt a static approach, analysing pairs of rules only. Rule r_1 causes a conflict on rule r_2 if there is at least one pair of transformations $t_1 : G \xrightarrow{r_1,m_1} H_1$ and $t_2 : G \xrightarrow{r_2,m_2} H_2$ where t_1 disables t_2. The outcome of this static analysis is a *conflict relation* between rules, i.e. rule pair (r_1, r_2) is in a conflict relation if r_1 causes a conflict on r_2 (or, equivalently, r_1 disables r_2). A conflict relation is represented by a table, whose entries in green refer to rule pairs without conflicting transformations, while entries in red indicate the existence of conflicting situations as described above. Numbers in red entries refer to different conflict reasons explained further below. A conflict relation can also be visualised as a graph where nodes represent rules and an edge from rule node r_1 to node r_2 means that pair (r_1, r_2) is the in conflict relation.

Example 4.3 (conflict table and graph). Figure 4.7 gives an overview of the conflicts between all rules shown in Fig. 2.7 and Fig. 2.8. The table was computed using AGG's critical pair analysis. For example, rule endSuper causes one conflict on rule linkClient, which we will analyse more closely below. We can also visualise the conflict relation by the graph in Fig. 4.8.   □

To gain a deeper understanding of the conflicts reported, we can ask which rule elements cause each conflict.

Example 4.4 (conflict-causing elements). For rule pair (endSuper, linkClient), Super node s is a conflict-causing element since it is deleted by rule endSuper and used by linkClient. We have seen one concrete sample application in Figure 4.1. For rule pair (newClient, newSuper), c:Client is a conflict-causing element created by the first rule and forbidden by the second.   □

To inspect a conflict in even more detail, we can ask which combinations of conflict-causing elements are possible. An answer to this question

first \ second	1: newS...	2: newCl...	3: linkCli...	4: promo...	5: redire...	6: endSu...	7: disco...	8: endCli...	9: endUn...
1: newSuper	2	1	0	0	0	0	0	0	0
2: newClient	1	1	0	0	0	0	0	0	0
3: linkClient	0	0	1	0	0	0	0	0	1
4: promoteClient	2	1	0	1	1	0	0	1	0
5: redirectClient	0	0	2	1	2	0	0	1	0
6: endSuper	2	0	1	0	1	1	0	0	0
7: disconnectSuper	0	0	0	0	0	0	6	0	0
8: endClient	0	0	0	1	1	0	0	1	0
9: endUnlinkedClient	0	0	0	0	0	0	0	0	1

Fig. 4.7. Overview of conflicts between the rules in Figs. 2.7 and 2.8

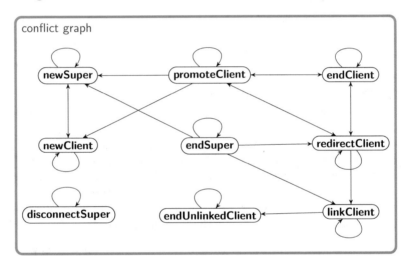

Fig. 4.8. Conflict graph for the rules in Figs. 2.7 and 2.8

is given by *critical pair analysis*. This technique is used in term rewriting to check for the confluence of rewrite systems. It was generalised to term graph rewriting in [230, 232] and to typed attributed graph transformations in [136]. A critical pair formalises the idea of two conflicting transformations $H_1 \xLeftarrow{r_1,m_1} G \xrightarrow{r_2,m_2} H_2$ in a minimal context. This means that the shared graph G is minimal with the property of allowing the application of each rule of the critical pair, such that the resulting transformations are in conflict.

From each critical pair, we can extract its *conflict reason* [184]. For delete/use conflicts, these are conflict-causing elements that rule matches overlap in. For a produce/forbid conflict, the conflict reason is an overlap of created elements in the right-hand side of rule r_1 with forbidden elements in a NAC of r_2.

Example 4.5 (critical pair for a conflict). Figure 4.9 shows a critical pair for a conflict of rule pair (endSuper, linkClient). The minimal graph G shows an overlap in node s: Super, which is deleted by rule endSuper and preserved by rule linkClient. Both rules are applicable to this graph, assuming that $1 < $ max. □

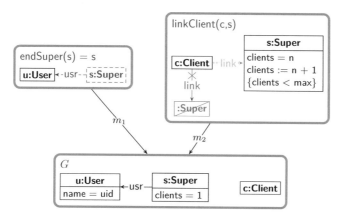

Fig. 4.9. Critical pair for (endSuper, linkClient) showing a delete/use conflict

Similar questions can be asked to understand dependencies at different levels of detail. The simplest one is whether rule r_2 depends on rule r_1. To answer this question, we have to check whether there is a pair of dependent transformations that apply the rules in this order. Analogously to the conflict notation, there is a dependency relation between rules which can be shown in a table or a graph, as illustrated by the next example.

Example 4.6 (dependency table and graph). Figure 4.10 shows which of the rules in Figs. 2.7 and 2.8 depend on each other. Table entries in green point to pairs of rules whose applications are always sequentially independent. Entries in blue show the number of dependent situations for a chosen rule pair. This table was computed using AGG's critical pair analysis for dependencies. For example, rule pair (endClient, newSuper) has one dependency, which we will analyse in more detail below. In Fig. 4.11, a graph illustrates all the rule dependencies in the example. □

To gain a deeper understanding of the dependencies reported, we can ask which rule elements cause the dependency of r_2 on r_1.

Example 4.7 (dependency-causing elements). For the pair of rules (endClient, newSuper), Client node c is a dependency-causing element, since it is deleted by endClient and forbidden by newSuper. We have seen one concrete application

first \ second	1: newS...	2: newCli...	3: linkCli...	4: promo...	5: redire...	6: endSu...	7: discon...	8: endCli...	9: endUn...
1: newSuper	2	0	1	0	2	0	2	0	0
2: newClient	0	0	0	0	0	0	0	0	1
3: linkClient	0	0	0	1	1	0	0	1	0
4: promoteClient	4	1	1	0	2	0	2	0	0
5: redirectClient	0	0	2	1	2	0	0	1	0
6: endSuper	1	1	0	0	0	0	0	0	0
7: disconnectSuper	0	0	0	0	0	0	0	0	0
8: endClient	2	1	0	0	0	0	0	0	0
9: endUnlinkedClient	1	1	0	0	0	0	0	0	0

Fig. 4.10. Overview of dependencies between rule pairs in Figs. 2.7 and 2.8

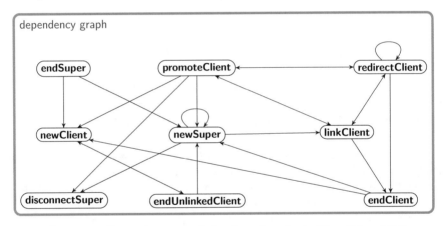

Fig. 4.11. Dependency graph for the rule pairs in Figs. 2.7 and 2.8

situation in Fig. 4.5. For rule pair (newClient, linkClient), c:Client is dependency-causing, since it is created by the first rule and used by the second.   □

To inspect a dependency of a given rule pair in even more detail, we can ask which combinations of dependency-causing elements are possible. An answer to this question is also given by critical pair analysis, applied to find consecutive rather than alternative transformations. To discover minimal dependent pairs of transformations $G \xrightarrow{r_1,m_1} H_1 \xrightarrow{r_2,m_2} X$, we have to consider all possible overlaps between the co-match $m_1' : R_1 \to H_1$ for r_1 and the match m_2 for r_2. Since rules and transformations are mostly invertible (see Section 2.4.7), a critical pair for a rule sequence $r_1; r_2$ can be reduced to a critical pair between rules r_1^{-1} and r_2.

Example 4.8 (critical pair for a dependency). Figure 4.12 shows a critical pair for a dependency in the rule sequence endClient; newSuper. The minimal in-

termediate graph H_1 contains a user that has just been disconnected and a
Super node to which users and clients can connect. Only by deleting the client
connected to the user does the addition of the Super node become possible. □

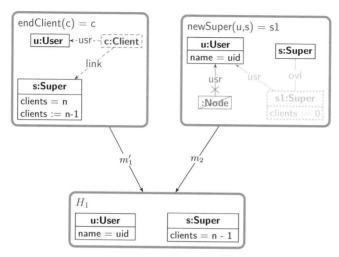

Fig. 4.12. Critical pair for (endClient, newSuper) showing a delete/forbid dependency

Our experience with a variety of applications shows that some rule pairs
can cause large numbers of critical pairs. Hence, we have investigated solutions
to present conflicts and dependencies more concisely using just a subset of all
critical pairs. Firstly, parallel applications of the same rule at the same match
are often in conflict. Such self-conflicts are resolvable by performing just one
of these applications. In order to not clutter the presentation unnecessarily
we may omit such self-conflicting pairs.

Secondly, the same combination of conflict- or dependency-causing elements may be reported in a number of very similar critical pairs. This may
happen if there are overlapping non-conflicting or non-depending graph elements as well, leading to all permutations of such overlaps being reported. To
avoid this, *essential critical pairs* were introduced in [184]. The smaller set of
essential critical pairs is still sufficient to show confluence of the transformation system. Indeed, Lambers et al. [183] showed that the set of critical pairs
needed to demonstrate confluence can be even more compact if the number
of overlapping elements is minimised. *Initial conflicts* and *initial dependencies*
allow a considerable reduction in the number of transformation pairs to be
considered.

4.2.3 Using Conflict and Dependency Analysis to Improve Graph Transformation Systems

The analyses described so far can have different objectives and their results can be used in different ways. Often, some or all conflicts or dependencies are undesirable, either because we want the system to be conflict-free or because certain conflicts or dependencies contradict given requirements. In this case it is possible to remove them by the following methods:

1. Modifying the relevant rules, for example by adding NACs to prevent particular transformations.
2. Adding control structures determining the order of conflicting rule applications, for example to first change an attribute and then move its containing element.
3. Adding new rules to resolve a conflict by making it confluent.

The last solution is especially interesting for the relational model, where confluence helps to guarantee functional behaviour. It can reduce non-determinism, thus removing the need for backtracking to find a valid output graph. In the following, we discuss criteria for confluence.

4.2.4 Confluence

Transformation sequences $H_1 \overset{*}{\Leftarrow} G \overset{*}{\Rightarrow} H_2$ are *confluent* if there are transformation sequences $H_1 \overset{*}{\Rightarrow} X \overset{*}{\Leftarrow} H_2$. A graph transformation system is confluent if this is the case for all pairs of sequences. It is *locally confluent* if all pairs of steps $H_1 \overset{r_1,m_1}{\Longleftarrow} G \overset{r_2,m_2}{\Longrightarrow} H_2$ are confluent.

The local Church-Rosser theorem [81, 85] states that parallel independent steps are trivially confluent by applying the same rules in different orders, i.e. given independent steps $H_1 \overset{r_1,m_1}{\Longleftarrow} G \overset{r_2,m_2}{\Longrightarrow} H_2$, there are steps $H_1 \overset{r_2,m_2'}{\Longrightarrow} X \overset{r_1,m_1'}{\Longleftarrow} H_2$ leading to the same result graph X.

Critical pairs allow us to formulate a condition for general confluence: a system is confluent if it is terminating and all critical pairs are (locally) confluent in a strict sense, agreeing not only on the resulting graph X but also on the tracking functions from their shared start graph G to X. A system is *terminating* if all its transformation sequences are finite. Criteria and techniques to analyse or ensure termination are discussed in Section 4.3 below. The set of critical pairs of a given graph transformation systems is *complete* in the sense that, given a pair of conflicting transformations, there is always a critical pair that can be embedded into this transformation pair. Assuming that the system is terminating, to prove that the system is confluent it is enough to check the strict confluence of all its critical pairs [136, 85]. Note that such a completeness property holds also for the set of all essential critical pairs [184] and even for the set of all initial conflicts [183].

Example 4.9 (confluence of the shutdown process for Super nodes). Example 3.4 presents rules disconnectSuperSd, redirectClientSd and shutdownSuperSd for implementing the shutdown of Super nodes without additional control constructs. To guarantee a unique result, we want to show local confluence. The first step consists in finding critical pairs. Then we have to show that each critical pair is strictly confluent. The only pair of rules with potential conflicts is (redirectClientSd, redirectClientSd), in particular if (1) the same client can be redirected to two different Super nodes (see the critical pair in Fig. 4.13), (2) the attribute clients of the ending Super node has to be updated twice to redirect two different clients and (3) two clients are moved to the same Super node such that its clients attribute has to be updated twice.

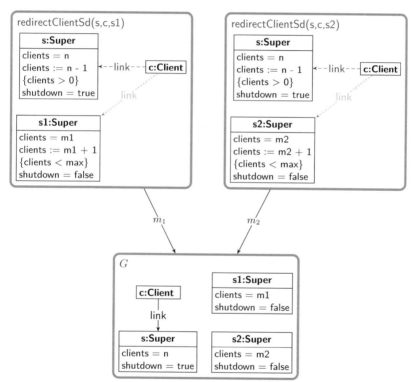

Fig. 4.13. Critical pair for (redirectClientSd, redirectClientSd) showing a delete/use conflict

We have to show the confluence of all critical pairs detected. The pair (1) depicted in Fig. 4.13 represents a situation where a client is redirected to one of two Super nodes. This means that, if two non-ending Super nodes are available, the choice is not unique. This conflict can be resolved by, for example, redirecting the client again to the other Super node. This solution is strictly confluent, as the corresponding tracking morphisms are equal.

The critical pairs reported in (2) and (3) are very easy to resolve. In both cases, an attribute is changed by both rule applications. These changes can also be performed sequentially in either order, since either "+1" or "−1" is performed twice, and this operation is commutative.   □

The process of establishing confluence through critical pairs can require several iterations. We try to show local confluence of the original set of rules. If this is not possible, we may decide to change or add rules and try again. To show (general) confluence by the way of local confluence, we also have to prove termination. This is discussed in the following section.

4.3 Termination

A graph transformation system is *terminating* if all its transformation sequences are finite. Graph transformation systems do not have this property in general. For example, a graph grammar that generates all graphs by creating single nodes and connecting them by edges is not terminating. Any generated graph can be extended by new nodes and edges at any time. In [231], Plump showed that termination is undecidable for graph transformation systems. This means that there is no algorithm which, for every given system, returns true if the system is terminating and false otherwise. Bereft of hope for a general solution, we can nevertheless develop sufficient (but not necessary) *termination criteria*: if a transformation system satisfies a termination criterion, we know that it terminates. Otherwise we can try other criteria or adapt the system.

In the following we give an overview of termination criteria for graph transformation systems.

4.3.1 Well-Founded Orders

A general approach to proving termination of rewrite systems is through well-founded partial orders. An order $>$ on a set S is well founded if it does not contain infinite descending chains, i.e. there is no infinite sequence $x_0, x_1, x_2, \ldots$ with $x_i > x_{i+1}$. If, in a rule-based system, there is a well founded order $L > R$ for all rules $r : L \to R$, we have to show that this order is *stable* under rule applications, i.e. that, for any rule application $G \xRightarrow{r,m} H$, $L > R$ implies $G > H$. A stable order is enough to show termination because it implies that the relation holds for all steps, so an infinite transformation sequence would result in an infinite descending chain.

For example, in a graph transformation system where the number of graph elements decreases at every step, the partial order on graphs given by "$G > H$ if G has more elements than H" would constitute a *termination order*. Rather than counting all elements, we could consider elements of certain node or edge types, or specific numerical attributes with decreasing values. More generally, we can count the number of occurrences of graph patterns, such as loops, or outgoing edges on certain types of nodes or triangular structures, or use combinations of the above.

Example 4.10 (termination of stepwise network deletion). Figure 2.8 shows a number of rules that delete network elements step by step. Let s_G and c_G be the numbers of Super and Client nodes and let o_G be the number of ovl edges in a network graph G. With $t_G = s_G + c_G + o_G$, it easy to see that each step reduces t_G, i.e. $t_G > t_H$ for any $G \xrightarrow{r,m} H$. Hence, given any network graph, only finitely many applications of the rules shown in Fig. 2.8 are possible. Once no more rule is applicable, the remaining network consists of User nodes only.   □

We should stress that termination checks based on order relations do not assume any control structures for rule applications. The situation is different when the following criteria are considered.

4.3.2 Layer Conditions

In [84], termination criteria for layered graph transformation systems (introduced in Chapter 3) were presented. Layering can be used to check termination if the creation and deletion of vertices and edges with certain types are coupled to layers. This is motivated by model-to-model transformations, where models are translated from one language to another (see also Chapter 12). Types of the source language are used by the given model, while instances of types of the target language are created by the model translation. This process can be controlled by layering.

In a *layered graph transformation system*, each rule r is assigned a layer $rl(r) = k$ with $0 \leq k \leq n$, $k, n \in \mathbb{N}$. Here, the overall number of layers is $n + 1$. This layering describes a simple control flow on rules in the sense that the rules of the lowest layer are applied first for as long as possible, then the rules of the next higher layer are applied, and so on.

To use layer conditions as termination criteria, each occurring node and edge type is equipped with a creation and a deletion layer. All types that are already used in the source language get the creation layer 0. The creation layer of any other type is equal to the layer in which it is used first. The deletion layer of a type is determined by the layer in which it is deleted first. All types occurring in the target language get the deletion layer $n + 1$.

Termination of the whole system can be shown by demonstrating termination for each layer separately. A layer is a *deletion layer* if (1) each of its rules deletes at least one element, (2) for each type occurring in one of its rules, the creation layer is lower than or equal to the deletion layer, (3) its rules delete only elements whose deletion layer is lower than or equal to the current layer, and (4) its rules create only elements whose creation layer is higher than the current layer.

A layer is a *non-deletion layer* if (1) each of its rules is non-deleting, (2) each of its rules can be applied only once at any given match (expressed by special NACs), (3) each rule only uses elements created in this layer or earlier, and (4) each rule creates an element with a creation layer higher than the current one. These conditions are summarised in Table 4.2.

Table 4.2. Conditions for deletion and non-deletion layers

Deletion layer conditions	Non-deletion layer conditions
If k is a deletion layer, for every rule r with $rl(r) = k$:	If k is a non-deletion layer, for every rule $r : L \to R$ with $rl(r) = k$:
1. Rule r deletes at least one element. 2. $0 \le cl(t) \le dl(t) \le n$ for all types t occurring in r. 3. If rule r deletes an element of type t, then $dl(t) \le rl(r)$. 4. If rule r creates an element of type t, then $cl(t) > rl(r)$.	1. Rule r is non-deleting. 2. At least one NAC of r can be embedded into R, extending the embedding of L into R. 3. For all $x \in L$, $cl(type(x)) \le rl(r)$. 4. If rule r creates an element of type t, then $cl(t) > rl(r)$.

Every layered graph transformation system is terminating, as illustrated the following example.

Example 4.11 (termination of layered graph transformation systems). To illustrate the termination criteria for layered graph transformation systems, we consider an extension of our running example of a VoIP network to graph-based stochastic simulation of networks to assess quality of service attributes. While this example concentrates on a translation of network graphs into a representation suitable for stochastic simulation, the simulation itself is presented in Chapter 9. In the following, we present this translation in more detail and show that it is terminating.

Figure 4.14 shows the underlying type graph. It consists of three parts: (1) the type graph of the original model (as presented in Fig. 2.25) on the left, (2) the type graph of the simulation model on the right, and (3) a trace type called Node2NN in the middle connected to types in the other two type graphs. The new type graph on the right distinguishes network nodes SN as super nodes and SC as client nodes, both are generalised by node type NN. For simulation purposes, SN nodes are equipped with information about bandwidth and SC nodes specify if they are hidden behind a firewall. The LK and OV node types model links between client and super nodes and links among super nodes, respectively, equipped with average delays. Note that attributed edges are avoided here, since they are less common than attributed vertices. To keep the network information, LK and OV vertices are used to represent links, equipped with edges to point to their incident network modes. Users are not needed in order to simulate network traffic.

In the following, four rules are shown for translating a VoIP network into a network simulation model. All the translation rules are non-deleting, i.e.

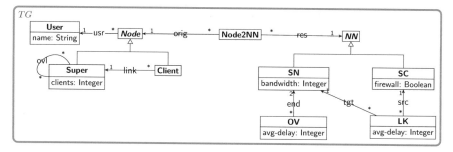

Fig. 4.14. Type graph for translating VoIP networks into network simulation models

they build up the new network model while keeping the original one. To keep track of the mapping of original to new network nodes, their relations are represented by vertices of type Node2NN and adjacent edges.

Rule translateSuper in Fig. 4.15 translates a Super node into a corresponding SN node with a random bandwidth. The operation randInt provides a normal distribution with mean m and variance v. Client nodes are translated very similarly using rule translateClient in Fig. 4.16 but, instead of setting the bandwidth, they are randomly hidden behind a firewall. In both cases, correspondences are kept by Node2NN vertices and adjacent edges.

When clients are added, the super node's spare bandwidth is reduced based on the clients' connectivity as in rule translateLink in Fig. 4.17. When serving a client behind a firewall, the super node has to route the audio traffic. Otherwise, it only establishes and monitors the connection, while audio packets are transferred directly between partners in a VoIP call.

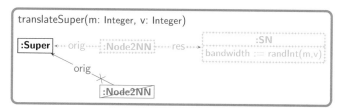

Fig. 4.15. Translation of Super nodes

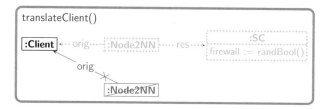

Fig. 4.16. Translation of Client nodes

The overlay information between Super nodes is translated with rule translateOvl in Fig. 4.18. As the average delay needs to be set for each overlay edge, an OV vertex is introduced for each ovl edge.

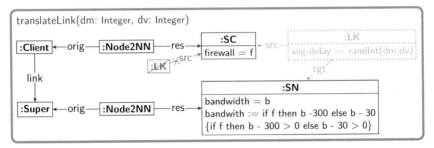

Fig. 4.17. Translation of link edges

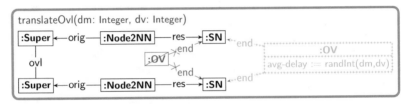

Fig. 4.18. Translation of ovl edges

Table 4.3. Rule layers

Rule	Layer
translateSuper	0
translateClient	0
translateLink	1
translateOvl	1

These four rules are applied in two layers as shown in Table 4.3. Links from clients to super nodes and overlay edges are translated after node translation. This means that rules translateSuper and translateClient are assigned to layer 0 and rules translateLink and translateOvl are assigned to layer 1. Given any VoIP network, we can show that all translations by the layered graph transformation system terminate. We can show this property by applying the termination criterion for non-deletion rules presented above. Table 4.4 shows a possible assignment of creation and deletion layers for all of the main types that occur in this example. All types of the original type graph get creation layer 0, since the translation assumes the existence of the original VoIP network. Network nodes and trace nodes are translated next and get creation layer 1 and connecting edges are created thereafter, i.e. they get creation layer 2. Given an additional set of deletion rules, it would be possible to delete the original network and trace structure, such that only the new network simulation model remains as input for the simulation. Such deletion rules would be assigned layer 2. Finally, any rules deleting elements of the network simulation model would be assigned layer 3. Deletion layers for types are assigned accordingly. The NACs ensure that each rule can only be applied once at a given match. Each application creates a structure that contains at least one of the rule's NACs. This means that the original match, extended to the derived graph, violates this NAC. Having all these assignments at hand, it is straightforward to check the termination conditions for layered transformation systems stated above.   □

Table 4.4. Creation and deletion layers for types

Original type	$cl(t)$	$dl(t)$	Trace type	$cl(t)$	$dl(t)$	Result type	$cl(t)$	$dl(t)$
Super	0	2	Node2NN	1	2	SN	1	3
Client	0	2				SC	1	3
User	0	2				LK	2	3
						OV	2	3

These termination conditions are helpful for showing the termination of transformation systems that translate graphs from one language to another. Layers can be interpreted as several passes in the model translation process and, of course, each pass has to terminate before the next ones can start. Note that, given a set of rules without layers, these termination criteria can also give hints about how to control rule applications by layers such that termination is ensured. In this case, the given graph transformation system can be improved (to a layered one) such that termination can be shown (using layer conditions).

4.4 Graph Constraints as Invariants

A type graph defines a set of instance graphs. But, even with subtyping and multiplicities, type graphs are not expressive enough to define more complex constraints on the structure of their instance graphs, especially when conditions on attributes are required. In Section 2.4.1, we introduced forbidden patterns to specify certain subsets of graphs. Here we will consider, in addition, positive and conditional constraints. Given a graph transformation system, graph constraints can be interpreted in a variety of ways. For example, constraints can be used as invariants to be satisfied by all reachable graphs. They can specify target graph classes of relational transformations or be part of more general temporal conditions. In this section we will focus on the view of constraints as invariants, as well as the problem of enforcing or verifying them for a given graph transformation system.

4.4.1 Positive and Conditional Constraints

When we require the presence of certain patterns in a graph G, there are two simple cases. A *positive constraint* is a pattern Q that we would like to occur somewhere in graph G. A *conditional constraint* generalises this idea by demanding that Q occurs relative to all occurrences of a smaller pattern $P \subseteq Q$. The occurrence of a pattern is expressed by the existence of an injective mapping $o : Q \to G$. In the conditional case, this means that for each occurrence $n : P \to G$ there should be an occurrence $o : Q \to G$ extending n. Since o is injective, it allows the counting of elements in the following sense. Imagine two elements x, y in pattern Q that are of the same type and have similar connections. Due to its injectivity, o is not allowed to map x and y to the same element in G. Hence, a subgraph $o(Q) \subseteq G$ has to be found with two distinct elements matching x and y.

Logically, we can write $\exists Q$ or $\forall P.\exists Q$, respectively. Positive constraints can be seen as a special case of conditional ones, with a trivial (i.e. empty) pattern graph P, i.e. $\forall \emptyset \exists Q$, with the empty pattern $\emptyset$ playing the role of *True* because it occurs in every graph. We also allow logical combinations such as $\forall P.(\exists Q_1 \vee \cdots \vee \exists Q_n)$, where one premise is followed by a disjunction of conclusions. With the empty disjunction equivalent to *False* this allows us to write $\forall P.\textit{False}$, which is equivalent to the forbidden pattern $\neg \exists P$.

More sophisticated constraints can be obtained by allowing propositional logic over multiple levels of conditionality, as in nested graph constraints [121]. However, as shown in the following example, negative and conditional constraints are sufficient to capture multiplicity constraints over edges.

Example 4.12 (multiplicity as graph constraint). The type graph in Fig. 1.16 shows multiplicities for several edge types, in particular for usr edges. The upper bound at the Node end tells us that no two Nodes are connected to the same User, while the lower bound at the User end requires that each Node is connected to at least one User. In addition, the upper bound at the User end demands that no two Users have the same Node.

While upper bounds represent negative existential constraints forbidding larger numbers of objects and links than allowed for, lower bounds represent conditional constraints. In Figs. 4.19 and 4.20, the first two multiplicities described above are formulated as graph constraints, called No2Nodes and AtLeast1User.   □

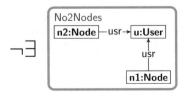

Fig. 4.19. Negative constraint: "No two Nodes are connected to the same User"

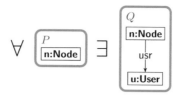

Fig. 4.20. Conditional constraint: "Each Node is connected to at least one User"

4.4.2 Enforcing Graph Invariants by Application Conditions

Graph constraints serving as invariants have to be satisfied globally, i.e. by all reachable graphs. In contrast, application conditions are local to rules, both in a temporal and in a spatial sense. As left or right application conditions of rules, they have to be checked before or after a rule is applied. They are therefore stated in the context of a rule's left- or right-hand side (see also Section 2.4.2) and checked at the time and place of its application.

An invariant is a graph constraint that has to be satisfied by all reachable graphs. To ensure that this is the case, we have to check that it is satisfied in the start graph and that every transformation step starting in a valid graph produces a valid graph as a result. Application conditions can help to ensure the second part of this requirement by disallowing transformations leading from valid to invalid graphs.

Here we describe a construction that takes a set of graph constraints and a graph transformation system as inputs and generates the application conditions required, so that each rule that can cause constraint violations is augmented by additional application conditions. The result is an improved graph transformation system whose transition relation coincides with the original one except for transitions between valid and invalid states. Moreover, given an invalid state, the augmented rule is only applicable if the resulting state is valid. Hence, transformations using augmented rules are not only *validity-preserving* but validity-guaranteeing.

Given a rule and a constraint, the construction works in two steps. The constraint is first localised to a right application condition of the rule. Then, this condition is transferred to an equivalent left application condition. We explain this construction in two parts: first, a negative constraint is handled and second, we consider the construction for a conditional constraint. Both cases are explained with the constraints presented in Example 4.12.

Example 4.13 (enforcing forbidden patterns). We reconsider the constraint No2Nodes in Fig. 4.19 asserting that no two Nodes are connected to the same User. To enforce constraint No2Nodes, we only have to check the rules that add usr edges, i.e. newSuper, newClient, promoteClient, endSuper and endClient. The check of rule newClient is shown below.

We start by analysing all situations where the application of the rule could violate the constraint. This is done by overlapping the constraint with the right-hand side of the rule in all ways, as shown for one example overlap in

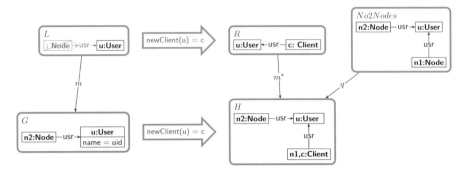

Fig. 4.21. Verifying constraint "No two Nodes are connected to the same User"

Fig. 4.21. The graph H in the bottom right is a gluing of R and No2Nodes merging the corresponding Users, Node n1 with Client c, and the usr edges in between. Other overlaps can be obtained by combinations of not merging the usr edges, only merging either Users or Nodes, using node n2 instead of n1, or taking the disjoint union of R and No2Nodes. Altogether, eight different overlaps are possible.

We rule out situations unobtainable by an application of rule newClient. For example, merging only n1 with c results in a graph where the Client node just created by the rule is already linked to another User. Since this link could neither have existed before the Client node was created nor have been created by the rule itself, this is not a situation where the application of the rule could have violated the constraint. Formally, the dangling condition for the inverse rule of newClient is not satisfied by this embedding of R into H and the corresponding left application condition is *False*.

The remaining overlaps constitute right application conditions. In particular, the gluing H in Fig. 4.21 represents the negative condition preventing an embedding of R where u is the target of a second usr edge.

To derive the equivalent left application condition, the inverse of rule newClient is applied, removing the Client node. The embedding of L into graph G shows the resulting application condition stating that the rule should only be applied if there is not already a Node connected to the User.

Other overlaps of R and No2Nodes either yield analogous results, fail to satisfy the dangling condition for the inverse rule or are subsumed by the condition depicted. The only other case of interest arises from the disjoint union of R and No2Nodes, which results in a precondition checking that No2Nodes does not occur before applying the rule. However, by assumption, this is not the case, so this condition is redundant. This means that the application condition depicted in Fig. 4.21 guarantees that this rule will never transform a graph satisfying No2Nodes into one that does not.   □

Unlike a negative constraint, a conditional $\forall P.\exists Q$ consists of two patterns, a *premise* P and a *conclusion* Q. This means that the construction described above has to be executed twice. The localisation of $\forall P.\exists Q$ to a right application condition requires the construction of all possible overlaps of the premise and the rule's right-hand side R. Each overlap $(R \cup P)_i$ is then extended by the conclusion yielding $(R \cup Q)_i$. Inside these graphs, elements of R and the conclusion may be glued, yielding T_{ij}. The resulting right application condition is

$$\bigwedge_i \left(\forall (R \cup P)_i \bigvee_{ij} \exists\, T_{ij} \right).$$

To translate this condition into a left application condition, we try to apply the inverse rule to each $(R \cup P)_i$. If this is not possible (i.e. because the dangling condition is not satisfied), this part of the condition is dropped. For all premises $(R \cup P)_i$ that can be translated, we try to translate the relevant conclusions T_{ij}. Again, if the dangling condition is not fulfilled, the corresponding conclusion becomes *False*. All remaining ones yield conclusions S_{lk} of the left application condition with translated premise $(L \cup P)_l$. The result is the left application condition

$$\bigwedge_l \left(\forall (L \cup P)_l \bigvee_{lk} \exists\, S_{lk} \right).$$

We illustrate this construction with the integration of the conditional constraint AtLeast1User into rule newClient.

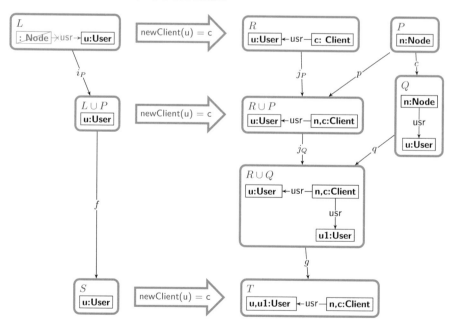

Fig. 4.22. Verifying constraint "Each Node is connected to at least one User"

Example 4.14 (enforcing conditional constraints). The conditional constraint
AtLeast1User states that at least one User is linked to each Node. Figure 4.22
augments rule newClient with a left application condition enforcing this constraint. Similarly to the negative case, we start by investigating gluings of
the right-hand side R and premise P and check for each gluing, if it could
be the result of applying the rule. Each such gluing yields the premise of a
right application condition, which can be transformed into the premise of a
left application condition by applying the reverse of newClient. In this case
there are only two possible gluings of P and R. Figure 4.22 shows the case in
which Node n is glued to Client c. The alternative is their disjoint union. Both
are possible result graphs $R \cup P$. The application of the inverse rule yields the
premise of the corresponding precondition.

In the second phase, the conclusion is derived analogously. Pattern Q is
glued to $R \cup P$ over the shared graph P, leading to $R \cup Q$. This gives us a
minimal gluing with one Client connected to two Users, which is merged further
to produce all possible graphs T into which $R \cup Q$ and Q can be embedded
while preserving the shared premise P. (Note that u:User is renamed to u1.)
Those embeddings into T that can be transformed by the inverse rule result
in conclusions of the precondition. In our case the only T derivable by the
rule is the one depicted in Fig. 4.22. Being isomorphic to the premise, this
yields a precondition that is trivially satisfied: a tautology, which is omitted.
In [229, 239] a number of simplification rules for application conditions are
introduced capable of recognising and removing such redundant cases.

If $R \cup P$ is the disjoint union, $L \cup P$ contains an additional Node. The
resulting left application condition states that any existing Node has to be
connected to a User, which again is a consequence of the assumption that
the constraint is valid in the given state. This means that the conditional
constraint does not produce any additional application conditions for this
rule. This reflects the fact that rule newClient can not create a violation of the
constraint that every Node must be connected to a User.   □

4.4.3 Verifying Invariants

Rather than using an invariant to construct a new application condition for a
given rule, the construction presented may also be used to verify the desired
property in the sense that a given rule always transforms legal graphs into legal
ones. This is the case if the constructed application conditions can be shown to
be redundant. To find redundancies, we simplify the resulting left application
conditions by as much as possible. (This is also useful for producing simpler
application conditions when enforcing graph constraints.)

A left application condition ac entails a condition ac' if, for every match
$m : L \rightarrow G$ that satisfies ac, it also satisfies ac'. In this case, if ac is an
existing application condition of a rule and ac' is derived from an invariant,
this means that ac' is redundant and does not have to be added to the rule.
Vice versa, we can remove ac if the derived application condition ac' is stricter.

An application condition can be simplified by refactoring its logical structure or finding that one graph pattern entails another one.

Example 4.15 (simplifying application conditions). Assume an application condition forbidding two nodes connected to a matched user. This application condition is entailed by the left application condition in Fig. 4.21 where one node connected to the matched user is forbidden. An application of the rule in Fig. 4.21 checks that there is no node connected to the user, which implies that there are no two nodes connected.   □

A calculus that allows one to compute the entailment relation, including the syntactic simplification of conditions and constraints, was provided in [229]. Additional simplification rules can be found in [239]. However, entailment is undecidable in general.

4.5 Model Checking

While graph constraints can be used as invariants, to be satisfied by any reachable graph, temporal constraints can specify which constraints are to hold on which graphs in a graph transition system. A liveness property, for example, may require a graph condition to become true on an execution path after finitely many transformation steps. Temporal properties can be verified using model checking.

The term "model checking" is used here in accordance with standard textbooks such as [32], as verifying a transition system (which describes all the potential ways in which a system can behave) against a formula in a temporal logic (which expresses some desirable property of that system). In the context of this book, such transition systems are *graph* transition systems, generated by graph transformation systems as described in Section 3.2.3.

4.5.1 System Properties

A *temporal logic* can express properties of states across a (graph) transition system, including the evolution of such properties over time or from one state to the next along a transition. Typical example properties that can be expressed are:

- Every message that is sent by some node in a network will eventually (certainly) arrive at the target node.
- An error message will be generated if and only if an error has actually occurred.
- Eventually the system will arrive at a stable state.

There are different families of temporal logic, dominant among which are *linear temporal logic* (LTL) and *computation tree logic* (CTL). These differ somewhat in the types of properties that can be expressed and in how concisely they can be stated:

- LTL expresses properties of *paths* (hence, is referred to as *linear*). Model checking an LTL formula involves making sure that the property expressed therein holds along *every* path allowed by the transition system.
- CTL expresses properties of *trees*; in particular, within a CTL property one can express that there may be a choice in the way the system can continue, due to the presence of multiple outgoing transitions of the current state. In other words, the choice of which path to follow is not made up front but during the evaluation of the formula, and there is no implicit universal quantification over all paths. This makes CTL less concise than LTL: a property that can be expressed in either logic will typically be much larger when expressed in CTL than it is in LTL.

The conciseness of LTL comes at a price: the time it takes to check an LTL formula, expressed as a function of the size of that formula, is exponential, whereas for CTL it is linear. Throughout the rest of this section, we stick to CTL over graph constraints. Hence, we may use temporal operators to formulate system properties for our graph transition systems. The most important operators are the following ones:

- A c (**A**ll): c holds on all paths starting from the current state graph.
- E c (**E**xists): There is at least one path starting from the current state graph where c holds.
- G c (**G**lobally): c holds on the entire subsequent path.
- F c (**F**inally): c holds eventually (in some state on the subsequent path).

We illustrate the use of these operators in the following example.

Example 4.16 (temporal properties). Considering the rules for joining the network and making connections shown in Fig. 2.7, the following properties are interesting for the resulting graph transformation system:

- *Liveness property:* All Users are connected to some Node eventually.
- *Safety properties:*
  - There is no Super node with more than max clients.
  - There is no Super node with clients = 0 and linked to some Client.
  - There is a Client link for all Super nodes with clients > 0.

All these properties are formulated as temporal formulas over graph constraints as presented in Fig. 4.23.   □

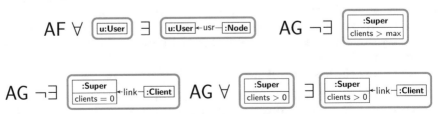

Fig. 4.23. Liveness and safety properties

It should be noted that the word *temporal* is potentially confusing in this context. Neither LTL nor CTL offer an ability to reason about *time*, in the sense of being able to specify the duration of computations. Rather, the term refers to the qualitative passing of time, i.e. the ability to express that one thing happens after another.

4.5.2 Model Checking Procedure

To check if a graph-based temporal formula holds for a graph transformation system, we explore its transition system for counterexamples. Starting from the start graph of the graph transformation system, all reachable graphs are investigated. Model checking of a graph transformation system is an automated technique which takes the transformation system and a system property as input and returns the first counterexample found [248]. The counterexample contains a path from the start graph to a state graph where the given property does not hold. If no counterexample is found, the system property holds for the complete transition system. During this process, it is important to know whether a state graph with equal structure and attribute values has been investigated before. Ideally, such isomorphic graphs are discovered and checked only once. Note that a transition system induced by a graph transformation system can be infinite. In that case, the non-existence of counterexamples cannot be inferred.

Example 4.17 (model checking). In the following, we consider a concrete setting for model checking. Take the graph transformation system given by graph IN in Fig. 2.6 as the start graph and consider the rules: newSuper, newClient and endClient depicted in Figs. 2.7 and 2.8. The resulting graph transition system contains 23 state graphs and 77 transitions. If we set max = 2 in the upper right constraint in Fig. 4.23, both upper constraints are satisfied in this transition system. If we were to choose max = 1, the upper right constraint in Fig. 4.23 would not be fulfilled. This would be true already for the start graph.   □

4.5.3 Potentials and Limits

Model checking of graph transformation systems allows to verify a range of system properties expressed in a temporal logic over graph patterns. All transformation concepts introduced so far, including different forms of rules (Chapter 2) and control structures (Chapter 3), may be used to specify the system under consideration. This means that rules may create and delete graph elements without limitation, and hence graphs may evolve dynamically. This last feature is a great advantage of model checking graph transformation systems over other model-checking techniques that often provide solutions only for more rigid structures.

A well-known problem of model-checking techniques is *state space explosion*. Even small systems can result in large or even infinite transition systems. Since all reachable states have to be investigated during model checking, the state space has to be reduced to make the problem more manageable. A number of techniques have been developed to achieve this, including partial order reduction and abstraction.

Partial order reduction exploits the commutativity of concurrently executed transitions, where several paths between the same pair of states may be reduced to one representative. For parallel independent transformations, for example, the local confluence theorem, a classical result of graph transformation theory, may be exploited. In abstraction techniques, a (potentially infinite) set of similar states is considered equivalent and therefore represented as a single state. Abstraction of graphs offers the opportunity to reduce a potentially infinite graph transition system to a finite one, making model checking feasible [247]. Node and edge identities can often be neglected in constraint checking, and thus we consider graphs up to isomorphism. If we want to refer to certain graph elements in temporal formulas, however, we have to trace the identity of at least those elements, for example by passing them as parameter values between rule applications. By exploiting graph isomorphism as a notion of equivalence, the state space of a graph transformation system can be considerably reduced [174]. Since graph transformation is defined up to isomorphism, this abstraction is sure to preserve the behaviour of the system. Graphs can be abstracted further by generalising similar structures into a shape graph [247] at the cost of over-approximating the behaviour of the system.

Stochastic model checking is used to verify properties of *stochastic graph transformation systems* as presented in Chapter 9 to investigate dynamic software architectures. Associating with each rule a probability distribution over time, the continuous-time Markov chains can be used that are obtained by adding rates of exponential distribution to the transitions of the resulting LTS.

4.6 Graph Parsing

Graph parsing is a technique for solving the membership problem for graph languages. One can phrase parsing as the search problem of finding a derivation from the start graph to the given graph using the rules of a grammar. One simple approach is to reduce the given graph to the start graph by applying the grammar rules in reverse. The resulting derivation records the syntactic structure of the given input graph. In this case, graph parsing is understood as graph reduction: given an input graph and a *stop graph, parsing rules* are applied to the input graph such that the stop graph is reached after finitely many steps. To solve the membership problem, the stop graph is the start of a given graph grammar and the parsing rules are the inverse grammar rules.

A naive *graph-parsing algorithm* is to apply the parsing rules in an arbitrary order for as long as possible. If the parsing process runs into a deadlock without reaching the stop graph, backtracking may be required to check if there is any other rule application sequence that reaches the stop graph. If all possible sequences can be explored and do not reach the stop graph, the input graph does not fulfil the reachability property. In general, there may be sequences that do not terminate, such that it cannot be decided if they are reducible to the start graph. Hence, the reachability problem is just semi-decidable. The membership problem can be reduced to the reachability problem, as an input graph is member of a graph language if it can be reached from the start graph.

Example 4.18 (parsing the network structure). Let us start with the graph grammar *GG* defined in Example 3.1, consisting of rules newSuper, newClient and linkClient (as shown in Fig. 2.7) as well as rules newUser and connectToSuper. To check if a given network graph specifies a valid peer-to-peer architecture, we invert these rules, yielding the rules deleteSuper, deleteClient, unlinkClient, deleteUser and unconnectSuper in Fig. 4.24. Note that all rules which delete nodes have the dangling condition as an additional application condition to remove the network systematically. Note further that the parameters are just informative; they do not restrict possible matches of parsing rules.

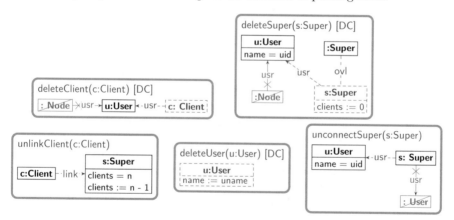

Fig. 4.24. Rules for parsing network structures

In parsing, for example, graph *H* in Fig. 2.9, we can apply these parsing rules in the following order: unlinkClient(c2); deleteClient(c2); deleteSuper(s2); unconnectSuper(s1); deleteUser(u1); deleteUser(u2); deleteUser(u3). The result is a graph with just one Super node which is equal to the start graph of *GG*. The following sequence of rule applications is also possible: unlinkClient(c2); deleteClient(c2); unconnectSuper(s2); unconnectSuper(s1). This yields the intermediate graph shown in Fig. 4.25, which can be further reduced by deleting all users, but two interconnected Super nodes remain. Hence, this rule application sequence does not yield the stop graph. The sequence deleteSuper(s2);

unconnectSuper(s1); unlinkClient(c2); deleteClient(c2), however, is also possible and can be continued towards the stop graph. Hence, rule deleteSuper should have a higher priority than unconnectSuper. Both delete a usr edge, but rule deleteSuper deletes even more structure. It is a common parsing strategy to prioritise rules that recognise larger structures over rules addressing smaller ones.   □

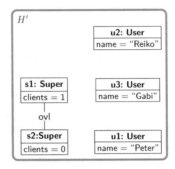

Fig. 4.25. Intermediate graph of a parsing process requiring backtracking

In Chapter 10, as a further example for graph parsing, we discuss the parsing of activity diagrams.

In the literature, sufficient criteria have been developed to avoid or reduce backtracking during the parsing process. In [47], the application of conflicting rules is delayed for as long as possible. This means that conflict-free rules should be applied first to reduce the input graph before applying conflicting rules. Following this strategy, the need for backtracking is reduced.

In [243], *layered graph grammars* help to identify several stages of parsing. In classical grammars, just two layers of recognition are identified, distinguishing terminal from non-terminal labels. Layered graph grammars allow a more fine-grained decomposition of label alphabets into several layers. After spatial relationships between visual elements are identified first in a bottom-up manner, they are mapped to higher-level syntax elements. The abstract syntax graph is recognised thereafter in a top-down phase. Each layer contains specific rules which are applied in that layer as often as possible. If no rule of the current layer is applicable any more, the parsing process continues with the next layer.

4.7 Comparison of Analysis Techniques

After having presented a range of analysis techniques, we conclude this chapter by discussing their commonalities and differences. We compare the techniques in terms of their inputs and outputs as well as the nature of the analysis performed. Each technique requires (a part of) a graph transformation system and a system property as inputs. Outputs may be analysis results of varying granularity and, potentially, repair actions. Moreover, we characterise the kinds of analysis provided. We refer to established work here, mostly with tool support. More advanced approaches, purely theoretical or prototypically implemented, are discussed in Section 4.8.

We refer to the analysis techniques as follows: conflict and dependency analysis (CDA), termination analysis (TA), constraint verification and enforcement (CV&E), model checking (MC), and graph parsing (GP).

4.7.1 Graph Transformation Systems

The two techniques that are state-based, requiring the start graph of the system, are model checking and graph parsing. In model checking, the underlying transition system has to be explored from its initial state. Graph parsing requires the entire graph grammar to check if the given graph can be reduced to the start graph.

All techniques work with the rules of a transformation system, some imposing restrictions on their features. While, in theory, model checking and parsing allow all transformation concepts, other techniques may support only simpler rules, for example without control or application conditions. Specific tools may impose additional limitations beyond what is possible in principle. For example, tool support for CDA supports simple application conditions only, while multipatterns are generally not allowed. Moreover, tools for CDA and CV&E often do not take into account control structures.

4.7.2 System Properties

We distinguish two kinds of system properties. *General properties* such as "Does the system terminate?"and "Does the system have conflicts or dependencies?" can be formulated independently of any concrete graph transformation system. A system is terminating if there are no infinite transformation sequences, i.e. each sequence ends in a graph where no further rules are applicable. A system does not have conflicts if all rule pairs are parallel independent, so they can be applied in any order. It does not have dependencies if all rule pairs are sequentially independent.

Specific properties are formulated for a given graph transformation system. Usually they require the type graph to specify state or temporal properties for the underlying transition system. *Invariants* can be considered as a special kind of temporal property: they have to be satisfied in all states, for all paths. The membership problem, whether a graph G is a member of a graph language (can be reached from the start graph), is another special case.

4.7.3 Analysis Outcomes

The results of analysis can be more or less verbose. All techniques provide binary answers, i.e. whether or not the desired property holds in the given system, but some techniques can give additional information about their result. CDA can show (increasingly more) information about concrete conflict or dependency situations. TA can provide reasons for, or examples of, non-termination, CV&E can return the rules not fulfilling the specified constraints, and MC can show a counterexample, i.e. a transition path not satisfying a constraint.

As discussed before, analysis techniques can also propose repair and improvement actions. TA can produce a layering for a set of rules such that the resulting layered graph transformation system would terminate. CV&E provides the user with additional application conditions for rules that would ensure that these rules can only be applied when they do not violate the invariants.

4.7.4 Kinds of Analysis

We distinguish between static and dynamic analysis techniques. *Static analysis* is performed on a graph transformation system, while *dynamic analysis* investigates the underlying graph transition system. Static analyses have the advantage of taking a concise description of the specified system as input but are often restricted in terms of the types of system supported. Dynamic analyses usually allow a large variety of system specifications and properties but suffer from state space explosion.

Furthermore, we can distinguish *push-button* techniques from *interactive* ones. While MC and GP are classical push-button techniques, the other analyses are more complex: CDA provides several granularity levels which present more and more detail of conflicts and dependencies to the user. TA and CV&E return their analysis results and support the adaptation of the original graph transformation system such that it satisfies the required property.

4.8 Summary and Further Reading

In this chapter, we have presented the most popular analysis and improvement techniques for graph transformation systems. Each of these techniques is formally defined, and most of them have been implemented and applied in a number of scenarios. We point to relevant literature for each of these techniques.

4.8.1 Conflicting and Dependent Transformations

The consideration of conflicts and dependencies between graph transformations is central in the gluing approach to graph transformation. The local Church-Rosser theorem about independence of graph transformation steps was first shown for coloured graphs in [81] in the DPO approach. It was later generalized to high-level replacement systems in [90] and instantiated to typed attributed graphs with node type inheritance in [140]. Critical pairs of (term) graph rules were extensively investigated by Plump in [231]. In [235], Plump introduced a sufficient criterion for critical pairs to be confluent. Tool support for critical pair analysis is available in AGG [98], Henshin [139] and Verigraph [29].

Recently, a *multigranular analysis* for conflicts and dependencies has been developed [186, 182, 30]. Several granularity levels were identified to reason about conflicts and dependencies. At the binary level, the user is just interested in knowing if a pair of rules has a conflict or dependency. At the coarse granularity level, information about the roots of conflicts and dependencies is given to the user, while the fine granularity level contains all necessary information to understand the conflicts and dependencies in detail. Obviously, critical pairs belong to the fine level. A user study showed that users often like to start at a higher-level of granularity in order to avoid being overwhelmed by information.

Conflicts and dependencies have been analysed for different use cases throughout the software engineering domain. Lambers et al. [186] have given an overview of these cases by their application domains, which are *analysis and design of software systems*, *model-driven engineering techniques*, *testing*, and *optimisation of rule-based computations*. We will go into more detail for the first three domains in Chapters 5, 7 and 11.

4.8.2 Termination

Since termination of graph transformation systems is undecidable in general, several sufficient but not necessary termination criteria have been developed. Besides the ones presented in this chapter, there was early work on termination orders for graph transformation systems by Aßmann [26]. A generalisation of termination orders to high-level replacement systems was presented in [46]. In [284], termination of graph transformation systems was shown based on Petri nets. A condition which ensures that the union of two terminating hypergraph transformation systems is terminating is presented was [236].

4.8.3 Graph Constraints as Invariants

In this chapter, we have focused on basic constraints and have presented how they can be enforced or verified for a given graph transformation system. The more general class of nested graph constraints [244, 121] is equivalent to first-order logic on graphs. For example, a forbidden pattern N yields the nested graph constraint $\neg \exists \emptyset \to N$, for short, $\neg \exists N$. A conditional constraint can be represented by $\forall \emptyset \to P, \exists P \to Q$, for short, $\forall P, \exists Q$. While $\neg \exists N$ does not show any nesting, i.e. it has depth 0, conditional constraints have nesting depth 1. Constraints with depth > 1 are also possible.

In Chapter 1, the properties of whole-part relationships were discussed. One of the main properties of all whole-part relationships is acyclicity. To express this property by nested graph constraints, an infinite constraint is needed of the form $\neg \exists C_1 \wedge \neg \exists C_2 \wedge \ldots$ with C_k denoting a cycle of length k (see also [85]).

A generalisation of the work in [138] to high-level replacement systems was presented in [83]. While constraints were first restricted to conditional ones, they were extended to nested graph constraints in [244]. Habel and Pennemann showed in [121] that nested constraints are expressively equivalent to first-order graph formulas. The correctness of graph transformation systems with respect to nested graph constraints in [121, 88] directly extends the original work in [138] and its generalisation in [83].

The translation of constraints in Object Constraint Language (OCL) to graph constraints was developed by Radtke et al. [239]. This is useful in model-driven engineering, for example to generate models or editing rules. The translation of OCL to graph constraints and their integration into rules as application conditions are supported by tooling [222] based on Henshin.

4.8.4 Model Checking

In software model checking, program states are represented by arrays or lists, as in JavaPathFinder [131]. Graphs, however, provide a more natural way to represent object structures. The theoretical basis for verifying graph transformation systems by model checking was laid in [134] and subsequent papers. The authors of these papers proposed that graphs can be interpreted as states and rule applications as transitions in a graph transition system (see also Section 3.2.3). This basic idea is used in all model-checking approaches to graph transformation systems. In [248], the two main approaches were compared: either traditional model-checking techniques are exploited by translating graph transformation systems to an input format of an off-the-shelf model checker [282] such as SPIN [148], or model checking is directly implemented on graph transition systems [246]. Both approaches have advantages and disadvantages, as stated in [248]:

- If the graphical structure is relatively stable and has limited symmetry, the translation to an off-the-shelf model checker seems superior. This is due to very efficient state space representations and mature technology.
- If the structures are inherently dynamic (since, in particular, nodes and edges are created at run time) and/or show a lot of symmetries, the direct implementation of model checking on the resulting graph transition system is a promising alternative. In particular, symmetry reduction in object structures requires isomorphism abstraction [155].

Model checking has been implemented in several graph-transformation-based tools, such as GROOVE [107], CheckVML [254] and Henshin [22]. While GROOVE implements model checking directly on graph transition systems, CheckVML and Henshin use external model-checking tools such as SPIN [148], CADP [55] and mCRL2 [203, 174].

4.8.5 Graph Parsing

Graph grammars are used to specify visual languages [11]. To parse visual representations, two kinds of graph parsers have been suggested. Context-free hypergraph grammars [213] use hypergraphs to specify the underlying abstract syntax of visual representations. Parsing rules are context-free in the sense that the left-hand side contains only a non-terminal hyperedge to be replaced by a hypergraph on the right-hand side. Context nodes are used to capture the connections of the non-terminal hyperedge, and connect the new hypergraph. Instead, Rekers and Schürr [243] used a graph-parsing approach based on typed attributed graphs as the abstract syntax. The form of rules is unrestricted, but their application has to follow a layering condition to ensure that the parsing process is terminating.

In contrast to text, there is typically no definite beginning or end point in a graph. The order in which graph elements are parsed depends on the applicability of rules and additional control structures. In general, therefore, parsing may require search and backtracking. This means that the time complexity of a graph parser can easily be exponential. Practical graph-parsing approaches are defined to avoid or at least, minimise backtracking. For example, Drewes et al. [75] study predictive shift-reduce parsing that yields efficient parsers for a subclass of hyperedge replacement grammar. They show that parsers of this kind run in linear space and time.

4.8.6 Further Analysis Techniques

There are more analysis techniques for graph transformation systems than we are able to discuss in detail, but we would like to mention the following.

Baldan et al. [33] analysed a graph transformation system by approximating its behaviour by a Petri net. Given a graph transformation system with somewhat restricted rules and some graph property, the tool Augur [171] over-approximates a system by a Petri graph (a Petri net with edges between its places) and translates a graph property into a property on Petri net markings. The analysis is performed directly on the Petri net structure underlying the Petri graph and checks all reachable graphs. If the property does not hold, a counterexample for the net is generated and translated back to the graph transformation system.

Non-functional requirements can be analysed with stochastic graph transformation systems [137]. These extend graph transformation by continuous time, associating a (random, exponentially distributed) application delay with each rule. From this extension, *continuous-time Markov chains*, a stochastic extension of transition systems, can be derived and used to analyse timed probabilistic properties. This is described in detail in Chapter 9.

Part II

Graph Transformation in Software Engineering

Software engineering[1] is "the application of a systematic, disciplined, quantifiable approach to the development, operation, and maintenance of software". This comprises the definition of engineering *processes* consisting of a set of interrelated *activities* which process *artefacts*. Engineering processes are not confined to forward engineering, i.e. the development of new software, but include reverse and re-engineering processes as they occur in continuous software evolution [249]. Agile processes have been developed to acknowledge and embrace change as an essential ingredient of software development.

Each activity of such engineering processes creates or modifies some artefacts; they are initiated and performed by stakeholders in different roles. For example, software requirements elicitation may contain an activity for finding inconsistencies in functional specifications (as presented in Chapter 5) while model-based testing (as presented in Chapter 7) may include activities for the specification of a test model and the generation of test cases.

In software engineering, a range of *languages* are used to represent software artefacts. There are, of course, programming languages such as Java and C, but also modelling languages such as UML and languages to exchange data such as XML and to present textual information such as HTML. Besides general purpose modelling languages, there are domain-specific modelling languages such as the Business Process Model Notation [1], the Web Services Description Language (Chapter 6), languages for feature models such as FeatureIDE [5], and languages for Model-Driven Engineering such as the Eclipse Modelling Framework [92]. All these languages have to be clearly defined in terms of their syntax and semantics. Moreover, they need comprehensive and user-friendly tool environments providing not only editors but also interpreters, compilers, analysers, and version management tools. Chapters 10–12 are dedicated to the engineering of domain-specific modelling languages.

According to the SWEBOK [262] "software engineering *methods* provide an organised and systematic approach to developing software for a target computer." It is important for software engineers to use appropriate methods for the chosen development process as "this choice can have a dramatic effect on the success of the software project". If software engineers want to specify, analyse, or verify software artefacts, formal methods are needed. In addition, software engineers may use other kinds of methods, such as model-based, agile or prototyping methods. This book promotes graphs and graph transformation as software engineering methods. Combining formal foundations, an intuitive, visual nature and an executable semantics, they may be used both as a formal modelling methods in their own right, but also to provide semantics to object-oriented or component-based analysis and design. In the following, we discuss in more detail how graphs and graph transformation can be used in software engineering.

---

[1] as defined in the Systems and Software engineering — vocabulary of the ISO/IEC/ IEEE std 24765:2010(E), 2010

Many activities in software engineering processes rely on models to support the specification, analysis, documentation and communication of different aspects of a software system and its development. When models play a relevant role throughout the engineering process, we refer to *model-based software engineering* (MBSE). In this second part of the book, we will present a number of engineering processes using graph transformation systems as models, i.e. using *graph transformation-based software engineering* (GTBSE) methods. Here, graph transformation itself is used as a modelling language.

To support the use of models in software engineering, various software modelling languages have been developed in academia and industry. The term *language engineering* describes the definition of languages in terms of their syntax and semantics as well as the concepts needed to design comprehensive tool environments. We will show how graph transformation can be used to support language definition leading to a range of methods, theoretical results and tools for *graph transformation-based language engineering* (GTBLE).

Graphs and diagrams provide a direct, yet implementation-independent representation of many of the complex structures we encounter in software systems, such as objects and references, software architectures, or network topologies. Their ability to model concepts and ideas in a direct and intuitive way makes them uniquely suited to support a variety of activities typical of software engineering, from the very early stages where we use blobs and arrows to sketch the architecture or process flow of an application, to, for example, detailed class and interaction models we use to generate code or test cases.

Unsurprisingly therefore, graphs are also the foundation of many of the diagrammatic languages we use in model-based development. Apart from general-purpose languages, such as UML, there are many customised domain-specific modelling languages (DSMLs) that provide both dedicated notational elements and semantic interpretations specific to their domain.

In both uses of graphs, directly as representations of software artefacts or indirectly as a foundation of diagrammatic languages, we encounter many situations where graphs have to be generated, queried, changed or translated. For example, object structures, software architectures and network topologies may evolve as a result of a system's normal operation or in order to adapt to changes in their environment. Diagrams have to be parsed, edited, checked for consistency, and mapped to, generated from or synchronised with implementations, etc. All these manipulations are examples of graph transformations, yet a comprehensive account of where and how to apply graph transformation in software engineering is still missing. This part is dedicated to providing such an overview of applications of graph transformation in this area.

Chapters 5–9 are concerned with examples of *graph transformation-based-software engineering* (GTBSE) using graph transformation systems as models. This includes the specification and analysis of functional and non-functional requirements, software architecture and service design, model-based testing, and program understanding. In all these activities we benefit from the formal foundations of graph transformations, their visual and intuitive nature, and their executable semantics. The result is a method that fits seamlessly into mainstream modelling languages such as UML while supporting sophisticated verification and analysis techniques. In particular:

- Chapter 5 is concerned with detecting inconsistencies between functional requirements following a use-case-driven approach. When requirements analysts specify use cases with activity diagrams, their actions may be refined by pre- and postconditions formulated as graph transformation rules, leading to an extension of the modelling language used. Since these *refined activity diagrams* have a formal semantics as graph transformation systems, we can use analysis techniques such as those introduced in Chapter 4 to detect inconsistencies between requirements.
- Chapter 6 presents a contract-oriented approach to service specification and matching. Service developers can specify graph transformation rules as constituents of *visual contracts* to describe service semantics and to match services offered to service requests. Again, the use of graph transformation is twofold: rules are used as interface specifications for services and their formal foundation allows a precise definition of service matching.
- Chapter 7 uses visual contracts to specify a test model. Dependency coverage is presented as a new form of test selection criterion to generate test cases. Test developers can also use the model to generate test oracles. Visual contracts are used here both to specify interfaces of operations and to analyse their interdependencies and derive relevant test cases.
- Chapter 8 presents a dynamic approach to reverse engineering visual contracts from Java programs by tracing the execution of Java operations. The resulting contracts give accurate descriptions of the observed object structure transformations. This reverse-engineering approach can be used to generate the visual contracts used by the methods in earlier chapters.
- Chapter 9 introduces stochastic graph transformations by modelling a simple dynamic peer-to-peer architecture. Analysts can specify non-functional requirements, such as availability or response time, as stochastic properties and verify them using model checking or simulation. Stochastic graph transformation systems are used as a formal method to analyse non-functional requirements of software systems.

Chapters 10–12 are concerned with *graph transformation-based language engineering* problems, in particular with the definition of domain-specific modelling languages in terms of their syntax and semantics and the transformation and analysis of their models. In particular:

- Chapter 10 considers an advanced definition of domain-specific modelling languages based on meta models and graph grammars. Focusing on the conceptual design of language tools, language engineers can use graph transformation rules to specify complex editor operations and interpreters for models.

- Chapter 11 presents the use of graph transformation to specify and analyse model improvements. It also shows how graph transformation can help modellers to understand complex model changes.
- Chapter 12 considers interrelated models and modelling languages. Here language engineers use graph transformation to specify model translations and model synchronisations, and to analyse their properties.

Each chapter introduces the field by referring to relevant literature and stating the challenges faced by existing solutions. Then, graph-transformation-based approaches are introduced and illustrated using running examples, before the chapter concludes with a summary and discussion of interesting extensions, tools, applications and further references.

5

Detecting Inconsistent Requirements in a Use-Case-Driven Approach

Requirements engineering is the process of gathering, structuring, analysing and validating requirements for a software system. The result is a requirements specification that provides the basis for design decisions. Therefore, the detection of requirement errors later in the development process can cause expensive iterations through all phases, emphasising the need for early validation and analysis. In the context of continuous software engineering, where software is developed, released and evaluated in very short cycles [45] and requirements change frequently as well, this analysis needs to be done repeatedly and quickly. Automation is therefore key.

Following the "separation of concerns" principle, a complex problem is decomposed according to different aspects or views to investigate them in more depth. While most engineers seem to be well trained in this decomposition task, the re-integration of partial models is more challenging (see e.g. [126, 101]). A well-known instance of this problem is the integration of requirements expressing different user views or aspects of a system. In the case of inconsistencies, both kinds of integration may lead to mis-developments, which are often detected much later in the process. In fact, since the workflow of *eliciting requirements* is followed by *analysing* them, and therefore decomposing them with respect to aspects or views, unresolved consistency problems tend to persist until the next big synthesis step: the *design*. It is thus advisable to detect and eliminate (or at least manage [225]) inconsistencies in the requirements model before progressing further in system development.

In object-oriented software development, UML [280] has become the standard notation for software models at different stages of the life cycle and different levels of abstraction, including the requirements specification. The result of requirements analysis usually includes a domain class diagram and a use case specification with scenarios, often combined within an activity diagram. This captures the dynamic aspect of the system, *when an action should be performed*. The functional aspect, *how it should be performed*, can be specified by pre- and postconditions of the actions in activity diagrams. Often these are just expressed in natural language. In that case the functional description is not formally integrated either with the dynamic or the static domain model. The intended connections between domain classes and activities can be indicated using meaningful names for classes and actions, but any formal checking of their correct use will remain hard to reliably automate. Even if diagrammatically specified, an early consistency check of activity diagrams using object structures and flow is made difficult by the informal nature of activity specifications. We consider an activity diagram to be consistent with an object structure if all flow paths specified in the diagram can be performed based on the actions' pre- and postconditions. A more precise specification of each action may enable a (semi-)automated consistency analysis. In particular, the following kinds of inconsistency may occur:

- *Type inconsistency:* Dynamic and functional requirements expressed by activity diagrams and their actions' pre- and postconditions may refer to terms of the problem domain that are not captured in the static domain model, or that have been renamed or redefined in the static model. As a consequence, the intended effect of executing an activity diagram may be unclear or violate constraints of the static model.

- *Inconsistency of dynamic and functional aspects:* Dynamic requirements expressed by activity diagrams may be inconsistent with the changes to the data and object structure specified by the actions' pre- and postconditions. In this case, the control flow in the activity diagrams or the pre- or postconditions may have to be adapted.

- *Inconsistency of views:* Use cases expressing the requirements of different stakeholders may overlap in scope. This may be intended if interaction is required in order to perform a common task, but it may also be a consequence of conflicting interests of different parties in the real world, or of undocumented dependencies between different use cases. We distinguish between *conflicts*, where the execution of one action may prevent the execution of another, and *dependencies*, where the execution of one action may require the prior execution of another.

If a model is suitably formalised, for example using class diagrams for domain models, activity diagrams for dynamic models and OCL for functional specifications, type consistency is easy to check statically. In our case, where the pre- and postconditions are expressed by graph transformation rules, this amounts to verifying that rules are correctly typed over the class diagram seen as a type graph. The remaining two consistency problems will be addressed as follows. First, we augment activity diagrams by specifying their actions in more detail. As suggested in [130], each action is modelled by pre- and postconditions specified by a pair of interrelated object diagrams, i.e. by a rule. This generalises the modelling of object flows to include object references.

Graph transformation systems provide a semantics for object-oriented models consisting of class models, use case and activity diagrams and their action specifications in terms of pre- and postconditions. In particular, activity diagrams specify control flow over rule applications, analogously to transformation units in Chapter 3.

This interpretation of object-oriented models allows (semi-)automated inconsistency analysis of aspects and views by formalising the intuitive notions of conflict and dependency of activity diagrams. Compared with logic-based approaches, which target critical systems where the cost of highly specialised experts for creating and verifying formal specifications is justified, we aim at models as they occur in mainstream business applications. Models in this domain are used by both domain experts and developers. Our aim is not to formally verify consistency, but to detect potential consistency problems. We run a plausibility check, which allows us to analyse an integrated behaviour model for *favourable* and *critical* signs of consistency [99]. *Favourable* signs may be, for example, situations where rules are triggered by other rules that precede them in the control flow. *Critical* signs are situations (1) where a rule application causes a conflict with another rule that should be applied after the first along the control flow, or (2) where a rule application depends causally on the effects of a second rule application scheduled by the control flow to occur after the first.

We will demonstrate with an example how the results of our analysis can be used to annotate use cases and activity diagrams to trigger a review of the requirements model to eliminate any undesired effects.

Before reading this chapter it is useful to be aware of the material in Chapters 1 and 2, in particular on typed attributed graph transformation systems. We will also make reference to control structures covered in Chapter 3 and use conflict and dependency analysis as introduced in Section 4.2 are used to compute favourable and critical signs for consistency.

5.1 Integrated Modelling of Static and Dynamic Requirements

Starting with an example of a lightweight, semi-formal requirements specification, first we demonstrate its shortcomings. Then, by enhancing the specification, we make it amenable to automated consistency analysis.

Object-oriented requirements specifications comprise both static requirements concerning the object structures of the problem domain and dynamic requirements concerning the intended behaviour. These can be expressed by UML class and use case diagrams [280]. Use case diagrams are employed to identify system boundaries. The main ingredients are actors and use cases, representing major functional units of the system under development. A use case may be refined by an activity diagram specifying its intended workflow. Thereby, the overall workflow is structured into clusters of activities.

Example 5.1 (structural requirements). To illustrate our approach, we choose a small, simple part of a shop and consider the domain model first, as it may be found in the glossary of a requirements specification. The shop has racks carrying goods and provides shopping carts for its customers. Customers hold a certain amount of cash, as do the cash boxes of the shop. A bill lists the goods collected by a customer, together with the total of their prices.

We start with a global view of the shop and its customers, which is intended to identify conflicts between different actors. Later, we will see what information has to be provided in what view, depending on the use cases that the customers and clerks perform.

All structural requirements are modelled in the class diagram in Fig. 5.1. Since we are at the level of requirements, classes do not have method signatures associated with them, i.e. the class diagram specifies only classes, associations, attributes and constraints [150]. An object diagram, as shown in Fig. 5.2, represents an object structure as an instance of this class diagram modelling a snapshot of a shop, i.e. a concrete state of the shop.   □

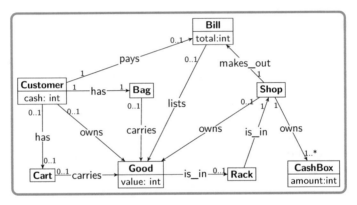

Fig. 5.1. A simple class model for a shop

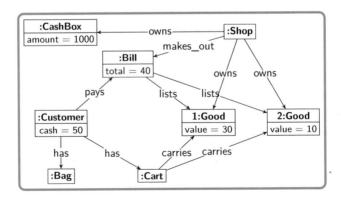

Fig. 5.2. Object diagram modelling a snapshot of a very small shop

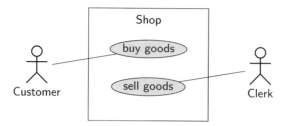

Fig. 5.3. Kernel use cases for selling goods

Example 5.2 (use case and activity diagrams). Dynamic requirements, here business processes, can be identified within use case diagrams, with each use case refined by an activity diagram. In this example, a shop offers goods to be bought by customers while clerks are waiting to sell goods. This excerpt of system behaviour is modelled by the use case diagram in Fig. 5.3. The essential information of the use cases buy goods and sell goods is given in the following:

- *Use case buy goods:* A customer buys a number of goods in a shop.
  - *Actor:* Customer
  - *Precondition:* A customer entity exists.
  - *Procedure:* The customer first takes a cart and selects all desired goods by taking them from the rack and placing them into the cart. After the customer has selected these goods, they are entered onto the bill and are paid for by the customer. Then the goods belong to the customer and no longer to the shop. The customer carries them home in a bag.
  - *Postcondition:* The customer owns all the goods they have bought.

- *Use case sell goods:* A clerk sells the goods in a shop.
  - *Actor:* Clerk
  - *Precondition:* A customer entity exists.
  - *Procedure:* The clerk creates a bill for the customer and bills every item the customer has in their cart. In doing so, the clerk takes one item after another out of the cart and lists it on the bill. The total sum of the bill is increased by the price of the item. Thereafter, the clerk settles the bill and adds the total sum to the cash box of the shop.
  - *Postcondition:* The customer owns all the goods they have bought.

To specify these use cases more precisely, we formulate them with activity diagrams. These diagrams model the intended control flow of the activities. The refinement of use case buy goods is given by the left activity diagram in Fig. 5.4, while use case sell goods is refined by the right diagram. Activity diagrams consist of actions connected by transitions modelling the flow of control. To buy goods, a customer first takes a cart, provided that they do not have one already, then selects goods repeatedly before paying the bill. To sell goods, the clerk creates a bill, takes the goods out of the cart and settles the bill.   □

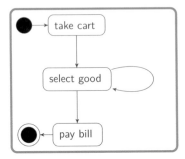 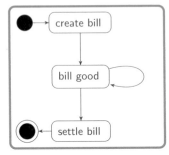

Fig. 5.4. Activity diagrams for buying goods (left) and selling goods (right)

So far, the only link between static and dynamic requirements is given by the names of the use cases and activities, such as buy goods or take cart, which make reference to the classes in the class diagram. A requirements specification of this kind cannot be used to find inconsistencies between the functional behaviours of use cases. To do so we need to clarify how activities change object structures. This information can be deduced, at least partly, from the use case descriptions given above.

An integration of static and dynamic requirements can be achieved by modelling the pre- and postconditions of activities. Some approaches, such as xUML [207], provide means for formal action specification using a high-level action notation. However, such formal notations require familiarity with programming concepts. For discussing requirements with domain experts or users, a diagrammatic action specification is more suitable. Catalysis [76], for example, advocates the use of collaborations for this purpose. The idea goes back to the Fusion method [60], where actions are specified by snapshots of the object configuration before and after the operation. Building on the latter approach, we propose a rule-based refinement of activities specifying a form of collaboration. In the following example, the compact notation of rules (as presented in Chapter 2) is adopted. This activity refinement summarises all checks and basic actions that can be identified on the level of requirements analysis.

Example 5.3 (activities modelled by dynamic object diagrams). For each activity in the diagrams in Fig. 5.4, a rule is given in Figs. 5.5 and 5.6. Activity bill good, for example, is specified in Fig. 5.6. It is applicable if the current object configuration comprises (instances of) Customer, Cart, Bill and Good such that the Customer is associated with a Bill and a Cart containing a Good. As a result of the application, the Good is taken from the Cart and added to the Bill. Also, the total amount of the Bill is increased by the value of the Good.

In order to make our point, we have included two inconsistencies which will be detected by formal analysis later. The first is between pay bill and settle bill. Both activities include the transfer of ownership of the goods, as described by the redirection of their links from the Shop to the Customer. This represents an overlap of responsibilities which requires further negotiation. Second,

Customer and Clerk seem to come from different continents: use case buy goods uses European standards, where customers have to collect their shopping by themselves after paying the bill, whereas use case sell goods acts according to the American custom, where goods are packed into bags by a clerk while they are being entered on the bill.   □

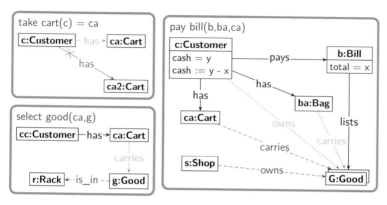

Fig. 5.5. Three rules forming the activity specification for use case buy goods

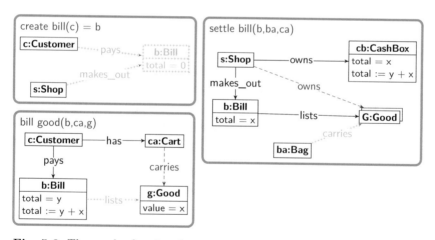

Fig. 5.6. Three rules forming the activity specification for use case sell goods

Refined activity diagrams provide an executable model which can visualise a system's behaviour at a high abstraction level. Considering a class model as a type graph with a set of graph constraints capturing multiplicities, it defines a set of object diagrams as instance graphs. A refined activity diagram can be specified by a transformation unit (see Section 3.3.3), where control flow is covered by constructs such as sequential composition, **alap** and **if –then–else**. This means that the static, functional and dynamic aspects of a model can be specified as a typed graph transformation system with control.

A use case represents a view of the overall model corresponding to the requirements of a particular actor (or a group of actors with the same role). A view of a graph transformation system representing the complete model is defined by a subgraph of the type graph (modelling the relevant fragment of the class diagram) and a subset of the rules acting on that restricted set of types [96].

Example 5.4 (views on the model). In our example, the view corresponding to the use case buy goods comprises the rules take cart, select good and pay bill. The relevant fragment of the class diagram excludes only the CashBox class and its association to the Shop. The use case sell goods consists of the rules create bill, bill good and settle bill. The corresponding class diagram excludes only the cash attribute of class Customer.

A use case in isolation may not constitute a complete behaviour specification, because it represents an incomplete view of the system's functionality from the perspective of a specific actor. Thus, interaction is required between the system's use cases. Executing the activity bill good of the clerk, for example, should depend on previously executing the activity select good of the customer.   □

One important integration problem is to fix interactions between use cases due to incomplete developer views. Moreover, there may be conflicts between use cases resulting from different opinions of the stakeholders about the intended behaviour or the scope of their responsibility. The next section is devoted to the analysis of such conflicts and dependencies. Before arriving there, we summarise how graph transformation is used to specify system requirements.

Note 5.1: Specifying activities on object structures. Object structures can be considered as a specific form of graph while type graphs support all the main features of class models. Graph transformation rules can specify activities on object structures by *if–then* patterns: *if* a specific object pattern exists *then* a number of change actions are performed. A set of rules extends the specification of object flow in activity diagrams.

5.2 Analysing Requirement Models

In the following, we investigate inconsistencies that may occur between dynamic requirements, given as use cases refined by activity diagrams, and functional aspects, given in the form of pre- and postconditions for actions, expressed in rules. First, we look for conflict and dependencies between functional requirements specified in actions. Then, we compare the conflicts and dependencies found with the specified control flow in activity diagrams to find favourable or critical sign for consistency between these two views.

5.2.1 Conflicts and Dependencies Between Functional Requirements

To find conflicts or dependencies, we consider activity diagrams and look for potential conflicts and dependencies between the rules specifying their actions. If two use cases belong to different viewpoints, this analysis may reveal an inconsistency between views as well.

We begin our consideration with an example that shows two conflicting state transitions formulated as graph transformation steps. Both steps start at the snapshot shown in Fig. 5.2.

Example 5.5 (conflicting state change). An example of a conflicting state change is shown by the conflicting applications of pay bill and settle bill in Fig. 5.7: both rule applications delete the owns links between the goods and the shop. Thus, they overlap in items that are deleted. As a consequence, each of the two applications disables the other one, i.e. they cannot be part of the same sequence of rule applications. This is unfortunate, because both rule applications capture important aspects of the intended overall behaviour. For example, pay bill updates the cash attribute of the Customer, while settle bill computes the new amount attribute of the CashBox. We will see below how these different views of the same process can be integrated.   □

We want not only to test actions on sample snapshots, but also to understand when they may be in conflict or dependency in general, with respect to all possible snapshots. For this reason, we consider the modelled control flow and check for potential conflicts and dependencies of participating actions by applying the conflict and dependency analysis presented in Chapter 4. Note that we also use rules with multiobjects for which the use of CDA has not been explained yet. As presented before, a rule containing a multiobject is interpreted as a rule schema yielding an infinite number of graph transformation rules. Obviously, this presents an obstacle to an exhaustive pairwise CDA. However, since rules resulting from the same scheme differ in the number of copies of the corresponding multiobject only, it is enough here to consider the rule instance where the multi-object is represented by one normal object. (The general case is more difficult; see [273, 44] for more details.) In the following, we will see that some of the analysis results are expected, i.e. they are *favourable signs* while others are not expected, i.e. they are *critical signs*.

5.2.2 Conflicts and Dependencies as Critical and Favourable Signs for Consistency

If an application of rule A may disable an application of rule B, and B should be applied after A, then this situation may lead to an incomplete functional behaviour. This is a *critical sign*, and the requirements engineer may consider switching the order of the corresponding actions in the activity diagram. On

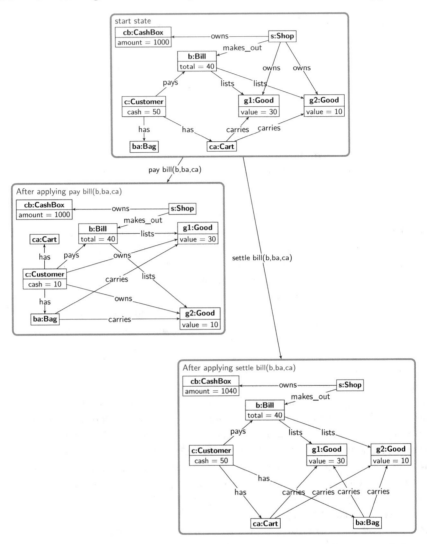

Fig. 5.7. A conflict situation between actions pay bill and settle bill

the other hand, if, for some application of rule A, no potentially disabling application of rule B is performed before A, then the application of rule A cannot be impeded. If the requirements engineer expects this analysis result, it is a *favourable sign*. The analysis of rule applications originating from different use case specifications helps to determine potential dependencies of use cases, as well as potentially conflicting ones.

Example 5.6 (potential conflicts between use cases buy goods and sell goods). Considering the use cases buy goods and sell goods, CDA results in two potential inter-use-case conflicts, as shown in Fig. 5.8. Binary analysis results are shown in the figure as follows. A red double arrow between two rule nodes indicates potential conflicts in both directions. If such an arrow does not exist between two rule nodes, there is no conflicting situation at all.

An application of rule **pay bill** may disable an application of **bill good**, and vice versa, since both rule applications take goods out of a cart, i.e. delete links between **Good** and **Cart** objects. These potential conflicts cannot be easily resolved by ordering the rule applications. Therefore, if we want to apply both rules on the same goods, we have to change at least one of the rules to make both views consistent.

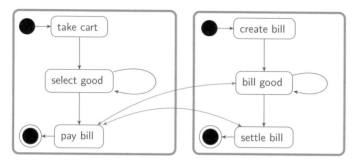

Fig. 5.8. Activity diagrams with conflict relations

Moreover, an application of rule **pay bill** may disable an application of **settle bill**, and vice versa, since both rule applications remove goods from the shop, i.e. delete links between **Good** and **Shop** objects. As before, consistency requires us to adapt at least one them such that they can both act on the same goods. All potential conflicts found for this example are critical signs, since they may impede intended rule applications. There are no further potential conflicts.

The absence of conflicts can also indicate possible errors in a specification, i.e. can also be a critical sign. Further analysis reveals that the application of **pay bill** does not disable **select good**. So, customers are able to continue shopping even though they have already paid. If this is regarded as unwanted behaviour, we can prevent this case by requiring that the cart should be returned when paying. This behaviour can be expressed by deleting the link between **Customer** and **Cart** in an improved version of rule **pay bill**.   □

If an application of rule B may depend on an application of rule A and B is applied after A, then the order of rule applications agrees with their causal dependencies. This is a *favourable sign* for the requirements engineer. If, for some application of rule B, however, no rule A is performed before B is enabled, this may lead to an incomplete functional behaviour. Hence, this is a *critical sign*, and the requirements engineer may decide to add some triggering rule application or to adapt some previous rule applications such that the needed trigger is created. As with conflicts, binary CDA results on dependencies are enough to discover these signs.

Example 5.7 (potential dependencies between buy goods and sell goods). Figure 5.9 shows the potential dependencies within and between our two example use cases. The dependencies between actions inside each of the use cases follow the specified control flow, and are favourable signs. They are depicted by green dashed arrows.

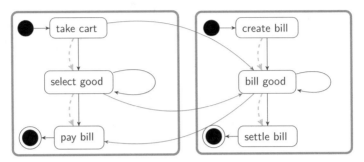

Fig. 5.9. Activity diagrams with dependency relations. Green arrows show favourable dependencies, and red ones show critical dependencies (since they are all interview dependencies)

In addition, Fig. 5.9 shows potential inter-use-case dependencies. For example, the customer has to take a cart and select goods before the goods are billed and the bill is settled. Moreover, all goods have to be billed before the bill is paid. Since no further dependencies have been found, this means that, for example, a bill may be created even if the customer has not yet selected any goods. Whether this is a mistake depends on the intention of the requirements engineer: how should the actions of the two use cases be interleaved to perform the overall task? All inter-use-case dependencies are critical signs, since we cannot ensure that the necessary rules have been applied early enough. To apply rule bill good, for example, rules take cart and select good have to be applied before as triggers. These dependencies are depicted by red solid arrows. There is also a dependency in this example running in the opposite direction, i.e. the use case interdependency is cyclic. □

In surveying the results of the analysis, the requirements engineer has to decide which dependencies or conflicts do actually represent errors or inconsistencies in the model. Owing to the semi-formal and incomplete nature of such analysis models, this decision must be based on the intention of the requirements engineer and cannot be taken mechanically. Nevertheless, the signs flagged up by the analysis can give valuable hints about changing the model in the next iteration or documenting the relevant decisions better.

Example 5.8 (resolving conflicts). The conflicts between the use cases buy goods and sell goods contradict the intuition that both use cases have to be performed in combination to achieve the desired effect. Having decided that there should not be conflicts between these two use cases, we have to correct this at the level of the actions associated with pay bill and bill good, and with pay bill and settle bill, respectively. In our case, the conflicts can be resolved by assigning the responsibilities for Cart and Shop to the clerk. Hence, deleting the links between Cart and Good and between Shop and Good is exclusive to the operation settle bill of the clerk. The revised rules pay bill2 and settle bill are shown in Figs. 5.10 and 5.11.

This rule adaptation is just the first step in resolving the conflict. Since settle bill and pay bill are not in the same control flow, other activities can be performed in between. If pay bill is applied first, for example, the customer's owns edges are created, but the shop's owns edges are still there. Another customer may buy the same goods as well, which is obviously an error. To avoid this situation, we could form the use cases differently. Activities take cart and select good would form a use case called selecting. Activity pay bill would form a separate one called pay goods, to be combined with the use case sell good into a larger case paying.   □

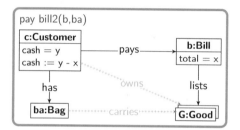

Fig. 5.10. Revised version of rule pay bill

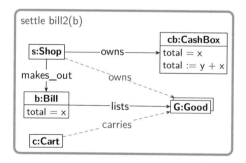

Fig. 5.11. Revised version of rule settle bill

We summarise the favourable and critical signs based on potential conflicts and dependencies of rule applications in Table 5.1. Potential conflicts and dependencies are considered in the context of the control flow in activity diagrams.

If rule A disables rule B and B is to be applied after A, this potential conflict is definitely a critical sign. If B should be applied after A, and A does

Table 5.1. Potential conflicts and dependencies in control flows: critical or favourable signs?

	With control flow	Against control flow	No control flow
Conflict	Critical sign	—	Critical sign
No conflict	Favourable sign	—	Favourable sign
Dependency	Favourable sign	Critical sign	Critical sign
No dependency	Critical sign	Favourable sign	Favourable sign

not cause a conflict on B, this is a favourable sign. If B occurs before A but not after it, the fact that A may cause a conflict on B does not have any effect. If A and B are not in a specific control flow, they are meant to be independent of each other. Therefore, a potential conflict between them is a critical sign; no potential conflict is a favourable sign.

If the application of rule B follows that of rule A in a control flow, a potential dependency of applying B on applying A fits the specified flow, i.e. it is a favourable sign. Conversely, if the control flow specifies that rule A should be applied after rule B or if both rule applications are not in a direct control flow, a potential dependency of B on A turns into a critical sign, since it may add a further restriction on applicability. If two rule applications cannot have any dependency, this can only be a critical sign if the first rule destroys a setting that is needed by the second one.

Up to now, we have interpreted binary CDA results only. In order to understand better the results of an analysis, the requirements engineer might be interested in the objects and links responsible for conflicts and dependencies. For this purpose, a combined presentation of control flow and data dependencies is helpful.

Example 5.9 (dependent objects and links). Consider, for example, the diagram in Fig. 5.12, where the dependencies between actions are depicted together with the essential objects and links where these dependencies manifest themselves. Note that not all objects and links are considered here and that link names have been omitted for better readability. A red, bent arrow from an activity such as take cart to a link such as the one between Customer and Cart represents the fact that the link is created by the action. Symmetrically, an arrow from a link or object to an activity indicates that the item is used, i.e. read or even deleted. Thus, the customer first has to take a cart, producing the corresponding link, before goods may be selected or billed, where the link is required, etc. Note that a diagram such as in Fig. 5.12 can be computed from a coarse granular analysis of conflicts and dependencies (see Section 4.2). □

We started this chapter with a consideration of three different forms of inconsistency that may occur in requirements specifications. Throughout this chapter we have investigated inconsistencies between dynamic and functional system aspects, finding that potential conflicts and dependencies between rules

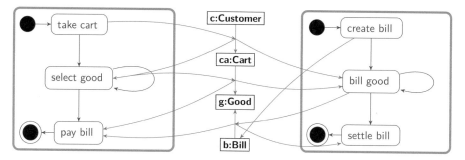

Fig. 5.12. Activity diagrams with dependent objects and links

may not be aligned with workflows described by activity diagrams. If two rules refine actions in two different workflows occurring in different views, this technique may also reveal inconsistencies between views.

Inconsistencies involving static requirements, i.e. with the types and structural invariants of the problem domain, can be discovered by type checking and are usually easier to correct. Inconsistencies between types and activity diagrams can be corrected by renaming types or activities. Functional requirements in the form of rules may show various forms of inconsistency with their class models, such as pre- and postcondition patterns that cannot be mapped to the defined class structure. This kind of inconsistency can be checked by establishing the existence of a typing morphism. If there is no graph morphism from a pre- or postcondition to the type graph defined by the class model, there is a type inconsistency. Furthermore, a rule application may yield a result state that does not fulfil all invariants specified in the class model. Such an inconsistency can be resolved by integrating the failed invariant into the rule as an additional application condition (see Section 4.4).

Inconsistency between views is not limited to the case where their respective workflows are inconsistent. The problem may also extend to their static requirements, for example, if the same type is specified by two different names or the same name is used to denote semantically different concepts. Such inconsistencies can be resolved, for example, by introducing a reference model to relate several views [96].

5.3 Summary and Further Reading

This chapter has shown that rules can be integrated into object-oriented requirement specifications based on UML. While workflows are described by activity diagrams, their actions can be refined by rules describing pre- and postconditions of actions. Since rules have to conform to the given class diagram, they build a bridge between static and dynamic requirements. This approach to integrated modelling of static and dynamic system concerns based on graph transformation, including their consistency analysis, was first presented in [130] and then elaborated on in several further publications.

The integrated modelling of static and dynamic system requirements allows a (semi-)automated consistency analysis of aspects and views, looking for favourable and critical signs with respect to control flow and functional behaviour [99]. In a similar line of research, sufficient criteria for applicability and non-applicability of rule sequences were presented [185]. Restricting the control for rule applications to sequencing only, precise sufficient criteria were presented to check in advance whether a rule sequence can be completely applied. These criteria were further developed in [153] to make them useful for consistent behaviour modelling with refined activity diagrams. In [154], refined activity diagrams were extended to allow the definition of object flow between rule applications. Rules may have input and output parameters that are objects or data; object flow is easily realised by passing parameters between actions and thus, between rule applications.

The concept of refined activity diagrams with related consistency analysis has been used not only for integrated requirements specifications but also in the context of aspect modelling. An analysis of aspect-oriented model weaving based on graph transformation was presented in [205, 206].

6

Service Specification and Matching

Service-oriented systems are developed by composing reusable services, often distributed and provided by external organisations. In addition, the familiar approach to building applications from reusable components is extended into runtime, raising the need to find and bind to required services automatically. At the business level, this means ensuring agreement on a range of functional and non-functional characteristics of services to enable cooperation between organisations. Owing to the dynamic nature of the composition, this agreement must be automated. At the technical level, standardisation and the specification of service interfaces ensure interoperability and support automation.

Web services are the most common realisation of the service-oriented paradigm. They provide programmatic access to application components distributed over the Web using ubiquitous W3C standards based on HTTP and XML, thus ensuring technical interoperability at the transport and messaging level. When the need arises, application software should be able to find and bind to services at runtime. Web services follow the service-oriented architecture (SOA) style, which defines the roles of *provider, requester* and *registry*. Providers advertise their services by publishing descriptions on a registry. When requesters need a particular kind of service, they query the registry and receive a list of suitable candidates. After selecting the preferred service, the requester is able to use it directly by contacting the provider.

To specify a service, an interface definition language such as the XML-based Web Services Description Language (WSDL) [290] is used. WSDL specifies the operation offered by a Web service at the technical level, defining the syntax of admissible service invocations and the protocols to be used to access them, but not their business semantics nor their effect. In traditional software development, a human developer may infer the semantics of an operation from a signature such as orderBook(isbn:String). Automatic service discovery requires a precise, machine-readable description.

Semantic service descriptions addressing this need are based on ontologies that standardise the terms used in such specifications. Ontologies are repre-

© Springer Nature Switzerland AG 2020
R. Heckel, G. Taentzer, *Graph Transformation for Software Engineers*,
https://doi.org/10.1007/978-3-030-43916-3_6

sented in Semantic Web languages such as RDF or OWL, based on which one can describe semantics as input–output behaviour [201], workflow [169] or the logical specification of pre- and postconditions. Non-functional properties are defined in terms of quality of service (QoS) properties. In addition, services may be classified by, for example, location, purpose and provider to be organised into categories in registries that support the automatic discovery of services.

Besides the centralised, repository-based model, alternative discovery protocols include a publish-subscribe model, where requesters can register their interest in being notified of the availability of a suitable service, and network-based methods, which use gossiping protocols to query the network about the services provided. However, since the matching of services based on semantic descriptions is largely independent of the discovery protocol, we will stick to one model which is the repository-based one.

Combined with the technical standardisation of service access, such descriptions provide the means to find and integrate services on a global scale. This means that standard software functions such as authentication, logging and payment but also real-world services such as shipment, hotel and transport reservations can be obtained from suitable service providers and combined to provide added value to clients. However, the dynamic and distributed nature of service composition poses a range of challenges in engineering such systems (see e.g. [72]):

- Some common concerns in distributed applications, such as security and fault tolerance, also apply to service-oriented computing. At the technology level these are addressed by dedicated protocols for secure service interaction, reliable messaging and transaction handling, such as WS-Security and WS-BPEL. However, solutions have to be decided on and specified at the business level before being implemented using these standards.
- The development of services is distributed in space, time and authority: individual components are developed by teams working at different times in different organisations. This impacts on software engineering activities at all levels, from capturing requirements via design and documentation through to testing. It also means that service interactions implement contracts between business partners rather than purely technical processes.
- Changes to requirements at any individual requester or provider may lead to evolution at both specification and implementation level, with the need to maintain consistency between requester and provider views.

Model-based software engineering can address these challenges using models at different levels for different purposes. At an informal level, models act as means of communication between distributed development teams. At a semi-formal level, they serve as documentation (communication over time) of designs or implementations. Formal models can be used to verify protocols and other architecture choices for security and reliability properties, or they can serve as a basis for automated code generation, making it easier to create and evolve applications that are correct by construction.

In this chapter, we describe the use of graph transformation as a model-based approach to service engineering, in particular for the specification and matching of services. Corresponding techniques for testing and reverse engineering are considered in Chapters 7 and 8, respectively.

Graph transformation rules are used to describe service semantics through *visual contracts* describing the preconditions and effects of an operation in terms of both its input and output, and the service's internal object structure. Owing to their use of graph transformation rules, visual contracts support, in particular, the specification of complex structural transformations, combining a semiformal visual representation with a rigorous formal semantics. Based on such a detailed yet technology-independent specification we can state precise conditions for matching required by provided services, both one to one and incrementally.

Visual contracts differ from contracts embedded in Java code using the JML or contracts in Eiffel, as well as from model-level contracts formulated in OCL. They are *visual*, using UML notation to model complex patterns and transformations intuitively and concisely, and *abstract*, providing a specification of object transformations at a high level of granularity to aid readability and scalability. Moreover, they are *deep*, capturing the transformation of internal object structures besides input/output behaviour. And last but not least, they are *executable*, yielding a graph transition system that can be used for simulating and analysing system behaviour.

Employing well-known visual notations based on UML [280], this approach integrates naturally with the model-based development of service-oriented systems on the requester as well as on the provider side. The principle of *design-by-contract* [212] is used as a basis for service specification and matching. In component-based development it supports reliable composition by specifying interfaces formally and validating interactions against such specifications. A core concept of design-by-contract is the formulation of pre- and postconditions for each operation. However, these conditions are usually expressed in a logical notation at programming-language level, making them hard to integrate into diagrammatic model-based development methods. Graph transformation rules provide a visual notation for pre- and postconditions that integrates easily into UML while providing a formal and operational semantics suitable for both verification and execution. They also allow a precise formulation of service matching along with semantic guarantees for the resulting composition of services.

Starting from an overview of the development of service-oriented systems in Section 6.1, we show how services and service requirements can be formulated using visual contracts in Section 6.2. In Section 6.3, we focus on the matching of service descriptions and requirements and discuss how service matching is interpreted at runtime. Finally, to address the case where one service does not fully satisfy a service requirement, we consider incremental service compositions in Section 6.4. Since visual contracts are specified by typed attributed graph transformation rules, it is worthwhile to be aware of the concepts introduced in Chapters 1 and 2 before reading this one.

6.1 Developing Service-Oriented Software

The most common implementations of the SOA paradigm are Web services. More recent developments include mash-ups, software-as-a-service and cloud computing [25]. In each case we distinguish two types of developmental activity: (1) on the requester side, the development of client applications that use required services, and (2) on the provider side, the development of the services themselves. Accordingly, in the following we distinguish *application developers* from *service developers*. In a typical service-oriented architecture as depicted in Fig. 6.1, service developers publish their implemented services to a registry to attract service users. Application developers use a discovery service or registry to find services with specific properties or satisfying a particular specification. To find the right service, an application developer sends their requirements to the registry, which tries to find a matching service and, if successful, sends the information to the requester, allowing them to contact the provider.

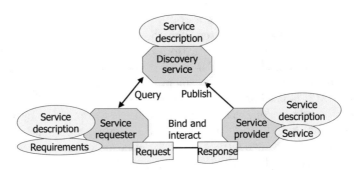

Fig. 6.1. Service-oriented architecture

This process of discovery works best if the matching of service requests to provided services yields precise and comprehensive results. A purely syntactical description of services does not allow semantic matching. Natural-language descriptions of their semantics are understandable by developers, but too ambiguous for precise automated matching. We are proposing an approach that is both understandable to humans and precise enough for automation. The concept of *design-by-contract* views services as software components with contractually specified interfaces. A provided service promises certain results as a *postcondition*, assuming that a *precondition* is met. A requester who wants to use this service has to ensure that this precondition holds before they use the service. Then, after invoking the service, the requester can assume that the postcondition holds as promised. We will present *visual contracts* based on graph transformation as an approach that is both easy to understand and precise, and thus represents a powerful realisation of design-by-contract at the model level.

To allow a semantic description of services and service requests, visual contracts are based on a common *ontology*, i.e. a shared conceptual data model agreed between application and service developers. To enable matching, both the service description and the requirement have to use the same concepts.

The shared ontology is used only for matching, i.e. the application and the service implementation may use different internal data models. In this case, the mapping between the internal and shared data models has to be documented, for example to allow the tracing of requirements to implementations.

6.2 Service Specification

According to our requirements, service matching must provide the flexibility of discovering the widest range of services satisfying the requester's requirements while ensuring interoperability of the application with all of these services. The first problem is the interrelation of the conceptual models behind the client application and the services. This is achieved using shared ontologies as standardised domain models.

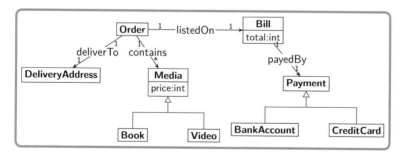

Fig. 6.2. Ontology for selling books and videos

At the conceptual level, ontologies can be represented by entity-relationship models or class diagrams with additional constraints. We will use visual contracts based on class diagrams to specify services. This combination translates naturally into a typed graph transformation system consisting of a set of rules over a fixed type graph.

Example 6.1 (service specification). Figure 6.2 shows a small sample ontology for media sales depicted as a class diagram. It defines the concept of an Order referring to one Bill, one DeliveryAddress, and any number of Books and Videos. A generalisation relationship indicates that CreditCard and BankAccount are specialisations of Payment, while Book and Video specialise Media. Classes Media and Bill both have attributes, and we can think of a constraint stating that, for all orders o, the total of a bill is greater than or equal to the sum of all prices of the media in its order.

If a vendor wants to express that their service is able to handle orders for books payable by credit card, they can formulate this as the visual contract expressed by the rule at the top left of Fig. 6.3. This rule says that the Web service needs data on the media to be ordered, the delivery address of the buyer and their credit card. It creates a new order for the item, and a bill for this customer reflecting the price of the item ordered in its total attribute. The link between the CreditCard and Bill objects denotes that the bill is paid by credit card after the execution of the service. Note that subsequent steps in selling the item, such as delivery and actual payment, are not covered by this ontology fragment. Further operations, such as adding items to an existing order or cancelling an order, can be specified in a similar way.

The precondition of a service is expressed by the left-hand side of a rule, while the service's effect comprises all creations and deletions formulated in the rule. Visual contracts are linked to the signatures of the operations offe-

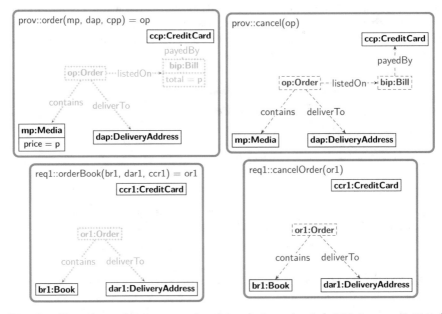

Fig. 6.3. Provider and requester rules for ordering a book (which is a media item)

red by the service. For example, the contract at the top left of Fig. 6.3 specifies an operation order(mp: Media, dap: DeliveryAddress, cpp: CreditCard): Order. At the top right, the operation cancel(op: Order) is specified to delete a specified order.   □

Visual contracts can be used for describing both services provided and services required. From a provider's point of view, the left-hand side of a rule specifies the precondition that must hold for its own internal state and the data sent by the requester for the operation to execute successfully. The right-hand side of the rule depicts the postcondition, i.e. a promise about the situation after a successful execution. The operation's effect consists of all creation and deletion actions specified by the rule.

From a requester's point of view, the left-hand side of a rule represents their assumption about the provider's state and the data they are willing to provide when invoking the service, and the right-hand side describes their expectations about the resulting state. In general, several rules may be needed to specify a service provided or required, since, depending on different preconditions, different effects may be expected.

Example 6.2 (specification of a service request). Visual contracts from a requester's point of view are shown in the bottom of Fig. 6.3. In contract req1::orderBook(br1: Book, dar1: DeliveryAddress, ccr1: CreditCard) = or1: Order, for example, if the client provides information about a book, a credit card and their delivery address, the service provider should create an order based on this information. This means that we are looking for a shop offering an operation to order books payable by credit card. Intuitively, the provider rule in Fig. 6.3 should be a candidate for this requirement, since this rule creates an order for media items, which, according to the ontology, include books. The next section provides a precise formulation of this intuition.   □

6.3 Matching of Service Specifications

The motivation for implementing a service is to satisfy some demand, formally expressed in a service requirement. When a requester application R finds and binds to a provided service P, R has to be sure that P provides its functionality in a way that is consistent with the assumptions about the required service made in R's implementation. These assumptions are expressed in a *requester contract* consisting of one or more rules. The registry compares these with available *provider contracts* which represent descriptions of actually implemented services. The desired result is the set of those provider contracts that fulfil the requirements. In this section, we give a more detailed explanation of what it means that provider rule p fulfils the requirements of requester rule r, or, briefly, that p *matches* r. Then, a provider contract C_P matches a requester contract C_R if for every rule r in C_R there exists a rule p in C_P such that p matches r. We give an operational interpretation of this statement and discuss its consequences and benefits for the testing of services.

6.3.1 Definition of Service Matching

A requester rule r declares the objects and links whose existence is *guaranteed* by R when a service is invoked. These are the objects and links that are preserved or deleted by the requester rule. The effects that R *expects* as a result of invoking a matching service are specified by the actions of r, i.e. any deletions and creations of objects and links and updates of certain attribute values. A provider rule p has a slightly different interpretation. It *expects* the existence of all objects and links in the left-hand side of p as a precondition, and *guarantees* as effects all deletions and creations specified by p. Matching provider and requester rules means comparing the guarantees given by either side with the expectations of the other: the requester's precondition must entail the provider's precondition and the provider's effects must entail the requester's effects.

Example 6.3 (specification matching). The rule for orderBook() at the bottom left of Fig. 6.3 says that, if the requester invokes the operation in a state where objects ccr1:CreditCard, br1:Book and dar1:DeliveryAddress are present, then or1:Order, with two links, should be created by the provider. Compare this with the provider rule for order() above it, where objects ccp:CreditCard, mp:Media and dap:DeliveryAddress are assumed, and then a guarantee is given that objects op:Order and bip:Bill and four links will be created. It is easy to see that, in this example, the requester's precondition entails the provider's precondition and the provider's effects entail the requester's effects. In particular, the br1:Book object guaranteed by the requester satisfies the expectation of mp:Media by the provider because Book is a subtype of Media.

However, such a match can not be found between the rules cancel() and cancelOrder() on the right side of Fig. 6.3 because the requester's precondition does not entail that of the provider. In particular, the provider expects the Order to be linked to the CreditCard via a Bill. This information may be needed to refund the price of the order to the correct card and we know from the cardinalities in the ontology that such a connection exists. Based on the visual representation it is easy to see that, in the requester's version of this rule, the Bill object is missing.

Instead, the effect expected by the requester, i.e. the deletion of the or1:Order object with its links, is correctly entailed by the provider rule which deletes the matching object op:Order and the bip:Bill object. Notice how the effects provided can exceed the effects requested in terms of both the creation and the deletion of elements.

Figure 6.4 shows a variant of the requester rule correcting the incomplete precondition. It is structurally equivalent to the provider rule, but guarantees the more specific Book object where a general Media object is expected.   □

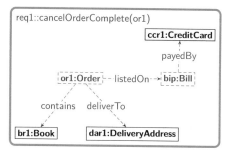

Fig. 6.4. Requester rule for cancelling orders, with completed precondition

In general, a provider rule $p : L_p \Rightarrow R_p$ matches a requester rule $r : L_r \Rightarrow R_r$ if we can establish a structure-preserving mapping relating their elements[1] such that the following conditions hold:

1. Every element in the left-hand side L_p of p is related to one element in the left-hand side L_r of r.
2. Every element deleted in r is related to an element deleted by p.
3. Each element in p related to a preserved element in r is preserved in p.
4. Every element created in r is related to an element created by p.

The difference between the statements of conditions 2 and 4 on the one hand and 3 on the other hand is necessary because the mapping between the elements of r and p can be partial. While all elements deleted and created by r must be part of the mapping, elements preserved by r may not be, but if they are, they are preserved as well.

The mapping of elements is subject to the same constraints as matches of the left-hand sides of rules into host graphs. In particular, while renaming of elements is possible, their types have to be compatible and the graph structure has to be preserved, i.e. matching links must have matching sources and targets.

Example 6.4 (specification matching continued). Let us apply this definition to the provider and requester rules p and r in Fig. 6.3. In order to satisfy condition 1, we consider a mapping m_1 defined by pairs {(ccp, ccr1), (mp, br1), (dap, dar1)}. Matching elements are of compatible types. Condition 2 requires an inclusion of the deleted elements of r in those of p, which is trivial because these sets are empty for both rules. The preserved elements of r are all matched by preserved elements of p, as requested by condition 3. Finally, condition 4 requires that all elements created in r (i.e. the object or1:Order with its two links) are in correspondence with elements created in p. Thus, the matching must be extended to include the pair (op, or1) as well as the links from or1 and the corresponding ones from op.

---

[1] Formally, this is a partial graph homomorphism from $L_p \cup R_p$ to $L_r \cup R_r$. Recall that, for each rule $L \Rightarrow R$, its deleted, created and preserved elements are given by $L \setminus R$, $R \setminus L$ and $L \cap R$, respectively.

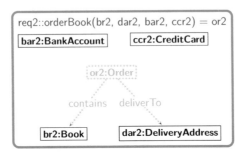

Fig. 6.5. A second requester rule for ordering a book

The situation is more subtle with the requester rule req2::orderBook() in Fig. 6.5, which provides an alternative payment mechanism. The correspondence $m_2 = \{(\mathsf{ccp}, \mathsf{ccr2}), (\mathsf{mp}, \mathsf{br2}), (\mathsf{dap}, \mathsf{dar2})\}$ satisfies condition 1 while the new object bar2:BankAccount in r is not part of this match, because this data is not assumed by the provider. However, it is included in the requester rule to make it as flexible as possible, thus returning more matches. The sets of deleted and created elements are similar to those of req1::orderBook(), but as elements required to be preserved by the requester we have bar2, ccr2, br2, dar2. The corresponding elements mp, dap, ccp of $p = \mathsf{prov::order}()$ are indeed preserved as required by condition 3 above. This illustrates the difference from conditions 2 and 4, where elements of the respective kind in r *must be in correspondence* with elements of the same kind in p, while in condition 3 elements *that are in correspondence* must be of the same kind. Thus, objects that are required to be preserved by the requester rule are optional in the sense that they need not be present in the provider rule, but if they are, they must not be deleted.   □

In order that an operation invocation by the requester can be processed by the provider, we have to make sure that all the necessary data is supplied. This is the case if, as stated in condition 1 above, all elements of p's precondition are matched by elements of the same or a more specific type in r's precondition. In particular, since an object of a subtype T is also an instance of a supertype S of T, the expectation of p to find an object of type S is satisfied by an object of type T.

While elements preserved by r are protected in p, the provider rule can delete additional elements outside the scope of r, such as bip:Bill in prov::cancel(). Such unexpected effects of the provider can be undesirable. For example, we would not want a matching provider rule p to delete any other orders we already have while creating or:Order, nor to add any more products to this or any other order. This can be specified on the requester side by declaring certain critical types as protected, ruling out any matches resulting in unspecified creation or deletion of its instances.

When the system is trying to negotiate a match between a requester and a provider, it may happen that the provider needs more information and guarantees than have been given by the requester. If the requester is able and willing to extend the precondition of their request, it can be matched with the provided service. The requester may also decide to use another service with a weaker precondition. If such a match covers only some of the requested effects, this provided service is only a partial solution and has to be completed from contributions of one or more further services. A process for such a composed service solution is presented in Section 6.4.

Note 6.1: Rule matching for service matching. Graph transformation rules can be used to specify *visual contracts*, i.e. pre- and postconditions of operations of services or components. Rule matching is used to check if contracts of service requesters and providers are compatible. In particular, the precondition of a provider rule must entail that of the requester rule, while a requester's effects must entail the provider's effects.

6.3.2 Operational Interpretation of Service Matching

Specification matching provides us with a static check of the interoperability of a provider and requester, assuming that the respective rules faithfully reflect the needs and provisions of their implementations. Their relation is illustrated in Fig. 6.6 from an operational point of view. This diagram shows the invocation of P by R, as well as P's reply, together with the relevant preconditions and effects:

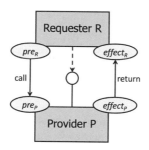

Fig. 6.6. Operational interpretation of service matching

1. When invoking the service, R guarantees that its precondition pre_R holds.
2. P can assume its precondition pre_P holds because it is entailed by pre_R.
3. P guarantees that its execution realises the effects described by its rule p.
4. R can assume the effects specified by its rule r, which are entailed by p.

With each service invocation, we avoid the need for the checks for conditions 2 and 4, which are guaranteed by the matching. This saves not only time but also, more importantly, implementation effort in checking and error handling. It also allows the developer of the requester to abstract from the actual service implementation by working with the assumption that a suitably matching service will be provided, thus decoupling the development processes between the requester and provider sides.

To ensure that the software implemented by R with the help of P works as expected, we have to verify that the guarantees given in conditions 1 and 3 are correctly implemented, and that the assumptions derived from conditions 2 and 4 are indeed sufficient to ensure the correct function of P and R. This is not a problem of matchmaking, but one of establishing the correctness of the implementations of P and R with respect to these specifications.

When one is testing a service-oriented application, specification matching can to some extent replace integration testing, as the correct interaction of services is analysed and guaranteed statically. The correctness of individual services, however, has to be tested with respect to their requirements and assumptions.

6.4 Incremental Service Composition

If a service requirement cannot be matched by a single offer, multiple services have to be composed for a complete match. This requires incremental service matching: a service request is matched partially at first, and then we compute the remainder of this request with respect to the service offered, containing all effects not yet realised, by identifying all effects the matched service shares with the specified request. These effects become additional preconditions in the remainder of the request. We iterate these steps until all required effects are satisfied or we run out of providers to match. Finally, we compose all offers into a global process summarising the overall set of preconditions and effects of the combined services provided.

Example 6.5 (service composition). If both a book and a video are ordered together, the combined request can be expressed as shown in Fig. 6.7. We assume that there is no single operation offering such an order. Hence these articles have to be purchased in two different steps, which means that two order operations have to be matched against the requirement, one for the book and one for the video.

In a partial match of requester operation req::orderBookAndVideo() with provider operation prov::order(), the order for one item (e.g. the book) can be covered but the order for the video remains open. As a result of this partial match, or1 and its outgoing edges are created by prov::order() as required. The remainder of the request can be expressed by adding the newly created elements to the precondition of the updated requester rule shown in Fig. 6.8, representing the remainder yet to be matched. Then, we can use the same provider rule with a mapping of mp to vr to cover the rest of the

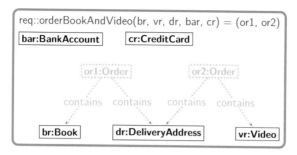

Fig. 6.7. Requester rule for ordering a book and a video

requirements of req::orderBookAndVideo(). This means that the matching of req::orderBookAndVideo(br, vr, dr, bar, cr) = (or1, or2) proceeds in two steps:

1. req::orderBookAndVideo(br, vr, dr, bar, cr) = (or1, or2) minus prov::order(br, dr, cr) = or1 yields req::orderVideo(vr, dr, bar, cr) = or2.
2. req::orderVideo(vr, dr, bar, cr) = or2 is matched by prov::order(vr, dr, cr) = or2.

This is done such that the overall request req::orderBookAndVideo(br, vr, dr, bar, cr) = (or1, or2) is matched by the composition prov::order(br, dr, cr) = or1 ; prov::order(vr, dr, cr) = or2.   □

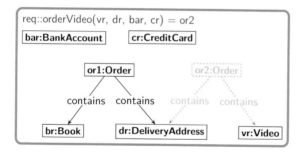

Fig. 6.8. Remainder requester rule for ordering a video

In general, several different providers may be needed to fulfil a single request. In more complex cases, they may produce additional (transient) object structure, which would occur in the remainder rule, but not necessarily in the composed contract. For example, think of a shopping cart object created in the first step in a series of multiple orders, which is updated by each order and finally deleted. This is an implementation choice that the requester may not want to anticipate, but it would be part of the provider rules and thus occur in the remainder rules of the intermediate stages. Formally, the construction is based on the notion of a concurrent or derived rule [85] which allows intermediate structures to be consumed in later steps. The relation between the composed rule and the original request is analogous so that between the provider and requester rules in a one-to-one match.

The iterative process of matching a requirement to one or more provided services either can be semi-automatic, requiring user input, or can be phrased as a search and optimisation problem. Matching services are computed automatically, but if there are multiple options we have to select the most suitable one, for example one that covers the required effects most comprehensively and efficiently. For example, our combined order request could also be matched by a sequence that orders a book, then cancels the order, and then orders another book and the video as in the solution above, but this sequence may be seen as less efficient than the shorter one consisting of the last two orders only.

The matching procedure is *complete* in the following sense: if there is a way of satisfying a request completely by a sequence of provided services, then there exists a composed service together with a complete match. In other words, if there is no match, the request cannot be satisfied. That means the desired functionality cannot be implemented unless the requester decides to adapt their requirements.

As a search and optimisation problem over a finite domain, the problem is *decidable but NP complete*, assuming that the number of provided services is finite and there are no complex constraints on attributes over unbounded domains. In particular, the process is *terminating*, since the number of effects in each service request is finite. If each partial match makes some progress, i.e. it covers at least one requested effect, after a finite number of iterations we will know if all requested effects can be matched, and which sequence of provided services forms a solution. However, if complex attribute conditions are used, the problem requires logical inference and will be semi-decidable only. These properties were demonstrated in more detail in [218], based on graph transformation theory.

In general, if we do not need full automation, several alternative combinations of offers computed for a given service request could be presented to the client to let them choose the most suitable one. Alternatively, the selection could be automated based on a specification of non-functional requirements, such as cost, response time or reliability of services. Once a combined offer has been computed, it can be stored in a repository of services, such that new requests can be served more quickly, by matching them against existing combined offers.

6.5 Summary and Further Reading

Services are software components that can be published and discovered in registries at runtime. Web services in particular are discovered and invoked over Web protocols. They allow adhoc global application integration based on changing business demands. At the technical level, standardisation and rigorous semantic specifications are required to enable the automated integration of services. In this chapter, we have described an approach using visual contracts to specify the operations offered by a service with their data types and constraints. Visual contracts support, in particular, the specification of changes to complex object structures. They combine a semiformal visual representation with a rigorous formal semantics enabling us to state precise conditions for matching required by provided services.

Visual contracts are sets of graph transformation rules that define pre- and postconditions of services based on a shared reference data model (ontology). The requester and provider contracts match if the requester's precondition contains the provider's precondition, and the provider's contract subsumes all effects (deletions, creations and updates) required in the requester's contract and preserves all of the matched context elements. The matching process can be incremental, supporting the combination of several offered services to satisfy a single requirement.

In Chapter 8, we will describe an approach to the reverse engineering of visual contracts from service implementations in Java. This can help the provider, who has access to the source or byte code, to create contracts for their services. If a description of a provided service is created manually, the service implementation can be validated by testing. This is supported by our approach to testing against visual contracts presented in Chapter 7. Contracts expressing service requirements arise from requirements analysis as presented in Chapter 5, decomposing high-level functional goals into requirements for individual components.

6.5.1 Tools and Evaluation

The technical feasibility of the approach described here has been validated in a prototypical tool that supports the visual editing of service descriptions and requests (Section 6.2) and their matching (Section 6.3) based on standard Semantic Web languages and tools. As presented in [128], this prototype uses AGG (the Attributed Graph Grammar system) [98] to develop graph transformation rules over a type graph created by importing an RDF ontology in DAML+OIL [61], a precursor to the Web ontology language OWL [286]. Rules are exported to RDF, so that ontologies, and pre- and postconditions are all present as RDF graphs. This means that the matching of rules can be described in terms of RDF graph matching. This has been implemented in Java based on the Semantic Web toolkit Jena [56] using the RDF query language RDQL.

Based on prototypical tool support, a study was conducted to explore the practical use of visual contracts for the specification of services in business-critical applications [97]. Natural language specifications of services were augmented by formal descriptions using visual contracts. The company sd&m, which led the study, was particularly interested in the visual nature of the description, its seamless embedding into UML and its expressiveness for specifying application interfaces concisely and in enough detail to support discovery and matching. The evaluation of a case study, which consisted of contracts for about 50 operations at both technical and business level, showed that, despite the limited tool support, visual contracts extended with advanced features such as multiobjects and attribute conditions satisfied these requirements.

6.5.2 Extensions

Further concepts, such as attribute conditions, NACs or multiobjects, can enhance the expressiveness and flexibility of rule-based specifications. For example, a requirement that we may be allowed to cancel an order only if it has not yet been delivered can be expressed by a negative condition over a suitable extension of the model. A multiobject could be required to say that we want to cancel all orders of a particular user. Such extensions require a more sophisticated notion of matching, which can be realised using the advanced graph transformation concepts discussed in Chapter 2. For example, [59] formalised the matching of visual contracts containing NACs. Such matching concepts can be implemented using more advanced logics [245], as supported by Semantic Web languages such as OWL [286].

The idea of model-based specification and matching of services to enable dynamic discovery has been the focus of a number of scientific publications using a range of modelling languages. It has been used to support the generation of service monitors in the Java Modelling Language (JML) in [194], where also attributes and NACs were considered. A service monitor allows one to verify the compliance of a service with its published specification throughout its life cycle. It can be used to bridge the gap between the high-level specification of services for service matching and their implementation in an object-oriented language.

Visual contracts were developed for the purpose of service interface specification in [129] and were used for model-based testing in [194, 118]. Using a formal interpretation in terms of typed graph transformation, they are executable and hence suitable for the generation of test oracles [167]. The theory and tools of graph transformation also provide support for the generation of test cases [253] and the definition and evaluation of coverage criteria [166]. These applications are explored in more detail in the following chapter.

From a logical point of view, Web services are a form of software component discovered and provided over the Internet. The approach to specification and matching presented here can also be used for discovering methods (operations) in APIs, frameworks or libraries, for choosing plug-ins, and for Android apps. Some of these domains use their own standards for interface specifications and registries, to which any language and tool support for visual contracts would have to be adapted. This is in line with the general idea of model-driven development, where essentially similar models can map to different implementation platforms.

7

Model-Based Testing

Software testing is the most important method for verifying the correctness of a system against its specification. This remains the case despite advances in formal verification methods such as model checking or theorem proving. Even if testing can not demonstrate the absence of errors, when carried out systematically it can increase our confidence that the number of errors is low.

However, testing in practice is often unstructured, not reproducible, poorly documented, lacking in detailed rationales for test design and dependent on the ingenuity of individual testers. Testing is also expensive, taking up a significant proportion of the development effort. A systematic approach to testing consists of activities such as *coverage analysis* to assess the quality and completeness of tests, the creation of *test oracles* to predict the expected results, and *test case generation* based on formal criteria. *Model-based testing* [281] helps to perform testing activities at a higher level of abstraction, making them traceable and supporting automation.

According to [281], model-based testing comprises the following steps (see Fig. 7.1). Based on informal requirements or an early design of the *system under test* (SUT), the developer extracts a model defining the structural and behavioural aspects of the SUT. Owing to its purpose, this model is called a *test model*. To be useful for testing, it is important that this model is independent of the SUT's implementation. The test model can be abstract in the sense that it neglects parts of the functionality or non-functional properties such as timing. However, it must be sufficiently precise and consistent to serve as a basis for automatically generating high-quality test cases and oracles. A test model may also contain *test selection criteria* to guide automatic test case generation. Typically, *coverage criteria* are formulated with respect to the SUT's behaviour as well as the input and output data. Once the test model and the test selection criteria are specified, a set of *test cases* can be generated such that the coverage criteria are met. The test model can be employed, moreover, to generate test oracles that are used to predict test results.

© Springer Nature Switzerland AG 2020
R. Heckel, G. Taentzer, *Graph Transformation for Software Engineers*,
https://doi.org/10.1007/978-3-030-43916-3_7

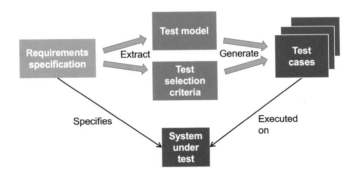

Fig. 7.1. Model-based testing

A *test model* can specify an SUT's behaviour in terms of the pre- and postconditions of its operations. Languages used for this purpose include Z [263], JML [58] and OCL [226]. We propose the use of visual contracts, which provide an intuitive but precise notation for pre- and postconditions. Visual contracts are able to specify the interfaces of operations of services, or components. As described in Chapter 6, they can be used for modelling (and matching) services. As executable, formal and visual models based on graph transformation, they provide the basis for model-based testing in this chapter, including the generation of test cases and oracles, and the definition of coverage criteria.

Test selection criteria are often defined in terms of the elements of a test model, such as states, transitions and branch conditions of state machines or activity diagrams. Such criteria are analogous to code coverage criteria based on control or data flow graphs, except that they work at the level of models. In this chapter, we are interested in testing the interaction of functional units such as operations specified by visual contracts. To test potential interactions, we have to observe their dependencies, i.e. situations where one operation is required before another one can be executed. This means that that the visual contracts serving as our test model will undergo a dependency analysis before coverage is defined based on the resulting dependency graph. This is reminiscent of white-box testing approaches based on data flow analysis, where coverage is defined on a data-flow graph extracted from the code. In contrast, we perform this process at model level. Full dependency coverage is achieved if all edges of the dependency graph correspond to dependencies observed when executing test cases [166, 253].

Given a test model and some test selection criteria, the objective of model-based *test generation* is to produce a set of test cases that fulfil those criteria. Since we are interested in dependencies between operation calls, we want to generate test cases covering their dependencies. Similar motivations have been considered in more specific settings, such as user sessions in Web applications [228]. The work presented in [221] discusses coverage analysis for object-oriented systems using dependencies. The authors of [221] proposed a call-based system dependency graph capturing control and data dependencies between statements, as well as operation calls. We present a language-independent approach to test case generation, in line with the principles of model-based development. Similarly, Briand et al. [49, 50] considered a model-based approach using UML artefacts for test case generation. There, dependencies have to be modelled explicitly at system level using activity diagrams. In our case they are extracted from specifications of individual operations (using visual contracts) by static analysis.

Given a set of visual contracts as part of a test model, their dependency graph as a coverage criterion, and an initial state, our generation of test cases will consist of two tasks: (1) generating a set of rule call sequences that cover the dependency graph, and (2) translating them to test cases for the SUT.

Software testing uses *test oracles* to predict expected test results. In the majority of projects, oracles are implemented manually, relying on the tester's understanding of functional requirements to decide the correct response of the system in every given test case. As a result, they are costly to create and maintain and their quality depends on their correct implementation. Alternatively, if suitable specifications are available, oracles can be generated automatically at lower cost and with better quality [181].

Visual contracts are directly executable and therefore suitable for automatically generating oracles. However, the gap in abstraction between service implementations and visual models may pose a number of challenges in implementing this basic idea. If we use a graph transformation engine to execute our test model, we need an adapter to present the model's functionality in a way that is comparable to the interface of the SUT. An adapter allows us to automate the decision about whether a test outcome is correct. Such information is present in visual contracts and should be reused rather than reimplemented. This is potentially relevant to all developers implementing tests, independently of any specific testing or debugging tools, even if the tests themselves are implemented manually.

This chapter is structured as follows. After defining a set of visual contracts as a test model and a notion of dependency cover as a test selection criterion in Section 7.1, we consider test case generation in more detail in Section 7.2. Thereafter, we present our generation of test oracles in Section 7.3. The chapter concludes with a summary and discussion of further work in Section 7.4.

Since visual contracts are specified as typed attributed graph transformation rules, it is worthwhile to be aware of the concepts introduced in Chapters 1 and 2 before reading this one. Dependencies between operation calls are used as test selection criteria. They are based on conflict and dependency analysis as presented in Section 4.2.

7.1 Test Models and Test Selection Criteria

Starting from a software requirements specification, the developer creates a test model based on defined interfaces. For example, when testing a service (see Chapter 6) the developer takes into account information about its input, output and basic workflow. For testing class or component operations, the developer starts out from operation signatures and any available documentation of their behaviour. In both cases, a test model consists of a class model and a set of visual contracts. This means that test models use the same basic structure and notation as the service models considered in Chapter 6, but provide a more detailed description of operations. As discussed in Chapter 6, such models can be formally represented as graph transformation systems.

The following small case study will serve to illustrate and evaluate the concepts and techniques of this chapter.

Example 7.1 (managing hotel guests). A registered guest can book a room, subject to availability. There are no booking charges, and the bill starts to accumulate once the room is occupied. Since payment details are already stored by the hotel, the amount of the bill is automatically deducted when the guest announces their intention to leave. They can check out successfully only when the bill is paid. In Listing 7.1, the core of a potential service interface in Java is depicted. It provides operation signatures that would typically occur in this context. A basic domain model for this service is shown in Fig. 7.2.

```
//...
public interface Hotel {
    // ...
    public Guest findGuest(String name);
    public String bookRoom(Room room, Guest guest, s:Date, e:Date);
    public String occupyRoom(Room room, Guest guest, Bill bill);
    public boolean updateBill( Bill  bill , int amount);
    public boolean clearBill ( Bill  bill ) throws Exception;
    public boolean checkout(Guest guest, Room room, Bill bill );
    // ...
}
```

Listing 7.1. Interface for hotel service

Fig. 7.3 contains the visual contracts for all the operations occurring in the listing. Given a name n, findGuest returns a guest g with this name. Given a room r, a guest g, and start and end dates s and e, bookRoom books this room for this guest if there is no overlapping reservation. When guest g arrives at the hotel and wants to occupy room r, there are two successful alternatives. Either a reservation exists starting from today so that the room can be occupied by the guest, or there is no such reservation and the room is still free. Then, a new reservation is created starting today. In both cases, occupyRoom occupies the

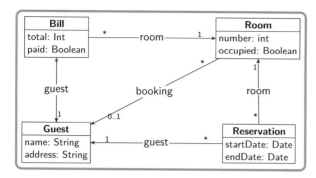

Fig. 7.2. Simplified class model for the hotel example

room and creates a new bill b. This means that occupyRoom is an example of an operation whose visual contract consists of two rules specifying alternative outcomes depending on the current state. Rule updateBill repeatedly updates bill b by amount a to cover the room price and additional expenses, such as breakfast and beverages. At the end of their stay, the guest clears the bill with clearBill and checks out. This is possible only if the bill is paid. Contract checkout deletes the reservation for room r, and this room is no longer occupied.

Signatures allow us to relate visual contracts to operations in the system and to represent their invocations with actual parameters and results as transformations [166]. This is illustrated by the transformation sequence in Fig. 7.4, which represents a series of system states changed by the invocation of operations, at model level.   □

If the implementation and model share the same signature, the expected output and actual output can be compared directly. However, there are cases where the signatures may deviate. If the implementation returns a complex object type, such as a collection, the response of a visual contract can be a set of nodes. Furthermore, an implementation signature may extend a model signature by providing an additional response to indicate if the operation was successful. This response can be in the form of a numerical error code, a Boolean value or an exception. One example is the operation checkout(), where a Boolean value is returned to indicate that the checkout was successful. The model may check the successful execution of a rule invocation instead.

At model level, a *test case* combines an initial state with a sequence of rule invocations. If the sequence is applicable, i.e. we can derive a corresponding sequence of transformations as a model-level equivalent of a test execution, this allows us to derive parameter bindings for the operations from the rules' matches. This leads to a *sequence of rule calls*.

Example 7.2 (test case). Consider the following sequence of rule invocations:

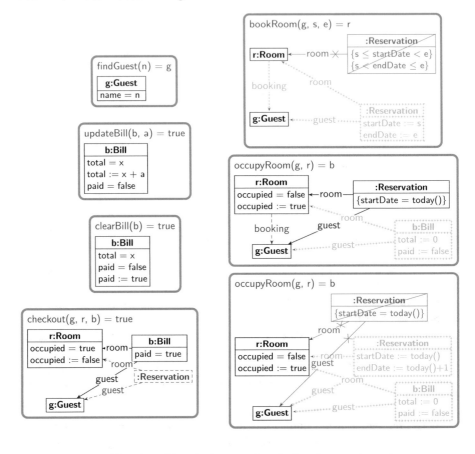

Fig. 7.3. Visual contracts for the hotel example

$$is : r = \mathsf{bookRoom(g, s, e)};$$
$$b = \mathsf{occupyRoom(g, r)};$$
$$\mathsf{updateBill(b, a)};$$
$$\mathsf{clearBill(b)};$$
$$\mathsf{checkout(g, r, b)}.$$

Given a graph G_0, we obtain the rule call sequence cs where variables g and r are bound to concrete values of G_0. Later a Bill is created binding variable b. The resulting rule call sequence is shown below and corresponds to the transformation sequence in Fig. 7.4.

$$cs : r1 = \mathsf{bookRoom(g1, 18\text{-}09\text{-}13, 18\text{-}09\text{-}20)};$$
$$b1 = \mathsf{occupyRoom(g1, r1)};$$
$$\mathsf{updateBill(b1, 250)};$$
$$\mathsf{clearBill(b1)};$$
$$\mathsf{checkout(g1, r1, b1)}.$$

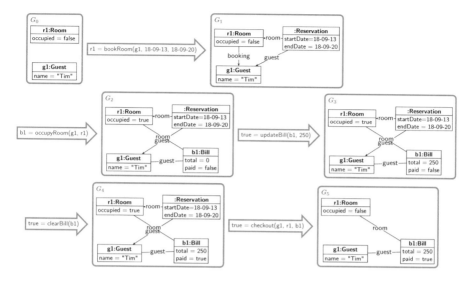

Fig. 7.4. An example transformation sequence

□

Since visual contracts are based on graph transformation rules, we can use dependency analysis to extract a dependency graph for the visual contracts in the test model as a basis for a coverage criterion. This graph differs slightly from a dependency graph over rules, since the nodes are labelled by the operation names identifying the contracts. A visual contract, specified by a set of rules, depends on another one if any of its rules depends on a rule of the other contract. Based on such a dependency graph, we use dependency coverage as a test selection criteria, i.e. test cases are designed to test all dependencies between visual contracts.

Example 7.3 (dependency graph). Using the visual contracts in Fig. 7.3, we compute a dependency graph as shown in Fig. 7.5. Considering, for example,

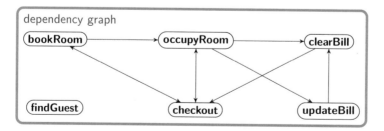

Fig. 7.5. Dependency graph for visual contracts in hotel Web service

the edge between nodes bookRoom and occupyRoom, we see that a Reservation created by bookRoom is read by (the first rule of) operation occupyRoom. The dependency between clearBill and checkout is due to the attribute paid. The first rule sets it to true and the second one requires this value. Rule occupyRoom may cause a dependency on checkout, since it may create a Reservation, deleted later. By deleting it, occupyRoom may create a new Reservation for the same room and the same guest again. So, occupyRoom may be dependent on checkout. Similar dependencies occur between bookRoom and checkout.   □

As a test selection criterion, our model-level dependency coverage resembles code-level data-flow coverage which is often complemented by control-flow based criteria. However, control flow is not usually specified at the level of service operations, but determined by the client program invoking them. This means that to test an interface independently of a client program we rely on the possible data flows between operations as represented by potential dependencies between their visual contracts.

The dependency relation itself is a very basic test selection criterion. It may be refined to take into account dependency-causing rule elements and their potentially combined occurrences. For even more thorough testing, we can require test cases to cover all minimal dependent transformation pairs computed by critical pair analysis (see Section 4.2).

7.2 Generation of Test Cases

In this section, we introduce an approach to generating test cases for our test model relying on dependency analysis for the test selection criterion. In particular, we define a notion of test coverage based on dependency graphs and present an algorithm generating rule call sequences that cover all dependency edges, i.e. all potential dependencies between visual contracts, that are reachable from a given state. We discuss how the approach can be extended by considering more refined dependencies (as presented in Section 4.2) and how conflict analysis and other analysis techniques for graph transformation systems can be used for generating test cases in general.

The following algorithm generates rule call sequences that exercise dependencies between visual contracts while recording coverage of the dependency graph:

1. Given a set of rules R, its dependency graph DG and an initial graph G_0, we first check which of the rules are applicable to G_0. Starting with one of these for the first step, we compute all paths through DG that cover at least one dependency, starting with the chosen rule and avoiding executing each cycle in DG more than once. This provides us with a set S of rule sequences. Note that this set depends on the initial graph G_0.
2. As long as the dependency graph has uncovered edges, we perform the following steps:

(a) We enrich the sequences in S to cater for rules with multiple dependencies. For example, dependencies (p, r) and (q, r) may lead first to a sequence $\ldots p; r \ldots$, which is then augmented to $\ldots p; q; r \ldots$. If this enrichment yields sequences that are subsumed by sequences covering a larger set of dependencies, we remove redundant sequences.

(b) Next, we iterate through the sequences in S, repeatedly choosing a sequence s that covers a maximal subset of dependency edges not covered before. We verify the applicability of s while choosing matches to maximise dependency coverage. The starting rule in s has a match on G_0 by assumption. After having applied a rule p of s, we look for a match of the next rule q in s into the resulting graph such that the co-match of p and the match of q overlap in dependency-causing elements. If no such match for q exists, we choose an arbitrary match. If the resulting sequence of rule calls can be fully applied to G_0, then we move it to T, the set of test sequences. Otherwise, s is removed from S. For successful sequences s, the coverage of new dependency edges is determined. We continue by considering the remaining sequences in S until full coverage is achieved or, by considering unmarked dependencies, no further unmarked dependencies can be covered.

(c) In order to derive the actual test cases, all unbound parameters remaining are instantiated with concrete values, such that the entire sequence remains applicable to G_0. The result s is an operation call sequence.

(d) We iterate through the steps above while there are unchecked starting rules in R, until the coverage is complete or cannot be improved any more. In addition, the user can be asked if they would like to continue for one more iteration. In each new iteration, we select only those additional sequences that improve coverage.

Throughout, we report progress by displaying which sequences have been added to T and what is the resulting coverage.

Example 7.4 (rule sequences). Considering the rules in Fig. 7.3 and graph G_0 in Fig. 7.4, we find that rules findGuest and bookRoom are the only applicable ones. Since findGuest is not involved in any dependency with other rules, we can neglect it and continue with bookRoom. Taking this rule as the initial one, we construct a set of possible sequences, say $\{s_1 = \text{bookRoom;occupyRooom},$ $s_2 = \text{bookRoom;checkout}\}$. Considering s_2, we need occupyRoom to be included, since there is a dependency (occupyRoom, checkout). Therefore, we extend s_2 to $s_2' = \text{bookRoom;occupyRoom;checkout}$. Then we find that s_2' subsumes s_1, so running s_1 would not improve coverage. Hence we drop s_1 from the set. For example, sequence s_2' results in the rule call sequence

$$r1 = \text{bookRoom(g1, 18-09-13, 18-09-20)};$$
$$b1 = \text{occupyRoom(g1, r1)};$$
$$\text{checkout(g1, r1, b1)}.$$

In executing this sequence, we observe an overlap between the co-match of the first step and the match of the second step in the form of a produce/use dependency. In particular, the booking edge created by bookRoom is read by occupyRoom.

To cover more of the dependency graph, further sequences are needed, such as

> r1 = bookRoom(g1, 18-09-13, 18-09-20);
> b1 = occupyRoom(g1, r1);
> updateBill(b1, 250);
> clearBill(b1);
> checkout(g1, r1, b1);
> bookRoom(g1, 18-09-13, 18-09-20).

Note that the last call of rule bookRoom is needed to cover the dependency of bookRoom on checkout. □

While this algorithm is eager to cover most of the edges in DG, some edges may not be coverable, either because the corresponding rules are not reachable from the start graph G_0 or because matches chosen earlier in a sequence prevent rules from being applicable. We can mitigate both problems by considering different start graphs, enabling a wider range of sequences. Such start graphs should be constructed such that the left-hand sides of at least two dependent rules can be matched in a way that both rules are applicable in sequence. The algorithm will always terminate, because the input is finite and processed systematically.

Once a set of rule call sequences modelling interesting test cases generated, the actual test cases have to be derived. A test case requires an object structure that corresponds to the initial graph G_0. Each rule call sequence generated by the algorithm above is translated to an operation call sequence. While most of this translation is straightforward, operations of the SUT may have return values that have to be taken into account. Test assertions are not explicitly modelled here. The simplest case is the successful execution of a complete operation call sequence. More sophisticated assertions, checking properties of the resulting object structure, could be realised by rules representing queries. This topic is elaborated on in the next section.

The algorithm presented here considers the existence of dependencies without distinguishing more detailed information (see the discussion within and after Example 4.7). The test selection criteria could be refined by representing each initial dependency (i.e. each cause for dependency) as a separate edge in the dependency graph and requiring coverage of this refined graph. Similarly to the above, the resulting algorithm would have to check which initial dependencies (given by transformation pairs) can be embedded into the sequence such that it is applicable to graph G_0. The aim would be to cover all initial dependencies. Analogously to dependencies, conflicts can be used as coverage criteria. This would allow us to guarantee that critical interactions are tested, for example conflicts in resource allocation such as trying to reserve a room that is already reserved. In [165], coverage of dependencies and conflicts was considered in more detail. Moreover, rules that are neither in conflict nor in dependency with any other rule could also be of interest for testing (considering, for example, favourable and critical signs of consistency as described in Chapter 5).

7.3 Models as Test Oracles

To determine if a test has been successfully passed, the results of the execution have to be verified by comparing them with the results predicted by the specification. Rather than predicting the results of all test cases beforehand, it is common to use a trusted source, often called a *test oracle* [167], to produce these results at execution time. In our approach, the role of the test oracle is played by an executable model.

7.3.1 Partiality of Visual Contracts

In general, a visual contract only partially specifies the intended behaviour of the implementation. If the oracle predicts success while the implementation reports a failure, this difference could be due to either an error in the implementation or an underspecified precondition of the contract. This potential failure should be reported to the developer as a warning, with all relevant details needed to interpret the result.

Example 7.5 (partially modelled behaviour). Assume that the system operation clearBill throws an exception if the payment cannot be performed, for example because the credit card details are wrong. Since payment is not modelled explicitly, the model predicts success and returns a result graph, while the SUT has to handle the exception.   □

7.3.2 Handling and Reporting Failure

There are different ways in which failures can be reported to the tester. We distinguish them by asking: (1) What is the origin of the failure? (2) How is the failure presented? (3) How is the failure interpreted? For example, in a service-oriented system, a failure may be due to a fault at the server or in client–server communication. Server-side failures can be due to logical or technical reasons. Logical failures occur if the precondition of an operation is not satisfied, i.e. the application is invoked, but not executed correctly or not executed at all. Technical failures can be down to a variety of reasons, such as the database being offline, server-side system failures, power outages or hardware issues. Communication failures may result from loss of network access, congestion causing delays, etc. A server-side failure presents itself as an exception, a fault message or an application-specific error code, while a communication failure shows up as an exception (timeout) on the client side. Taking all these failures into account, the following test outcomes are possible:

1. The test oracle and the execution are both successful and yield the same result.
2. The test oracle and the execution are both successful but yield different results.
3. The test oracle and the execution both show failures, and hence yield the same result.
4. While the test oracle predicts success, the test execution fails. This outcome could be due to either a faulty implementation or an underspecified precondition of the visual contract, i.e. a weaker precondition than in the implementation.
5. While the test oracle predicts failure, the test execution succeeds. This is a failure, since the precondition of the visual contract should not be stronger than that of its implementation.

Example 7.6 (diverse test results). We take the transformation sequence shown in Fig. 7.4 as test oracle and start our consideration with the first transformation step. If bookRoom is implemented as modelled, we have an example of case 1. Its implementation may do more, for example requiring a deposit for a reservation. In that case, the test oracle is weaker, i.e. we have case 2. In Example 7.5, we have already covered case 4. While we cannot book a room twice for overlapping dates in the model, this may be possible in the SUT if a reservation can be changed by the same guest. In this case, the test oracle would predict a failure while the test execution on the SUT would succeed (case 5). We could fix this situation by relaxing the precondition of bookRoom in the model. A precondition checking that there is no overlapping reservation by another guest would be weaker than the original one. If such a reservation is not possible in the SUT, i.e. the operation fails in both the model and the SUT, we have an example of case 3.   □

Test oracles can be used to check assertions expressed by additional query rules. In this way, by checking for successful execution, we can encode a check for the existence or non-existence of certain patterns.

7.4 Summary and Further Reading

Visual contracts provide a diagrammatic notation for pre- and postconditions as an alternative to OCL or code-level contract languages. When using visual contracts for testing, we benefit from their executability and formal background in graph transformation, allowing us to provide model-based coverage criteria and test oracles.

We have provided a comprehensive approach aimed at automating the three major challenges of testing through the use of models. In particular, we can

- define coverage based on the structure of the dependency graph and analyse potential dependencies between operations,
- deploy such a dependency graph to generate test cases, and
- use graph transformation to produce test oracles predicting the correct outcomes of tests.

By extending our approach towards conflict coverage, testing of concurrent threads could be tackled. To increase the expressiveness of test models, the approach needs to be extended to advanced rule concepts such as multiobjects. Finally, after having considered a coherent set of separate components, it is worthwhile to investigate the use of model-based testing within a larger testing process. Alternative ways of interleaving test case generation, execution, oracles and coverage analysis may be investigated to support, for example, explorative testing at runtime.

7.4.1 Tooling

The generation of test cases and the computation of oracles have been prototypically implemented based on AGG, as discussed in more detail in [166, 167]. To evaluate the scalability of the test case generation process presented and the completeness of the generated test suite, the resulting test cases were executed on the implementation. NCover[1] was used as a tool to calculate code-based coverage for a test set that provides a full dependency cover. Evaluation results for a variant of the hotel service example and a larger case study of a bug-tracking service (with 31 visual contracts) were reported in [166, 165]. Both systems, however, are relatively small compared with industry-size applications. While larger benchmark applications are available for software testing, they do not come with visual contracts, making larger-scale experimentation difficult.

7.4.2 Extensions

Visual contracts were used for testing in, for example, [195, 166, 165] and, more specifically, for the generation of test cases in [118, 175, 257]. The approach proposed in [118] used visual contracts as system specifications and translates them to the Java modelling language to create test oracles. In order to translate logical into executable test cases, these test generation approaches derive concrete prestates of the system from model-level representations and automate the checking of poststates against postconditions.

In [165], test case generation and coverage were driven not only by dependencies but also by conflicts between rules. A conflict graph was used to represent potential conflicts, where test cases produced by critical pair analysis were generated to cover all potential conflicts.

---

[1] Available at http://www.ncover.com/.

One popular method of model-based testing [281] uses model checking for test case generation. Given a requirement in temporal logic, and deriving a labelled transition system from the test model, a model checker can be used to generate counterexamples as a source for generating test cases. As presented in Section 4.5, graph transition systems can be used for model checking. In this context, counterexamples are rule call sequences. This approach was investigated for service-oriented systems in [114] based on a platform metamodel for SOA and graph transformation rules describing the behaviour of the platform. Rule sequences were generated as counterexamples using GROOVE as a model checker.

The work in [257], in contrast, used visual contracts and translated them into the planning domain definition language PDDL, so that planning tools could be used for generating tests. Sequences of rules were computed based on an encoding of the initial system state in order to reach a state satisfying a given requirement. The authors of [257] compared their approach with the alternative of using a model checker to generate the state space and to find test sequences. They observed that the use of heuristics allowed them to not generate the full state space, mitigating the state space explosion problem of model checking. Note that our approach in this chapter is not state-based at all, but focuses on a static analysis of the dependencies between rules.

8

Reverse Engineering: Inferring Visual Contracts from Java Programs

When working on an existing software system, we face the challenge of developing a high-level understanding of its implementation. This is necessary for both finding and correcting errors, and for adding or revising features or improving the architecture through refactoring. This is especially difficult in large systems that have undergone many changes during their lifetime and where the original design information is no longer visible or documented in the code. *Reverse engineering* aims to address this problem of extracting high-level information about the structure and behaviour of programs, often represented by visual models to support understanding and communication. In this way, reverse engineering can help us to cope with the complexity of the implementation.

To be scalable, and allow one to keep models consistent with evolving software systems, reverse engineering has to be automated. We distinguish between approaches based on static and dynamic analysis. The static approach, exemplified by [277, 251], examines the source code with the intention of extracting the possible behaviours. This approach is well established but limited in its ability to detect dynamic object-oriented behaviour, such as dynamic binding. The dynamic approach [294, 295] uses test runs to explore the software. It can detect dynamic object behaviour, but the extracted model represents only those behaviours actually executed. The resulting behavioural models are often UML diagrams, such as sequence diagrams [251, 294], but there is also work using graph grammars for representing sets of nested call graphs [295].

In a service-oriented system, providers have to document the use of their services while protecting the technology behind it. Visual contracts, as presented in Chapter 6, describe preconditions and effects on object structures. They allow a detailed yet technology-independent specification of methods and operations, that can be used for both service matching and testing.

In this chapter, we present a dynamic approach to reverse engineering visual contracts from sequential Java programs by tracing the execution of Java operations [15]. The resulting contracts give accurate descriptions of observed object transformations, i.e. their precondition and effects in terms of object structures, and parameter and attribute values. The restriction to sequential Java makes it easy to associate each object access to a unique operation invocation during tracing, but is not essential for the remaining steps in the inference of visual contracts.

Given a Java application, the reverse engineering starts with (1) defining the type model (extracting the set of classes to be observed) and the scope of the observation. We proceed by (2) observing the behaviour under test using AspectJ instrumentation of the Java bytecode and synthesising rule instances as pre/post snapshot graphs of individual invocations; (3) combining the instances into higher-level rules by abstracting from non-essential context; (4) generalising further by introducing multiobjects and patterns; (5) deriving logical constraints and assignments over attribute and parameter values; and (6) identifying universally shared conditions and structures as invariants that are captured separately. The following section describes this process in more detail, before we discuss the correctness and completeness of the extracted contracts.

This chapter is structured as follows. The extraction of visual contracts from code is presented step-by-step in Section 8.1. This extraction procedure is analysed concerning correctness and completeness in Section 8.2. The chapter concludes with a summary and a discussion of the approach with respect to tooling, evaluation, extensions and applications in Section 8.3. Since visual contracts are specified as typed attributed graph transformation rules, it is worthwhile to be aware of the concepts introduced in Chapters 1 and 2 before reading this one.

8.1 Extraction of Visual Contracts

We start the reverse engineering of visual contracts by extracting a class diagram from the Java code. This extraction is based on a straightforward mapping between the object-oriented concepts of Java and UML class diagrams. Then we describe how the execution of a method is traced and how such a trace is translated into a rule instance reflecting the objects accessed and changed by this specific execution. From rule instances we infer general visual contracts and augment them first by attribute conditions and calculations, then by multiobjects and multipatterns to further raise the level of abstraction.

8.1.1 Type Model and Scope

All classes of a package of interest, their fields and their inheritance relations can be extracted into a type graph, where an object-valued field is shown as an edge to the target class with cardinality 0..1, while fields that are arrays or collections of objects are represented by edge types with cardinality * or 1..*.

If the target class belongs to the package, the reference is extracted as an edge type between node types that correspond to the source and target classes. If the target is a data type or a class that does not belong to the package, the corresponding reference gives rise to an attribute of the source class.

Example 8.1 (extracting type information). Let us start by considering the implementation of a car rental service. The package rentalService shown in Fig. 8.1 gives rise to the type graph in Fig. 8.2. An object-valued field is represented, for example, by the edge type labelled car from Reservation to Car. Edge type reservations has target cardinality *, since a collection of reservations is allowed. Note that the class diagram does not contain operations, but represents a type graph defining node and edge types and attributes.   □

On this class model, we can now define the scope of our observation as the subset of classes whose access will be traced. In our case we choose to observe the entire model.

8.1.2 From Tracing Object Access to Rule Instances

We want to observe all accesses to objects of interest, i.e. objects that are instances of classes within our scope, during the execution of an operation invocation. Observations are enabled by instrumentation of the Java bytecode following an aspect-oriented approach. In particular, we use unrestricted pointcuts such as `pointcut stateTriggers(): !within(Tracing.*);` to access the object state before and after each instruction to observe and log their effects. An operation invocation thus yields a trace recording all object creations as well as read and write accesses to objects and fields caused by this invocation. For each operation invocation, we extract a rule instance capturing the recorded behaviour.

In a sequential execution, all actions observed between the start and the return of a method invocation can be attributed to this invocation. Concurrent invocations make it more difficult to identify the inducing invocations for each action. Therefore, we stick to sequential programs here. We aggregate all observations of the same invocation into a *rule instance* capturing the overall precondition and effect. Along with the instance, we collect traceability data for its elements, such as the line numbers of corresponding statements in the code. This is used later to validate the extraction, for example to assess which code fragments are captured by which contracts.

Example 8.2 (Java methods in class Rental). We consider class Rental in Listing 8.1, which provides all main services as methods, listed with their signatures only. The implementation of method dropOffCar() is shown in Fig. 8.3. There are three possible paths, depending on the evaluation of the two if statements in lines 4 and 10. Hence, three test cases are enough to cover the complete code of this method. (1) If an invalid reservation index is passed,

```
1    package rentalService ;
2
3    public class Rental {
4      public Branch[] branches;
5      public ArrayList <Reservation> reservations ;
6      public String  registerClient (String  city , String clientName) {..}
7      public String makeReservation(String  clientId , String pickup, String dropoff) {..}
8      public Boolean cancelReservation (String  resId) {..}
9      public Boolean cancelClientReservation (String  clientId ) {..}
10     public Boolean pickupCar(String  resId ) {..}
11     public Boolean dropoffCar( String  resId ) {..}
12     public ArrayList <Reservation> showReservationsForClient(String  clientId ) {..}
13     // further methods to access rental information
14   }
15
16   public class Branch {
17     public ArrayList <Car> at =new ArrayList<Car>();
18     public ArrayList <Client> ofClients=new ArrayList<Client>();
19     public String city =null;
20     public int cMax;
21     public int rMax;
22   }
23
24   public class Client {
25     public String cName;
26     public String cID;
27   }
28
29   public class Car {
30     private String  registration =null;
31     private Branch ownedBy=null;
32   }
33
34   public class Reservation {
35     public String  reference ;
36     public Client made=null;
37     public Branch pickup=null;
38     public Branch dropoff=null;
39     public Car For=null;
40   }
```

Fig. 8.1. Fragments of classes from package rentalService

the execution breaks (at line 5). (2) If the index is valid, i.e. the corresponding Reservation object exists but the car has not been picked up yet, the execution breaks (at line 11). This case can be recognised using the reference pickup, which would have been deleted otherwise. (3) If the index exists and

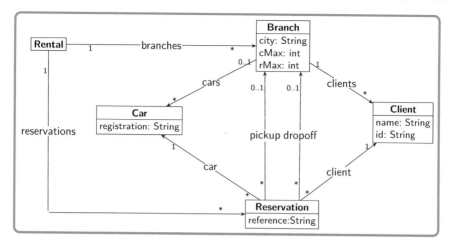

Fig. 8.2. Type graph for the Rental example

the car has been dropped off, the car is returned to the branch where it has to be dropped off and the Reservation object is removed from the list of reservations. Figure 8.4 presents an implementation of method showReservati-

```
1   public  Boolean dropoffCar( String  resId ){
2
3           int  resIndex  = this . getReservationIndex ( resId );
4           if  ( resIndex ==−1){
5               return  false ;
6           }
7
8           Reservation  reservation  = this . reservations .get( resIndex );
9           // check  if  the  reserved  car  has  been  picked  up  already
10          if  ( reservation .pickup!=null){
11              return  false ;
12          }
13
14          // return  reserved  car  to  the  dropoff  branch
15          reservation . dropoff . cars .add( reservation . car );
16          // remove  reservation  object
17          this . reservations .remove(resIndex );
18          return  true ;
19      }
```

Fig. 8.3. Implementation of method Rental.dropOffCar()

onForClient. Given a clientId, the list of all existing reservations is traversed to find all those reservations made by the client with clientId. These reservations are returned.   □

```
1   public ArrayList <Reservation> showReservationsForClient(String  clientId ){
2
3          ArrayList <Reservation> cReservations = new ArrayList<Reservation>();
4          for (Reservation  reservation :   reservations ){
5              if ( reservation . client . cId . equalsIgnoreCase( clientId )){
6                  cReservations . add( reservation );
7              }
8          }
9          return  cReservations ;
10      }
```

Fig. 8.4. Implementation of method Rental.showReservationsForClient()

By invoking a method of interest, we can analyse its trace with respect to the objects and fields accessed. The object referred to by this() and all objects reachable from it define the scope of the execution. They are needed to construct the rule instance representing this execution. Read access determines the additional context whose existence is required in order to execute the method. Calls of getter and setter methods are used to observe read and write accesses at field level, yielding corresponding actions on attribute values or objects and references dependent on target types.

Collections such as sets and lists have to be treated in a special way. A getter call yields a complete collection, while calls of add and remove result in adding or removing references between the collection and corresponding objects. Additionally, the call of collection methods elements() and size() require read access to a collection.

Example 8.3 (rule instances). Figure 8.5 shows four rule instances extracted from four calls to method dropOffCar() with different arguments and in different internal states. The topmost instance reflects the behaviour when the ArrayList of reservations is empty. This leads to a failure of the search for a reservation matching the given resId in lines 1–6 in Fig. 8.3. The execution breaks, and therefore the instance does not have any action, nor any further context. In the second instance, the Reservation object Leicester_12 exists, but the execution breaks as well, since the car has not been picked up yet. This can be seen from the presence of the reference pickup, which would have been removed by an invocation to pickupCar(). Since this execution of dropOffCar() stops in line 11 in Fig. 8.3, the resulting second rule instance does not contain any action either.

The third instance reflects an execution of the third path in a state where the Reservation object Leicester_8 is the only object accessed by the call to getReservationIndex() in line 3 of Fig. 8.3. This method is responsible for searching through the ArrayList of reservations and returning the index of the object matching the given resID. The conditions in lines 4 and 10 are false, so there is no return from the method there, and the last lines of this method are

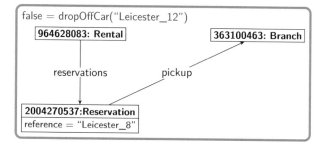

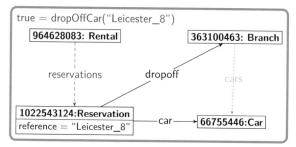

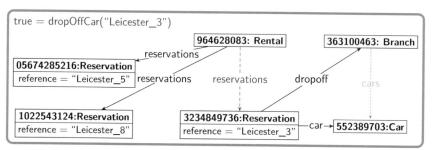

Fig. 8.5. Rule instances extracted from three calls of the method in Fig. 8.3

reached. In particular, the two statements in lines 15 and 17 are transferred to actions in the contract instance.

The bottommost rule instance is the result of a similar execution except for the fact that getReservationIndex() needs to access three Reservation objects in order to find the one whose reference equals Leicester_3. As a consequence, two additional Reservation objects appear in the rule instance as context.   □

8.1.3 General Rules and Contracts

Information about objects, references and attributes created, deleted or modi-fied in a rule instance allows us to create a *minimal rule* describing the effect of the execution without any additional context. Two rule instances realising the same effect share the same minimal rule.

A minimal rule is constructed by cutting out all context not needed to achieve the observed changes and not required as the this object, input or return parameters. Concrete attribute or parameter values are replaced by variables. The result is a classification of instances by effect. Considering a set of all instances with the same minimal rule, they have the same overall effects in terms of the creation or deletion of objects and links, but potentially different preconditions.

Example 8.4 (minimal rules). The minimal rule describing the effect of the first two rule instances in Fig. 8.5 is shown in the left of Fig. 8.6. There is no effect, so the this object of type Rental is the only element. The variable resId for the input parameter is chosen to match that in the operation signature.

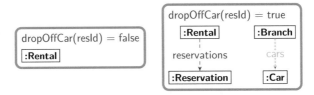

Fig. 8.6. Minimal rules derived from the rule instances in Fig. 8.5

The last two rule instances in Fig. 8.5 share the minimal rule in the right of Fig. 8.6. This rule contains the two effects of removing the reservations link from the this object and adding the cars link to an existing Branch, the respective source and target objects required for these links, and the attribute of the Reservation object matched by the input parameter. □

To generalise the preconditions of a set of rule instances sharing the same minimal rule, we infer one so-called *maximal rule*, which extends the minimal rule by all context that is present in all rule instances, essentially the intersection of all its instances' preconditions. A maximal rule represents a general specification of one possible case of executing the operation, typically corresponding to a path through the method's code.

Example 8.5 (maximal rules). The maximal rules inferred from the rule instances in Fig. 8.5 are shown in Fig. 8.7. The first one, in the left of the figure, is identical to its minimal rule, because the smallest rule instance with this minimal rule, shown in the in top of Fig. 8.5, does not contain any further context. The rule in the right of Fig. 8.7 is the maximal rule derived for the last two rule instances in Fig. 8.5, sharing the minimal rule in the right of Fig. 8.6. This maximal rule is also structurally identical to the smaller instance with the single Reservation object, omitting the two additional Reservation objects only occurring in the last instance. □

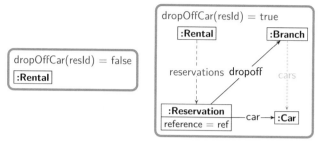

Fig. 8.7. Maximal rules derived from the rule instances in Fig. 8.5

8.1.4 Universal Context

Preconditions present in all contracts are candidates for global invariants. To identify and cut out such invariant context, we compare the preconditions of all maximal rules across all contracts to identify structures that are universally present. Universal context presented as global invariants (and therefore removed from the rules) can reduce the size of contracts, making them more concise and readable.

Example 8.6 (extracting universal context). The Rental object occurs in each rule, so it is a candidate for being moved into a global invariant. Note that it is still needed as part of the effect specification in the rightmost maximal rule in Fig. 8.7, since the link to the reservation with reference resId has to be removed. □

8.1.5 Attribute Conditions and Assignments

While the structural view is naturally expressed by graphical patterns, constraints or assignments over basic data types are more adequately expressed in logical terms. Let us consider how attribute constraints for rules can be inferred. Suppose a rule instance $op(a_1, \ldots, a_n)$ has attribute and parameter values $a_1, \ldots, a_n$. A maximal rule $r = op(x_1, \ldots, x_n)$ generalising a number of instances with identical effect has a set of local variables and formal parameters $x_1, \ldots, x_n$. Since the maximal rule r is embedded by a match into every rule instance it subsumes, this match defines an assignment of the local variables $x_1, \ldots, x_n \rightarrow a_1, \ldots, a_n$. If we fix the order of $x_1, \ldots, x_n$, each assignment becomes a vector of values to be fed into a machine learning tool capable of deriving logical constraints.

A set of logical constraints can be generated that are valid for all those assignments provided. These constraints are integrated into the graphical part of the contract where each constraint becomes part of the pre- or postcondition depending on whether the variables used occur in the left- or right-hand side or both, or if they refer to the operation's parameters.

Example 8.7 (resulting visual contracts). Starting from the rule instances in Example 8.3, we can derive the visual contracts as follows. We abstract from concrete object identifiers and arguments and introduce formal parameters. For the sake of clarity, in this example their names are chosen to correspond to parameter names in the code. Moreover, the Rental object can be removed partly as described in Example 8.6.

The resulting visual contract is shown in Fig. 8.8. The left rule is empty because it represents cases without any effect. It is obtained by dropping the Rental objects from the corresponding rule in Fig. 8.7. The right rule is structurally identical to its maximal rule, because the Rental object is part of the effect specification, but has the additional constraint {resId = ref}. This is derived as an attribute condition because it holds in all rule instances associated with the corresponding maximal rule.   □

The visual contract derived in the example does not fully capture the control flow of operation dropOffCar but only the conditions relevant to the specific case captured by each rule. This could be addressed by additional control structures, such as a negative application condition or a transformation unit, which could be derived from the control flow of the code.

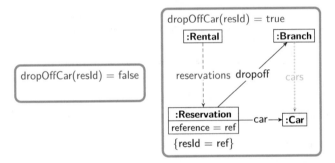

Fig. 8.8. Visual contract for dropOffCar() derived from the maximal rules in Fig. 8.7

8.1.6 Multiobjects and Multipatterns

The contracts extracted so far may use many rules to describe a single operation. When iterating over containers, for example, the set of rules is potentially unbounded. Some of them may differ only in the number of objects manipulated while performing the same actions on all of them. Multiobjects and multipatterns are introduced as a concise way to specify constraints and actions across sets of similar structures, i.e. to summarise sets of similar rules.

To extract rules with multiobjects, we have to discover sets of equivalent objects (that have the same structure and behaviour) and represent them by a multiobject node. We consider only multiobject nodes that are part of minimal rules, because their typical use is to describe universally quantified effects (rather than preconditions). If several rules with multiobjects are isomorphic after inferring multiobjects, the original rules can be replaced by a single rule with appropriate cardinalities reflecting the generalised case.

Two objects are *equivalent* if (1) they are of the same type, (2) they are part of the minimal rule, and (3) they have the same context (incident edges of the same type connected to the same nodes) in the pre- and postcondition (and thus specify the same actions). Assuming for every operation *op* a set of maximal rules as constructed above, we derive contracts with multiobjects in two steps as follows:

- *Merge equivalent objects:* For each rule r in a given set of maximal rules and each non-trivial equivalence class of objects in r, one object is chosen as the representative for that class and added to the set of multiobject nodes for r, while all other objects of that class are deleted with their incident edges. The cardinality of the multiobject node is defined to be the cardinality of its equivalence class (the number of objects it represents).
- *Combine isomorphic rules:* A maximal set of structurally equivalent rules constructed as above, differing only in their object identities and the cardinalities of their multiobject nodes, forms an equivalence class. For each such class, we derive a single rule by selecting a representative for this class and assigning to each of its multiobject nodes the union of the cardinalities of the corresponding nodes in all the rules in the same class.
- *Multipattern inference:* Occasionally we require universal quantification not just on a single object but on a more general structure. Multipatterns provide this extension. To derive contracts with multipatterns, we discover equivalent graph fragments within a rule r that can be represented by a multipattern. A graph fragment consists of nodes and edges that do not necessarily form a graph themselves, because edges in the fragment may be connected to nodes outside the fragment, called *boundary nodes*. Two fragments f and f' in r are equivalent if (1) they are isomorphic (share the same shape, typing and attributes), and (2) they have the same external connections within r, i.e. they share the same boundary nodes. We choose one representative of a set of equivalent fragments to infer the multipattern.

Example 8.8 (visual contracts with multipatterns). Two rules for the operation showReservationForClient can be deduced for the method shown in Fig. 8.4. They are depicted in Fig. 8.9. The topmost rule shows one reservation for client c1, while the middle shows two reservations for client c2. The derived rule is shown at the bottom of Fig. 8.9. It contains a multiobject R of reservations for client c. According to the semantics of multiobjects in rules, R is applied to all reservations that a matched client has made.   □

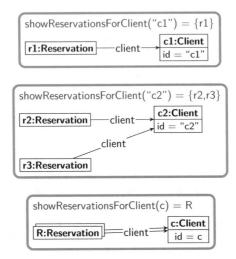

Fig. 8.9. Two maximal rules (top) and the resulting multiobject rule (bottom) for showReservationsForClient()

8.2 Correctness and Completeness

We want to understand to what extent the contracts extracted provide an accurate description of the software's behaviour. We answer this question by considering the correctness and completeness of derived contracts.

For every state s in the implementation, there exists a corresponding object graph $G(s)$ at model level, obtained by representing all objects in the scope of observation (i.e. that are instances of the classes selected for tracing) as nodes, with object-valued attributes as edges and data-valued attributes as node attributes. A model is *correct*, if for every valid state s and every valid contract invocation, a step from $G(s)$ to some graph H in the model implies a step in the implementation from state s to a new state s' such that $H = G(s')$. This means that the model does not allow behaviour that is not implemented by the system. Conversely, *completeness* means that for each valid state s, a step caused by an operation invocation of the implementation leading to a state s' must be matched by a step from graph $G(s)$ to graph $G(s')$ in the model, i.e. all the system's behaviour is captured by the model.

Extracted models are usually neither correct nor complete. Correctness may fail because the model is extracted for a part of the system only as identified by the implementation classes selected for tracing. Anything outside this scope of observation is not recorded and therefore not represented by the model. This means that if the implementation checks a condition that is defined on an object outside that scope, this check is not reflected in the precondition of the contract. If this check fails, a corresponding step in the model may not be reflected by this step in the implementation. However, we can expect that whenever both, the implementation and the model preconditions are satisfied, the observable effect of the implementation-level step matches the effect of the model-level step. The comparison is moderated via the mapping G of implementation states to object graphs, which takes account of the selected scope.

Completeness may fail because test runs usually do not reflect the complete behaviour of a system. The dynamic approach to extracting contracts is inherently dependent on the range of behaviours observed. System behaviour that has not been observed will not be reflected in the model. So, what can we realistically hope to achieve? A restricted form of completeness should require that the observed behaviour is present in the model. This means that, when we execute the tests that the model was extracted from, all steps in the implementation should be matched by the model.

Example 8.9 (reflecting on visual-contract extraction from dropOffCar()). In the following, we reason about the correctness and completeness of our example contract extraction. Figure 8.2 shows the classes selected for tracing. Test runs for method dropOffCar were chosen such that the complete body of this method was covered. If we invoke method dropOffCar() with any reservation id on some state s yielding state s', one of the corresponding visual contracts in Fig. 8.8 is applicable to $G(s)$ yielding a graph isomorphic to $G(s')$. Hence, the restricted form of completeness can be shown for this example.   □

More generally, owing to the method of model extraction, we can assert that the model and implementation should show the same behaviour at least for the test runs used. In particular,

- a contract instance captures precisely the preconditions and effects relevant to the invocation it is derived from, within the scope of observation;
- a minimal contract instance captures exactly the effect of the contract instances it is extracted from;
- a maximal contract instance subsumes all contract instances it is derived from, i.e. every contract instance can be replicated as an application of the maximal contract instance;
- a contract with multipatterns is (more concise, but) equivalent to the set of maximal contract instances it is derived from, i.e. by retaining the original contracts' cardinality information, they describe exactly the same set of transformations, and
- the parameter and attribute constraints derived do not invalidate any of the contract instances their maximal instance originates from.

8.3 Summary and Further Reading

This chapter has presented an automated reverse engineering approach for Java programs yielding visual contracts that specify pre- and postconditions of operations. This approach is dynamic, as visual contracts are inferred from tracing the execution of Java operations. The reverse engineering process requires us to define the scope of observation and to provide test cases for the relevant operations. It proceeds by synthesising rule instances, combining them and generalising them to general specifications of the operations by means of attributed graph transformation rules.

8.3.1 Tooling

The inference of visual contracts from Java programs as presented in this chapter has been implemented in a proof-of-concept tool [15] supporting the following steps. A tracer observes test runs of a given Java program within a specific scope defined on the basis of AspectJ. It produces visual-contract instances that are generalised afterwards using graph matching. The inference of generalised contracts uses Daikon [100], a machine learning tool that is capable of deriving logical constraints. The resulting visual contracts can be exported to Henshin [22, 139], a model transformation language and tool based on graph transformation.

8.3.2 Evaluation

In [15], experiments were reported on two case studies to evaluate the scalability of the presented approach to both large numbers of invocations and large object graphs. The case studies were based on NanoXML and JHotDraw,[1] both popular benchmarks for software testing and analysis, and representative of the kind of system our method would be appropriate for, i.e. with significant and dynamic object structures in their core model. In NanoXML, this is the object representation of the XML tree; for JHotDraw, it is that of graphics objects.

NanoXML is a small non-validating XML parser for Java, which provides a lightweight, standard way to manipulate XML documents. The experiments were based on version 2.2.1, which consists of three packages and 24 Java classes, focusing on two classes, XMLElement and XMLAttribute, which provide the functionality to manipulate XML documents. In particular, all XMLElement methods were monitored, executing 5605 test cases in order to evaluate the handling of large numbers of invocations.

These tests covered 2099 out of 5836 instructions. Each test generated a single rule instance from which minimal and maximal rules, multiobjects, and constraints were extracted. The results showed that the efforts for tracing, rule instance construction and extraction of minimal rules were essentially linear, as was the derivation of constraints and multiobjects. The construction of maximal rules requires one to compare all rule instances with shared minimal rules, which is quadratic in the number of rule instances that share the same effect.

---

[1] See http://nanoxml.sourceforge.net/orig/ and www.jhotdraw.org/.

JHotDraw is a Java GUI framework for technical and structured graphics, developed as an exercise in good software design using patterns. Here, version 5.3 was used, which has 243 classes, focusing on the top-level methods for the manipulation of graphs. Test cases were created by GUI testing using WindowTester[2] to generate tests by recording user interactions. This resulted in 405 test cases covering 9284 of 34710 instructions. Based on the recorded test cases, the total run time of the extraction was about 3 hours 15 mins. The scalability is analogous to that of NanoXML, but the quadratic component of maximal-rule extraction was less significant owing to the smaller overall number of rule instances.

The evaluation also showed a proportionality between model accuracy and code coverage, in particular branch cover. Moreover, a user study was conducted to find out how visual contracts can help developers in assessing test reports and localising faults. This confirmed an important benefit of visual contracts, i.e. that they are not linear but able to correlate items of information across more than one dimension.

8.3.3 Extensions

In this chapter, we considered typed attributed graphs with subtyping between node types. Extracted rules can have attribute conditions, multiobjects and multipatterns. It is possible to extend the approach to generate basic control structures such as negative application conditions and simple transformation units. For example, in the case of operation dropOffCar() in Fig. 8.8 we could use negative conditions, priorities or a control expression to prefer the rule on the right, considering the two identity rule on the left as failure case.

Owing to the way executions are logged, the approach is limited to sequential programs. To extract contracts from a concurrent execution, where more than one invocation can be active in parallel, we would have to find a way to allocate access to objects and attributes to one of the active invocations. Thereafter, the synthesis and generalisation of rules could proceed as presented here. It would be interesting to consider how closely the concurrent semantics of graph transformations matches the behaviour of concurrent Java programs.

8.3.4 Applications

The automatic inference of visual contracts can be applied in several ways such as to specify services in the context of service-oriented computing (see Chapter 6), to document the behaviour of Java libraries, to generate further

---

[2] A tool to record GUI tests for Swing applications; see `https://developers.google.com/java-dev-tools/wintester/html/gettingstarted/swing_sampletest`.

test cases (see Chapter 7) and to provide a visual form of debugging of Java programs. We go into more details for three of these applications.

Given the implementation of a provided service together with representative example runs, a correct-by-construction service description by means of visual contracts can be extracted. With s service request specified as a visual contract, Chapter 6 presents how such specifications can be used for matching.

To understand the relation between visual-contract extraction as presented here and testing using visual contracts discussed in the previous chapter, observe that this is a reverse engineering approach, while testing is part of forward engineering. Testing software against contracts extracted by running the same version of the code is an interesting way to evaluate the correctness of the overall approach, but otherwise redundant. Instead, testing and extraction can be combined in a reengineering cycle, extracting visual contracts from an old version of the software to generate regression tests for a new version.

Another application of reverse engineering Java programs is debugging [15]. Debuggers are used to inspect the behaviour of a program step by step. Starting at a specified breakpoint, changes in the program state are inspected. As users are interested only in part of the program's behaviour, they could use visual contracts to observe localised changes. Besides providing a visual form of debugging, this can also raise the level of abstraction from the code to a model.

9

Stochastic Analysis of Dynamic Software Architectures

The high-level structure of a software system is referred to as its *software architecture*. Apart from the functionality to be supported, its design is determined by non-functional requirements, such as platform and location independence, scalability, and reliability. In this chapter, we want to consider a method that uses graph transformation for probabilistic and stochastic modelling of systems such that non-functional requirements can be analysed. We will illustrate the approach by means of a model of our VoIP application.

Let us consider some examples of non-functional requirements for such an application:

1. The VoIP services should be provided in a *location-independent* way to allow access from mobile or fixed devices through a range of different types of connection.
2. The system should be highly *scalable* while remaining free of charge, thus imposing limits on the allowable infrastructure cost to the provider.
3. The system should be *reliable* in the sense that, at any time with high probability, everyone in the network should be able to call everyone else.

The first requirement calls for the use of a ubiquitous underlying transport network, such as the Internet, so the application is designed as an overlay voice-over-IP network, i.e. an application-level network where VoIP clients maintain their own connections. Requirement 2 suggests the use of a peer-to-peer architecture, where management tasks, such as establishing connections, are performed by clients, minimising the need for central infrastructure. Requirement 3 calls for a mechanism to ensure fault tolerance, such as maintaining an appropriate level of redundancy to cope with loss of connections or clients.

In general, designing a software architecture means making fundamental structural choices that are hard to change once implemented. It is therefore imperative to document the architecture of a system unambiguously and clearly, both to facilitate discussion and agreement between stakeholders and to assess if functional and non-functional requirements will be met. To sup-

© Springer Nature Switzerland AG 2020
R. Heckel, G. Taentzer, *Graph Transformation for Software Engineers*,
https://doi.org/10.1007/978-3-030-43916-3_9

port both purposes, an architectural description needs to be readable and to support suitable analysis techniques.

In particular, non-functional properties are difficult to assess before an application is fully developed and deployed and many failures in software projects have been attributed to a lack of understanding of the impact of early design choices on non-functional aspects [110]. In distributed and mobile applications, factors such as the availability and bandwidth of network connections, computing resources, and the behaviour of end users have a major impact on the overall performance. For example, the time taken to establish a VoIP connection in a P2P network will depend on the length of the shortest path between the caller and the callee, which will vary over time owing to peers joining and leaving the network.

Such factors, which are external to the application, are often unpredictable at an individual level. However, assumptions about external factors can be formalised using probabilistic or stochastic methods. For example, while we may not know for an individual user if they will accept a connection request or for how long they will remain connected, we may be able to get statistical information about their probability of accepting requests or the average time connected. In the first case we have a probabilistic model, probabilities being used to *specify alternative actions or outcomes* available in a given state. In the second case, to model uncertainty in timing, we use a stochastic model equipped with a continuous notion of time to describe the probabilities of *certain delays or durations of actions.*

It follows from this discussion that any approach to documenting and analysing software architectures of the type encountered in today's mobile and distributed applications should have the following characteristics:

- understandability to domain experts, software architects and developers;
- ability to model distributed structure and dynamic changes in the network;
- support for expressing non-functional requirements, including probabilistic or stochastic properties;
- capability for probabilistic or stochastic modelling and analysis.

Architectural description languages typically use graphical notations, for example based on UML, to support understandability by a wide range of stakeholders. To specify the set of all possible configurations of a system, structural models describe the types of components and connectors available and the constraints governing their composition, e.g. using variants of class and object diagrams for the type and instance levels, respectively. The ability to model structural changes at a similarly high level is often limited. Dynamic reconfiguration may be programmed or scripted but is rarely expressed graphically.

To support the specification and analysis of non-functional properties, architectural designs are often mapped to low-level semantic models such as stochastic transition systems (or Markov chains [16, 224]), automata-based languages such as UPPAAL [39], stochastic Petri nets [223, 217, 14, 38] or process calculi [71, 237, 51]. Most of these describe behaviour in terms of the ordering of events, neglecting aspects of data transformations and changes to software architecture or network topology. The stochastic π-calculus [237], which allows one to describe dynamic reconfigurations, is an adequate semantic framework for programming, but too low-level for expressing designs in an implementation-independent way, i.e. *what* changes are required, instead of *how* they are achieved.

The properties themselves can be expressed using probabilistic or stochastic logics. For example, the reliability requirement 3 in the P2P example can be formalised by a so-called *steady-state property* saying that, in the long run, the probability of the network being disconnected must be below a certain threshold. The scalability requirement 2 can be expressed, for example, by the requirement that the time for a peer to connect to the network should not increase significantly with the number of peers in the network. This is called a *transient property* which states the probability that an event occurs within a certain time interval, for example 99% of connection requests are answered within 2 seconds.

Such properties can be verified through model checking based on stochastic automata, transition systems or Markov chains, or by simulating the system model and observing its performance. Model checking requires a translation from the high-level modelling language to the semantic language used for analysis. Simulations can be performed on the model directly, in a variant of model-level testing coupled with a statistical analysis of the test results.

We have argued before that graph transformations are unique in providing an intuitive visual modelling technique for structural and data transformations, equipped with both an operational semantics and a formal mathematical interpretation that supports analysis. Rules specify pre- and postconditions of operations in terms of complex patterns describing *what* transformations should be achieved rather than *how* they should be realised. While other languages or formalisms share some of these characteristics, graph transformations are unique in having this combination of features.

Stochastic graph transformation systems (SGTSs) [133, 132] add the ability to specify and analyse non-functional properties, such as the performance and reliability of these models. They extend graph transformation systems by continuous time, associating a random application delay with each rule. As a result, we are able to derive semantic representations for stochastic analysis, such as continuous-time Markov chains (CTMCs) [224], a stochastic extension of transition systems. By allowing one to specify timed probabilistic properties, such as the probability of being connected to the service within 20 seconds after start-up or the long-term probability that a service will be available, CTMCs form the basis for powerful analysis techniques and tools. SGTSs enable the use of these techniques for models of dynamic networks, where, as argued above, time-based probabilistic performance properties are particularly relevant.

For example, in the VoIP model this will allow us to answer questions about the availability of network services in the case of different connection protocols running at different speeds. Availability is interpreted as the probability of the network being connected, so that every participant can communicate with every other one. The high-level effects of protocols are specified by rules. Their relative speed is defined by probability distributions governing the delay of their application. We will discuss the use of simulation and model checking to analyse this system in order to assess different alternative protocol.

In this chapter, we illustrate the use of stochastic graph transformation systems by modelling a simplified version of the VoIP network. From a software engineering perspective, we follow a methodology that starts by identifying the high-level requirements to be verified. These requirements inform our architectural modelling, which includes a structural dimension as well as the rules for architectural adaptation. The model is validated using sample state graphs and transformations. For the resulting graph transformation system, we define distributions for the timing of rules, resulting in a stochastic system. We then formalise the stochastic properties and verify them using model checking or simulation.

After recalling the functional model of the VoIP network in Section 9.1, we introduce and illustrate stochastic graph transformation systems in Section 9.2. Section 9.3 explains how such models can be analysed using simulation and model checking and Section 9.4 summarises the methodology of stochastic modelling and analysis using graph transformation systems. We conclude this chapter with a discussion of tools and relevant theoretical problems. Since stochastic graph transformation systems extend typed attributed graph transformation systems, it is worthwhile to be aware of the concepts introduced in Chapters 1 and 2 before reading this one. We will refer to analysis techniques such as model checking of graph transition systems as discussed in Section 4.5.

9.1 A Peer-to-Peer Network Model

Peer-to-peer (P2P) networks are decentralised, self-organising application-level networks. Owing to the lack of global control and the unreliability of the underlying network infrastructure, P2P networks are prone to dependability problems. One common solution consists in creating sufficient redundancy to ensure that, when a node unexpectedly leaves the network or is unreachable, its role in storing and routing information can be taken over by other nodes. For example, the VoIP network Skype used to be based on a P2P architecture before it was hosted on Microsoft's cloud services. The P2P architecture provided a scalable solution without the need to invest heavily in infrastructure.

Mariani [198] proposed an algorithm which, when executed asynchronously by each peer, adds redundant connections to the network to guarantee that the disappearance of a peer does not unduly affect the overall performance and routing capabilities of the network. It does so by querying the local context of a node up to a given depth to expose potential weaknesses in the network topology. The assumption is that this happens fast enough to prevent loss of connectivity owing to the disappearance of a node before extra links can be added. The desired result is increased fault tolerance.

The idea is to compare the level of fault tolerance achieved by this systematic approach with that obtained by the simpler solution of adding a limited number of references at random. For this purpose, we model two protocols, a random protocol and a systematic one following Mariani [198], by stochastic graph transformation systems and analyse different variants to find out, for each version of the model, the probability of encountering a state where the network is disconnected.

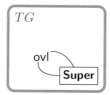

Fig. 9.1. Type graph for simple P2P model

Example 9.1 (P2P network rules). We first recall the structure and operations of the VoIP network model introduced as our running example in Chapter 2. In that model, graphs represent configurations, modelling network nodes as vertices and links between them as edges. For simplicity we consider only the super node network, ignoring client peers and users, so our type graph in Fig. 9.1 contains only one node and one edge type.

The rules for the P2P network model are shown in Fig. 9.2. Rule new creates a new node of type Super and links it to an existing node s with a new edge of type ovl. Rule end models the deletion of a node s with all its ingoing and outgoing edges. This may cause the network to become disconnected.

The rule disconnected detects such situations. It is applicable if two nodes s1, s2 are *not* connected by a path of ovl edges. Note that the application does not have any effect on the graph. It is used only to generate a loop in the transition system on every state whose graph is disconnected. This is achieved by a negative application condition containing a path expression.

The rule smart models the approach of adding redundant links where the network is weak, i.e. where the removal of a node would result in lengthening the shortest path between two remaining nodes. It is identical to the shortcut rule in Fig. 2.17. The rule random models the naive approach of adding links at random as long as the number of additional ovl edges attached to either s2 or s3, beyond the ones linking them to s1, does not exceed two. Hence, the rule will not increase the degree of any node beyond three. This condition is expressed by negative conditions too, each involving a multiobject with a cardinality constraint.

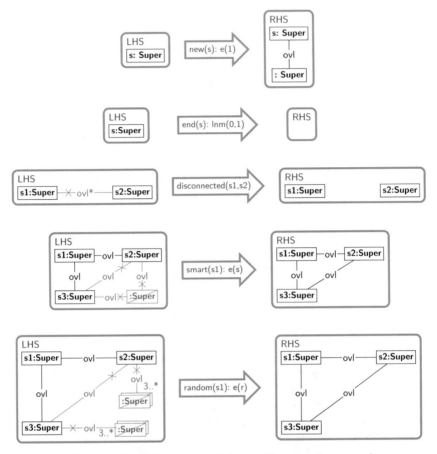

Fig. 9.2. Rules for nodes joining and leaving the network

Let us consider the different effects of rules smart and random. In the network graph shown in Fig. 9.3, for example, there are several possible applications of the random rule such as to three of the outer corners of the square of nodes, that would create additional edges. However, only the edge from s2 to s4 will improve the resilience of the network against loss of connectivity in the event of the removal of a single node. This is indeed the only edge added by the smart rule, while the random rule is not applicable to this match because s2 already has three connections.   □

Recall that the timing of operations such as those modelled by rules new and end is unpredictable, because it depends on user behaviour. This is captured by probability distributions specifying random delays for the application of these rules. For example, for rule new, which is always applicable as long as there is at least one node to connect to, we use an exponential distribution with rate 1 that defines the *average frequency* at which new nodes will join while allowing for random intervals between consecutive applications. The end

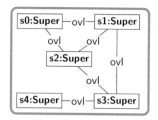

Fig. 9.3. P2P network graph

rule is applicable to any node in the network, representing either the decision of the user to terminate the node or a loss of the network connection. It has a log-normal distribution, representing the time a node remains in the network.

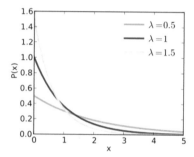

Fig. 9.4. Exponential probability density functions with different rates $c = \lambda$.[1]

We usually consider exponential distributions $e(c)$ or log-normal distributions $lnm(m, d)$. *Exponential distributions* are specified by a positive real number c, representing the rate of the exponentially distributed delay of the application. This means that the rate c defines an *average delay* of $1/c$ for the application of a rule r once a match for r exists in the current graph. The exponential distribution describes a random process in which events occur independently of each other, at a given rate per unit of time. Examples of such phenomena include radioactive decay, occurrences of a rare disease in a large population and the arrival of a packet of information on the Internet. The probability density functions for a range of rates $c = \lambda$ in Fig. 9.4 show how higher rates lead to lower values of the delay x being more likely.

Log-normal distributions are a typical model for the response times of both humans and software performing or controlling a given task. Such a distribution is characterised by a location parameter m and a scale parameter d, the standard deviation on a logarithmic scale. Examples of probability density functions with $m = \mu = 0$ are shown in Fig. 9.5. We can see how higher standard deviations lead to a higher likelihood of longer delays. In contrast to

---

[1] From Wikipedia Commons, `commons.wikimedia.org/wiki/File:Exponential_pdf.svg`

exponential distributions, where the probability of an event occurring in the next time interval decreases uniformly over time (accounting for the increasing probability that it has already happened), a log-normal distribution has a peak where the event is most likely (for example the most common duration of a phone call), with both shorter and longer delays less likely.

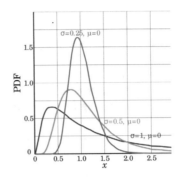

Fig. 9.5. Log-normal probability density functions with identical parameter $m = \mu$ but but differing parameters $d = \sigma$.[3]

Pragmatically, this means that if only the average delay d of an event is known (e.g. customers arrive at a supermarket queue at average intervals of d), we choose an exponential distribution with rate $1/d$. If, in addition, we know that delays closer to the average are more likely than those further away from it, we use a log-normal distribution. Given a set of data points representing sample delays, there are statistical methods to calculate the distribution's mean and standard deviation parameters. For example, for the mean we apply the natural logarithm to each sample delay value and then take their average.

In our example, where we do not have sample data, we are not interested in any specific delay values but in the effects of the relative timing between the rules for creating and ending of peers and the repair operations of the network. Therefore, we use rate 1 and mean 0, both describing an average delay of 1 for their respective operation.

Example 9.2 (distribution rates). In Fig. 9.2 we indicate exponential distributions by $e(c)$, with the rates c being constants or variables, following the parameterised rule name inside the arrow. For example, new(s): e(1) indicates an exponential distribution with a rate of 1, which means that on average this rule will be applied once per unit of time for each match of the left-hand side to an existing node s.

Since rule new is applicable to a node in the network throughout its lifetime, this means that the delay (the time between the rule becoming applicable and its eventual application) is on average $1/1 = 1$ unit of time. Since this rule

---

[3] From Wikipedia Commons, `commons.wikimedia.org/wiki/File:PDF-log_`
`normal_distributions.svg`?

is applicable again and again at the same match, this delay represents the average time between two applications, i.e. a node receives a new neighbour on average once every unit of time.

The rates s, r for smart(s1), random(s1) are variables ranging from 1 to 10000 when the model is analysed for the effect of different relative speeds of operations on the quality of the network. Rule disconnected does not model an operation but a query. It is not assigned a distribution, because it is not meant to be applied, but only used to observe a property of the state graph.

Rule end is also applicable to a node as soon as it is created. A lognormal distribution lnm(0, 1) with mean 0 and standard deviation 1 specifies an average delay of 1 unit, with delays around the average more likely than longer or shorter ones. In our model, this delay represents the average time a node remains in the network. The distribution of end(s): lnm(0,1) is visualised in the lowest (blue) line in Fig. 9.5.

□

9.2 Stochastic Graph Transformation

A stochastic graph transformation system is a typed graph transformation system that associates with each rule a probability distribution over time describing by how much its application is delayed once a match becomes available. Formally, a stochastic graph transformation system $SG = \langle TG, R, F \rangle$ consists of a graph transformation system $\langle TG, R \rangle$ and a mapping F assigning each rule $r \in R$ a continuous probability distribution $F(r) : \mathbf{R} \rightarrow [0, 1]$ such that $F(r)(0) = 0$.

The operational interpretation of stochastic graph transformation is based on simulation. With the start graph G_0 as the initial current state G, and setting the simulation time to $t = 0$, we first determine the set $E(G)$ of enabled events, i.e. all rule matches $e = r(m)$ of rules $r \in R$ and matches m for r in G.

For each enabled event, a scheduling time t_e is computed by a random number generator (RNG) based on the probability distribution assigned to the event. Timed events are collected in a schedule (a list ordered by time). Then, at each simulation step:

1. The first element (e, t) is removed from the schedule.
2. The simulation time is increased to t.
3. The rule match $r(m)$ is applied, changing the current state graph.
4. The new schedule is computed, based on the new current state graph, removing all events past the current time, as well as those that are no longer enabled in the current state graph, and adding to the schedule an event for each newly enabled rule match $r(m)$ with time $t = t + d$, where d is provided by the RNG depending on r's distribution.

An RNG draws a random value from a given probability distribution, in this case a distribution over time of the delay of the event after it has been enabled. The probability of a particular value being drawn depends on the type and parameters of the distribution. The result is a timed sequence of transformation steps

$$(G_0, t_0) \xrightarrow{r_1(m_1)} (G_1, t_1) \xrightarrow{r_2(m_2)} \cdots \xrightarrow{r_n(m_n)} (G_n, t_n),$$

where t_1 is the time of the application of $r_1(m_1)$ and $d_1 = t_1 - t_0$ is its delay.

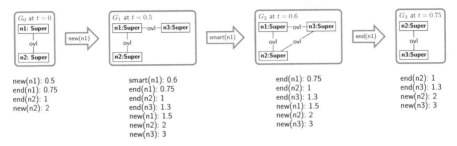

new(n1): 0.5
end(n1): 0.75
end(n2): 1
new(n2): 2

smart(n1): 0.6
end(n1): 0.75
end(n2): 1
end(n3): 1.3
new(n1): 1.5
new(n2): 2
new(n3): 3

end(n1): 0.75
end(n2): 1
end(n3): 1.3
new(n1): 1.5
new(n2): 2
new(n3): 3

end(n2): 1
end(n3): 1.3
new(n2): 2
new(n3): 3

Fig. 9.6. A timed step sequence simulating the P2P model

Example 9.3 (P2P model simulation). In Fig. 9.6 we illustrate the idea of a timed sequence arising from a simulation of the P2P example. The start graph G_0 has two linked Super nodes, which each allow matches for rules new and end. The four rule matches are scheduled by the RNG for the times shown in the list below the graph; for example, new(n1): 0.5 means that rule match new(n1) is scheduled for $t = 0.5$. According to the simulation algorithm, we choose this as the earliest event and apply it, leading to graph G_1.

The new node n3 enables additional rule matches new(n3) and end(n3). Their delays, as determined by the RNG, are 2.5 and 0.8, respectively, to which we add the current time 0.5 to get their scheduled times 3 and 1.3. There is also a match for rule smart now, which is scheduled for 0.6 and becomes the next event to be applied.

The resulting graph G_2 at time 0.6 has an additional edge, which disables another application of smart but retains all other rule matches and their times. The next step is therefore end(n1) which leads to G_3 at $t = 0.75$, where node n1 disappears and therefore all events relying on this node are cancelled. Again there are no new matches, so no new events are added and the next step will be end(n2) followed by end(n3) after which the simulation ends.

Note that the choice of rules and matches depends solely on the RNG. If shorter delays for rule new had been created, it might have been applied before end, leading to additional matches and a potentially longer simulation sequence.   □

In the final discussion in Chapter 4 we stressed that analysis techniques are limited, by their underlying theory or tool support, to certain features of graph transformation systems. In terms of the features introduced in Chapter 2, our model is a typed graph transformation system with negative application conditions. In addition, to express the graph property of connectedness, path expressions are used inside negative conditions. We do not support explicit control flow here, because our operational semantics is based on stochastic simulation, which chooses available rules and matches randomly.

A consequence of this interpretation is that rule matches in different parts of the graph are scheduled independently, reflecting the nature of a distributed system. Therefore, stochastic graph transformation systems tend not to allow globally programmed control structures, but are limited to rule-level control such as application conditions. To increase expressivity it could be beneficial to support transformation units representing strictly local control flow.

Data attributes are possible, depending on the type of analysis required. If a graph transformation system is to be simulated as above, attributes do not pose a fundamental problem. Analysis techniques that rely on generating the state space of the system, such as stochastic model checking, will often struggle with attributes of arbitrary data types because they can lead to an infinite number of states.

9.3 Stochastic Analysis

In this section, we discuss two common approaches to verifying properties of dynamic architectures specified by stochastic graph transformation systems. The first is stochastic simulation as described above, and the second is based on stochastic model checking.

9.3.1 Simulation

A *stochastic simulation* executes the model, generating a timed transformation sequence that can be seen as a test. However, owing to the random nature of the process, a single test run does not allow us to draw meaningful conclusions about stochastic properties. Instead, by running a batch of simulations with the same start graph we can collect statistics, for example on:

- how many runs terminate after a limited number of steps, as in the example above;
- what is the average number of peers or links in the network;
- how often certain rules are actually applied, for example to assess the frequency of use of the smart or random rule;
- what is the proportion of runs that eventually lead to disconnected graphs, and how long it takes until that happens.

By varying the model and the rule parameters, we can gain valuable insights about the effect of design decisions. For example, to compare the effectiveness of the rules smart and random in creating redundancy to prevent disconnected network graphs, we can run a batch of simulations using rules $R_{random} = \{\text{new, end, random}\}$ and another one with the same distributions using $R_{smart} = \{\text{new, end, smart}\}$. We can also analyse the effects of different delays by modifying the distribution parameters, for example, to find how quickly the rules random and smart have to react to weaknesses in the network in order to repair them in time.

9.3.2 Model Checking

While simulations allow us to sample the range of possible system behaviours and so gain statistical information, model checking allows a comprehensive analysis of the labelled transition system generated. Our approach to *stochastic model checking* is based on so-called Markov chains [16, 224], in particular continuous-time Markov chains obtained by adding the rates of exponential distributions to the transitions of an LTS generated from a graph transformation system.

The restriction to exponential distributions is worth noting. In fact, when we are aiming at stochastic model checking, we work with a simplified notion of stochastic graph transformation system where, for each rule p, instead of an arbitrary distribution $F(p)$ we provide the rate $\rho(p) = c$ of an exponential distribution. This allows us to derive a CTMC which supports efficient simulation and model-checking techniques.

As introduced before, exponential distributions are single-parameter distributions that have a wide range of applications in analysing the reliability and availability of systems. For example, modelling a component's reliability with an exponential distribution presupposes that the failure rate is stable, which is generally true for electronic components during the main portion of their useful life. This means that the chance of a component breaking down during the next unit of time is independent of its current age: the *memoryless property*. A similar assumption is often used for the arrival of customers at a supermarket queue or, as in this case, users starting their VoIP clients to join the network.

Operations such as end, which we have deemed to be governed by lognormal distributions, have to be approximated by an exponential distribution with similar expected values (means) of the delay. This may lead to systematic errors, which can be assessed by comparing the results of simulations on (a small version of) the original model and simulations or model checking analyses on the CTMC model. For example, in the case of the P2P model we could simulate the version with log-normal distributions for a small number of peers, then replace the log-normal by exponential distributions and simulate the model again to see if we get similar results. If this is the case for the small model, we could expect this to hold also for models with larger numbers of peers.

The questions that can be answered by stochastic model checking fall into two categories:

- *Transient property:* Assuming that the current state has a given property P, what is the probability of reaching a state with property Q within a certain period of time?
- *Steady-state property:* What is the long-term probability of finding the system in a state that satisfies a given property P?

Properties of the first kind are called *transient* because they depend on the passage of time. For example, in the case of a system capable of reconnecting a disconnected network graph, a transient property could state a probability for the system being reconnected within a certain time limit. A *steady-state* property refers to a system's long-term behaviour. Such a property could describe the probability of the system being disconnected over its entire life time.

For analysis methods to be able to answer such questions, they require information about both the states and transitions in a system and their timing or probability. Such information will be captured in the CTMC derived from the transition system of the given GTS. While it is possible to specify small Markov chains directly, for example using a finite state machine notation, we describe large and complex CTMCs over states representing network graphs by a stochastic GTS.

In the context of this book, a CTMC is a simple transition system labelled with positive real numbers, called transition rates. This means that for every pair of states s, s' there exists at most one transition $s \xrightarrow{c} s'$ labelled by its rate constant c.[4]

The operational interpretation is as follows. If a transition $s \xrightarrow{c} s'$ is the only one starting in s, the time for it to happen is exponentially distributed with rate constant c and mean $1/c$. If there is more than one transition starting in state s, the time for leaving s is exponentially distributed with the *total exit rate* $O(s)$, given by the sum of all rates of outgoing transitions. In this case there is a competition, or *race*, between the outgoing transitions. The probability that transition $s \xrightarrow{c} s'$ wins the race is $c/O(s)$, the ratio of c and the total exit rate of s.

Given an initial state s, a CTMC can be used to analyse a system's behaviour at two levels. Its *transient solution* $P(t)(s, s')$ is defined as the probability that, starting out in s, we are in state s' at time t. Its *steady-state solution* $S(s)$ defines, for each state s, the long-term, invariant probability of finding the system in s.

---

[4] This is an intuitive representation of CTMCs but not the most common or mathematically most convenient one. In general, they are defined as a continuous-time, discrete-state random process, represented by a *Q-matrix*, i.e. the "incidence matrix" of its transition system (cf. [224]).

A stochastic graph transformation system can be translated into a CTMC by first deriving its graph transition system and then augmenting it with rates. We already know how to construct the uncontrolled graph transition system. Its CTMC has the same set of states. It has a transition $s \xrightarrow{c} s'$ if and only if there is a transition $s \xrightarrow{p} s'$ using rule p in the LTS, where the rate c is the sum of all rates of rules applied in transitions from s to s'.

Note that, in the original transition system, there may be multiple transitions linking two given states. Since the CTMC is based on a simple transition system, it can hold only a single transition for every pair of states. The rates of all rules leading to transformations between s and s' are therefore added up. For example, assume that in a state s consisting of two nodes n1, n2 only, both can decide to end their operation. This leads to two different transitions end(n1), end(n2) whose resulting states are isomorphic graphs represented by a single state s'. In this case, if the rate of end is 1, the transition $s \xrightarrow{c} s'$ has a rate $c = 2 * 1 = 2$.

We can use a graph transformation tool (such as GROOVE [107] or Henshin) to generate the labelled transition system of a graph transformation system. After augmenting it with rates as described above, the resulting CTMC can be analysed by a probabilistic model checker or analysis tool (such as PRISM [180]).

As usual, the size of the state space to be generated and analysed is a limiting factor for the model-checking approach. Simulations are more scalable in principle. Here the reliability of the result depends on the number of simulation runs, so we avoid a hard limit by trading accuracy against effort.

Example 9.4 (stochastic model checking). The results of steady-state analysis of the two stochastic graph transformation systems defined in the previous section (using rule sets R_{random} and R_{smart}) are visualised in Fig. 9.7. Both systems were restricted to a maximum of seven peers. The bottom graph represents the behaviour of $\mathcal{SG}_{smart}$ based on rules R_{smart}, whose transition graph has 798 states and 16293 transitions. We observe that, when we increase the rate of rule smart by a factor of 10 we decrease the long-term probability of a disconnected network by about the same factor: from 0.225300 for $\rho(\text{smart}) = 10$ to 0.000244 for $\rho(\text{smart}) = 10000$. Indeed, for rates at least 10 times higher than those of rules end and new, the probability seems to follow $2.4 \cdot \rho(\text{smart})^{-1}$. This means that an estimate of the average time it takes to execute (the implementation of) smart as a function of the rate of peers entering and leaving the system would provide us with an estimate of the network's reliability.

The upper graph in Fig. 9.7 represents the system $\mathcal{SG}_{random}$ based on rules R_{random} which has 487 states and 9593 transitions. We observe that the added redundancy does not have a relevant effect on the reliability, even if the number of additional edges created is roughly the same as in the other system (the overall number of states is only slightly smaller). This shows the superiority of $\mathcal{SG}_{smart}$.   □

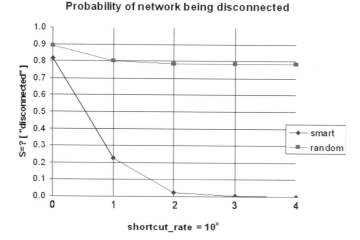

Fig. 9.7. Results of stochastic model checking

9.4 Methodology

To give a better idea of where, when and how software engineers could use the techniques described in this chapter, we summarise the overall methodology of stochastic modelling and analysis using graph transformation systems.

The methodology works best if we focus on architecture modelling, in particular structural reconfiguration and related data, rather than the communication or computation aspects. While lower-level network traffic could be modelled, for example using message nodes passed between components, this may lead to scalability problems with simulation or stochastic model checking. Apart from this, as usual, the scope of the model is determined by its purpose. This means that to analyse a particular property, the relevant information needs to be present. For example, in the current model we cannot capture how client nodes connect to super nodes, because clients are not part of the model, which focuses on super-node connectivity.

9.4.1 Identify High-Level Requirements to Be Verified

The purpose of a formal model is to be able to verify its properties, so we start by collecting relevant requirements. In particular, when modelling using stochastic graph transformation, we consider measurable, non-functional requirements which can be expressed in architectural terms and which are determined at least in part by architectural design choices. Examples include availability, performance, response time and throughput. We start by expressing these properties in natural language, in terms of architectural concepts. For example, in our P2P model, availability can be described as the probability that every network node can reach all other nodes, i.e. that the network is connected.

9.4.2 Architectural Modelling

We model different types of architectural elements, such as client or server components, network nodes and communication links by a type graph with attributes and constraints. To validate the type model, we show desirable sample configurations as instance graphs and check that undesirable ones are ruled out by the constraints.

9.4.3 Architectural Adaptation

We identify the operations that change the structure or data of configurations, such as network nodes joining or leaving, and connections being established or broken. We formulate these operations as rules over the architecture model type graph and define their parameters, i.e. which nodes, edges or attributes determine their matches or outcomes. For example, new(n: Super) is the operation to create a new Super node and to connect it to an existing node n.

9.4.4 Validate the Model

To test the type graph, configurations and rules, we apply rules to sample configurations and validate their effects. This can be done using a graph transformation tool, which may also support more elaborate state space exploration, manually guided or automated, to test and debug the model.

9.4.5 Determine Distributions

As described earlier, we consider exponential or log-normal distributions for the delay in the application of our rules. The choice depends on the nature of the operations described and the data we have available. For example, if we know only the average delay d of an operation, as in the case of new, this translates into an exponential distribution with rate $1/d$. If we know that an operation has a certain likely duration, as in the case of rule end, we may use a log-normal distribution. There are models based on real data collected from existing systems, from which distributions are derived, while other models are hypothetical, created as part of the development of a new system where no such data is available.

Recall that stochastic simulation is possible for a range of distributions, while model checking is generally limited to exponential ones, so the choice of analysis approach also determines which distributions we can use.

9.4.6 Formalise and Encode Stochastic Properties

From informal descriptions of the requirements, we derive the stochastic properties to be analysed. Typical formats include steady-state properties (in the long term, the probability that state property P will hold is at least p) or transient properties (the probability that property P will hold within a certain period of time is at least p), but other kinds of properties such as the frequency of certain events or the probability that a run contains an event can also be used to express requirements. More complex temporal properties can be expressed using logics such as continuous stochastic logic [31].

To express state properties, such as the (non)existence of certain structures or the fact that a graph is (dis)connected we may need the addition of observer rules, i.e. rules to observe state properties, for example disconnected in our P2P example.

9.4.7 Analyse the Model

Using stochastic model checking we can analyse models with small state spaces, such as networks with a small number of nodes or where the state space is otherwise limited. This allows us to validate the model, including its stochastic aspects, and give a first indication of whether the properties we are interested in are formalised correctly and are true in small models.

Simulation can explore larger instances, but can also be used to compare simulation and model-checking results on small models. This is important in particular if, for example, log-normal distributions in a simulation model are simplified to exponential ones and we need to assess if this change has a significant impact on the analysis results.

Generally, simulation avoids the state space explosion problem and is therefore more scalable than model checking. The typical tradeoff is between the accuracy of results, which increases with the number of simulations run, and the run time required to execute large numbers of simulation runs.

9.5 Summary and Further Reading

In this chapter, we have introduced stochastic graph transformation systems and developed a small case study to demonstrate their modelling and analysis capabilities. Two protocols for adding redundant links in a P2P network have been analysed.

For stochastic model checking, a simple tool chain uses GROOVE [107] to generate the transition system and PRISM [180] for the actual analysis. A similar solution has been created using the Henshin state space tools to generate the transition system [22]. Stochastic simulation has been supported by several tools. The algorithm presented here was first implemented in [278]. Kasim [69] is a stochastic simulator for the domain-specific graph transformation language Kappa which specialises in formal executable models for computational biology.

Let us conclude this chapter by discussing some of the shortcomings, further work and lessons learned. First, the model presented in this chapter captures only a simplified version of the original protocol. More comprehensive models including the selection of and connection to super nodes by clients and the promotion of clients to super nodes have been studied in [163, 164].

Second, P2P networks often contain thousands or even millions of nodes. Hence, the validity of the results of our analysis, which considers only seven peers, can be questioned. However, this is not so much an issue of the formalism itself, but of the analysis techniques and tools. More realistic cases can be anlysed by complementing model checking with stochastic simulation [278].

Finally, not all user behaviour, as expressed in rules such as new and end, or system behaviour, such as in smart and random, is exponentially distributed. The general notion of stochastic graph transformation [188] allows for more general distributions, but such models are harder to analyse using simulation or model checking.

SGTSs follow the example of approaches such as stochastic Petri nets [200] in adding stochastic information to an existing behavioural modelling language. A transition system (generated by a behavioural model, e.g. a GTS or a Petri net) is augmented by probability distributions describing the time it takes for a transition to occur. Such a transition system yields a CTMC, providing the input to stochastic analysis techniques.

A simpler approach may augment transitions by probabilities rather than rates, capturing the choices between transitions but not their timing. Discrete-time Markov chains, the probabilistic analog of CTMCs, support probabilistic analysis and model checking. Extending this approach further, Markov decision processes allow one to combine non-deterministic choice (by the system) of an action followed by probabilistic selection (by the environment) of a successor state. Such a combination has been introduced for graph transformation systems in [173] and further generalised to include stochastic time in [202].

More domain-specific approaches to stochastic graph transformation have been used in computational biology. Notably, Kappa [176] provides a range of specific theoretical results, analysis capabilities and tools, some of which have been adopted into the mainstream [70]. Targeting probabilistic graph algorithms, the graph-programming language GP2 has been extended by probabilistic features [28].

Advanced Modelling-Language Definition: Integrating Metamodelling with Graph Transformation

Models are used in software development as abstract representations of systems, to focus on specific aspects, sketch new developments or create a high-level view of an existing system. In Chapter 5, for example, class diagrams and refined activity models were used to capture functional requirements. Supporting different problem domains and implementation technologies, a variety of domain-specific notations have been developed. In business modelling, for example, business process models are used. Models may be represented in textual or graphical forms, depending on their purpose. For example, OCL constraints are textual while UML class diagrams are visual. Textual languages are typically closer, in both appearance and tool support, to programming languages and are, therefore, often used by software developers. Domain experts, analysts and designers tend to prefer graphical notations to represent complex structures at a high level of abstraction. To separate the structure from the presentation of models, we commonly distinguish between their concrete and abstract syntax. This allows, for example, the same concepts to be represented differently in different models.

To better support modelling for a given application domain or platform, a *domain-specific modelling language* (DSML) provides dedicated concepts and constraints, raising the level of abstraction and improving productivity. Working efficiently with DSMLs requires tools such as editors, interpreters and compilers. However, the manual implementation of such tools for each new language is prohibitively expensive. Hence, language engineers need an approach to engineering DSMLs which can automatically generate language-specific tools from a language definition.

A DSML can be a textual or visual language. While the abstract syntax of textual languages is typically tree-like, visual models are generally represented by object graphs, often equipped with spanning trees as in EMF [264]. Both types of definition abstract from concrete element shapes and layout. However, tree-like and graph-like abstract syntax differ in how they represent references that go beyond the parent–child relations in trees. While tree-like representations use special attributes, such as IDREF in XML [9], graph-like structures use edges to represent references more directly. As a consequence, graphs are a natural choice for defining (not only) the syntax of visual languages.

The syntax of textual languages can be defined constructively by string grammars, such as the Extended Backus–Naur form (EBNF), describing how instances of the language can be generated from a start symbol. Visual languages are typically defined in a declarative way, by meta-models. But what are the reasons for such a divergence of methods? Looking back, grammar-based methods have been used for visual languages, too. For example, in the approaches presented in [199], multidimensional representations are coded into one-dimensional strings. Such encodings allow the use of string grammars at the cost of a wider gap between concepts and their representation.

The awkwardness of such encodings may have been the reason that designers of visual languages have looked for an alternative, which they found in *metamodels*, i.e. models specifying the abstract syntax of modelling languages. However, when limited to defining object and link types only, metamodels are too weak to define exactly the language of interest. To further restrict the set of models defined by a metamodel, several forms of constraints have been considered, such as multiplicities and OCL constraints. However, even metamodels with constraints often allow too many models. The problem is that an exact specification of a non-trivial language can require a number of constraints of significant complexity.

Let us illustrate this issue using the language of well-formed activity models, i.e. activity models whose control flow is a combination of nested imperative control structures. We will use this example to show how difficult it is to give an exact specification of a language using metamodels with constraints only.

Example 10.1 (well-structured activity models). Well-structured activity models specify workflows which correspond to simple imperative programs using control constructs, such as sequential composition, if–then–else and while-loops. A sample activity diagram is depicted in Fig. 10.1. It models a typical workflow arising as a result of a new sales order in a Web-based order management system. For each product ordered, the following workflow is specified. After receiving an order, a distributor checks the availability of the product. If it is not available, the client is notified, otherwise its price is calculated and a receipt sent. Attempting to define well-structured activity models using metamodels with constraints only, we will demonstrate the limitations of this approach.   □

A constructive way to define a DSML, circumventing the complexity of a constraint-based declarative solution, is the use of graph grammars (defined in Chapter 3). Similarly to the EBNF, the specification is rule-based, but in this case graph grammar rules are used to manipulate the graph representations of models. We start with a metamodel, formally presented as a type graph, to define the types of nodes and edges allowed. Then, picking the smallest model

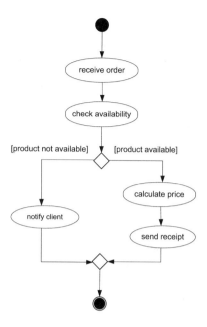

Fig. 10.1. Example activity model for a product-ordering workflow

of the DSML as the start graph, further models are constructed by applying
grammar rules such that each rule application results in a new model. This
means that there are no non-terminal types (whose instances can not be part
of any model), i.e. all types in the metamodel are terminal.

By combining metamodels and graph grammars to generate the subset of
valid models from a basic start graph, we inherit the best features of both
methods. The definition of a language by a generating grammar is inductive,
building domain-specific models of increasing complexity. A DSML defined by
a graph grammar is a subset of the language specified by the metamodel, i.e.
all generated model graphs are well typed and satisfy the constraints.

In this way, we combine two technological spaces [178] with their individual advantages and disadvantages: while metamodels support an intuitive
approach to language design, especially for languages with shallow structures
such as class models, grammars are better suited for defining models with
complex dependencies as they arise, for example, in programming languages.
Furthermore, graph grammars support the design of DSML-specific tools. In
analogy to string grammars, they can be used to generate model parsers.
We distinguish between graph grammars with and without non-terminals. As
pointed out in Section 4.6, classical grammars have two layers of recognition,
using terminal and non-terminal labels. In this chapter, we focus on grammars
with terminal labels only, which means that each derived model graph has to
represent a valid language instance. This design decision restricts the choice

of parsers; however, domain-specific models are usually created and modified in syntax-based editors that integrate constraint-validity checks. The use of graph grammars for developing model editors is discussed below.

By defining the syntax of a DSML, we create a basis for the definition of its semantics. For programming languages we can distinguish denotational *interpreter semantics* from operational *compiler semantics*. An interpreter executes a model directly based on its abstract syntax. A compiler translates the model into another language. Unlike with syntax, there is no standard way to define the semantics of a DSML. The UML specification, for example, defines the semantics of UML using OCL and informal text. A formal definition of an operational semantics is given by *semantic anchoring* [57] using Abstract State Machines (ASMs). Another obvious way to define operational semantics is by means of model transformations, such as in [189] based on graph transformation or in [250] using MAUDE, an object-oriented language based on rewriting logic.

Using a graph transformation system to define the operational semantics of a DSML provides us with a *visual* definition which is easier to understand at an intuitive level; it is also *formal*, so amenable to automated analysis; and *executable*, and thus usable for implementing an interpreter. In this chapter, we will define an interpreter for well-structured activity models, which executes their workflow step by step.

Compilers for DSMLs are usually defined as model-to-model or model-to-text transformations. We will consider compilers for DSMLs in more detail in Chapter 12, translating well-structured activity models to Petri nets for analysis purposes.

The specification of a DSML should allow the generation of an editor for the language. A metamodel can be used to generate a basic model editor. Distinguishing between basic and advanced editor operations, basic operations include creating and deleting individual model elements and relations, updating attributes, and moving model elements. Models produced or manipulated by such operations may not automatically belong to the language; they may require further editing to become valid language instances.

Basic editors can be enhanced by advanced editor operations and quick fix facilities to make manual editing more efficient. Providing a graph grammar in addition to a metamodel, its rules can be used to generate advanced editor operations and quick fixes.

This chapter is concerned with engineering methods for the definition of the syntax and operational semantics of DSMLs and the generation of tool support. More advanced aspects of language engineering such as model quality assurance, version management, translation to and synchronisation with other domains are considered in Chapters 11 and 12. We present these topics in separate chapters because graph transformation techniques are particularly useful there. Summarizing, this chapter makes the following contributions:

- We position graph grammars for the syntax definition of DSMLs in relation to metamodelling. Graph grammars allow a constructive approach to language definition. They generalise Chomsky grammars [13] and allow the generation of model parsers and further language-specific tools. The semantics of DSMLs can be defined intuitively yet precisely by graph transformation systems. While an interpreter is specified as an in-place model transformation, a compiler is given by a model-to-model or model-to-text translation (see Chapter 12).

- Graph transformation systems are well suited for the conceptual design of language tools, such as domain-specific editors and interpreters, because transformation rules can naturally specify editor operations and interpreter steps. Since rule applications may render the resulting models invalid with respect to the language definition, rules can be restricted by augmenting them with application conditions deduced from language constraints (see Section 4.4).

This chapter is structured as follows. We present a structured language design process in Section 10.1, which starts with eliciting requirements as presented in Section 10.2, followed by defining the syntax of a DSML using graph grammars in Section 10.3. This syntax definition is utilised for developing user-friendly DSML editors in Section 10.4. Finally, we discuss how an interpreter semantics can be defined using graph transformations in Section 10.5.

Since graph grammars in this chapter are based on typed attributed graph transformation systems, it is useful to be aware of this material in Chapters 1 and 2. We will also refer to some of the semantic concepts introduced at the start of Chapter 3 and to analysis techniques in Chapter. 3

10.1 Language Design Process

To support the language engineer in developing a DSML, we provide a structured methodology, starting with the gathering of requirements and leading to the development of the relevant DSML tools, in particular an editor. In Fig. 10.2 we outline the main tasks of language development.

To elicit the requirements for a DSML, we identify the basic building blocks of models and the constraints for their combination. The basic building blocks are the model elements and relations specified in the *language alphabet*. A DSML for process design, for example, requires activities and transitions. Initially, there is no need to specify how they are represented visually or how they are connected: the logical relations between elements of the alphabet are defined in the abstract syntax model of the DSML, while the concrete, visual syntax is defined by mapping domain elements to their concrete representations. In our example, we choose a graph-like representation using ellipses for simple activities and arrows for transitions. Moreover, we have to define how attributes and relations are represented. A transition running between

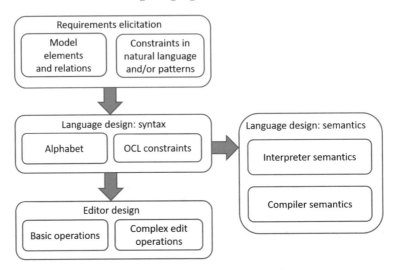

Fig. 10.2. Main tasks of language design

two activities, for example, is visually represented by an arrow starting at the border of one ellipse and ending at the border of another one. This concludes the definition of the DSML alphabet with its abstract and concrete syntax.

Next, we specify which models over the alphabet are considered valid. First, constraints are formulated in natural language. For example, each activity model has to start with a single activity without incoming transitions. Typically OCL [226] is used to formalise such constraints. Visual patterns as they are supported by the graph constraints introduced in Chapter 4 help to formulate and illustrate more complex constraints, expressing required or forbidden combinations of elements.

Such a language specification can be used directly for deriving a DSML editor with *basic editing operations*, displaying all elements of the alphabet in a palette. Models created or manipulated in such a basic editor have to be validated against the language constraints defined. This can be done either in batch processing or incrementally. Since edited models can violate constraints, it can be helpful to compute a set of editing operations for repairing invalid models. These repair operations are also known as *quick fixes*. Grammar rules may be used to deduce quick fixes: once basic editing operations have been applied, leaving the editor with an invalid model, the rule corresponding to the last operation applied is matched against the grammar rules, and so-called residual rules are constructed specifying possible quick fixes. For example, after the insertion of an unconnected activity, the model can be repaired by several quick fixes which connect the new activity to existing activities in the model, in line with the rules of the grammar.

To make the editing of models more efficient and less error-prone, advanced editors support *complex editing operations*, for example, implementing modelling guidelines such as the splitting of end activities to produce less tangled diagrams, refactorings such as the sequentialisation of concurrent actions, and optimisations such as the deletion of unnecessary activities. Conceptually, these operations are in-place model transformations, i.e. transformations performed on and modifying a single model rather than transformations between models. Graph transformations are well suited to specifying such *endogenous* transformations because a rule application typically modifies just a small portion of a graph while leaving the rest unchanged. Conceptually, we have to make sure that additional editing operations do not lead to models outside the defined language. Analysis techniques for graph transformation systems are vital in verifying such properties of language consistency.

After defining the syntax of DSMLs, we turn towards specifying their semantics. Languages for behaviour modeling can be equipped with an *interpreter semantics*. Alternatively, DSMLs may be given a *compiler semantics*, translating them into other languages serving as semantic domains. These target languages may be formal specification languages or logics supported by tools for validating interesting properties, or implementation languages supported by an execution engine. We show how graph transformations can be used to define both kinds of semantics: the interpreter semantics is considered in this chapter, while a compiler semantics designed as a model-to-model transformation is presented in Chapter 12.

Language design is often a continuous process, repeatedly producing new versions of a language. Hence, domain-specific models can become obsolete and require migration to newer versions. We will discuss this problem at the end of the chapter.

10.2 Requirements Elicitation

When starting on the design of a new DSML, a language engineer has to understand its requirements in terms of the types of model elements needed and their visual representation. For example, when one is designing a language for high-level process modelling, activity models may be a good choice. Figure 10.3 shows a set of model elements to define activity models. The language engineer distinguishes various forms of activities as well as transitions. Textual annotations on transitions and in activities add information to these model elements.

Then, a definition is required of the legal combinations of elements and their relations. In our example, each transition runs between two activities or as a loop at a single activity. More precisely, well-structured activity models have to fulfil the following language constraints (stated in natural language first):

1. Each activity model has exactly one start and one end activity.
2. (a) A start activity does not have incoming transitions, but has one outgoing transition. (b) An end activity does not have outgoing transitions, but has one incoming transition.

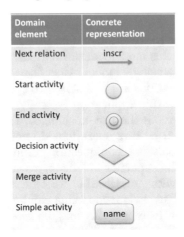

Fig. 10.3. Concrete representations of activity model elements and relations

3. (a) A decision activity has one incoming and two outgoing transitions. (b) A merge activity has one outgoing and two incoming transitions.
4. A transition has a guard (i.e. a non-empty inscription) if and only if it begins in a decision activity.
5. A simple activity has exactly one incoming and one outgoing transition.
6. A transition starts at one activity and ends at one activity.
7. The control flow graph so defined is connected and acyclic.

10.3 Abstract Syntax Design

Following requirements elicitation, a language engineer defines the abstract syntax of their DSML by a metamodel. Here, language elements and their relations form a domain-specific alphabet specified by a class structure. Additional constraints restricting the set of instances can be formulated in OCL. In our graph-based approach, type graphs are used to specify the alphabet, while graph constraints are well suited to restricting the set of instance graphs through required and forbidden patterns.

In addition to this declarative method of language design, we have discussed a constructive approach based on graph grammars. In analogy to string grammars, a model is an element of a language if it can be derived by a series of rewriting steps starting from the start graph. We will see below that graph grammars are of special interest when it comes to the design of domain-specific model editors.

10.3.1 Alphabet Definition

As the conceptual and structural foundation of a DSML, the definition of an alphabet is a crucial part of its design. As an example, consider the abstract syntax definition of an alphabet for activity models. This approach directly follows the metamodelling idea, where language elements with their attributes and relations are specified by class structures, here represented by a type graph. Informal constraints are formalised by graph constraints as illustrated below.

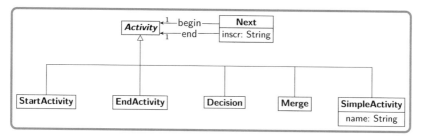

Fig. 10.4. Type graph for simple activity models

The type graph for activity models introduces two kinds of concepts: activities and transitions which begin and end at activities. Activity is an abstract type, so each Activity node is of one of its subtypes SimpleActivity, StartActivity, EndActivity, Decision or Merge. In addition, simple activities may be named. Moreover, transitions may have inscriptions, which are used as guard conditions. This type graph is shown in Fig. 10.4. Transitions are realised by the type Next.

10.3.2 Language Constraints

The most common way to describe conditions over a metamodel is by OCL constraints; they have to be satisfied by all instance models. Two sample OCL constraints formalising our conditions given above are the following:

- Constraint 1: context Activity inv:
  allInstances()→select(oclIsTypeOf(StartActivity))→size() = 1 and
  allInstances()→select(oclIsTypeOf(EndActivity))→size() = 1
- Constraint 4: context Next inv:
  if begin.oclIsTypeOf(Decision) then inscr <> ' ' else inscr = ' ' endif

Not all the language constraints of activity models stated above, however, can be formulated in OCL straightforwardly. Constraint 2(a), for example, is formulated over all start activities and their incoming and outgoing transitions. Interpreting the edge types begin and end as unidirectional associations, Constraint 2(a) cannot be specified in OCL directly. In [125], Hanysz et al. presented an extension of OCL to navigate across non-navigable associations by annotating these associations with opposite roles. Using that idea, we introduce the opposite roles outgoing with begin and incoming with end. Then, Constraint 2(a) can be specified in OCL as follows:

- Constraint 2(a): context StartActivity inv:
  self.incoming→empty() and self.outgoing→size() = 1

Graph constraints, as presented in Chapter 4, are a visual way to formalise language constraints. They show graph structures directly without using navigation expressions and hence, provide a more direct representation of structural conditions. The navigability of associations does not play any role. In Figs. 10.5–10.10, the informal constraints for activity models listed above are formalised as graph constraints. Figure 10.5 shows a graph constraint for constraint 1 which requires the existence of exactly one start activity and one end activity. It is formalised by atomic graph constraints demanding at least one and at most one such activities. In this way, the whole constraint can be expressed by the existence and non-existence of simple graph patterns.

Fig. 10.5. Graph constraint formalising language constraint 1

More complex conditions starting with a universal quantification have to be formulated as conditional constraints consisting of two graphs $P \subseteq Q$. Such a constraint is satisfied by a graph G if each occurrence of pattern P in G can be extended to an occurrence of pattern Q. We can use propositional operators over constraints sharing the same pattern P to state more specific conditions, as shown in Figs. 10.6–10.10.

We do not draw a direct relation between OCL and graph constraints here. The interested reader is referred to [239] for a translation of Essential OCL invariants to nested graph constraints. We also do not specify acyclicity of activity diagrams, since such a constraint is not expressible in first-order logic, and hence cannot be specified by the graph constraints introduced here. In [238] Radke presented an extension of graph constraints where hyperedge replacement is used to specify constraints with variable parts allowing one to express second-order conditions.

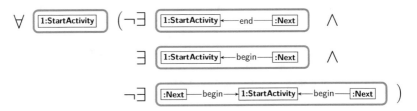

Fig. 10.6. Graph constraint formalising language constraint 2(a); constraint 2(b) can be formalised analogously

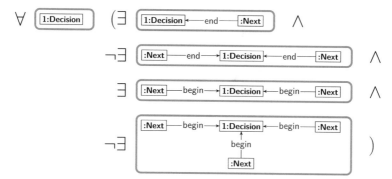

Fig. 10.7. Graph constraint formalising language constraint 3(a); constraint 3(b) can be formalised analogously

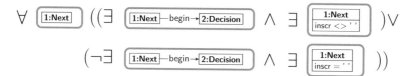

Fig. 10.8. Graph constraint formalising language constraint 4

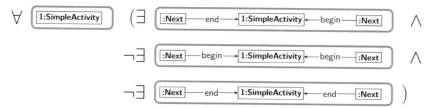

Fig. 10.9. Graph constraint formalising language constraint 5

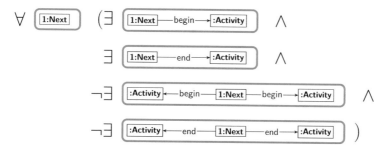

Fig. 10.10. Graph constraint formalising language constraint 6

10.3.3 Language Instances

Figure 10.11 shows the model graph *ASG* of the activity diagram shown in Fig. 10.1. It is typed over the type graph shown in Fig. 10.4 with the mapping indicated by corresponding type names inside all nodes and at all edges. Moreover, it fulfils all of the language constraints depicted in Figs. 10.5–10.10. Hence, this instance represents a well-structured activity model.

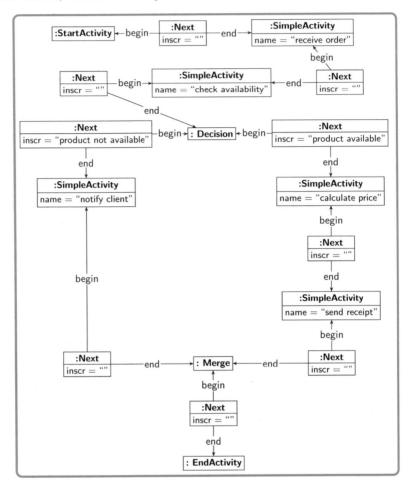

Fig. 10.11. Model graph of activity diagram in Fig. 10.1

10.3.4 Language Grammar

An alternative way to define the syntax of a DSML is a graph grammar. In contrast to a metamodel with constraints, a grammar is a constructive specification, using an instance of the language as the start graph and deriving all other instances by successively applying graph grammar rules.

In the following, we consider a simple graph grammar for well-structured activity diagrams. As above in the context of constraints, we have chosen a simple but meaningful subset of activity diagrams. Recall that our set of well-structured activity diagrams does not have cycles and is connected.

We consider the graph grammar shown in Fig. 10.12, given informally in concrete syntax first. The start graph is the smallest activity diagram that satisfies our constraints. It consists of a start activity directly followed by an end activity. The grammar contains three rules. Rule insertSimpleActivityAfterStart inserts a simple activity, directly after the start activity. The name of the new activity is given by the input parameter n. This rule can only be applied to insert a simple activity. Rule insertDecision inserts a decision activity with two branches. Each branch contains a simple activity, potentially to be rewritten later. The branches are joined by a merge activity. This rule has four input parameters: two transition inscriptions x and y as guards for the decision, and two names n and m for the simple activities in both branches. Note that activity a in the left-hand side is replaced by the decision structure in the right-hand side. Lastly, rule insertSequentialActivity handles the insertion of a second simple activity following the given one.

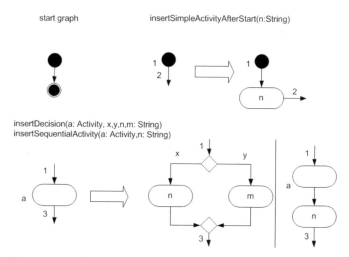

Fig. 10.12. Graph grammar in concrete syntax representation

This concrete syntax representation is useful for illustrating the idea of the generation process, but it is not fully formal. For an exact definition of the language, we require the abstract syntax, presenting a graph grammar for well-structured activity diagrams typed over the abstract alphabet graph in Fig. 10.4. This graph grammar is shown in Fig. 10.13. As a simple activity can be inserted after the start activity and after a simple activity in a similar way and since it should be possible to insert a simple activity also after a merge activity, the grammar in abstract syntax is slightly more general than the one in concrete syntax. Figure 10.13 contains just two rules since the rules insertSimpleActivityAfterStart and insertSequentialActivity are integrated into one rule called insertSimpleActivity. Activities after which a new simple activity can be inserted may be of any type except for decision activities. While we explicitly have to prohibit that the activity is a decision, this is not needed for end activities as there is no transition which begins at an end activity. Hence, there is no match for insertSequentialActivity such that a is an end activity.

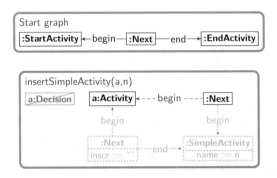

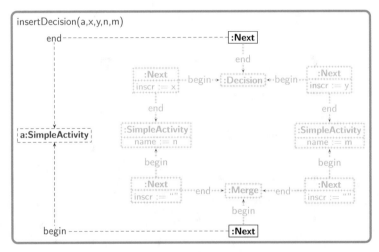

Fig. 10.13. Graph grammar in abstract syntax representation

Example 10.2 (generating the abstract syntax graph of an activity diagram). To illustrate the process of generating an abstract syntax graph by a graph grammar, we consider the transformation sequence that creates the graph in Fig. 10.11. Beginning with the start graph in Fig. 10.13, the following rule sequence is applied:

1. insertSimpleActivity(start,"receive Order");
2. insertSimpleActivity(receiveOrder, "Check Availability");
3. insertSimpleActivity(checkAvailability,"Decision");
4. insertDecision(decision,"product not available", "product available", "notify client", "calculate price");
5. insertSimpleActivity(calculatePrice,"send receipt");

We assume that for activities receiverOrder, checkAvalability, decision and calculatePrice, their object identifiers equal the values of their name attribute. The object identifier of the start activity is just start.   □

Given two language specifications, one by a metamodel with constraints and one by a graph grammar over the same metamodel, the question arises how the corresponding modelling languages are related. According to our language design process, we define a superset of the language by a metamodel first, to further constrain it by a graph grammar afterwards. Therefore, we need to check if all graphs derived by the grammar fulfil the constraints given in the metamodel.

To show that the constraints in Figs. 10.5–10.10 are fulfilled by all graphs derived by the abstract syntax grammar, we apply consistency checking as presented in Chapter 4. First we have to show that the start graph fulfils all constraints. For constraints 1 and 2 this is straightforward. Constraints 3 and 5 do not apply, and constraints 4 and 6 are easily checked.

For the rules, we have to show that, if graph G fulfils constraint c and a transformation $G \Longrightarrow_r H$ takes place, then graph H fulfils constraint c as well. Since none of the two rules change the number of start and end activities or the number of their connections, constraints 1 and 2 are obviously fulfilled by graph H.

1. insertSimpleActivity: This rule inserts a new Next relation between two activities without an inscription. Therefore, constraints 4 and 6 are fulfilled and constraint 5 is obeyed, since new parts are directly connected to existing ones. Constraint 3 does not apply since the activities occurring in this rule cannot be decision activities.
2. insertDecision: A new decision structure is added to the graph. The Decision-activity has exactly one incoming edge and two outgoing ones. The Merge-activity has exactly two incoming edges and one outgoing edge. Therefore, constraint 3 is fulfilled. The Next-relations going out from the Decision-activity have non-empty inscriptions, and thus constraint 4 is obeyed. Since each new branch has one new simple activity with one incoming and one outgoing edge, constraint 5 is also obeyed.

Hence, our graph grammar is consistent with the given metamodel. However, there are models which fulfil all constraints of our metamodel but cannot be constructed by the graph grammar. For example, a model with a decision structure that does not contain any simple activity, i.e. with transitions that go directly from the decision activity to the merge activity, cannot be derived from the start graph.

10.3.5 Language Parsing

Graph parsing is the application of inverse grammar rules to a given instance graph in order to reduce it to the start graph (see also Section 4.6). Considering the example above, all rules can be inverted and applied in reverse order. Note that the inverse applications of insertSimpleActivity(start,"receive Order") and insertSimpleActivity(receiveOrder, "Check Availability") could also occur earlier as they are independent of the parsing of the decision structure, i.e. the simple parsing process described is non-deterministic.

Note 10.1: Language definition using graph grammars. The abstract syntax of a DSML instance is naturally presented as a graph, in particular if there is no dominant tree structure containing all its elements. Unlike metamodelling, graph grammars define the abstract syntax graphs of a DSML in a constructive way. While textual parsers process input text in a definite order, graph parsers do not fix the order of pattern recognition. This means that, in general, there is neither a defined starting point for parsing nor a designated order of processing a graph.

10.4 Model Editors

In order to create and modify models we require operations for creating, deleting and changing model elements. Grammar rules are a good indication of how models can be constructed using an editor. If each create operation corresponds to a rule of the grammar, and deletion and change rules are deduced from grammar rules, the editor is syntax directed, guaranteed always to produce models specified by the grammar. However, such an editing style is often considered as too restrictive.

If inconsistent models are allowed temporarily, editing operations can be more flexible. Often, in this case, they correspond to subrules of grammar rules. An operation may cover, for example, the insertion and deletion of a single element or relation or the modification of an attribute. Applying such a simple operation can lead to models outside the language. A comparison of the underlying simple rules with the original grammar rules can determine residual rules that indicate quick fixes for inconsistent models.

Conversely, editing operations may be more complex than grammar-induced operations, to perform larger modifications such as refactorings. To ensure that their application always leads to models in the DSML, they should be assembled from editing operations that preserve well-formedness. These operations include grammar rules, deduced inverse rules and change rules.

10.4.1 Simple Editing Operations

A straightforward way to develop editing operations is to think of the rules of the grammar as specifying the set of editing operations. However, allowing just these operations may restrict the editing process too much. A convenient editor should also support *basic operations*. These are editing operations that support the insertion of single elements and relations, their deletion, and their modification. In Fig. 10.14, the specification of the basic operation rename-Activity by a rule is shown, which identifies an activity by a parameter a and renames it to m.

Fig. 10.14. Editing rule RenameActivity

Operations that insert, move and delete single model elements and references, set and update attributes are considered basic. They can be deduced from a given metamodel or type graph. Often, basic operations do not preserve the consistency of graphs; we will discuss below how to deal with inconsistencies.

10.4.2 Complex Editing Operations

Typical candidates for complex operations are refactorings and other domain-specific transformations combining several basic operations. Since our grammar of well-structured activity diagrams has quite elaborate rules already, there are not very many combined operations that are both useful and general enough. A reasonable candidate for an additional operation is insertDecision-AfterActivity shown in Fig. 10.15, which combines sequential applications of insertSimpleActivity and insertDecision. Further examples of complex operations are the splitting and merging of activities and the deletion of unnecessary activities. These are all examples of refactoring operations on activity diagrams.

10.4.3 Living with Inconsistencies

Since we have restricted our DSML to well-structured activity models, consistency-preserving editing operations are quite complex. If inconsistent activity models are allowed temporarily, basic operations may be applied freely. For example, when an isolated simple activity is inserted, the activity model becomes inconsistent. To repair this problem, the isolated activity has to be integrated into an existing control flow. There are several ways to fix such an invalid situation. We can design corresponding editing operations, called *quick fixes*, from the given graph grammar. For example, the rule integrateSimple-Activity in Fig. 10.16 can be used to connect an existing simple activity to some activity (which is not a decision activity). It checks if an existing simple activity is isolated, i.e. has neither an incoming nor an outgoing transition, as expressed by two negative application conditions. If this precondition holds,

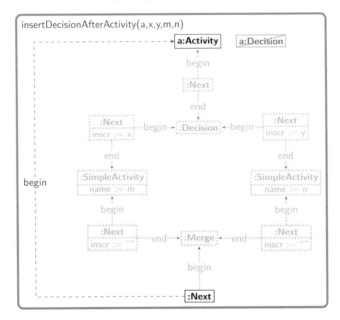

Fig. 10.15. Specification of editing operation insertDecisionAfterActivity

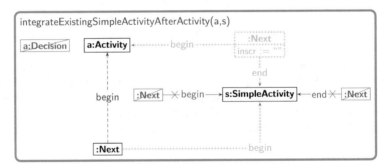

Fig. 10.16. Quick fix operation integrateExistingSimpleActivityAfterActivity

the simple activity is integrated into the control flow immediately after a specified activity.

In the following we show how this quick fix operation is derived from rule insertSimpleActivity in Fig. 10.13. Consider rule InsertIsolatedSimpleActivity, which specifies the insertion of an isolated simple activity, with an empty left-hand side and a simple activity on the right-hand side. The fact that this simple activity is isolated can be made explicit by two NACs saying that there are not transitions beginning or ending at this activity. A composition (formally a concurrent rule, see [85]) of InsertIsolatedSimpleActivity and IntegrateExistingSimpleActivityAfterActivity overlapping in the complete right-hand side of the first rule yields the original grammar rule InsertSimpleActivity. Note that the left-hand side of such a composed rule is the union of the left-hand sides of the original rules except for the transient part, i.e. the elements created by the first rule and consumed by the second. The right-hand side of the rule is created analogously. Here, the right-hand sides of both original rules are joined, again without the transient part. Furthermore, the NACs of both rules are added appropriately. As the two NACs expressing the isolation of the simple activity s to be integrated cannot be translated to the left-hand side of InsertSimpleActivity since s does not exist there, they are dropped.

In this setting, rule IntegrateExistingSimpleActivityAfterActivity is a *residual rule* of the basic rule InsertIsolatedSimpleActivity and the grammar rule InsertSimpleActivity. All residual rules of basic and grammar rules can specify quick fixes. It is up to the editor designer to decide which subset of residual rules should be offered to the user.

10.4.4 Editor Generation

A model-driven approach to DSML editor development allows one to generate fully functional model editors, making it easier to develop DSMLs and use them in model-based software development. The underlying editor specification can use a metamodel or a graph grammar. Since it is tedious to define the operations of an editor by hand, these specifications should be inferred automatically from the underlying language specification.

In the following, we summarise which operations can be deduced from a metamodel or a graph grammar. Given a metamodel, language-specific basic operations can be generated. Remember that these operations do not necessarily preserve the well-formedness of models. Two useful types of complex operations are refactorings and quick fixes. They cannot be deduced automatically from metamodels, but have to be added programmatically.

Given a graph grammar, all its rules specify consistency-preserving editing operations. Delete operations can be deduced by inverting grammar rules. For each type of model element, a change operation such as renameActivity can be added. In addition, complex editing operations can be specified manually by composing existing operations. New operations are specified as additional transformation rules that are composed from existing ones. Finally, quick fix rules can be deduced by subdividing the rules mentioned above into basic and residual rules.

10.5 Interpreter Semantics

For a DSML modelling behaviour, an executable interpreter semantics can be adequate. Requirements for operational semantics can be captured informally first. To design an interpreter semantics, an example-based approach is helpful, where example patterns before and after its execution are specified for each action. These examples can be considered as preliminary steps towards the precise definition of an interpreter semantics.

In the following, we present the definition of an interpreter semantics by graph transformation rules. The approach is closely related to dynamic metamodelling as presented in [95], using collaboration diagrams typed over the language meta-model to specify interpreter steps. Collaboration diagrams can be specified as graph transformation rules.

To define system behaviour, we extend the abstract syntax of the DSML to represent the current state. To interpret, for example, an activity diagram, it is necessary to mark the current activity to be executed. This means that a marker is set at the start activity at the beginning and moved along the specified control flow as the execution proceeds. As an example, the interpreter semantics of well-formed activity diagrams is shown below. We assume that all the diagrams to be interpreted are syntactically correct, i.e. belong to the (slightly extended) DSML defined.

Of the different kinds of semantics for graph transformation systems presented in Chapter 3, labelled transition systems are the most appropriate to represent the behaviour of an interpreter. All possible states and transitions are specified, branching and termination can be studied directly, and parameters can provide additional detail about transitions. Transformation units can be useful for specifying complex interpreter steps that should not be interrupted. An interpreter of statecharts, for example, may combine several state changes into one larger step to implement a *run-to-completion* semantics [127].

Example 10.3 (interpreting well-formed activity models). To define an interpreter semantics of well-formed activity diagrams, we need a slight extension of the alphabet. We choose a "current" marker to point to the current activity. It is depicted in activity diagrams by an additional arrow in the upper left corner of an activity, as seen in Fig. 10.17. Alternative visualisations, for example, using a different fill colour or border, are also possible.

The execution of an activity diagram starts with marking the current state. We always begin at the start activity, and thus the marker is set there. This action (specified by rule start()) and all other interpreter actions are specified by the rules in Fig. 10.17. After marking the start activity, rule nextAfterStart() can be applied. Its target activity is a simple one. Similar rules can handle decision or end activities. Rule next() executes a sequence of simple activities while rule decision(x:String) handles a decision, causing a branching of control flow. Since we do not formalise the syntax and semantics of guard conditions here, the choice of branch is an input parameter. A rule for joining the control flow would look similar to rule next() where the target is a merge activity. A separate rule is needed to handle end activities. Once the end activity is reached, the current state marker is deleted by rule finish() and the current interpreter run is finished.

To see that all interpreter runs terminate, consider that rule start() can be applied to a well-formed activity diagram only once and all other rules process exactly one activity. We never insert additional markers, so the number of markers is at most one. Moreover, rule finish() deletes a marker at an end

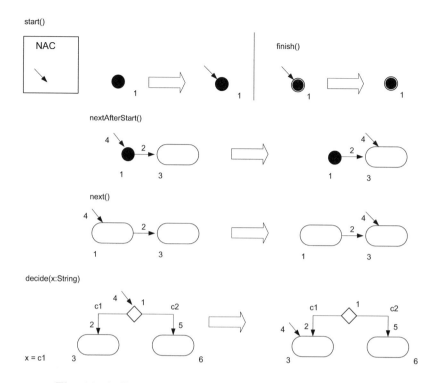

Fig. 10.17. Interpreter rules for well-formed activity diagrams

activity, and there is always at least one end activity in a well-formed activity diagram. The simple activity diagrams we consider here do not contain cycles, and thus they all describe finite control flows.

With a fully interpreted language for guards, it could happen that interpreter runs cannot terminate in an end activity, i.e. if neither of the two guards at a decision holds. However, assuming that c2 is always the negation of c1, in each state exactly one of the two conditions is true and the execution can proceed deterministically. This can be achieved by setting c2 to otherwise. □

As with the informal grammar rules in Fig. 10.12, we have presented the interpreter rules using the concrete syntax of activity diagrams, extended by a current state marker. It is easy to see how they could be translated into a representation based on a suitably extended metamodel.

10.6 Language Evolution

A DSML has to adapt to changing requirements, for example, due to new demands or an improved understanding of the target domain. DSML evolution affects the language specification as well as its tool support. This can render existing models invalid, so they have to be migrated to the new version of the language. If the DSML is specified by a metamodel, we consider the new version of the abstract syntax as a target metamodel for a model transformation implementing the migration.

Example 10.4 (language evolution). Based on the abstract syntax graph in Fig. 10.4, we want to elaborate further the Next relations between activities. They will be called Transitions and their inscriptions will be removed (because they are empty apart from decision branches). Instead, inscriptions will be moved to guards, a new type of element. Furthermore, fork and join activities will be included in activity diagrams. The metamodel in Fig. 10.4 can be transformed by the applications of suitable evolution rules to perform all desired changes. These evolution rules include renaming a type, extracting an attribute to a new type, and adding new types and relations. The result is shown in Fig. 10.18.

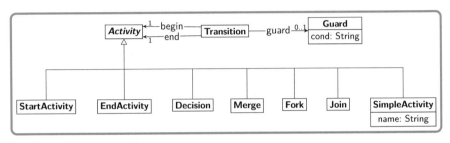

Fig. 10.18. Abstract syntax graph for simple activity models after evolution

New types of activities require new language constraints, extending the set of constraints on page 221:

8. (a) Each fork activity has one incoming and two outgoing transitions.
   (b) Analogously, each join activity has one outgoing and two incoming transitions.

Additionally, we need a rule insertForkJoin, similar to the rule insertDecision but substituting decision and merge activities by fork and join activities.   □

To migrate an existing model to this new language version, we distinguish several cases. (1) New types and relations represent new language features. Existing models do not have to be changed to incorporate them. In our example, this applies to fork and join activities. (2) A type renaming (such as Next to Transition) can be easily performed everywhere the type is used. (3) Migration is a little trickier when it comes to the incorporation of guards. Only if an inscription is non-empty, it should be replaced by a guard. Otherwise, the inscription should just be removed. Further cases of model migration are imaginable. In general, we should keep as much as information as possible from the existing model. In [116], Gruschko et al. classified metamodel changes into *non-breaking, breaking and resolvable*, and *breaking and unresolvable*. Changes are non-breaking if instance models do not have to be migrated at all, as in our case (1). They are breaking and resolvable if model migrations can be performed automatically, as in cases (2) and (3). If a metamodel change is classified as unresolvable, model migrations need further information and guidance.

10.7 Summary and Further Reading

The contribution of this chapter has been to show that graph grammars are a natural means to define DSMLs. A graph grammar based on a metamodel may offer a constructive view of a language. A grammar is of direct practical use for the design of editing operations, not only for create operations (as specified by the grammar rules) but for all standard operations. In addition, graph transformation is well suited to defining an interpreter semantics for a given DSML.

In the following, we relate our graph-grammar-based approach to prominent methods for DSML specification in the literature. In [199], Mariott and Meyer discussed two types of approach to defining visual languages: while logic-based approaches such as metamodelling have their roots in artificial intelligence, grammar-based approaches originate in theoretical linguistics and formal language theory. The focus of this chapter is on abstract syntax. Concrete syntax either is partly integrated (e.g. through the visual representation of model elements) or has to be specified separately in a concrete syntax structure related to the abstract syntax. A comprehensive overview of existing approaches to syntax definition for visual modelling languages was given by Tveit in her dissertation [279]. Owing to their popularity, she focussed on metamodel-based approaches.

The metamodelling approach to the definition of domain-specific languages has been widely adopted. It is declarative, with structural information and well-formedness constraints specified in a logic-based form, and has resulted in a variety of tool environments supporting visual editor generation, among others. As a representative, MetaEdit+ [211, 276] supports the definition and generation of different kinds of visual editor such as diagram, table and matrix editors. Moreover, it supports multilanguage integration and multi-user modelling. In addition, there are generation facilities for code and documentation. Further tool environments of this kind are GME [111] and Marama [210]. EMF [264] and the Graphical Modelling Framework (GMF) are in the same category.

Grammar-based approaches to define domain-specific modelling languages are established for textual languages. For example, Xtext [291] uses EBNF-like grammars to define the syntax of domain-specific languages. Such a grammar is translated to a metamodel for the definition of model transformations, for example, for interpreting and translating domain-specific models. It may also be used as a basis to develop a visual editor for the specified DSML, as in the GMF approach.

In the literature, there are various forms of grammar-based approaches to visual-language definition extending string or tree grammars as in, for example, [65], [156] and [256]. In these approaches, multidimensional structures are encoded in strings or trees, usually via special attributes referring to other model elements. The approach DEViL [255] presented by Schmidt, for example, is based on tree grammars and distinguishes three kinds of attributes to represent data values, references and container structures. Similarly to EMF, a visual model is represented in a tree structure induced by containers. String-based grammars are less established as a means to specify visual domain-specific languages, possibly because the need for complex encodings to capture multidimensional representations hampers usability and results in scalability issues for parsers and other tools.

Graph grammars allow one to express multidimensional structures more directly as graphs. The main graph-grammar-based approaches to visual-language definition were presented and compared in [11]. Although this approach is feasible in principle, we are convinced that an integration of metamodelling and graph transformation has the highest potential to enable advanced DSML definition. To support, for example, instance generation, a graph grammar can be deduced from a metamodel as presented in [91, 271]. To capture OCL constraints, they are translated to graph constraints in [239], and further to preconditions of graph grammar rules in [121]. Corresponding tool support was presented in [222].

Since graphs and graph transformation can be applied on different levels of abstraction, they can also be used in continuous language engineering. Co-evolution based on graph transformation of metamodels and instance models has been investigated in [275, 274] and [197]. In this line of research, transformation rules for metamodel evolution are used to automatically deduce default migration rules, which may be customised as long as well-formedness of models is preserved.

Improving Models and Understanding Model Changes

In model-based software development, models are primary artefacts that represent many aspects of a software system. In software evolution in particular, models are used to provide an overview of the current version of the software, to redesign it and to generate code from the redesigned model. Evolution may be driven by changes in the environment, new feature requests or the need to improve the software. In model-based software engineering, especially the last two phenomena lead to model changes. When one is comparing models before and after evolution, it is important to understand their differences. This chapter presents the use of graph transformation to specify and analyse model improvements as well as to understand complex model changes.

Software quality assurance frequently leads back to the quality assurance of the models involved. While there are standards for software quality and quality assurance processes in general, such standards do not exist for *model quality assurance*. A widely accepted approach is the 6C goals of Mohagheghi et al. [215], who proposed six quality categories for models. It remains open how they can be applied to DSMLs.

Refactoring [103] is a widely adopted technique to improve the structure of object-oriented software systems while preserving their behaviour. To identify design issues, the concept of code smells has been developed. Both concepts have been transferred to models, especially those using UML. Here, we propose a quality assurance approach that can be adapted and applied to any DSML.

In [24], a model quality assurance process was presented that can be adapted to project-specific and domain-specific needs. This process is based on static model analysis using model smells. Based on the analysis results, appropriate model refactoring steps may be performed. To define domain-specific model smells and refactorings, Arendt et al. followed the Goal–Question–Metric (GQM) approach [35]. A model quality aspect is stated as a goal, and then specific questions have to be developed, resulting in the definition of model smells. These are used to find out if a model has to be refactored. This means that, for a given refactoring to be applicable, a specified set of smells has to be detected.

© Springer Nature Switzerland AG 2020
R. Heckel, G. Taentzer, *Graph Transformation for Software Engineers*,
https://doi.org/10.1007/978-3-030-43916-3_11

Although smell detection and refactoring can be automated, deciding what to refactor and which refactoring to apply remains a difficult manual process, made more complex by conflicts and dependencies between refactoring operations. If language engineers specify refactorings by graph transformation rules, they can use the CDA technique (as presented in Section 4.2) to detect potential conflicts and dependencies that are implicit in their causal relations [208]. The results of this analysis can help a modeller to make an informed decision about which refactoring is most suitable in a given context and for what reason. Concretely, the following questions may be answered:

- What are the alternatives to a selected refactoring, i.e. are there other mutually exclusive refactorings that address the same design smell?
- What other refactorings need to be applied first in order to make the selected refactoring applicable?
- What other refactorings are still applicable after applying the selected refactoring?

With respect to smells, additional questions occur:

- What refactoring is able to resolve a selected smell?
- What new smells may occur after a refactoring has been performed?

A language engineer can specify a model smell by a graph pattern. Such a pattern can be regarded as an identical graph transformation rule with the pattern as both its left- and right-hand side. A dependency analysis of all rules specifying smells and refactorings is able to answer the questions above.

Complex refactoring processes lead to an evolution of both models and software systems. A basic prerequisite for managing the evolution of model-based software is to *detect and understand changes at model level*. The currently available model differencing tools, however, operate on low-level, sometimes even tool-specific model representations. Line-based differencing tools group changes line by line. While this is acceptable for textual models, it is not adequate for visual models. Storing a visual model in a textual format allows one to exchange models between tools, but such a textual format does not represent the model at the right level of granularity to be understood by the user or analysed effectively by a differencing tool.

A better way to represent a model is an abstract syntax tree. Such a representation is usually not shown to the user either, so a model in abstract syntax will be difficult to understand. Using a tree-based format, model differences reported elementwise are still difficult to understand. A more concise and syntax-independent form is needed to report complex model changes.

Investigating model editing processes more closely, we consistently found certain recurring atomic changes. Hence, it makes sense to encapsulate them as editing operations (see also Chapter 10) and to use those to communicate changes. This means that, instead of reporting changes in each model element individually, editing operations are reported together with their arguments. Linking model differencing to model editing, they can be presented at a higher level of abstraction. Editing operations have been shown to form adequate building blocks for understanding of complex model changes [158, 159].

Our second contribution in this chapter is to show how graph transformation can help modellers to understand complex changes. Editing operations encapsulate semantically connected model changes. As pointed out in Chapter 10, the specification of an editing operation by a graph transformation rule appears natural, since model editing is usually pattern-based and local. Larger model changes are reported by so-called editing scripts, i.e. partially ordered sets of operations with their arguments. Their partial order stems from their causal dependencies. Note that a resulting script does not need to reflect the actual editing process performed. It is a representative, but optimised version of editing processes with the same outcome. This representation is minimal in the sense of using the smallest number of operations to yield the change considered. Instead of reporting various small model changes, such a script reports the building blocks of a change process.

This chapter starts with an example of refactoring in Section 11.1. Thereafter, we consider a widely used definition of model quality as a basis to specify model smells and refactorings by graph transformation rules in Section 11.2. These specifications are used as a prerequisite for analysing refactoring dependencies in Section 11.3. Finally, we consider high-level model differencing based on editing operations in Section 11.4.

Since this chapter uses typed attributed graph transformation systems with control, it helps comprehension to be aware of the material in Chapters 1 to 3. In addition, CDA introduced in Section 4.2 is used to analyse conflicts and causal dependencies between refactorings and editing operations.

11.1 An Example of Model Refactoring

Class models are basic ingredients of model-based software development. They are often used to design the core structures of a software system, starting with the domain model of high-level concepts and relations. In the following, we consider a simple domain model for a university calendar which shows some bad smells. They may be erased by refactoring the model. There are several possible refactorings that would improve the model, but to choose an effective refactoring process it is necessary to know how individual refactoring steps interact, i.e. what their conflicts and dependencies are.

Our example domain model deals with lecturers who give courses and students who attend them. Courses consist of lectures, which may have additional tutorials. This model is shown in Fig. 11.1 using the standard notation for UML class diagrams. It contains some model smells, which may point to design problems:

1. Classes Student and Lecturer have similar attributes, namely firstName and forename as well as familyName and surname. This creates redundancy,

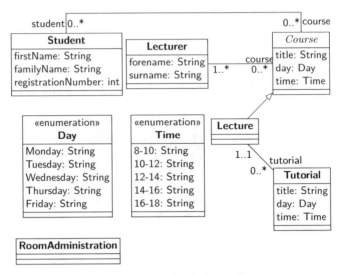

Fig. 11.1. Class model before refactoring

which may be reduced by introducing a common superclass holding these common attributes just once.

2. Similarly, class Tutorial has the same attributes as class Course.
3. There is an abstract class Course, which has just one subclass. This points to *speculative generality*, i.e. a design decision which is not transparent, introducing unnecessary complexity.
4. Class RoomAdministration is not connected to any other class. The class model seems to be incomplete.

To improve this model, several *refactorings* may be performed:

1. Rename Student.firstName to forename.
2. Rename Student.familyName to surname.
3. Create a superclass Person for classes Student and Lecturer.
4. Pull up attribute forename from classes Student and Lecturer to class Person. This refactoring presumes the first renaming mentioned above, as well as a common superclass.
5. Pull up attribute surname from classes Student and Lecturer to class Person. This refactoring presumes the second renaming mentioned above, as well as a common superclass.
6. Delete the unused class RoomAdministration to resolve the incompleteness.
7. Pull up the association tutorial from class Lecture to class Course.
8. Delete the empty subclass Lecture. This refactoring presumes that association tutorial has already been pulled up.
9. Insert an inheritance relation from class Tutorial to class Course and delete all attributes of class Tutorial.

This list of potential refactorings is quite long, even though the example model is small. As already stated, some refactorings need others to be performed beforehand, i.e. some of the refactorings presented are *dependent* on others. For example, refactorings 4 and 5 are dependent on refactorings 1 – 3. All five refactorings are needed to erase the redundancy detected.

At the same time, some of the listed refactorings are mutually exclusive: either association tutorial is pulled up and class Lecture is deleted as in refactorings 7 and 8, or the attributes of class Tutorial are pulled up as in refactoring 9. In the first case, we decide that class Lecture indicates a *speculative generality* and delete it, while the second solution keeps class Lecture for future enhancements.

Furthermore, we could also think of renaming Student.firstName and Student.familyName to forename and surname, creating a superclass Person and finally pulling up both attributes to this new superclass. These refactorings are in conflict with refactorings 1 – 5. We have to decide one way or the other:

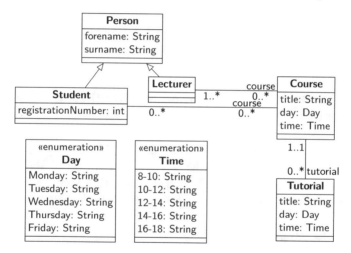

Fig. 11.2. Class model after refactoring

Figs. 11.2 and 11.3 show two possible results of refactoring:

1. Starting with the model in Fig. 11.1 and applying refactorings 1 – 8 yields the model in Fig. 11.2.
2. Starting with the model in Fig. 11.1 and applying refactorings 1 – 6 and 9 yields the model in Fig. 11.3.

It is clear that tool support is needed to perform complex model refactorings. Even in this small example, a number of refactorings are needed to erase a design flaw. In the following sections, we discuss definitions of model quality and how modellers can be improved it by detecting model smells and performing refactorings. Moreover, we show how language engineers can specify smells and refactorings by graph transformation rules and how the

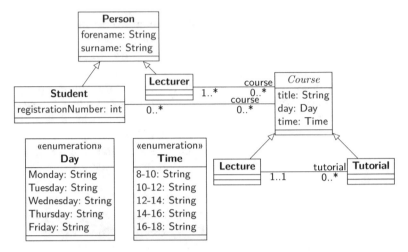

Fig. 11.3. Class model after an alternative refactoring

analysis of conflicts and dependencies can help modellers to make informed decisions about their refactoring processes.

11.2 Model Quality Assurance by Smell Detection and Refactoring

In the following, we present how model quality and quality assurance can be defined on the basis of graph transformation. We recall the established definition of model quality by Mohagheghi et al. [215], which will be used as guideline for defining domain-specific model smells and refactorings.

11.2.1 Model Quality

While software quality is concerned with the software system, model quality focuses on the quality of models in model-based development. A prominent approach to model quality are the 6C goals of Mohagheghi et al. [215]. Based on a systematic literature review, these authors identified six classes of model quality goals. Here, we recall part of the summary given in [24]:

1. *Correctness:* A model is *correct* if it meets the syntax and semantics of the given modelling language. Model elements should be used in the way defined and semantic ambiguities should not occur in models.
2. *Completeness:* A model is *complete* if it contains all relevant information, and if it is detailed enough according to its purpose.
3. *Consistency:* A model is *consistent* if it does not contain contradictions. This definition covers *horizontal consistency*, concerned with models or diagrams on the same level of abstraction, *vertical consistency*, covering

aspects of the model on different levels of abstraction, and *semantic consistency*, focusing on the meaning of the same element in different models or diagrams.

4. *Comprehensibility:* A model is *comprehensible* if it is understandable to the intended user, be they a human or a tool. In most of the literature, the focus is on comprehensibility to humans, including aspects such as the aesthetics of a diagram, the simplicity or complexity of the model, and using the correct type of diagram for the intended audience. This goal is also referred to as *pragmatic quality* in the literature.

5. *Confinement:* A model is *confined* if it suits the modelling purpose and the kind of system it represents. This definition also includes using the relevant diagrams on the right abstraction levels. Furthermore, a confined model does not have unnecessary information and is as simple as possible. Developing the right model for a given system and purpose also depends on selecting an adequate modelling language. This means that the modeller uses language concepts that are suitable for the intended purpose. Additional concepts should be used very sparsely or omitted entirely.

6. *Changeability:* A model is *changeable* if it can be evolved easily and continuously. This is important, since system requirements and context may evolve over time. Changeability should be supported by modelling languages and modelling tools as well.

Depending on the purpose of the model, some quality aspects may have higher priority than others. For example, comprehensibility of models is very important if the main purpose of modelling is to communicate between different stakeholders. In model-driven development, correctness plays an important role since code is generated from models.

To assess model quality, the methods proposed in the literature range from inspections, via metrics, errors and bad smells, to controlled experiments [215]. In the following, we focus on smell detection and show how graph transformation can help language engineers to specify smells. Since refactoring is the technique of choice to fix recognised model smells, we will later consider the specification of refactorings. Each specified smell serves as a precondition for at least one model refactoring. Therefore, it makes sense to analyse interdependencies between smells and refactorings. If specifications for both are given by graph transformation rules, this analysis is supported by CDA.

Assessing model quality by smells is a heuristic approach. Smells are just indications that certain parts of a model may violate specific quality aspects. To find out which smells are helpful for assessing a given quality, we follow the goal/question/metric (GQM) approach [35]. For stating an aspect of model quality as a goal, characteristic numbers have to be defined to assess this quality. An accepted approach is to formulate a range of questions which quantify the quality by specific metrics. For example, to measure confinement of class models for requirements elicitation, we may be interested in the following questions (based on [24]):

- Are there classes that are not used by any other model element? This is a typical case of unnecessary information in the model.
- Are there abstract classes not doing much? Again, this might be an indicator of unnecessary information in the model.
- Do similar attributes occur in more than one class? This might be a hint that the modeller is not using the inheritance concept of class models enough.

Model smells which can answer these questions are specified in the next section. They can serve as the basis for metrics measuring the number of smell occurrences in the model. The smaller these numbers are, the better is the quality of the model.

11.2.2 A Sample Modelling Language

As we have seen in the previous chapter, the internal structure of models is naturally specified by graphs while model changes can be specified by graph transformation rules. Moreover, we have seen how type graphs are used to define the types and relations of modelling languages.

In the following, we present the type graph for the simple class models used to analyse an application domain. It contains classes with attributes and associations, but no operations. Associations may hold multiplicities and roles, but are not further distinguished as, for example, aggregations or compositions. Multiplicities are given by lower and upper bounds in the form of natural numbers, or **unlimited** upper bounds. In addition, enumerations and primitive types are defined, but packages and comments are not. The resulting type graph is shown in Fig. 11.4.

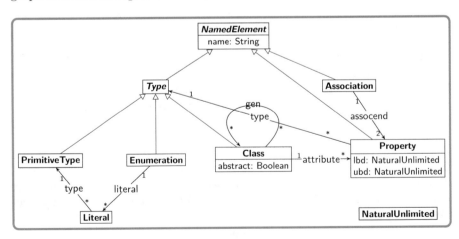

Fig. 11.4. Type graph for simple class models

The underlying structure of the class model in Fig. 11.1 can be considered as an instance graph of the type graph in Fig. 11.4. A snippet of this instance graph is shown in Fig. 11.5. This shows the abstract syntax of the association between classes Lecturer and Course, as well as the subclass Lecture. Note that title is the only attribute of class Course shown. The attributes of class Lecturer are omitted completely.

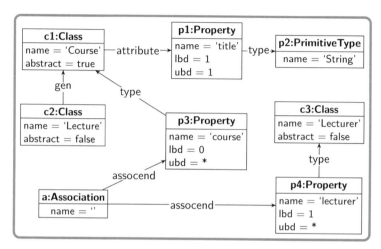

Fig. 11.5. Snippet of instance graph for the simple class diagram in Fig. 11.1

Example 11.1 (smells specification). Figure 11.6 shows how model smells can be specified by graph transformation rules. All these rules are graph queries, i.e. they do not change the graph but check for the existence or non-existence of graph patterns. If such a rule is applicable, its parameters are set. These are output parameters reporting the smells found, to be used in possible subsequent refactorings. Rule checkRedundantAttributes() = (p1,p2) reports on two different attributes with the same name and type in two different classes. Rule checkSpeculativeGenerality() = c checks for an abstract class c with fewer than two subclasses. Note that the separate NAC is needed here to express that two subclasses do not exist but one may exist, i.e. the whole structure in red shown in N must not exist. Finally, rule checkUnusedClass() = c checks if there is a class c that neither has attributes nor is used as the type of some property (attribute or association end). □

11.2.3 Specification of Model Refactorings

Effective tool support for refactoring should indicate continuously which refactoring operations are applicable to the current model. This involves checking the pre-conditions of these operations, initially without specifying any input parameters. If this check is passed and a refactoring is selected, it is followed

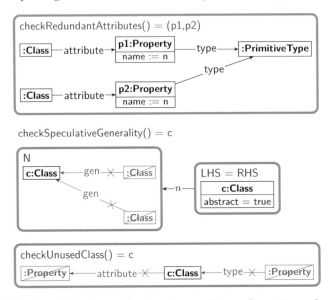

Fig. 11.6. Smell specification by graph transformation rules

by a conclusive precondition check taking into account the actual parameter values. This means that the initial precondition check determines if the basic pattern of the refactoring is present in the model. Once a refactoring is selected, its input parameters are set and the instantiated precondition is verified before the actual model manipulation takes place. Hence, we consider a refactoring as a three-step process, consisting of an *initial precondition check*, a *final precondition check* and the actual *model change*. This procedure presented in [24] was originally proposed and implemented in the Eclipse-based LTK technology [8] to specify program refactorings.

Example 11.2 (renaming). As a first example, we consider what is probably the most popular refactoring: renaming, in particular, the renaming of attributes. To apply this refactoring, we need to know the attribute to be renamed and the new name. The initial precondition AttributeExists() (shown on the left of Fig. 11.7) checks if there is at least one attribute in the model. In this case, this refactoring is applicable. The final precondition is specified by a controlled rule application, shown on the right of Fig. 11.7. This takes the selected attribute p and the new name n and checks that neither the owning class c nor any transitive parent or child class contains an attribute with the new name. This requires two loops, applied for as long as possible to transitively reach all parents and children. Note that in each new loop c is set to c' to go one step higher or lower in the inheritance hierarchy. Moreover, the new name should be non-empty (checked by rule checkClass()). If the final precondition is satisfied, the name of the attribute can be changed to the new name. This is done by rule renameAttribute, depicted on the left of Fig. 11.7. □

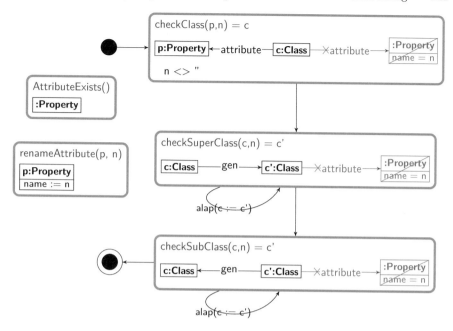

Fig. 11.7. Specification of refactoring renameAttribute

Example 11.3 (creating a superclass). Another popular refactoring is CreateSuperclass. This creates a new class as a superclass of one or more existing classes. This is necessary, for example, to eliminate redundant attributes or associations by pulling them up to a superclass, if such a superclass does not already exist. To apply this refactoring, we have to know the class(es) C that should get a new superclass and the name n of this new class. The initial precondition ClassExists() checks if there is at least one class in the model. If not, the refactoring is not applicable. The final precondition takes the new name n as input and checks if a class with this name already exists. If not, the actual model change by rule createSuperclass(C,n) creates a new class with name n as a superclass of the indicated classes C. (Note that C is a set parameter used in a multiobject.) The whole specification of this refactoring is shown in Fig. 11.8.   □

Example 11.4 (pulling up an attribute). To eliminate redundant attributes occurring in several subclasses of a common superclass, the refactoring pullUpAttribute can be used. It is applicable if there is any situation where an attribute may be pulled up. To do this, the attribute's name n has to be specified as well as the class s to which it should be moved. The initial precondition PullableAttributeExists() checks if there is an attribute in a subclass which may be pulled up. The final precondition, checkSubclasses(), takes the attribute name n and class s as input and checks if the corresponding attribute

Fig. 11.8. Specification of refactoring createSuperclass

is in all subclasses of class s and is not used by some association. With the final precondition satisfied, the attribute can be pulled up. This is done by rule pullUpAttribute() in Fig. 11.9, which moves the attribute from one subclass to its superclass and deletes the attributes with the same name from all other subclasses.   □

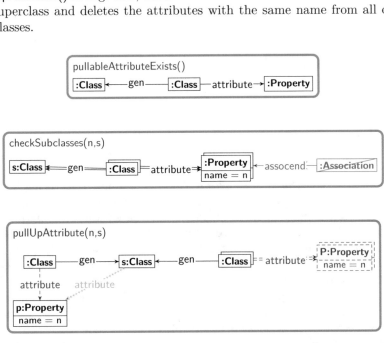

Fig. 11.9. Specification of refactoring pullUpAttribute

11.2.4 Discussion

Smell specification by graph transformation is useful for pattern-based smells. The pattern of interest can be directly specified in a rule using the abstract model syntax. Graph transformation is less useful for metrics-based smells, since counting of model elements is not specifically supported. If metrics-based smells focus on specific numbers of element occurrences, such as 0 or 1, or exactly, at most or at least n, however these are easy to encode in the left-hand side patterns of graph transformation rules.

As shown above, we follow the threefold specification approach for refactorings. The arguments given for smell specification carry over to the specification of preconditions. Thus, graph transformation is well suited for specifying pattern-based preconditions and potentially less suited for metrics-based ones. The specification of model changes by graph transformation rules is very natural.

For each model smell, several refactorings may be relevant. These are not necessarily all the refactorings applicable to the model, but a suitable subset able to eliminate the smell. For an unused class, for example, the renaming of this class is applicable, but would not eliminate the smell. The deletion of the unused class or the creation of contained properties would address the smell. The application of a refactoring poses the risk of creating new model smells. Hence, it is worthwhile to check the relationship between model refactorings and smells. An example of a refactoring that causes a smell is the insertion of a new element that completes a partial smell.

11.3 Analysing the Interplay of Refactorings

After having shown how model smells and refactorings can be specified by graph transformation rules, we now reason about the order in which refactorings should be performed. By considering their potential conflicts and dependencies, engineers can learn how design goals may be reached by refactorings. For example, the refactoring pullUpAttribute may require the refactoring renameAttribute to equip with the same name all those attributes being pulled up. Table 11.1 shows potential dependencies between selected refactorings. Whenever a refactoring shown in the top row may be dependent on a refactoring shown on the left, the table entry is +, otherwise −.

Note that a refactoring is dependent on another one if at least one rule of the first refactoring is dependent on a rule of the second one. Refactoring pullUpAttribute, for example, may be dependent on refactoring renameAttribute since its rule checkSubclasses may be dependent on rule renameAttribute. It may be necessary for attributes to be renamed before the check, such that all subclasses have an attribute with the same name.

Table 11.1. Overview of potential dependencies between selected refactorings

Potential dependencies	renameAttribute	createSuperclass	pullUpAttribute
renameAttribute	+	−	+
createSuperclass	−	+	+
pullUpAttribute	−	−	+

Potential conflicts indicate (possibly mutually exclusive) choices in the refactoring process. Potential conflicts between the set of refactorings considered above are shown in Table 11.2. If an attribute is pulled up, it cannot be renamed as an attribute of the original class, but only of the new one. Hence, despite a conflict, subsequent refactorings may still be applicable but not with the original parameters, i.e. they have to be adapted. If an attribute with name n is pulled up to a class with an attribute that should be renamed to n, this renaming cannot take place at all. So, either one or the other refactoring can take place, but not both. However, we have to keep in mind that these are only potential conflicts, i.e. they may or may not occur in actual refactoring scenarios. For example, not all renamings are in conflict, just those that rename the same model element (attribute).

Table 11.2. Overview of potential conflicts between selected refactorings

Potential conflicts	renameAttribute	createSuperclass	pullUpAttribute
renameAttribute	+	−	+
createSuperclass	−	+	−
pullUpAttribute	+	−	+

In the following, we consider some selected dependencies and conflicts in more detail.

Example 11.5 (dependency of pullUpAttribute on renameAttribute). The refactoring pullUpAttribute can only be performed if each subclass has an attribute with the same name. This check is done by rule checkSubclasses which is a rule with multiobjects. To find potential dependencies, here it is enough to consider dependencies of a rule where all multiobjects are replaced by single objects. We call the resulting rule checkSubclass. (Note, however, that this reduction to a simpler rule is not always possible; see [273, 44].) Figure 11.10 shows a change/use dependency of rules renameAttribute and checkSubclass. Rule renameAttribute prepares the attribute name such that it is found as an attribute of a subclass. Note that graph H_1 shows a minimal situation where rule renameAttribute has been applied and rule checkSubclass is applicable. In a similar way, rule renameAttribute is dependent on rule pullUpAttribute.   □

Example 11.6 (dependency of pullUpAttribute on createSuperclass). The refactoring pullUpAttribute can only be performed if there is already a superclass to which an attribute can be pulled up. Hence, there is a potential produce/use dependency with rule createSuperclass, as shown in Fig. 11.11. The first rule of the refactoring pullUpAttribute, i.e. rule pullableAttributeExists, is already dependent. Graph H_1 shows a minimal situation where rule createSuperclass has been applied and rule pullableAttributeExists is applicable such that its match uses the newly created superclass. Similarly, rules checkSubclass and pullUpAttribute are dependent on rule createSuperclass.   □

Example 11.7 (conflicts between renameAttribute and pullUpAttribute).
Figure 11.12 shows a conflict between rules renameAttribute and checkSubclass.

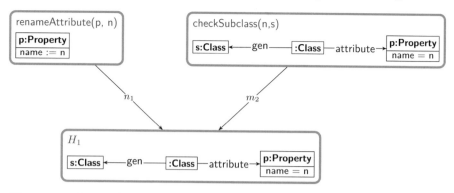

Fig. 11.10. Change/use dependency between refactorings renameAttribute and pullUpAttribute

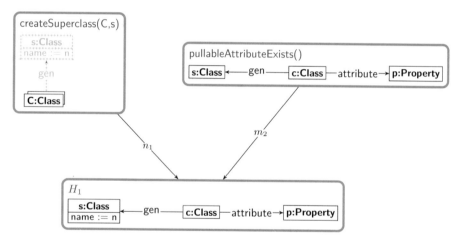

Fig. 11.11. Produce/use dependency between refactorings createSuperclass and pullableAttributeExists

(Again, we do not consider rule checkSubclasses, which contains multiobjects, but restrict our consideration to the basic rule checkSubclass, which is enough to find conflicts.) The conflict is caused by rule renameAttribute and can be solved by performing just one of the two refactorings. One solution is to not perform the renaming or to take it back, i.e. to rename the attribute back to its original name. In that case, the attribute can still be pulled up. Another solution is to perform the renaming and not to pull up the attribute.

In turn, rule pullUpAttribute can cause conflicts with rule checkClass of the refactoring renameAttribute. Figure 11.13 shows a delete/use conflict where an attribute link is deleted but is needed to check the existence of the attribute in a given class. This conflict can be resolved by deciding on one or the other refactoring and omitting the other one, or by first pulling up the attribute and renaming it in the context of the new class.

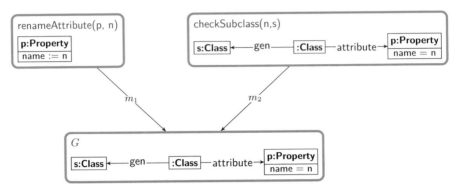

Fig. 11.12. Conflict between refactorings renameAttribute and pullUpAttribute

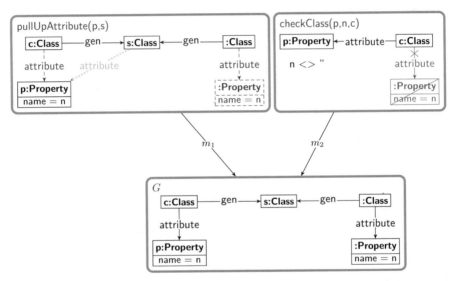

Fig. 11.13. Delete/use conflict between refactorings pullUpAttribute and renameAttribute

Rule pullUpAttribute may also cause produce/forbid conflicts with rule checkClass, as shown in Fig. 11.14. The application of rule pullUpAttribute creates an attribute link such that the superclass does get an attribute with name n. Hence, rule checkClass is not applicable any more, since its negative application condition is no longer satisfied. This conflict can be resolved by not applying one or the other refactoring, or by renaming the attribute to another name.   □

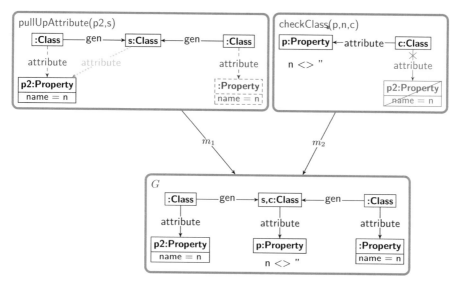

Fig. 11.14. Produce/forbid conflict between refactorings pullUpAttribute and renameAttribute

11.4 Understanding Model Changes

In model-based software development, models continuously evolve, not only due to refactoring but also in response to changing requirements, software changes or other external factors. Therefore, models can have many versions during a system's lifetime. A clear picture of all model versions, of their successor relationships and other dependencies, and of the changes between revisions is essential to understand and plan the co-evolution of a system and its model. This means that developers need adequate tools for model comparison, patching and merging. However, the tools currently available typically display and operate with low-level model changes based on their internal model representations. Presenting a large number of low-level changes to the user does not help their understanding of model evolution histories.

11.4.1 Model Differencing

In [158, 159], the calculation and propagation of model changes was lifted to a higher abstraction level. Semantically connected model changes are encapsulated and reported as invocations of editing operations. Moreover, several such invocations may be grouped together to edit scripts used as model patches. A prerequisite for this approach is to specify all the editing operations of interest. This is typically the task of language designers, supported by modellers if specific operations are needed.

   As demonstrated in this and the previous chapter, graph transformations are useful for specifying editing operations for models, especially refactorings.

This is advantageous not only for developing user-friendly model editors, but also for user-friendly model differencing tools. Editing operations are designed to encapsulate semantically connected model changes. Therefore it is worthwhile to present reports on model changes at this level. This means that for each DSML, one needs to specify all relevant editing operations. As shown in [162], most of the standard editing operations can be generated from a metamodel, i.e. this work can be largely automated.

Example 11.8 (model change). Considering the model versions in Figs. 11.1 and 11.2, a modeller wants to be informed which editing operations have led to this evolution. As refactorings 1 – 8 have taken place, they result in the following set of low-level changes:

- changeValue(firstName,"name","forename")
- changeValue(familyName,"name","surname")
- addNode("Class","Person",true)
- addReference(student,"gen",person)
- addReference(lecturer,"gen",person)
- deleteNode("Class",roomAdministration)
- deleteReference(lectureProp,"type",lecture)
- addReference(lectureProp,"type",course)
- deleteReference(lecturer,"attribute",forename)
- addReference(person,"attribute",forename)
- deleteReference(student,"attribute",firstName)
- deleteNode("Property",firstName)
- deleteReference(lecturer,"attribute",surname)
- addReference(person,"attribute",surname)
- deleteReference(student,"attribute",familyName)
- deleteNode("Property",familyName)
- deleteReference(lecture,"gen",course)
- deleteNode("Class",lecture)

Different types of low-level changes are represented with corresponding details. Value changes are shown by referring to the model node (a metaclass instance), its meta-attribute and the new value. A new model node is added by setting its type, name and further meta-attributes. References are added or deleted, each referring to its source node, type and target node. In this example, we use the following identifiers for nodes: if unique, we use their name in lower case; for properties whose names refer to association roles equalling the lowercase variant of their type, names are extended by "Prop".

As this example shows, a few changes in a small model can already result in a long list of low-level updates. For better understanding, we want to infer higher-level editing operations. For example, the last two changes in the list are caused by the refactoring deleteEmptySubclass.   □

To find out which low-level changes belong together and form so-called semantic change sets, a language engineer specifies editing operation rules first. Since each operation leads to a characteristic pattern of low-level change actions, a modeller tries to find occurrences of these patterns. To do so, each editor rule is translated to a *recognition rule*. Note that recognition rules operate on a data structure of low-level changes, while editor rules are applied to domain-specific models.

Example 11.9 (recognition of editing operation). For rule pullUpAttribute in Fig. 11.9, its pattern of low-level changes is

- deleteReference(c, "attribute", p)
- addReference(s, "attribute", p)
- deleteReference(c', "attribute", p')
- deleteNode("Property", p')

where s is a class, p is a property of class s, c is a subclass of s, for all c' in C (the set of subclasses of s except c) and all p' in P (a set of properties in subclasses of s with the same name as p). Since C or P may be empty, at least two low-level changes are recognised as editing operations. Depending on the number of sub-classes of s, there may be many more. If s has, for example, three sub-classes, eight low-level changes are grouped.   □

Since a recognition rule just adds information about a pattern found and checks application conditions on model elements and references only, the applications of such rules are always conflict free. Hence, they can be applied in parallel. Considering the set of all possible applications of recognition rules to a given low-level change set, some low-level changes may be recognised in two or even more editor steps while others may not be recognised at all.

If one operation creates an element which is deleted by a subsequent one, this transient effect is not recognisable by comparing the initial version of the model with the final one. This means that not all low-level changes of the corresponding editor steps can be recognised by an algorithm that works without backtracking. Hence, the corresponding steps cannot be recognised. In cases where a complete editing operation is undone, many transient effects occur that do not affect the new version of the model and hence are not isolated as low-level changes. In such a case, neither the original editor step is recognised nor its inverse. This means that a language engineer has to check that the initial editor rule set does not have transient effects other than those due to applying inverse rules. We call such a rule set well-formed.

Given a well-formed rule set, it can still happen that some low-level changes are matched to two or more editor steps. However, we are looking for a complete partitioning of the set of low-level changes into editor steps. It is possible that some recognised editor steps have to be ruled out in order to find an optimal set partition. For example, a combination of actions that delete and add a reference can be interpreted as a move of a reference. Hence, pulling up an attribute can also be considered as moving a reference and deleting a set of properties. However, a modeller typically wants to find the minimum number of editor steps, because understanding model changes is easier for a smaller number of reported steps.

In [158], the following strategy was presented: First, all low-level change sets are recognized that do not overlap with any other and can be associated to a unique editing operation. Second, all low-level change sets that are entirely included in other sets and do not overlap with further ones, are discarded. This fits our overall strategy of finding the minimum number of editor steps. This case occurs whenever a complex operation is composed from smaller ones or a core operation has one or more extensions. Finally, the remaining low-level change sets are partially overlapping. This reduced set-partitioning problem has to be solved by combinatorial optimisation. From a practical point of view, this is not a problem since case studies have shown that this case occurs very rarely.

11.4.2 Model Patching

If a modeller wants to patch model changes to another version, it is not enough to infer a set of editing operations; the actual arguments are needed to execute the actual steps. Moreover, it has to be clear in what order the steps have to be applied, such that all of them are applicable and there is no need for backtracking. If an output parameter of one operation is used directly by a subsequent one as an input parameter, the sequential dependency is obvious. However, it cannot be reduced to parameter passing in general. The execution of an operation call may also depend on other operation calls if, for example, elements are deleted which are forbidden by subsequent steps. To analyse all possible sequences of two editing operation calls by hand can be tedious. Instead, a modeller can apply CDA to find all potential dependencies between operations. Thereafter, the list of potential dependencies is traversed with respect to the corresponding recognition rules. The corresponding minimal difference graphs is tried to be embedded into the actual model difference graph: given two editor steps $G \Longrightarrow_{r_1,m_1} H_1$, $H_1 \Longrightarrow_{r_2,m_2} H_2$, they are actually dependent if the co-match $m_1' : R_1 \to H_1$ and match m_2 overlap in at least one element. All the information gathered is synthesised in an *editing script*, i.e. a partially ordered set of editing operation calls. In the following, we present an example of an editing script deduced from the set of low level changes presented above.

Example 11.10 (editing script). The low-level changes shown in the previous example can be grouped into the following editing steps, forming a partially ordered set of operation calls. All operation calls in item 1 can take place immediately in any order. Thereafter, operation calls in item 2 become executable. Note that these calls are not dependent with respect to parameter passing, but are dependent owing to pattern-based dependencies:

1. renameAttribute(firstName,"forename"),
   renameAttribute(familyName,"surname"),
   createSuperclass({student,lecturer} ,"Person"),
   deleteUnusedClass(roomAdministration),
   pullUpAssociation(tutorial,course)
2. pullUpAttribute(forename,person),
   pullUpAttribute(surname,person),
   deleteEmptySubclass(lecture)

We see that all the refactorings performed are reported as model changes. Note that only their actual change rules are listed. Precondition checks are not reported, since they do not cause any model changes. Abstract syntax objects are referred to by their internal names (usually equal to their class names). If two model elements (especially attributes and associations) have the same name, their name spaces are given as well to distinguish them, for example, Course.title and Tutorial.title (not needed in this example).   □

An editing script summarises model changes in a compact way. Such a script can be used to report on model differences or to provide a patch to be applied to another model version. A patch is applicable to a model version if there is at least one transformation sequence that applies all editing rules along the dependency-induced partial order. This technique is correct in the sense that a patch can always be applied to the original model version it was deduced from. Trying to apply it to any other model version may, of course, fail [160]. Several kinds of problem may occur. If a modeller chooses an argument of an editor step incorrectly, the step may be performed in the wrong context of the model version or may not be executable at all. If a required model element does not exist or a forbidden one does exist, the step involved, as well as any dependent steps, cannot be performed.

If an editing script can be applied only partly, automatic model patching should be enhanced by user interaction. A modeller may solve these problems in different ways: either the script is not applied at all; the editing script is applied partially, leading to a meaningful result; or problematic editor steps are adapted manually such that the script can be applied completely.

11.5 Summary and Further Reading

Since models play an important role in model-based software engineering, modellers need to be supported in working with them. This chapter shows how models can be improved by detecting model smells and performing refactorings. Larger refactoring processes can consist of a number of basic refactoring steps which have to be arranged such that the intended overall redesign can performed. We have seen that CDA can help to find causal dependencies between refactorings to help planing the redesign process. Moreover, it supports the modeller in finding conflicts between alternative refactorings that have to be resolved.

After a period of model evolution, including but not limited to refactoring, stakeholders such as system analysts, model engineers and software developers need to understand the changes performed. This chapter also shows how graph transformation can help in providing a high-level view of model changes, by grouping semantically connected changes into *editing operations*. A partial order of editing operations, called an *editing script*, represents a minimal editing process leading from one major model version to the next one. CDA can be used again, to find causal dependencies between operations.

11.5.1 Improving Models

The initial idea of specifying refactorings by graph transformation to analyse their conflicts and dependencies by critical pair analysis was due to [208]. It was taken up by Arendt et al. to specify not only refactorings but also model metrics and smells, as a basis for a model quality assurance process [23, 24, 21]. The semantics preservation of refactorings based on graph transformation was further investigated in [241, 240]. The authors of those publications showed that all the specified refactorings preserve the given semantics. This consideration also covers the case in which a refactoring consists of several steps that are not semantics-preserving individually, but only as whole. The refactoring of architectural models based on graph transformation was presented in [43]. The main contribution was to show behaviour preservation using CSP [146] as the semantic domain. Heckel et al. used refactoring by graph transformation to transform legacy software architectures to service-oriented ones [135].

11.5.2 Understanding Model Changes

The second part of this chapter presents an approach to lifting low-level model differences to a higher level using editing operations. Kehrer et al. presented more details of this approach in [158, 159, 160, 157], especially the construction of recognition rules from editor rules. Kehrer et al. [160] addressed the parallel evolution of model variants as they occur in automation engineering. Local improvements occurring in one variant have to be propagated to other variants or back-ported to a central base version.

High-level model differencing has been applied in a number of case studies to show the flexibility of the approach and the usefulness of lifting model differences. The parallel evolution of model variants in industrial plant automation was considered in [160]. Complex differences between feature models were investigated to reason about software product-line evolution [53]. The semi-automatic co-evolution of architecture and fault tree models was considered in [106]. As the use of textual domain-specific modelling languages is an important trend in model-driven engineering, Kehrer et al. showed that high-level differencing can also be adapted to a textual modelling language using simple Web models as an example [161]. This approach is also useful for reversing engineering Java software systems to obtain model histories to be analysed. The purpose of that work was to synthesise realistic test models [293].

11.5.3 Tool Support

The concepts and methods presented in this chapter have led to Eclipse-based tools, namely EMF Refactor [3] for quality assurance of models. EMF Refactor supports language engineers in specifying metrics, smells and refactorings for domain-specific modelling languages, not only in a graph-transformation-based manner provided by Henshin, but also in Java, OCL and other model transformation languages such as EWL [4].

For high-level model differencing, the tool environment SiLift [7] has been developed. As a prerequisite, it supports the specification of editing operations for DSLs. For a given change as reported by, for example, EMF Compare [2], an editing script is generated. Several evaluations have been presented in [159, 53, 106] to show that the proposed techniques and tools are correct and useful. The generated editing scripts were shown to be correct in the sense that they are always applicable to the original model and lead to the new model version. Moreover, it was shown that a script raises the level of abstraction in the sense that the algorithm finds as many complex operations as possible.

Translating and Synchronising Models

In model-based software engineering, models are used to represent systems on a higher level of abstraction. They allow developers to abstract from implementation details, focussing on expressing solutions in terms of domain concepts. Model translations to one or more implementation platforms support a *model-driven* approach, allowing reuse across platforms, reducing development costs and improving software quality. Model translations have also been used for analysing models by translating them to formal specification languages and analysing the corresponding formal models. Based on their visual representation and mathematical background, graph transformations can be used to specify model-to-model and model-to-text transformations in an intuitive and precise way supporting execution and formal analysis.

Individual models can represent specific but potentially overlapping views of a system. For example, class models and sequence diagrams both contain information about operations. In order to provide a basis for further development and analysis, such overlapping views have to be kept consistent with each other as well as with the software artefacts they model. In a forward engineering scenario, this consistency can be achieved *by construction* when transforming models into implementations automatically. If there is a change on either side, for example, in the class model or the code, the consistency relation between them can break, and the views are not consistent any more.

Updating a view manually after each change of the other view is tedious and error prone. Instead, we need a mechanism to translate and synchronise models automatically. Model transformation languages and tools have been developed for this purpose. Their intention is to provide dedicated support for the development of model translation and synchronisation tools, at a higher level of abstraction than a general-purpose programming language. Graph transformation provides one such high-level model transformation approach.

As indicated above, *model translations* can be performed for different reasons. They are required for realising mappings between models, from models to code or other implementation-level artefacts, or vice versa, or for mapping

© Springer Nature Switzerland AG 2020
R. Heckel, G. Taentzer, *Graph Transformation for Software Engineers*,
https://doi.org/10.1007/978-3-030-43916-3_12

software models to mathematical models used for analysis. Model transformations can relate models at the same level of abstraction, for example, if they describe different components or aspects of the same system. Transformations between models at the same level are called *horizontal*. In contrast, *vertical* transformations describe mappings between models and other artefacts at different levels of abstractions, such as a mapping from a model to code [209]. In both cases it is typical that the source and target artefacts are expressed in different languages, i.e. they are defined over different metamodels. This type of model transformation is called *exogenous* [209] or a *model translation*.

As a running example throughout this chapter, we will use an exogenous vertical transformation that is one of the most popular case studies in the literature: the translation of object-oriented models into relational database schemas, also known as *object–relational (O–R) mapping* [40, 37].

The alternative to exogenous model transformations are *endogenous* ones, between models over the same metamodel. Such transformations have been used in the previous two chapters to describe DSMLs by graph grammars, derive basic and advanced model editor operations and model fixes, and specify smell detection and model refactoring, as well as model differencing.

When applying model transformations to generate models, a new model is produced after each transformation step, i.e. such a transformation is performed *out-place*. All other usage scenarios modify the current model and therefore require *in-place* transformations. Endogenous model transformations may be performed in-place or out-place, dependent on their purpose. Model translations are intentionally out-place, since new artefacts are computed. However, they may be implemented as in-place transformations computing an extension of the given model to represent the translation result. To access this result, it may be read out from the derived graph using a projection to the types of the target metamodel.

There are many model transformation approaches and languages [68] targeting different kinds of transformations. Since our focus is on model translations, we consider out-place transformation languages, such as ATL [152], ETL [170], QVT (both QVT–O and QVT–R) [177, 266] and triple graph grammars [260]. Alternatively, language engineers can use general-purpose programming languages to specify model translations. The choice of a specific transformation language may depend on objective characteristics, such as expressiveness, user-friendliness and tool support, but language engineers also tend to stick with languages they are familiar with. A strong argument for choosing a graph-transformation-based language is that it allows a declarative definition of model translations in the sense that the way graph patterns are navigated does not have to be specified. The underlying pattern matcher implements strategies to find patterns. Furthermore, the visual layout of transformation rules may be helpful in developing and maintaining translations of complex structures as they can occur in models. Based on their mathematical background and theory, graph transformation languages also come with powerful analysis techniques to reason about model translations.

For a model translation to be well defined we expect that, given a valid input model, the translation yields a correct model as a result. To verify that this is the case, the following questions may be important:

- Is the result model syntactically correct?
- Is the result model semantically correct with respect to the input model?
- Can every syntactically correct input model be translated?
- Does the model translation always terminate?
- Does the model translation always yield a unique result model?

Translations based on graph transformation allow the use of tools for the verification of such properties based on the analysis techniques discussed in Chapter 4. Especially in critical applications, this is an important advantage over translations implemented in programming languages and many model transformation approaches. In the example case of an O–R mapping (which may or may not be critical) we expect a translation to produce a unique relational schema for each valid class model. This schema has to be syntactically correct, i.e. it has to belong to the modelling language of relational schemas. Moreover, to be semantically correct the relational schema has to represent a flattened structure of its input class model. Conversely, the same relational schema may be the result of translating several class diagrams if they differ only in their class inheritance relations.

To (re-)establish of consistency between related software artefacts we require *model synchronisations*. The consistency of related artefacts may break owing to changes in just one artefact, or changes in several artefacts during the same cycle. For example, a class diagram may be changed to reflect new requirements while related code is updated to repair bugs. We limit ourselves to the case of just two interrelated artefacts, leaving the problem of consistency in dynamic artefact networks for the future [267].

In complex scenarios, achieving full consistency may not be possible. Then, the problem becomes one of achieving maximum consistency. The basic form of model synchronisation is unidirectional, where changes on one side are propagated to the other side. In addition, we consider concurrent model synchronisation, where both models are modified and changes have to be propagated in both directions. This is the case, for example, if a new class is added to the class model while the relational schema is improved by splitting a table.

In an integrated tool environment, we would expect synchronisation to be automatic once the developer has performed a change. As in the case of model translation, this raises questions of syntactic and semantic correctness, completeness, termination, and uniqueness of the result. In addition, we expect model synchronisation to be *Hippocratic*[1], i.e. not to change models that are already consistent. As in the verification of model translations, we would like

---

[1] The term is derived as a metaphor from the Hippocratic Oath, stating that a doctor should not harm patients [265].

to benefit from the analysis techniques and tools of graph transformation systems to establish such properties.

Most graph transformation approaches to model synchronisation are based on *triple graph grammars* (TGGs) [260]. A TGG is a graph grammar that derives graph triples consisting of source, target and correspondence graphs, the latter relating the source and target graphs. A triple graph grammar can be projected to two graph grammars, one for the source and one for the target modelling language. The language of interrelated models generated by a TGG defines all consistent interrelated models. This provides us with a declarative specification of model consistency. A TGG can be *operationalised* automatically to create forward (source-to-target) or backward (target-to-source) translations, each resulting in consistent pairs of interrelated models. These translations are syntactically correct, terminating and yield unique results under reasonable assumptions. A TGG can also be used to generate correct and Hippocratic model synchronisations.

This chapter is structured as follows. In Section 12.1 we consider interrelated models and modelling languages based on an example of object–relational mapping before studying model translations and their properties in Section 12.2. TGGs and their operationalisation are introduced in Section 12.3. Finally, we discuss model synchronisation in Section 12.4.

Since this chapter uses typed attributed graph transformation systems, it is useful to be aware of the material in Chapters 1 and 2. In addition, analysis techniques presented in Chapter 4 (i.e. CDA, termination analysis, constraint checking and graph parsing) are used to show relevant properties of model translations and synchronisations.

12.1 Interrelated Models and Modelling Languages

Models can be linked in several ways. Apart from the use of shared *names* or certain naming conventions, a simple method is to add *references* between elements of different modules. Such links are easy to maintain when working with models representing different views. UML diagrams, for example, often refer to model elements defined in other diagrams, such as an object in a behaviour diagram pointing to its defining class. Remote references realise tightly coupled model relations, which require a close integration between the manipulations of related models. A more loosely coupled relation is achieved through *correspondence links* between elements of different models. This leaves the source and target models, often belonging to different languages and possibly held in different tools, independent of each other while allowing one to represent their relation in a way that is navigable from both ends. In the following example, we will relate class models and relational schemas by correspondence links, giving us the option to modify each model independently.

Example 12.1 (classes to tables: requirements). This example provides a baseline scenario for model-driven development. It served as a reference case study to compare a number of model transformation approaches [54]. Subsequently, various model transformation techniques and tools have been applied to variants of it to illustrate and assess their features. Conceptually, an O–R mapping is a translation between the two paradigms of object-oriented and relational data modelling.

We will introduce this (slightly simplified) example by presenting its source and target metamodels first. Note that multiplicities allow models with incomplete information, in order to support a stepwise translation of class models while keeping intermediate inter-related models consistent with each other.

The Class metamodel is shown in Fig. 12.1. Its principal metaclass is Class, which contains a set of Attributes and has a super reference pointing to a superclass, if it exists, for modelling inheritance trees. An Attribute points to a DataType and can be primary. Primary attributes are used to identify objects. Note that subclasses do not have additional primary attributes. The metaclass DataType models primitive data types. In addition, there is the metaclass Association pointing to its source and destination classes with src and dest. All these metaclasses are named. We forgo pulling up the name into an abstract metaclass, for the sake of simplicity.

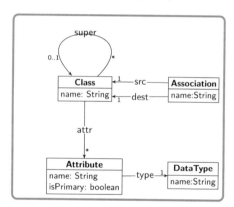

Fig. 12.1. Class metamodel

The principal metaclass of the Relational metamodel in Fig. 12.2 is Table, containing a set of Columns and a set of ForeignKeys stored in columns. Table points to the metaclass Column with the references pkey for its primary key and col for all its columns. It may have at most one column functioning as the primary key. A ForeignKey refers to a Table; it is represented by the Column it refers to with fcol. Furthermore, a Column may have a reference to Type. Tables, columns and types are named. (Again, we intend to keep the metamodel simple, and forgo pulling up the name into an abstract metaclass.) The translation of class to relational models is specified as follows:

- For each Class instance, which is not a subclass, a Table instance has to be created with the same name. A complete class hierarchy is translated into

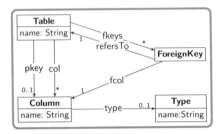

Fig. 12.2. Table metamodel

one table, i.e. a subclass is not mapped to a separate table but corresponds to the table of its superclass. This design decision is well suited for small inheritance hierarchies with little variance between classes, while large hierarchies with large variance are better split up into several tables.

- For each DataType instance, a Type instance has to be created. Their names have to correspond.
- For each Attribute instance typed over a DataType, a Column instance has to be created. Their names and their types have to correspond. If the Attribute is primary, the Table refers to this Column by a pkey reference. In any case, the Table has to refer to the Column with a col reference.
- For each Association instance, a ForeignKey instance has to be created. In addition, a Column is created which belongs to the table that corresponds to the source class; the ForeignKey refers to it by fcol. The ForeignKey also points to the table that corresponds to the destination class. This is indicated by a refersTo reference.

A very small example is depicted in Figs. 12.3 and 12.4. Note that both models are depicted in their abstract syntax. The Class model contains two classes, Family and Person. The class Family has an attribute name, which is primary. The class Person has an attribute firstname, which is primary as well. Furthermore, there is an association members, which refers to all family members. Another association, called closestFriend, points to a person who is the closest friend of a given person. This class model is to be translated to a relational schema: This schema contains two tables, called Family and Person. Table Family has two columns, called name (this one is the primary key) and members_firstname, pointing to persons stored in table Person. That table also has two columns, one is called firstname (this one is the primary key here) and closestFriend_firstname, pointing to a person in the same table.   □

To design a translation from one metamodel to another, developers often start with identifying which metaclasses correspond to each other. Such metaclass correspondences can be expressed by correspondence links.

Example 12.2 (correspondences between metamodels). The Class and Table metamodels are both shown in Fig. 12.5. To design a model translation from class models to relational ones, we identify correspondences between metaclasses first. The translation should map a Class to a Table, an Association to

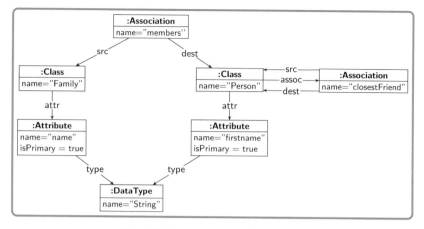

Fig. 12.3. An example Class model

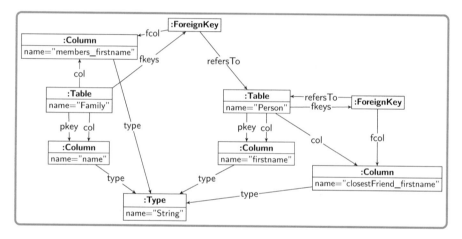

Fig. 12.4. An example Table model

a ForeignKey, an Attribute to a Column, and a DataType to a Type. To keep track of the translation, we make these correspondences explicit by the use of correspondence nodes and their references into the source and target models. Depending on which node types correspond to each other, correspondence nodes are typed by CT (class–table), AC (attribute–column), DT (datatype–type), or AF (association–foreignKey). In addition, there is ST (subclass–table) to relate a subclass to the table of its parent class. This is a special kind of correspondence between classes and tables indicated by an inheritance relation from ST to CT. Note that, for the sake of simplicity, adjacent edges of correspondence nodes are not typed explicitly but are typed implicitly by their source and target node types (see [113] for details of this approach).   □

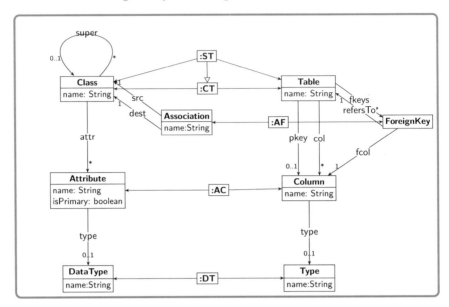

Fig. 12.5. Example metamodels with correspondence links

12.2 Model Translation

Defining correspondences between metamodels is a valuable first step in developing a model translation. It clarifies at the type level how elements should be translated. Next, we identify model patterns to specify how instances should be translated. Since ultimately we have to design rules to translate entire models, we also have to consider the order in which model patterns are translated. This will remain implicit in the sequential dependencies between rules, however. We design the model translation for class models first, deriving their corresponding relational schemas. Then we discuss important properties of such model translations.

Example 12.3 (translation of classes to tables). Figure 12.6 shows the model translation rules that are needed to translate a class model to a relational one. We assume that well-formed input models are given, in particular that a subclass does not have a **primary** attribute if a superclass already has one.

Rule translateClassToTable() translates a class without superclass to a table with the same name. Similarly, rule translateDataTypeToType() translates a datatype of the class model to a type in the relational schema. Rule translateAttributeToColumn() translates an attribute if its container class has already been translated. In this case a new column is created with the same name as the attribute and a corresponding type. This column belongs to the translated table. Rule translatePrimary() sets a column to be the primary key if its corresponding attribute is primary. Rule translateSubclassToTable() translates a subclass of an already translated class to the same table. This means that

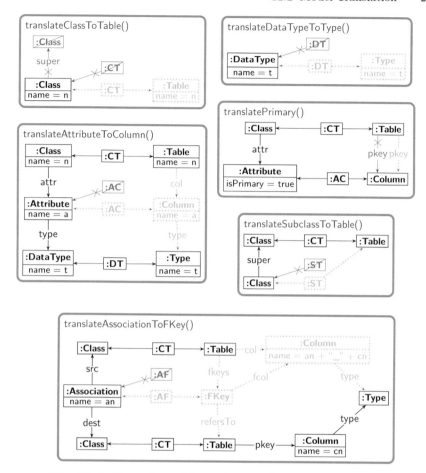

Fig. 12.6. Example model translation rules for O–R mapping

a complete inheritance tree is flattened into one big table. This strategy to handle class inheritance is not the only possibility. More details of this problem can be found in [37]. Finally, an association is translated to a foreign key by rule translateAssociationToFKey(), which also creates another column belonging to the same table. This table corresponds to the source class of the translated association. The foreign key refers to the table corresponding to the destination class of the association. The type of the new column is the corresponding type used by the primary key of the destination table, since it should contain those keys. Two further rules for translating associations are not shown in Fig. 12.6. If an association runs from and to the same class, a variant of rule translateAssociationToFKey() is needed where the upper and lower classes, linked CT nodes, and tables as well as edges in between, are merged. For associations between classes related to the same table due to inheritage, we need a further variant of rule translateAssociationToFKey() to merge the two tables.

Note that each class model element can only be translated once, since we keep track of the translation in correspondence links. If we require the translation rules in Fig. 12.6 to be applied to a class model for as long as possible, each rule match can be used only once, owing to negative application conditions. This solution can be used as long as there are n-to-1 relationships between source and target elements. For the backward translation mapping relational schemes to class models, this would fail, as a table may correspond to more than one class. In that case, markings would help, as introduced in [190].

By applying the model translation rules presented in Fig. 12.6 to the class model in Fig. 12.3, we obtain a related model pair with the relational model in Fig. 12.4 as the target and a correspondence model linking it with the source. □

12.2.1 Properties of Model Translations

A model translation is implemented with special requirements on its input and output: given a valid model as input, the translation result should be *correct, syntactically* with respect to its language definition and *semantically* in relation to the input model. This means that the output model is syntactically correct if its target model is an element of the target modelling language. Semantic correctness is harder to formalise. Often, semantic equivalence is postulated, for example, before and after a refactoring step that improves the structure of a model while preserving its semantics. For translations (exogenous transformations between models in different languages), a *compiler semantics* can be used to map both the input and the output model into a common semantic domain where their relation can be formalised. Furthermore, the translation should yield a result after *finitely* many steps. And often, the translation should yield a *unique result*.

The analysis techniques in Chapter 4 can be used to demonstrate some of the desired properties. The syntactic correctness of output models can be checked by parsing the corresponding model graph, as discussed in Section 4.6. If we just want to see if the multiplicities of the target metamodel are observed, we can interpret them as graph constraints and verify these as presented in Section 4.4.

Semantic correctness is often difficult to demonstrate. If both, the source and the target language have a formal semantics in a shared domain, a useful technique is to show semantic equivalence or refinement. For example, in the case of behavioural models, the operational semantics of the input and output models can be given by labelled transition systems S_1 and S_2. In this case we could ask if they are bisimilar, or if one simulates the other [149].

Systems S_1 *simulates* S_2 if there exists a relation R between their states such that for every pair of related states s_1 in S_1 and s_2 in S_2 and transition

$s_1 \xrightarrow{p} s_1'$, there is a transition $s_2 \xrightarrow{p} s_2'$ where s_1' is related to s_2'. Relation R is called a *simulation*, and if its inverse R^{-1} is a simulation too, R is a *bisimulation* and S_1, S_2 are *bisimilar*.

Ehrig and Ermel [86] described an approach, for example, where the transition systems associated with both models are described by an interpreter semantics, using operational rules executing the model. Then, each operational semantics rule of the source language is translated into a corresponding rule of the target language. This is used to show that a transition in S_1 can always be matched by one in S_2, and vice versa. If either of the two modelling languages involved lacks a formal semantics, correctness of the translation can only be validated by testing, as outlined below.

To show termination, we will see in the following example that the layer conditions presented in Section 4.3 can be used. To argue that the result is unique for any input model, we consider all potential conflicts (computed by conflict analysis) and demonstrate how they can all be resolved.

Example 12.4 (functional behaviour of class model translation). To show the termination of the forward translation above, we check if any termination criteria are fulfilled and find that the forward translation satisfies the non-deletion layer conditions presented in Section 4.3:

- All forward translation rules are non-deleting.
- Each rule has a NAC which can be embedded into its right-hand side.

We define four rule layers. Rules translateClassToTable() and translateDataTypeToType() are in layer 0. Rule translateSubclassToTable() is in layer 1. Rule translateAttributeToColumn() is in layer 2. All other rules are in layer 3. All types of class models have creation layer 0. Types CT, Table, DT and Type and adjacent edge types have creation layer 1. Type ST and adjacent edge types have creation layer 2. Types AC and Column and all types of adjacent edges have creation layer 3. All other types have creation layer 4. With this layer assignment, each translation rule creates at least one element whose type has a creation layer greater than the rule's and uses only elements with types of creation layers lower than or equal to the rule's.

To show the confluence of our model translation, we start by reasoning about potential conflicts. Each rule is applicable at a given match only once. This means that, if we want to apply the same rule twice at the same match, these two applications are in conflict. More precisely, all such application pairs have produce/forbid conflicts. Since such rule applications would lead to the same result, we can ignore these kinds of conflicts. Applying the same rule at two different matches does not lead to conflicts provided that all instance graphs fulfil the upper bound constraints of the input metamodel. A similar argument applies to pairs of applications using two different rules. Hence, we do not have any real conflicts during model translation, so the result is unique for any input model.   □

12.2.2 Testing a Model Translation

To test a model translation, we have to check if it yields correct results for a set of representative input models. This involves the following activities [36]: (1) select test adequacy (or coverage) criteria to be reached, (2) generate test models and (3) construct a test oracle to decide if a test yields the correct result.

The language metamodel can be used as a basis for test adequacy criteria. Typical coverage criteria are based on the instantiation of metaclasses and a category partition for their attribute values. The effectiveness of these criteria for finding errors, however, has not been systematically established. This means that large numbers of test cases have to be created for comprehensive testing, making manual model creation impractical, hence an automated generation of test models is needed. This step is challenging because, if the input and output languages are complex, the corresponding models can be large and complex as well.

Input models have to be valid; in particular, they have to fulfil the well-formedness constraints of their metamodel. Models can be generated automatically based on the structure of a metamodel [52], but ignoring its well-formedness constraints. If the language is described by a graph grammar, this can be used to generate language instances satisfying complex constraints (see also Chapter 10).

A further obstacle is the potential complexity of the resulting models. Combined with the potentially confusing layout of automatically generated models, this makes them hard to inspect and assess by hand. A test oracle can automate this task, for example by comparing the output model with a model provided as the expected result of the test. To compare two models, their underlying graph structures have to be compared, which involves finding a graph isomorphism between them. In practice, this problem can be solved efficiently if the model graphs are extensively typed and attributed, and by exploiting the containment hierarchy over model elements that is present in many models. Another way of assessing output models is to query them to check properties such as syntactic correctness, size and the (non-)existence of specific patterns.

Example 12.5 (testing an O–R mapping). The class model in Fig. 12.3 nearly covers the whole metamodel in Fig. 12.1, but it remains to test the translation of class inheritance. Additionally, not all categories of attribute values and (non-)existence of instances are covered by this class model. In particular, non-primary attributes still have to be considered. We need to also check what happens for a class without a primary attribute. It turns out that an association to a class without a primary attribute cannot be translated, since the corresponding table needs a primary column. This situation can be fixed by extending the model translation with a further rule shown in Fig. 12.7.

After extending the O–R mapping with this rule, we have to check again if the required properties still hold. To fulfil the termination criteria, we set

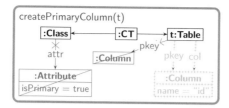

Fig. 12.7. Additional model translation rule for O–R mapping

the rule layer of our new rule createPrimaryColumn() to 2. The rule then uses types of lower or equal layers only and creates element types of upper layers. Moreover, one of its NACs can be embedded into its right-hand side. The arguments above for the uniqueness of results are still valid, and it is obvious that this rule does not violate the syntactic correctness of the output models.

In view of the (non-)existence of instances of certain types, the translation of associations is most interesting. Associations can occur in various settings: (1) between two classes without an inheritance relation, (2) in only one class (forming a loop), and (3) between two classes that are in an inheritance relation where (a) the source class inherits the target class and (b) vice versa. This example shows that the pure coverage of a given metamodel is often not enough but has to be extended to cover all relevant patterns that can occur in input models.   □

12.3 Triple Graph Grammars

When working with model pairs linked by a correspondence relation, we need to maintain the consistency of both, the source and the target model, and the relation. *Bidirectional transformation* languages simplify the task of maintaining the consistency of two or more artefacts. Triple graph grammars [260, 19] are a graph-transformation-based bidirectional transformation language. A triple graph grammar constructs two models and their correspondences, i.e. an interrelated model, simultaneously. After each derivation step, the resulting triple graph represents a consistent interrelated model. As inter-related models are often not changed simultaneously but independently of each other, rules are needed to edit source and target models separately. As a triple graph grammar may be projected to its source and target grammars, these rules can be automatically constructed, defining the source and target modelling languages. In addition, rules for translating source models to target models, and vice versa, can be automatically constructed from a given TGG. And finally, for maintaining consistency, rules can be derived that construct correspondence relations between unrelated source and target models and repair already established correspondence relations. For model transformations implemented by general-purpose programming languages, TGGs can serve as high-level specifications of such implementations to generate test cases and oracles.

TGG rules are graph transformation rules over an interrelated metamodel used as a type graph. Typically, they are monotonic (i.e., non-deleting) to enable efficient parsing. They may include NACs, often to control synchronisation processes, such as model translations (as in Example 12.3). Those NACs are restricted such that they include instances of either the source or the target metamodel [89] but not both, because such more complex conditions cannot easily be associated to one or the other side.

To set and interrelate attribute values, the data types used need according operations. We will discuss later the fact that a TGG rule using non-invertible operations may not be usable in all contexts.

Example 12.6 (triple graph grammar for O–R mapping). Figure 12.8 shows all triple graph rules needed for our O–R mapping. They can be used to create class models and their corresponding relational schemas simultaneously, starting from the empty triple graph. While most of the rules are simple, there are four rules we want to consider in more detail. Rule setPrimary() does not create a new source model element but changes an attribute value related to the creation of a new reference in the target model. Rule createSubclass() creates new source model elements, but no new target elements. Rule createAssociationAndFKey() creates a new column in the target model whose name is constructed from two other names using string concatenation. Finally, rule createPrimaryColumn() contains two NACs separately matching parts of the source and target models.

Two further TGG rules are needed to create specific associations, but not shown in Fig. 12.8. If an association is a loop at one and the same class, a variant of rule createAssociationAndFKey() is needed where the upper and lower classes, CT nodes, and tables, as well as the adjacent edges, are merged. For associations between classes that are related to the same table because of inheritance, we need a further variant of rule createAssociationAndFKey() where the two tables are merged. □

Note 12.1: Interrelation of patterns. Triple graph grammars provide a declarative, rule-based description of models linked by a correspondence relation. A triple graph rule describes a pattern of interrelated models, and shows how it can be extended by additional elements and relations.

12.3.1 Operationalisation of TGGs

To support a wide range of scenarios for the management of evolving interrelated models, not only model translations but additional operations are required such as for creating intermodel relations, checking their consistency, and synchronising related models where one or both sides may have changed. TGGs can be operationalised in a variety of different ways to support all these situations. This means that dedicated operational rule sets can be derived from

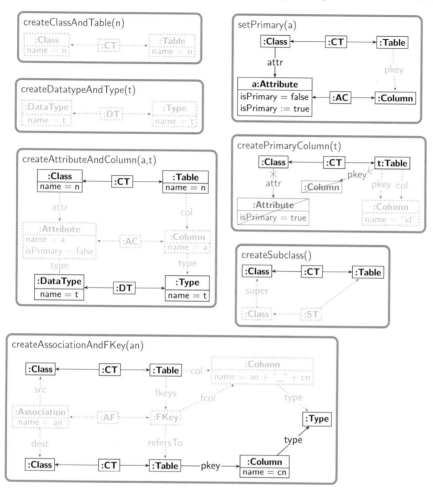

Fig. 12.8. A triple graph grammar for O–R mapping

a TGG automatically, realising the following operations, which we list first before explaining how they are derived:

- *Source construction:* Given a model of the source modelling language, an application of *source rules*, i.e. rules over the source metamodel, to the empty start model (graph) constructs a derivation sequence for this model.
- *Target construction:* Given a model of the target language, an application of *target rules*, i.e. rules over the target metamodel, to the empty start model construct a derivation sequence for this model.
- *Forward translation:* A model of the source language can be translated to an interrelated model containing a model of the target language using *forward rules*. Each forward rule takes a source model pattern and completes it to obtain its corresponding target pattern.

- *Backward translation:* A model of the target language can be translated to an interrelated model containing a model of the source language using *backward rules*. Each backward rule takes a target model pattern and completes it to obtain its corresponding source pattern.
- *Consistency creation:* Given a model of the source language and a model of the target language, they are consistent if they can be generated as part of an interrelated model using TGG rules. *Consistency-establishing rules* build up the correspondence interrelation between a source and a target model.
- *Consistency checking:* Given an interrelated model, *consistency-checking rules* are used to check if all the correspondence relations are consistent, i.e. can be generated by the grammar. These rules just check for consistency, but do not change anything.
- *Synchronisation:* Given a valid interrelated model and model updates on the source and/or target model, the output is a valid interrelated model where model updates have been propagated. If both, the source and the target model have been changed, we call this synchronisation *concurrent*. Hence, *synchronisation rules* propagate model changes.

We will illustrate the derivation of operational rules using selected operations. *Source rules* are easy to construct by projecting TGG rules to their source metamodel. Analogously, *target rules* are projections of TGG rules to their target metamodel. *Forward rules* assume that the source model part is given, and thus the source part of the forward translation rule is the identity on the right-hand side. The correspondence and target parts of the TGG rule are inherited by the forward rule. Additionally, all the target NACs of the TGG rule have to be carried over. If the TGG rule creates a target node without a correspondence to some source node, however, source NACs have to be added to the forward rule as well. Furthermore, we have to ensure that forward rules do not translate source parts several times, which is often done with additional NACs. *Backward rules* are constructed dually to forward rules. *Consistency-establishing* rules take the source and the target parts of a TGG rule as given and just create correspondence links, while *consistency-checking* rules just check the existence of interrelated patterns, i.e. they are identical on the right-hand sides of the TGG rules. These constructions of operationalised rules are presented in [191] in detail.

Example 12.7 (deriving forward rules from TGG rules for O–R mapping). The triple rules in Fig. 12.8 are in a direct relation with the model translation rules in Fig. 12.6. In fact, these model translation rules can be automatically derived from the TGG rules following the recipe described above.

While the construction is largely straightforward, there are three translation rules which deserve more explanation. There are two rules in the TGG which create classes, namely createClassAndTable() and createSubclass(). Rule createClassAndTable() creates a class without a superclass. The corresponding translation rule translateClassToTable() has to explicitly exclude this case by an additional NAC, since the source model exists already completely. Rule setPrimary() creates just an edge, and therefore rule translatePrimary() needs an additional NAC preventing it from creating such an edge more than once. Rule createPrimaryColumn() creates a column containing the primary key of the table. This column is not connected to any attribute, since there is no primary attribute in the class. Therefore, the source NAC has to be included in the forward rule as well, as seen already in Fig. 12.7.

Note that not all backward translation rules can be deduced automatically, since the string concatenation in rule createAssociationAndFKey() cannot be translated into a canonical string decomposition. Nevertheless, it is possible to define a suitable inverse manually, by taking the column name and stripping off "_" + cn.   □

TGG operationalisations have been shown to be sound: a model is *consistent*, i.e. it is syntactically correct if it can be generated by the grammar of its language. An interrelated model is *consistent* in this sense if it can be generated by the rules of its TGG. If an application of a set F of forward rules can extend a given source model to an interrelated model M such that M is consistent, the set F is *correct*. A set of forward rules is *complete* if there is a forward translation with these rules to a consistent interrelated model for every model of the source language [87, 112]. Moreover, forward translations are *information-preserving* in the sense that, given a consistent source model S, a forward translation guided by the derivation of S has an inverse backward translation yielding interrelated models whose source model is again S [82].

12.4 Model Synchronisation

Once the correspondence between two models is established, further changes can be propagated through model synchronisation to preserve consistency. Model updates are propagated either *unidirectionally* in the case of changes in only one model, or *bidirectionally* in the case of *concurrent* changes.

To perform a model synchronisation, one or both of the interrelated models are checked for modifications. If one model has been modified, we have to check if the resulting interrelated model is consistent, i.e. can be generated by our TGG rules. If this is the case, there is no need for further synchronisation. Otherwise, the modification has to be propagated to the other model.

A naive approach to synchronisation might remove all inconsistent parts of the model and all elements depending on them, and reconstruct them again in a consistent way. However, this solution is not only inefficient, but may also delete consistent model information that should have been kept. In the following, we are looking for a solution that discards as little information as possible.

TGG rules often realise a hierarchical definition of consistency in the sense that model elements are in correspondence if the model elements they are dependent on are already in correspondence. An association is in correspondence with a foreign key, for example, if its adjacent classes are in correspondence with the tables the foreign key belongs to and refers to. If one of these classes changes, this modification might have implications for adjacent associations and foreign keys. If the primary key changed, for example, the column for the foreign key will get a different name. In our running example, the hierarchy is rather flat. In general, such hierarchies can be much more elaborate, which increases the synchronisation effort considerably. Since model synchronisation is of special interest for concurrent model editing, synchronisation procedures have to be quick to not obstruct the user too much [108]. To decrease synchronisation time, all unnecessary model modifications must be avoided. Hence, deleting all dependent correspondences and building up correspondences from scratch is not an efficient solution. So, we have to find a minimal set of correspondences to be reconsidered for fixing the inconsistent situation. In general, our strategy for a unidirectional (without loss of generality forward) synchronisation is as follows. For each match of a forward translation rule that is changed by the model modification, the effect of the corresponding rule application has to be reversed. This can lead to a cascade of element deletions in the target model. Then, forward rules are applied again to build up a modified target model. If target models can be fixed locally, this strategy may be optimised by finding suitable *shortcut* rules [104] to perform the modification directly. Instead of deleting and recreating columns for foreign keys, for example, a possible repair would be a suitable renaming of foreign-key columns taking new primary-key names into account.

Example 12.8 (model synchronisation with TGG rules). We consider two examples of synchronisations triggered by modifications using the rules shown in Fig. 12.9. (1) After an attribute has been renamed using rule renameAttribute(), it is no longer in correspondence with a column, since their names are no longer the same. If this attribute is a primary one, this renaming has additional implications for associations in correspondence with foreign keys since the corresponding columns also have to change their names. (2) After an attribute has been set to be non-primary with rule setNonPrimary(), the corresponding pkey edge has to be deleted in the relational schema.

Fig. 12.9. Two modification rules for source models

Both situations have to be postprocessed, since associations may refer to the attribute-containing class as their target. The conservative strategy is to take back all applications of the rule translateAssociationToFKey() where the association points to the class with the changed primary key. Then, this rule is applied at new matches creating columns with new names to hold foreign keys. The optimised strategy is to modify these names directly, which can be done by applying rule modifyPrimaryColumn() in Fig. 12.10, combining the "net effects" of rules translateAssociationToFKey() applied inversely, createPrimaryColumn() and translateAssociationToFKey(). "Net effects" are all those rule actions that remain when we do not consider deletion and re-creation of model elements. Note that application conditions of the original rules may not occur in such a composed rule if they cannot be translated. One of the NACs of rule createPrimaryColumn, forbidding a primary-key column, cannot be translated, since the table has a primary key at the beginning which is replaced by a new one.   □

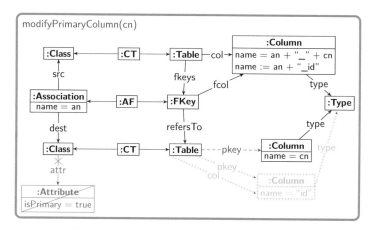

Fig. 12.10. A shortcut synchronisation rule

12.4.1 Properties of Synchronisation

A number of interesting properties have been identified for model synchronisation, including *correctness* (also called *soundness*), *Hippocraticness*, and *completeness* [266, 141]. A model synchronisation is *correct* if the resulting interrelated model is consistent assuming that the triggering model modification was consistent. Remember that *consistency* of an interrelated model means that this model can be generated by our TGG rules. A triggering model modification is consistent if it yields an interrelated model with consistent source and target models (but their correspondence may be inconsistent). A source or target model is consistent if it can be obtained as a source projection or target projection of a consistent interrelated model, respectively.

A model synchronisation is *Hippocratic* if it does not change interrelated models that are not modified. Finally, a model synchronisation is *complete* if it produces a consistent interrelated model, provided that one exists.

In addition, invertibility is often desired to allow an immediate "undo" of a modification. A model synchronisation from A to B is *invertible* if there is an opposite synchronisation from B to A such that their composition leads back to the original interrelated model. Often, a model synchronisation is just *weakly invertible*, meaning that the first synchronisation may not be invertible because of some initial information loss, but the inversion of the inverted synchronisation and continued inversions do not cause any further loss of information.

Another property of model synchronisations is *incrementality* [67, 192]. Intuitively, a synchronisation is incremental if, after a source model modification, it does not translate the entire modified model again, but modifies only a minimal part of the model affected by the change. To actually decide if a least change has been performed, one would need some metric to measure the size of change. An additional requirement of incremental model synchronisations is often that they *preserve recent changes*, assuming that these were intended by the modeller despite additional changes needed to rebuild a consistent model.

Example 12.9 (properties of model synchronisations). Both modification rules in Fig. 12.9 are consistent source rules, since attributes with arbitrary names can be generated and attributes can be set to primary or non-primary. The shortcut modification rule in Fig. 2.17 induces correct model synchronisations: it creates a new column containing the primary key id if there is no primary attribute in the class corresponding to the column's table, and adapts the column name of a foreign key that refers to this table, assuming that there is exactly one foreign key pointing to this table. Further modification rules are needed for cases where no foreign key points to this table, or more than one does so. All these modifications can be summarised in a rule where the association, its class, the foreign key, its table and its column, both correspondence links in between and all edges in between are in a multipattern (Section 2.4.4). With this rule, we can perform correct model synchronisations only. Owing to its NAC, the synchronisation rule in Fig. 2.17 is not applicable if an attribute is not set to non-primary. Hence, this rule is Hippocratic.

Finally, the synchronisation rule is minimal in the sense that it needs to move the pkey pointer to a new column, since the corresponding class is without a primary attribute after the modification. Also, the names of all foreign-key columns have to be adapted to the new primary key. All actions performed by the rule are required to reach a consistent interrelated model that preserves the triggering change, i.e. keeps the attribute non-primary. ☐

12.5 Summary and Further Reading

Model translation and synchronisation are core functions of model-based development activities such as code generation from or reverse engineering of models, co-evolution of models and code, and mappings between models. Especially model synchronisation is in the focus of the *bx community* which considers bidirectional transformations (bx) as a mechanism for maintaining the consistency of two (or more) related sources of information[2].

In this chapter, we have shown that triple graph grammars provide a powerful mechanism to support the translation and synchronisation of models in a declarative way. A triple graph rule extends a related model pair assuming the existence of a given related model pattern. A TGG can be operationalised to implement forward and backward translations, rules for consistency checking and consistency creation, and for model synchronisation. Under certain assumptions, analysis techniques for graph transformation systems can be used to show that model translations yield correct and unambiguous results.

Since interrelated models can become inconsistent if one or both models change, automated model synchronisation is essential to support evolution in model-based software projects. Synchronisations realised by TGGs may be shown to be correct, complete, deterministic, Hippocratic and invertible [142]. Repair rules can be constructed automatically to improve the efficiency of model synchronisation processes [104].

12.5.1 Extensions

As presented in this chapter, TGGs use simple rules without multipatterns. However, a universal quantification of certain rule parts can be useful, for example, when flattening hierarchical structures as they occur in class models with inheritance or in hierarchical statecharts. TGG rules with multipatterns as defined in [193] can handle these situations conveniently. TGG rules with multi-patterns can be operationalised to forward and backward translation rules as shown in [193]. In addition, they increase the true expressiveness of TGGs: if we restrict ourselves to TGG rules that do not add source elements, TGGs with simple rules only are less expressive than TGGs with rules allowing multipatterns. Without multipatterns, each TGG rule can relate only a fixed number of model elements. Multipatterns allow one to create variable numbers of interrelations. For example, when flattening class structures, a class property can be translated and linked to a variable number of properties, which depends on the number of (transitive) subclasses.

12.5.2 Tooling

There are several tools implementing the main features of TGGs. In [145, 192], three tools were compared in terms of their usability, expressiveness and analysis techniques. They all support the definition of TGG rules and the automatic deduction of forward and backward translation rules. MoTE [144] is an EMF-based tool which also supports incremental synchronisations. Simple TGG rules may be equipped with attribute assignments and conditions in

---

[2] The wiki of the bx community can be found at http://bx-community.wikidot.com

OCL or Java. NACs and multipatterns are not supported. The TGG interpreter [115] is an Eclipse-based tool allowing incremental synchronisations, too. Conditions are generally formulated in OCL. Both tools implement synchronisations that are correct, but not complete. eMoflon [18, 287] is a tool suite for TGGs based on EMF. It supports unidirectional and bidirectional translations. TGG rules may have NACs and bidirectional attribute manipulations. eMoflon is able is to handle model generation, forward translation and consistency checking.

12.5.3 Applications

TGGs have been developed in a number of industrial applications, for example to support the integration of modelling tools. In complex industrial projects, modelling tools have to work together based on different model representation formats. This leads to the need for translations between such formats [172]. TGGs have been used to implement model translations between different formats. When working with textual formats, TGGs are used to translate abstract syntax trees to models to be further translated to models in another format. In turn, these are mapped to another abstract syntax tree. Parsers and pretty-printers are used to translate a textual format to an abstract syntax tree and vice versa.

The possibly largest application of TGGs has been the automated translation of satellite procedures [143]. Here, domain experts were able to specify translations over a metamodel consisting of 140 types using a TGG with about 250 rules, for which they also demonstrated correctness. Savings of 1–2 person years, compared with manual conversion and validation, showed that TGGs can be used effectively in practice. Further industrial applications of TGGs were, for example, reported in [109] where SysML and AUTOSAR models were synchronised, and in [20], to support concurrent model-driven automation engineering.

References

1. Business Process Modeling Notation. `http://www.bpmn.org`
2. EMF Compare. `http://www.eclipse.org/emf/compare`
3. EMF Refactor. `http://www.eclipse.org/emf-refactor`
4. Epsilon Wizard Language. `http://www.eclipse.org/epsilon`
5. FeatureIDE. `http://fosd.de/fide`
6. The Fujaba tool suite. `www.fujaba.de`
7. SiLift: Semantic Lifting of Model Differences. `http://pi.informatik.uni-siegen.de/Projekte/SiLift`
8. The Language Toolkit (LTK). `http://eclipse.org/articles/Article-LTK/ltk.html`
9. XML. `www.w3.org/standards/xml`
10. XSL Transformations Version 3.0. `http://www.w3.org/standards/xml/transformation`
11. Application of graph transformation to visual languages. In: Bardohl, B., Minas, M., Schürr, A., Taentzer, G. (eds.) Handbook of Graph Grammars and Computing by Graph Transformation: Vol. 2: Applications, Languages, and Tools. World Scientific Publishing Co., Inc., River Edge, NJ, USA (1999)
12. AGG: `http://www.user.tu-berlin.de/o.runge/agg/`
13. Aho, A.V., Lam, M.S., Sethi, R., Ullman, J.D.: Compilers: Principles, Techniques, and Tools (2nd Edition). Addison-Wesley (2006)
14. Ajmone-Marsan, M., Balbo, G., Conte, G., Donatelli, S., Franceschinis, G.: Modelling with Generalized Stochastic Petri Nets. Wiley Series in Parallel Computing, John Wiley and Sons (1995)
15. Alshanqiti, A.M., Heckel, R., Kehrer, T.: Visual contract extractor: A tool for reverse engineering visual contracts using dynamic analysis. In: Proceedings of the 31st IEEE/ACM International Conference on Automated Software Engineering, ASE 2016, Singapore, September 3-7, 2016. pp. 816–821. ACM (2016), `https://doi.org/10.1145/2970276.2970287`
16. Anderson, W.G.: Continuous-Time Markov Chains. Springer (1991)
17. Andries, M., Engels, G., Habel, A., Hoffmann, B., Kreowski, H.J., Kuske, S., Plump, D., Schürr, A., Taentzer, G.: Graph transformation for specification and programming. Science of Computer Programming 34(1), 1–54 (1999)
18. Anjorin, A., Lauder, M., Patzina, S., Schürr, A.: Emoflon: leveraging EMF and professional CASE tools. In: Informatik 2011: Informatik schafft Communities, Beiträge der 41. Jahrestagung der Gesellschaft für Informatik e.V.

© Springer Nature Switzerland AG 2020
R. Heckel, G. Taentzer, *Graph Transformation for Software Engineers*,
https://doi.org/10.1007/978-3-030-43916-3

(GI), 4.-7.10.2011, Berlin, Deutschland (Abstract Proceedings). LNI, vol. 192, p. 281. GI (2011), `http://subs.emis.de/LNI/Proceedings/Proceedings192/article314.html`

19. Anjorin, A., Leblebici, E., Schürr, A.: 20 years of triple graph grammars: A roadmap for future research. ECEASST 73 (2015), `http://journal.ub.tu-berlin.de/eceasst/article/view/1031`

20. Anjorin, A., Yigitbas, E., Leblebici, E., Schürr, A., Lauder, M., Witte, M.: Description languages for consistency management scenarios based on examples from the industry automation domain. Programming Journal 2(3), 7 (2018), `https://doi.org/10.22152/programming-journal.org/2018/2/7`

21. Arendt, T.: Quality Assurance of Software Models: A Structured Quality Assurance Process Supported by a Flexible Tool Environment in the Eclipse Modeling Project. Ph.D. thesis, Philipps-Universität Marburg (2014)

22. Arendt, T., Biermann, E., Jurack, S., Krause, C., Taentzer, G.: Henshin: Advanced Concepts and tools for In-Place EMF Model Transformation. In: Model Driven Engineering Languages and Systems, 13th International Conference, MoDELS 2010, Oslo, Norway. Proceedings. LNCS, vol. 6394, pp. 121–135. Springer (2010)

23. Arendt, T., Kranz, S., Mantz, F., Regnat, N., Taentzer, G.: Towards syntactical model quality assurance in industrial software development: Process definition and tool support. In: Reussner, R.H., Grund, M., Oberweis, A., Tichy, W.F. (eds.) Software Engineering 2011: Fachtagung des GI-Fachbereichs Softwaretechnik, 21.-25. Februar 2011 in Karlsruhe. LNI, vol. 183, pp. 63–74. GI (2011), `http://subs.emis.de/LNI/Proceedings/Proceedings183/article6301.html`

24. Arendt, T., Taentzer, G.: A tool environment for quality assurance based on the Eclipse Modeling Framework. Automated Software Engineering 20(2), 141–184 (2013), `http://dx.doi.org/10.1007/s10515-012-0114-7`

25. Armbrust, M., Fox, A., Griffith, R., Joseph, A.D., Katz, R., Konwinski, A., Lee, G., Patterson, D., Rabkin, A., Stoica, I., Zaharia, M.: A view of cloud computing. Commun. ACM 53(4), 50–58 (Apr 2010), `http://doi.acm.org/10.1145/1721654.1721672`

26. Aßmann, U.: Graph rewrite systems for program optimization. ACM Trans. Program. Lang. Syst. 22(4), 583–637 (Jul 2000)

27. Aßmann, U., Bartho, A., Bürger, C., Cech, S., Demuth, B., Heidenreich, F., Johannes, J., Karol, S., Polowinski, J., Reimann, J., Schroeter, J., Seifert, M., Thiele, M., Wende, C., Wilke, C.: DropsBox: the Dresden Open Software Toolbox - Domain-specific modelling tools beyond metamodels and transformations. Software and System Modeling 13(1), 133–169 (2014)

28. Atkinson, T., Plump, D., Stepney, S.: Probabilistic graph programs for randomised and evolutionary algorithms. In: Lambers and Weber [187], pp. 63–78, `https://doi.org/10.1007/978-3-319-92991-0_5`

29. Azzi, G.G., Bezerra, J.S., Ribeiro, L., Costa, A., Rodrigues, L.M., Machado, R.: The Verigraph System for Graph Transformation. In: Graph Transformation, Specifications, and Nets - In Memory of Hartmut Ehrig. Lecture Notes in Computer Science, vol. 10800, pp. 160–178. Springer (2018), `https://doi.org/10.1007/978-3-319-75396-6_9`

30. Azzi, G.G., Corradini, A., Ribeiro, L.: On the essence and initiality of conflicts in M-adhesive transformation systems. Journal of Logical and Algebraic Met-

hods in Programming 109 (2019), `https://doi.org/10.1016/j.jlamp.2019.100482`

31. Baier, C., Haverkort, B.R., Hermanns, H., Katoen, J.: Model Checking Continuous-Time Markov Chains by Transient Analysis. In: Emerson, E.A., Sistla, A.P. (eds.) Computer Aided Verification, 12th International Conference, CAV 2000, Chicago, IL, USA, July 15 - 19, 2000, Proceedings. Lecture Notes in Computer Science, vol. 1855, pp. 358–372. Springer (2000), `https://doi.org/10.1007/10722167_28`

32. Baier, C., Katoen, J.: Principles of Model Checking. MIT Press (2008)

33. Baldan, P., Corradini, A., König, B.: A static analysis technique for graph transformation systems. In: CONCUR 2001 - Concurrency Theory, 12th International Conference, Aalborg, Denmark, August 20-25, 2001, Proceedings. Lecture Notes in Computer Science, vol. 2154, pp. 381–395. Springer (2001), `https://doi.org/10.1007/3-540-44685-0_26`

34. Baresi, L., Heckel, R.: Tutorial introduction to graph transformation: A software engineering perspective. In: Graph Transformation, First International Conference, ICGT 2002, Barcelona, Spain, October 7-12, 2002, Proceedings. Lecture Notes in Computer Science, vol. 2505, pp. 402–429. Springer (2002), `https://doi.org/10.1007/3-540-45832-8_30`

35. Basili, V.R.: Software modeling and measurement: the goal/question/metric paradigm. Tech. rep., College Park, MD, USA (1992), `http://portal.acm.org/citation.cfm?id=137076`

36. Baudry, B., Ghosh, S., Fleurey, F., France, R., Le Traon, Y., Mottu, J.M.: Barriers to systematic model transformation testing. Commun. ACM 53(6), 139–143 (Jun 2010), `http://doi.acm.org/10.1145/1743546.1743583`

37. Bauer, C., King, G., Gregory, G.: Java Persistence with Hibernate. Manning Publications Co., Greenwich, CT, USA, 2nd edn. (2015)

38. Bause, F., Kritzinger, P.S.: Stochastic Petri Nets. Vieweg Verlag, 2nd edn. (2002)

39. Behrmann, G., David, A., Larsen, K.G., Pettersson, P., Yi, W.: Developing UPPAAL over 15 years. Softw., Pract. Exper. 41(2), 133–142 (2011), `https://doi.org/10.1002/spe.1006`

40. Bézivin, J., Rumpe, B., Schürr, A., Tratt, L.: Model transformations in practice workshop. In: Bruel, J.M. (ed.) Satellite Events at the MoDELS 2005 Conference. pp. 120–127. Springer, Berlin, Heidelberg (2006)

41. Biermann, E., Ermel, C., Taentzer, G.: Formal foundation of consistent emf model transformations by algebraic graph transformation. Software and System Modeling 11(2), 227–250 (2012)

42. Biggs, N., Lloyd, E., Wilson, R.: Graph Theory. Oxford University Press (1986)

43. Bisztray, D., Heckel, R., Ehrig, H.: Verification of architectural refactorings by rule extraction. In: Fiadeiro, J.L., Inverardi, P. (eds.) Fundamental Approaches to Software Engineering, 11th International Conference, FASE 2008, Held as Part of the Joint European Conferences on Theory and Practice of Software, ETAPS 2008, Budapest, Hungary, March 29-April 6, 2008. Proceedings. Lecture Notes in Computer Science, vol. 4961, pp. 347–361 (2008), `http://dx.doi.org/10.1007/978-3-540-78743-3_26`

44. Born, K., Taentzer, G.: An algorithm for the critical pair analysis of amalgamated graph transformations. In: Graph Transformation - 9th International Conference, ICGT 2016, in Memory of Hartmut Ehrig, Held as Part

of STAF 2016, Vienna, Austria, July 5-6, 2016, Proceedings. Lecture Notes in Computer Science, vol. 9761, pp. 118–134. Springer (2016), `https://doi.org/10.1007/978-3-319-40530-8_8`

45. Bosch, J.: Continuous Software Engineering: An Introduction, pp. 3–13. Springer International Publishing, Cham (2014), `https://doi.org/10.1007/978-3-319-11283-1_1`

46. Bottoni, P., Hoffmann, K., Parisi-Presicce, F., Taentzer, G.: High-level replacement units and their termination properties. J. Vis. Lang. Comput. 16(6), 485–507 (2005)

47. Bottoni, P., Taentzer, G., Schürr, A.: Efficient parsing of visual languages based on critical pair analysis and contextual layered graph transformation. In: 2000 IEEE International Symposium on Visual Languages, VL 2000, Seattle, Washington, USA, September 10-13, 2000, Proceedings. pp. 59–60. IEEE Computer Society (2000), `https://doi.org/10.1109/VL.2000.874351`

48. Bravenboer, M., Kalleberg, K.T., Vermaas, R., Visser, E.: Stratego/xt 0.17. A language and toolset for program transformation. Sci. Comput. Program. 72(1-2), 52–70 (2008), `https://doi.org/10.1016/j.scico.2007.11.003`

49. Briand, L., Labiche, Y.: A UML-Based Approach to System Testing. In: Gogolla, M., Kobryn, C. (eds.) UML 2001 — The Unified Modeling Language. Modeling Languages, Concepts, and Tools. pp. 194–208. Springer, Berlin, Heidelberg (2001)

50. Briand, L., Labiche, Y.: A UML-Based Approach to System Testing. Software and Systems Modeling 1(1), 10–42 (Sep 2002), `https://doi.org/10.1007/s10270-002-0004-8`

51. Brinksma, E., Hermanns, H.: Process algebra and markov chains. pp. 183–231. Springer-Verlag New York, Inc., New York, NY, USA (2002), `http://dl.acm.org/citation.cfm?id=567305.567310`

52. Brottier, E., Fleurey, F., Steel, J., Baudry, B., Traon, Y.L.: Metamodel-based test generation for model transformations: An algorithm and a tool. In: Proceedings of the 17th International Symposium on Software Reliability Engineering. pp. 85–94. ISSRE '06, IEEE Computer Society, Washington, DC, USA (2006), `http://dx.doi.org/10.1109/ISSRE.2006.27`

53. Bürdek, J., Kehrer, T., Lochau, M., Reuling, D., Kelter, U., Schürr, A.: Reasoning about product-line evolution using complex feature model differences. Autom. Softw. Eng. 23(4), 687–733 (2016), `https://doi.org/10.1007/s10515-015-0185-3`

54. Bézivin, J., Rumpe, B., Schürr, A., Tratt, L.: Model transformations in practice workshop. In: Satellite Events at the MoDELS 2005 Conference: MoDELS 2005 International Workshops Doctoral Symposium, Educators Symposium Montego Bay, Jamaica, October 2-7, 2005 Revised Selected Papers. pp. 120–127 (01 2006)

55. CADP: Construction and Analysis of Distributed Processes. `http://cadp.inria.fr`

56. Carroll, J.J., Dickinson, I., Dollin, C., Reynolds, D., Seaborne, A., Wilkinson, K.: Jena: Implementing the Semantic Web Recommendations. Tech. Rep. HPL-2003-146, Hewlett Packard Laboratories (24 2003), `http://www.hpl.hp.com/techreports/2003/HPL-2003-146.html;http://www.hpl.hp.com/techreports/2003/HPL-2003-146.pdf`

57. Chen, K., Sztipanovits, J., Abdelwalhed, S., Jackson, E.: Semantic anchoring with model transformations. In: Hartman, A., Kreische, D. (eds.) Model Driven

Architecture – Foundations and Applications. pp. 115–129. Springer, Berlin, Heidelberg (2005)

58. Cheon, Y., Leavens, G.T.: A Simple and Practical Approach to Unit Testing: The JML and JUnit Way. In: Proceedings of the 16th European Conference on Object-Oriented Programming. pp. 231–255. ECOOP '02, Springer-Verlag, Berlin, Heidelberg (2002), `http://dl.acm.org/citation.cfm?id=646159.680018`

59. Cherchago, A., Heckel, R.: Specification Matching of Web Services Using Conditional Graph Transformation Rules. In: Ehrig, H., Engels, G., Parisi-Presicce, F., Rozenberg, G. (eds.) Graph Transformations, Second International Conference, ICGT 2004, Rome, Italy, September 28 - October 2, 2004, Proceedings. Lecture Notes in Computer Science, vol. 3256, pp. 304–318. Springer (2004), `https://doi.org/10.1007/978-3-540-30203-2_22`

60. Coleman, D., Arnold, P., Bodof, S., Dollin, C., Gilchrist, H., Hayes, F., Jeremes, P.: Object Oriented Development, The Fusion Method. Prentice Hall (1994)

61. Connolly, D., van Harmelen, F., Horrocks, I., McGuinness, D.L., Patel-Schneider, P.F., Stein, L.A.: DAML+OIL (March 2001) reference description. W3C note, W3C (Mar 2001), `http://www.w3.org/TR/daml+oil-reference`

62. Cordy, J.R.: The TXL source transformation language. Sci. Comput. Program. 61(3), 190–210 (2006), `https://doi.org/10.1016/j.scico.2006.04.002`

63. Corradini, A., Heckel, R.: Canonical derivations with negative application conditions. In: Graph Transformation - 7th International Conference, ICGT 2014, Held as Part of STAF 2014, York, UK, July 22-24, 2014. Proceedings. Lecture Notes in Computer Science, vol. 8571, pp. 207–221. Springer (2014), `https://doi.org/10.1007/978-3-319-09108-2_14`

64. Corradini, A., Heindel, T., Hermann, F., König, B.: Sesqui-pushout rewriting. In: Graph Transformations, Third International Conference, ICGT 2006, Natal, Rio Grande do Norte, Brazil, September 17-23, 2006, Proceedings. Lecture Notes in Computer Science, vol. 4178, pp. 30–45. Springer (2006)

65. Costagliola, G., De Lucia, A., Orefice, S., Tortora, G.: Positional grammars: A formalism for LR-like parsing of visual languages. In: Marriott, K., Meyer, B. (eds.) Visual Language Theory. pp. 171 – 192. Springer (1998)

66. Czarnecki, K.: Domain engineering. In: Encyclopedia of Software Engineering. Wiley (2002)

67. Czarnecki, K., Foster, J.N., Hu, Z., Lämmel, R., Schürr, A., Terwilliger, J.F.: Bidirectional transformations: A cross-discipline perspective. In: Proceedings of the 2nd International Conference on Theory and Practice of Model Transformations. pp. 260–283. ICMT '09, Springer-Verlag, Berlin, Heidelberg (2009), `http://dx.doi.org/10.1007/978-3-642-02408-5_19`

68. Czarnecki, K., Helsen, S.: Feature-based survey of model transformation approaches. IBM Systems Journal 45(3), 621–646 (2006)

69. Danos, V., Feret, J., Fontana, W., Krivine, J.: Scalable simulation of cellular signaling networks. In: Shao, Z. (ed.) Programming Languages and Systems, 5th Asian Symposium, APLAS 2007, Singapore, November 29-December 1, 2007, Proceedings. Lecture Notes in Computer Science, vol. 4807, pp. 139–157. Springer (2007), `https://doi.org/10.1007/978-3-540-76637-7_10`

70. Danos, V., Heckel, R., Sobocinski, P.: Transformation and refinement of rigid structures. In: Giese, H., König, B. (eds.) Graph Transformation - 7th International Conference, ICGT 2014, Held as Part of STAF 2014, York, UK, July

22-24, 2014. Proceedings. Lecture Notes in Computer Science, vol. 8571, pp. 146–160. Springer (2014), https://doi.org/10.1007/978-3-319-09108-2_10

71. D'Argenio, P.: Algebras and Automata for Timed and Stochastic Systems. IPA Dissertation Series 1999-10, CTIT PhD-Thesis Series 99-25, University of Twente (November 1999)

72. Di Nitto, E., Dustdar, S.: Principles of engineering service oriented systems. In: 31st International Conference on Software Engineering, ICSE 2009, May 16-24, 2009, Vancouver, Canada, Companion Volume. pp. 461–462. IEEE (2009), https://doi.org/10.1109/ICSE-COMPANION.2009.5071062

73. Diestel, R.: Graph Theory, vol. 5th ed. Springer (2017)

74. Drewes, F., Kreowski, H.J., Habel, A.: Handbook of graph grammars and computing by graph transformation. chap. Hyperedge Replacement Graph Grammars, pp. 95–162. World Scientific Publishing Co., Inc., River Edge, NJ, USA (1997), http://dl.acm.org/citation.cfm?id=278918.278927

75. Drewes, F., Hoffmann, B., Minas, M.: Formalization and correctness of predictive shift-reduce parsers for graph grammars based on hyperedge replacement. J. Log. Algebr. Meth. Program. 104, 303–341 (2019), https://doi.org/10.1016/j.jlamp.2018.12.006

76. D'Souza, D.F., Wills, A.C.: Objects, Components and Frameworks with UML: The Catalysis Approach. Addison-Wesley Longman Publishing Co., Inc., Boston, MA, USA (1999)

77. Ehrig, H., Engels, G., Kreowski, H.J., Rozenberg, G.: Handbook of Graph Grammars and Computing by Graph Transformation, Vol. 2: Applications, Languages and Tools. World Scientific (1999)

78. Ehrig, H., Kreowski, H.J.: Parallel graph grammars. In: Lindenmayer, A., Rozenberg, G. (eds.) Automata, Languages, Development, pp. 425–447. Amsterdam: North Holland (1976)

79. Ehrig, H., Kreowski, H.J., Montanari, U., Rozenberg, G. (eds.): Handbook of Graph Grammars and Computing by Graph Transformation. Vol. 3: Concurrency, Parallelism, and Distribution. World Scientific (1999)

80. Ehrig, H., Pfender, M., Schneider, H.: Graph grammars: an algebraic approach. In: 14th Annual IEEE Symposium on Switching and Automata Theory. pp. 167–180. IEEE (1973)

81. Ehrig, H.: Introduction to the algebraic theory of graph grammars (a survey). In: Graph-Grammars and Their Application to Computer Science and Biology. Lecture Notes in Computer Science, vol. 73, pp. 1–69. Springer (1979)

82. Ehrig, H., Ehrig, K., Ermel, C., Hermann, F., Taentzer, G.: Information preserving bidirectional model transformations. In: Fundamental Approaches to Software Engineering, 10th International Conference, FASE 2007, Held as Part of the Joint European Conferences, on Theory and Practice of Software, ETAPS 2007, Braga, Portugal, March 24 - April 1, 2007, Proceedings. Lecture Notes in Computer Science, vol. 4422, pp. 72–86. Springer (2007), https://doi.org/10.1007/978-3-540-71289-3_7

83. Ehrig, H., Ehrig, K., Habel, A., Pennemann, K.H.: Constraints and application conditions: From graphs to high-level structures. In: Graph Transformations, Second International Conference, ICGT 2004, Rome, Italy, September 28 - October 2, 2004, Proceedings. LNCS, vol. 3256, pp. 287–303. Springer (2004)

84. Ehrig, H., Ehrig, K., de Lara, J., Taentzer, G., Varró, D., Varró-Gyapay, S.: Termination criteria for model transformatio. In: Proc. Fundamental Approa-

ches to Software Engineering (FASE). LNCS, vol. 2984, pp. 214 – 228. Springer (2005)

85. Ehrig, H., Ehrig, K., Prange, U., Taentzer, G.: Fundamentals of Algebraic Graph Transformation. Monographs in Theoretical Computer Science. An EATCS Series, Springer (2006)

86. Ehrig, H., Ermel, C.: Semantical correctness and completeness of model transformations using graph and rule transformation. In: Proceedings of the 4th International Conference on Graph Transformations. pp. 194–210. ICGT '08, Springer-Verlag, Berlin, Heidelberg (2008), http://dx.doi.org/10.1007/978-3-540-87405-8_14

87. Ehrig, H., Ermel, C., Hermann, F., Prange, U.: On-the-fly construction, correctness and completeness of model transformations based on triple graph grammars. In: Model Driven Engineering Languages and Systems, 12th International Conference, MODELS 2009, Denver, CO, USA, October 4-9, 2009. Proceedings. Lecture Notes in Computer Science, vol. 5795, pp. 241–255. Springer (2009), https://doi.org/10.1007/978-3-642-04425-0_18

88. Ehrig, H., Habel, A., Lambers, L., Orejas, F., Golas, U.: Local confluence for rules with nested application conditions. In: Graph Transformations - 5th International Conference, ICGT 2010, Enschede, The Netherlands, September 27 - October 2, 2010. Proceedings. LNCS, vol. 6372, pp. 330–345. Springer (2010)

89. Ehrig, H., Hermann, F., Sartorius, C.: Completeness and correctness of model transformations based on triple graph grammars with negative application conditions. ECEASST 18 (2009), http://journal.ub.tu-berlin.de/index.php/eceasst/article/view/270

90. Ehrig, H., Padberg, J., Prange, U., Habel, A.: Adhesive high-level replacement systems: A new categorical framework for graph transformation. Fundam. Inform. 74(1), 1–29 (2006)

91. Ehrig, K., Küster, J.M., Taentzer, G.: Generating instance models from meta models. Software and System Modeling 8(4), 479–500 (2009)

92. EMF: Eclipse Modeling Framework. http://www.eclispe.org/emf

93. eMoflon: . https://emoflon.org/

94. Engels, G., Gall, R., Nagl, M., Schäfer, W.: Software specification using graph grammars. Computing 31, 317–346 (1983)

95. Engels, G., Hausmann, J.H., Heckel, R., Sauer, S.: Dynamic meta modeling: A graphical approach to the operational semantics of behavioral diagrams in UML. In: «UML» 2000 - The Unified Modeling Language, Advancing the Standard, Third International Conference, York, UK, October 2-6, 2000, Proceedings. Lecture Notes in Computer Science, vol. 1939, pp. 323–337. Springer (2000), https://doi.org/10.1007/3-540-40011-7_23

96. Engels, G., Heckel, R., Taentzer, G., Ehrig, H.: A combined reference model- and view-based approach to system specification. International Journal of Software Engineering and Knowledge Engineering 7(4), 457–477 (1997), http://dx.doi.org/10.1142/S0218194097000266

97. Engels, G., Hess, A., Humm, B., Juwig, O., Lohmann, M., Richter, J., Voß, M., Willkomm, J.: A method for engineering a true service-oriented architecture. In: ICEIS 2008 - Proceedings of the Tenth International Conference on Enterprise Information Systems, Volume ISAS-2, Barcelona, Spain, June 12-16, 2008. pp. 272–281 (2008)

98. Ermel, C., Rudolf, M., Taentzer, G.: The AGG approach: Language and tool environment. In: Ehrig et al. [77], pp. 551 – 601

99. Ermel, C., Gall, J., Lambers, L., Taentzer, G.: Modeling with plausibility checking: Inspecting favorable and critical signs for consistency between control flow and functional behavior. In: Fundamental Approaches to Software Engineering - 14th International Conference, FASE 2011, Held as Part of the Joint European Conferences on Theory and Practice of Software, ETAPS 2011, Saarbrücken, Germany, March 26-April 3, 2011. Proceedings. pp. 156–170 (2011), http://dx.doi.org/10.1007/978-3-642-19811-3_12

100. Ernst, M.D., Perkins, J.H., Guo, P.J., McCamant, S., Pacheco, C., Tschantz, M.S., Xiao, C.: The Daikon System for Dynamic Detection of Likely Invariants. Science of Computer Programming 69(1-3), 35–45 (Dec 2007), http://dx.doi.org/10.1016/j.scico.2007.01.015

101. Eshuis, R., Gorp, P.V.: Synthesizing object life cycles from business process models. In: Conceptual Modeling - 31st International Conference ER 2012, Florence, Italy, October 15-18, 2012. Proceedings. Lecture Notes in Computer Science, vol. 7532, pp. 307–320. Springer (2012), https://doi.org/10.1007/978-3-642-34002-4_24

102. Fischer, T., Niere, J., Torunski, L., Zündorf, A.: Story Diagrams: A New Graph Rewrite Language Based on the Unified Modeling Language and Java. In: Theory and Application of Graph Transformations, 6th International Workshop, TAGT'98, Paderborn, Germany, November 16-20, 1998, Selected Papers. Lecture Notes in Computer Science, vol. 1764, pp. 296–309. Springer (2000), https://doi.org/10.1007/978-3-540-46464-8_21

103. Fowler, M.: Refactoring – Improving the Design of Existing Code. Object Technology Series, Addison-Wesley (1999), http://martinfowler.com/books/refactoring.html

104. Fritsche, L., Kosiol, J., Schürr, A., Taentzer, G.: Efficient model synchronization by automatically constructed repair processes. In: Fundamental Approaches to Software Engineering - 22nd International Conference, FASE 2019, Held as Part of the European Joint Conferences on Theory and Practice of Software, ETAPS 2019, Prague, Czech Republic, April 6-11, 2019, Proceedings. Lecture Notes in Computer Science, vol. 11424, pp. 116–133. Springer (2019), https://doi.org/10.1007/978-3-030-16722-6_7

105. Geiß, R., Batz, G.V., Grund, D., Hack, S., Szalkowski, A.: GrGen: A Fast SPO-based Graph Rewriting Tool. In: Proceedings of the Third International Conference on Graph Transformations. pp. 383–397. ICGT'06, Springer-Verlag, Berlin, Heidelberg (2006), http://dx.doi.org/10.1007/11841883_27

106. Getir, S., Grunske, L., van Hoorn, A., Kehrer, T., Noller, Y., Tichy, M.: Supporting semi-automatic co-evolution of architecture and fault tree models. Journal of Systems and Software 142, 115–135 (2018), https://doi.org/10.1016/j.jss.2018.04.001

107. Ghamarian, A.H., de Mol, M.J., Rensink, A., Zambon, E., Zimakova, M.V.: Modelling and analysis using GROOVE. International journal on software tools for technology transfer 14(1), 15–40 (February 2012)

108. Giese, H., Hildebrandt, S.: Efficient model synchronization of large-scale models. Tech. rep. (2009)

109. Giese, H., Hildebrandt, S., Neumann, S.: Model Synchronization at Work: Keeping SysML and AUTOSAR Models Consistent, pp. 555–579. Springer Berlin Heidelberg (2010), https://doi.org/10.1007/978-3-642-17322-6_24

110. Gilb, T.: Principles of Software Engineering Management. Addison-Wesley (1988)

111. Generic Modeling Environment. `http://www.isis.vanderbilt.edu/projects/gme`

112. Golas, U., Ehrig, H., Hermann, F.: Formal specification of model transformations by triple graph grammars with application conditions. ECEASST 39 (2011), `http://journal.ub.tu-berlin.de/eceasst/article/view/646`

113. Golas, U., Lambers, L., Ehrig, H., Giese, H.: Toward Bridging the Gap between Formal Foundations and Current Practice for Triple Graph Grammars – Flexible Relations between Source and Target Elements. In: Graph Transformations – 6th International Conference, ICGT 2012, Bremen, Germany, September 24-29, 2012. Lecture Notes in Computer Science, vol. 7562, pp. 141–155. Springer (2012), `https://doi.org/10.1007/978-3-642-33654-6_10`

114. Gönczy, L., Heckel, R., Varró, D.: Model-based testing of service infrastructure components. In: Testing of Software and Communicating Systems, 19th IFIP TC6/WG6.1 International Conference, TestCom 2007, 7th International Workshop, FATES 2007, Tallinn, Estonia, June 26-29, 2007, Proceedings. Lecture Notes in Computer Science, vol. 4581, pp. 155–170. Springer

115. Greenyer, J., Kindler, E.: Comparing relational model transformation technologies: implementing query/view/transformation with triple graph grammars. Software and System Modeling 9(1), 21–46 (2010), `https://doi.org/10.1007/s10270-009-0121-8`

116. Gruschko, B., Kolovos, D., Paige, R.: Towards synchronizing models with evolving metamodels. In: Proceedings of 1st International Workshop on Model-Driven Software Evolution. pp. 1–9 (2007)

117. Guha, S., Daswani, N., Jain, R.: An Experimental Study of the Skype Peer-to-Peer VoIP System. In: Proceedings of the 5th International Workshop on Peer-to-Peer Systems (IPTPS). pp. 1–6. Santa Barbara, CA, USA (February 2006)

118. Güldali, B., Mlynarski, M., Wübbeke, A., Engels, G.: Model-based system testing using visual contracts. In: 35th Euromicro Conference on Software Engineering and Advanced Applications, SEAA 2009, Patras, Greece, August 27-29, 2009, Proceedings. pp. 121–124. IEEE Computer Society (2009)

119. GXL: Graph eXchange Language. `http://www.gupro.de/GXL/`

120. Habel, A., Heckel, R., Taentzer, G.: Graph grammars with negative application conditions. Fundam. Inform. 26(3/4), 287–313 (1996)

121. Habel, A., Pennemann, K.H.: Correctness of high-level transformation systems relative to nested conditions. Mathematical Structures in Computer Science 19(2), 245–296 (2009)

122. Habel, A., Plump, D.: Computational completeness of programming languages based on graph transformation. In: Honsell, F., Miculan, M. (eds.) Foundations of Software Science and Computation Structures. pp. 230–245. Springer, Berlin, Heidelberg (2001)

123. Habel, A., Sandmann, C., Teusch, T.: Integration of Graph Constraints into Graph Grammars, pp. 19–36. Springer International Publishing, Cham (2018), `https://doi.org/10.1007/978-3-319-75396-6_2`

124. Hans-Jörg Kreowski, Renate Klempien-Hinrichs, S.K.: Some Essentials of Graph Transformation, pp. 229–254. Springer, Berlin, Heidelberg (2006), `https://doi.org/10.1007/978-3-540-33461-3_9`

125. Hanysz, M., Hoppe, T., Uhl, A., Seibel, A., Giese, H., Berger, P., Hildebrandt, S.: Navigating across non-navigable ecore references via OCL. ECEASST 36 (2010), https://doi.org/10.14279/tuj.eceasst.36.440

126. Harel, D., Kugler, H.: Synthesizing state-based object systems from LSC specifications. Int. J. Found. Comput. Sci. 13(1), 5–51 (2002), https://doi.org/10.1142/S0129054102000935

127. Harel, D., Kugler, H.: The Rhapsody Semantics of Statecharts (or, On the Executable Core of the UML), pp. 325–354. Springer, Berlin, Heidelberg (2004), https://doi.org/10.1007/978-3-540-27863-4_19

128. Hausmann, J.H., Heckel, R., Lohmann, M.: Model-based discovery of web services. In: Proceedings of the IEEE International Conference on Web Services (ICWS'04), June 6-9, 2004, San Diego, California, USA. pp. 324–331. IEEE Computer Society (2004), https://doi.org/10.1109/ICWS.2004.1314754

129. Hausmann, J.H., Heckel, R., Lohmann, M.: Model-based development of web services descriptions enabling a precise matching concept. International Journal of Web Service Research 2(2), 67–84 (2005)

130. Hausmann, J.H., Heckel, R., Taentzer, G.: Detection of conflicting functional requirements in a use case-driven approach: A static analysis technique based on graph transformation. In: Proceedings of the 22rd International Conference on Software Engineering, ICSE 2002, 19-25 May 2002, Orlando, Florida, USA. pp. 105–115 (2002), http://doi.acm.org/10.1145/581339.581355

131. Havelund, K., Pressburger, T.: Model checking Java programs using Java PathFinder. International Journal on Software Tools for Technology Transfer 2(4), 366–381 (Mar 2000), https://doi.org/10.1007/s100090050043

132. Heckel, R.: Stochastic analysis of graph transformation systems: A case study in P2P networks. In: Van, H.D., Wirsing, M. (eds.) Proc. Intl. Colloquium on Theoretical Aspects of Computing (ICTAC'05), Hanoi, Vietnam. LNCS, vol. 3722. Springer (October 2005), invited paper

133. Heckel, R., Lajios, G., Menge, S.: Stochastic graph transformation systems. In: Ehrig, H., Engels, G., Parisi-Presicce, F., Rozenberg, G. (eds.) Proc. 2nd Intl. Conference on Graph Transformation (ICGT'04), Rome, Italy. LNCS, vol. 3256, pp. 210–225. Springer (October 2004)

134. Heckel, R.: Compositional verification of reactive systems specified by graph transformation. In: Astesiano, E. (ed.) Fundamental Approaches to Software Engineering. pp. 138–153. Springer Berlin Heidelberg (1998)

135. Heckel, R., Correia, R., Matos, C.M.P., El-Ramly, M., Koutsoukos, G., Andrade, L.F.: Architectural transformations: From legacy to three-tier and services. In: Mens, T., Demeyer, S. (eds.) Software Evolution, pp. 139–170. Springer (2008), http://dx.doi.org/10.1007/978-3-540-76440-3_7

136. Heckel, R., Küster, J.M., Taentzer, G.: Confluence of typed attributed graph transformation systems. In: Graph Transformation, First International Conference, ICGT 2002, Barcelona, Spain, October 7-12, 2002, Proceedings. Lecture Notes in Computer Science, vol. 2505, pp. 161–176. Springer (2002)

137. Heckel, R., Lajios, G., Menge, S.: Stochastic graph transformation systems. Fundam. Inform. 74(1), 63–84 (2006), http://content.iospress.com/articles/fundamenta-informaticae/fi74-1-04

138. Heckel, R., Wagner, A.: Ensuring consistency of conditional graph rewriting - a constructive approach. Electr. Notes Theor. Comput. Sci. 2, 118–126 (1995)

139. Henshin: http://www.eclipse.org/modeling/emft/henshin

140. Hermann, F., Ehrig, H., Ermel, C.: Transformation of Type Graphs with Inheritance for Ensuring Security in E-Government Networks. In: Fundamental Approaches to Software Engineering, 12th International Conference, FASE 2009, Held as Part of the Joint European Conferences on Theory and Practice of Software, ETAPS 2009, York, UK, March 22-29, 2009. Proceedings. LNCS, vol. 5503, pp. 325–339. Springer (2009)

141. Hermann, F., Ehrig, H., Ermel, C., Orejas, F.: Concurrent model synchronization with conflict resolution based on triple graph grammars. In: Fundamental Approaches to Software Engineering - 15th International Conference, FASE 2012, Held as Part of the European Joint Conferences on Theory and Practice of Software, ETAPS 2012, Tallinn, Estonia, March 24 - April 1, 2012. Proceedings. Lecture Notes in Computer Science, vol. 7212, pp. 178–193. Springer (2012), https://doi.org/10.1007/978-3-642-28872-2_13

142. Hermann, F., Ehrig, H., Orejas, F., Czarnecki, K., Diskin, Z., Xiong, Y., Gottmann, S., Engel, T.: Model synchronization based on triple graph grammars: Correctness, completeness and invertibility. Software and System Modeling 14(1), 241–269 (2015), https://doi.org/10.1007/s10270-012-0309-1

143. Hermann, F., Gottmann, S., Nachtigall, N., Ehrig, H., Braatz, B., Morelli, G., Pierre, A., Engel, T., Ermel, C.: Triple graph grammars in the large for translating satellite procedures. In: Theory and Practice of Model Transformations - 7th International Conference, ICMT 2014, Held as Part of STAF 2014, York, UK, July 21-22, 2014. Proceedings. Lecture Notes in Computer Science, vol. 8568, pp. 122–137. Springer (2014), https://doi.org/10.1007/978-3-319-08789-4_9

144. Hildebrandt, S., Lambers, L., Giese, H.: The MDELab tool framework for the development of correct model transformations with triple graph grammars. In: Proceedings of the First Workshop on the Analysis of Model Transformations, AMT@MODELS 2012, Innsbruck, Austria, October 2, 2012. pp. 33–34. ACM (2012), http://doi.acm.org/10.1145/2432497.2432504

145. Hildebrandt, S., Lambers, L., Giese, H., Rieke, J., Greenyer, J., Schäfer, W., Lauder, M., Anjorin, A., Schürr, A.: A Survey of Triple Graph Grammar Tools. ECEASST 57 (2013), http://journal.ub.tu-berlin.de/eceasst/article/view/865

146. Hoare, C.A.R.: Communicating Sequential Processes. Prentice-Hall (1985)

147. Hoffmann, B., Plump, D.: Implementing term rewriting by jungle evaluation. RAIRO Theoretical Informatics and Applications 25, 445–472 (1991)

148. Holzmann, G.J.: The Model Checker SPIN. IEEE Transactions on Software Engineering 23(5), 279–295 (May 1997), http://dx.doi.org/10.1109/32.588521

149. Hülsbusch, M., König, B., Rensink, A., Semenyak, M., Soltenborn, C., Wehrheim, H.: Showing full semantics preservation in model transformation: A comparison of techniques. In: Proceedings of the 8th International Conference on Integrated Formal Methods. pp. 183–198. Springer, Berlin, Heidelberg (2010), http://dl.acm.org/citation.cfm?id=1929463.1929477

150. Jacobson, I., Booch, G., Rumbaugh, J.E.: The Unified Software Development Process - The Complete Guide to the Unified Process from the Original Designers. Object Technology Series, Addison-Wesley (1999)

151. Janssens, D., Rozenberg, G.: On the structure of node-label controlled graph grammars. Information Science 20, 191–216 (1980)

152. Jouault, F., Allilaire, F., Bézivin, J., Kurtev, I.: ATL: A Model Transformation Tool. Science of Computer Programming 72(1–2), 31–39 (Jun 2008), http://dx.doi.org/10.1016/j.scico.2007.08.002
153. Jurack, S., Lambers, L., Mehner, K., Taentzer, G.: Sufficient criteria for consistent behavior modeling with refined activity diagrams. In: Model Driven Engineering Languages and Systems, 11th International Conference, MoDELS 2008, Toulouse, France, September 28 - October 3, 2008. LNCS, vol. 5301, pp. 341–355. Springer (2008), http://dx.doi.org/10.1007/978-3-540-87875-9_25
154. Jurack, S., Lambers, L., Mehner, K., Taentzer, G., Wierse, G.: Object flow definition for refined activity diagrams. In: Fundamental Approaches to Software Engineering, 12th International Conference, FASE 2009, Held as Part of the Joint European Conferences on Theory and Practice of Software, ETAPS 2009, York, UK, March 22-29, 2009. LNCS, vol. 5503, pp. 49–63. Springer (2009), http://dx.doi.org/10.1007/978-3-642-00593-0_4
155. Kastenberg, H., Rensink, A.: Model checking dynamic states in GROOVE. In: Model Checking Software, 13th International SPIN Workshop, Vienna, Austria, March 30 - April 1, 2006, Proceedings. Lecture Notes in Computer Science, vol. 3925, pp. 299–305. Springer (2006), https://doi.org/10.1007/11691617_19
156. Kastens, U., Schmidt, C.: VL-Eli: A generator for visual languages - system demonstration. Electr. Notes Theor. Comput. Sci. 65(3), 139–143 (2002)
157. Kehrer, T.: Calculation and Propagation of Model Changes Based on User-Level Edit Operations. Ph.D. thesis, Universität Siegen (2015)
158. Kehrer, T., Kelter, U., Taentzer, G.: A rule-based approach to the semantic lifting of model differences in the context of model versioning. In: Alexander, P., Pasareanu, C.S., Hosking, J.G. (eds.) 26th IEEE/ACM International Conference on Automated Software Engineering (ASE 2011), Lawrence, KS, USA, November 6-10, 2011. pp. 163–172. IEEE Computer Society (2011), http://dx.doi.org/10.1109/ASE.2011.6100050
159. Kehrer, T., Kelter, U., Taentzer, G.: Consistency-preserving edit scripts in model versioning. In: Denney, E., Bultan, T., Zeller, A. (eds.) 2013 28th IEEE/ACM International Conference on Automated Software Engineering, ASE 2013, Silicon Valley, CA, USA, November 11-15, 2013. pp. 191–201. IEEE (2013), http://dx.doi.org/10.1109/ASE.2013.6693079
160. Kehrer, T., Kelter, U., Taentzer, G.: Propagation of software model changes in the context of industrial plant automation. Automatisierungstechnik 62(11), 803–814 (2014), http://www.degruyter.com/view/j/auto.2014.62.issue-11/auto-2014-1102/auto-2014-1102.xml
161. Kehrer, T., Pietsch, C., Kelter, U., Strüber, D., Vaupel, S.: An adaptable tool environment for high-level differencing of textual models. In: Brucker, A.D., Egea, M., Gogolla, M., Tuong, F. (eds.) Proceedings of the 15th International Workshop on OCL and Textual Modeling co-located with 18th International Conference on Model Driven Engineering Languages and Systems (MoDELS 2015), Ottawa, Canada, September 28, 2015. CEUR Workshop Proceedings, vol. 1512, pp. 62–72. CEUR-WS.org (2015), http://ceur-ws.org/Vol-1512/paper05.pdf
162. Kehrer, T., Taentzer, G., Rindt, M., Kelter, U.: Automatically deriving the specification of model editing operations from meta-models. In: Theory and Practice of Model Transformations - 9th International Conference, ICMT 2016,

Held as Part of STAF 2016, Vienna, Austria, July 4-5, 2016, Proceedings. Lecture Notes in Computer Science, vol. 9765, pp. 173–188. Springer (2016), https://doi.org/10.1007/978-3-319-42064-6_12

163. Khan, A., Heckel, R.: Evaluating Super Node Selection and Load Balancing in P2P VoIP Networks Using Stochastic Graph Transformation. In: Obaidat, M.S., Sevillano, J.L., Filipe, J. (eds.) E-Business and Telecommunications: International Joint Conference, ICETE 2011, Seville, Spain, July 18-21, 2011, Revised Selected Papers. Communications in Computer and Information Science, vol. 314, pp. 60–73. Springer (2011), https://doi.org/10.1007/978-3-642-35755-8_5

164. Khan, A., Heckel, R.: Model-based Stochastic Simulation of Super Peer Promotion in P2P VoIP using Graph Transformation. In: Obaidat, M.S., Sevillano, J.L., Ortega, E.C. (eds.) DCNET 2011 and OPTICS 2011 - Proceedings of the International Conference on Data Communication Networking and International Conference on Optical Communication Systems, Seville, Spain, July 18-21, 2011. pp. 32–42. SciTePress (2011)

165. Khan, T.A.: Model-based testing using visual contracts. Ph.D. thesis, University of Leicester (2012)

166. Khan, T.A., Runge, O., Heckel, R.: Testing against visual contracts: Model-based coverage. In: Graph Transformations - 6th International Conference, ICGT 2012, Bremen, Germany, September 24-29, 2012. Proceedings. Lecture Notes in Computer Science, vol. 7562, pp. 279–293. Springer (2012), https://doi.org/10.1007/978-3-642-33654-6_19

167. Khan, T.A., Runge, O., Heckel, R.: Visual contracts as test oracle in AGG 2.0. ECEASST 47 (2012), http://journal.ub.tu-berlin.de/eceasst/article/view/728

168. Klop, J.W., Bezem, M., Vrijer, R.C.D. (eds.): Term Rewriting Systems. Cambridge University Press, New York, NY, USA (2001)

169. Klusch, M., Kapahnke, P., Schulte, S., Lécué, F., Bernstein, A.: Semantic Web service search: A brief survey. Künstliche Intelligenz 30(2), 139–147 (2016), https://doi.org/10.1007/s13218-015-0415-7

170. Kolovos, D.S., Paige, R.F., Polack, F.A.C.: The epsilon transformation language. In: Vallecillo, A., Gray, J., Pierantonio, A. (eds.) Theory and Practice of Model Transformations. pp. 46–60. Springer, Berlin, Heidelberg (2008)

171. König, B., Kozioura, V.: Augur 2 - A new version of a tool for the analysis of graph transformation systems. Electr. Notes Theor. Comput. Sci. 211, 201–210 (2008), https://doi.org/10.1016/j.entcs.2008.04.042

172. Königs, A., Schürr, A.: Tool integration with triple graph grammars - A survey. Electronic Notes in Theoretical Computer Science 148(1), 113–150 (2006), https://doi.org/10.1016/j.entcs.2005.12.015

173. Krause, C., Giese, H.: Probabilistic graph transformation systems. In: Ehrig, H., Engels, G., Kreowski, H., Rozenberg, G. (eds.) Graph Transformations - 6th International Conference, ICGT 2012, Bremen, Germany, September 24-29, 2012. Proceedings. Lecture Notes in Computer Science, vol. 7562, pp. 311–325. Springer (2012), https://doi.org/10.1007/978-3-642-33654-6_21

174. Krause, C., Neumann, S.: Instance-aware Model Checking of Graph Transformation Systems using - and mCRL2 (2012), www.eclipse.org/modeling/emft/henshin/documents/henshin_mcrl2.pdf

175. Krenn, W., Aichernig, B.K.: Test case generation by contract mutation in spec#. Electr. Notes Theor. Comput. Sci. 253(2), 71–86 (2009)

176. Krivine, J., Danos, V., Benecke, A.: Modelling Epigenetic Information Maintenance: A Kappa Tutorial. In: Bouajjani, A., Maler, O. (eds.) Computer Aided
Verification: 21st International Conference, CAV 2009, Grenoble, France, June
26 - July 2, 2009. Proceedings. Lecture Notes in Computer Science, vol. 5643,
pp. 17–32. Springer (2009), https://doi.org/10.1007/978-3-642-02658-4_3

177. Kurtev, I.: State of the Art of QVT: A Model Transformation Language Standard. In: Schürr, A., Nagl, M., Zündorf, A. (eds.) Applications of Graph Transformations with Industrial Relevance: Third International Symposium, AG-
TIVE 2007, Kassel, Germany, October 10–12, 2009, Revised Selected and Invited Papers, LNCS, vol. 5088, pp. 377–393. Springer, Berlin, Heidelberg (2008),
http://dx.doi.org/10.1007/978-3-540-89020-1_26

178. Kurtev, I., Bézivin, J., Aksit, M.: Technological spaces: An initial appraisal.
In: International Symposium on Distributed Objects and Applications, DOA
2002 (2002)

179. Kuske, S.: Transformation Units—A Structuring Principle for Graph Transformation Systems. Ph.D. thesis, University of Bremen (2000)

180. Kwiatkowska, M., Norman, G., Parker, D.: PRISM 4.0: Verification of probabilistic real-time systems. In: Gopalakrishnan, G., Qadeer, S. (eds.) Proceedings
of 23rd International Conference on Computer Aided Verification (CAV'11).
LNCS, vol. 6806, pp. 585–591. Springer (2011)

181. Lamancha, B.P., Polo, M., Caivano, D., Piattini, M., Visaggio, G.: Automated
generation of test oracles using a model-driven approach. Inf. Softw. Technol.
55(2), 301–319 (Feb 2013), http://dx.doi.org/10.1016/j.infsof.2012.08.
009

182. Lambers, L., Born, K., Kosiol, J., Strüber, D., Taentzer, G.: Granularity of
conflicts and dependencies in graph transformation systems: A two-dimensional
approach. Journal of Logical and Algebraic Methods in Programming 103, 105–
129 (2019), https://doi.org/10.1016/j.jlamp.2018.11.004

183. Lambers, L., Born, K., Orejas, F., Strüber, D., Taentzer, G.: Initial conflicts
and dependencies: Critical pairs revisited. In: Graph Transformation, Specifications, and Nets - In Memory of Hartmut Ehrig. Lecture Notes in Computer
Science, vol. 10800, pp. 105–123. Springer (2018), https://doi.org/10.1007/
978-3-319-75396-6_6

184. Lambers, L., Ehrig, H., Orejas, F.: Efficient conflict detection in graph transformation systems by essential critical pairs. Electr. Notes Theor. Comput. Sci.
211, 17–26 (2008)

185. Lambers, L., Ehrig, H., Taentzer, G.: Sufficient criteria for applicability and
non-applicability of rule sequences. ECEASST 10 (2008), http://eceasst.cs.
tu-berlin.de/index.php/eceasst/article/view/139

186. Lambers, L., Strüber, D., Taentzer, G., Born, K., Huebert, J.: Multi-granular
conflict and dependency analysis in software engineering based on graph transformation. In: Proceedings of the 40th International Conference on Software
Engineering. pp. 716–727. ICSE '18, ACM, New York, NY, USA (2018),
http://doi.acm.org/10.1145/3180155.3180258

187. Lambers, L., Weber, J.H. (eds.): Graph Transformation - 11th International
Conference, ICGT 2018, Held as Part of STAF 2018, Toulouse, France, June 25-
26, 2018, Proceedings, Lecture Notes in Computer Science, vol. 10887. Springer
(2018), https://doi.org/10.1007/978-3-319-92991-0

188. de Lara, J., Guerra, E., Boronat, A., Heckel, R., Torrini, P.: Domain-specific discrete event modelling and simulation using graph transformation. Software and System Modeling 13(1), 209–238 (2014), https://doi.org/10.1007/s10270-012-0242-3

189. de Lara, J., Vangheluwe, H.: Defining visual notations and their manipulation through meta-modelling and graph transformation. Journal of Visual Languages & Computing 15(3), 309 – 330 (2004), http://www.sciencedirect.com/science/article/pii/S1045926X04000138

190. Leblebici, E., Anjorin, A., Fritsche, L., Varró, G., Schürr, A.: Leveraging incremental pattern matching techniques for model synchronisation. In: Graph Transformation - 10th International Conference, ICGT 2017, Held as Part of STAF 2017, Marburg, Germany, July 18-19, 2017, Proceedings. Lecture Notes in Computer Science, vol. 10373, pp. 179–195. Springer (2017), https://doi.org/10.1007/978-3-319-61470-0_11

191. Leblebici, E., Anjorin, A., Schürr, A.: Inter-model consistency checking using triple graph grammars and linear optimization techniques. In: Fundamental Approaches to Software Engineering - 20th International Conference, FASE 2017, Held as Part of the European Joint Conferences on Theory and Practice of Software, ETAPS 2017, Uppsala, Sweden, April 22-29, 2017, Proceedings. Lecture Notes in Computer Science, vol. 10202, pp. 191–207. Springer (2017), https://doi.org/10.1007/978-3-662-54494-5_11

192. Leblebici, E., Anjorin, A., Schürr, A., Hildebrandt, S., Rieke, J., Greenyer, J.: A comparison of incremental triple graph grammar tools. ECEASST 67 (2014), http://journal.ub.tu-berlin.de/eceasst/article/view/939

193. Leblebici, E., Anjorin, A., Schürr, A., Taentzer, G.: Multi-amalgamated triple graph grammars: Formal foundation and application to visual language translation. J. Vis. Lang. Comput. 42, 99–121 (2017), https://doi.org/10.1016/j.jvlc.2016.03.001

194. Lohmann, M., Mariani, L., Heckel, R.: A model-driven approach to discovery, testing and monitoring of web services. In: Baresi, L., Di Nitto, E. (eds.) Test and Analysis of Web Services, pp. 173–204. Springer (2007), https://doi.org/10.1007/978-3-540-72912-9_7

195. Lohmann, M., Sauer, S., Engels, G.: Executable visual contracts. In: VL-HCC '05: Proceedings of the 2005 IEEE Symposium on Visual Languages and Human-Centric Computing. pp. 63–70. IEEE Computer Society, Washington, DC, USA (2005)

196. Löwe, M.: Algebraic approach to single-pushout graph transformation. Theoretical Computer Science 109, 181–224 (1993)

197. Mantz, F., Taentzer, G., Lamo, Y., Wolter, U.: Co-evolving meta-models and their instance models: A formal approach based on graph transformation. Sci. Comput. Program. 104, 2–43 (2015), https://doi.org/10.1016/j.scico.2015.01.002

198. Mariani, L.: Fault-tolerant routing for P2P systems with unstructured topology. In: 2005 IEEE/IPSJ International Symposium on Applications and the Internet (SAINT 2005), 31 January - 4 February 2005, Trento, Italy. pp. 256–263. IEEE Computer Society (2005), https://doi.org/10.1109/SAINT.2005.30

199. Marriott, K., Meyer, B.: Visual Language Theory. Springer (1998)

200. Marsan, M.A.: Stochastic Petri nets: An elementary introduction. In: Rozenberg, G. (ed.) Advances in Petri Nets 1989. pp. 1–29. Springer, Berlin, Heidelberg (1990)

201. Martin, D., Paolucci, M., McIlraith, S., Burstein, M., McDermott, D., McGuinness, D., Parsia, B., Payne, T., Sabou, M., Solanki, M., Srinivasan, N., Sycara, K.: Bringing semantics to Web services: The OWL-S approach. In: Proceedings of the First International Workshop on Semantic Web Services and Web Process Composition (SWSWPC 2004), July 6-9, 2004, San Diego, California, USA. (2004)

202. Maximova, M., Giese, H., Krause, C.: Probabilistic timed graph transformation systems. In: de Lara, J., Plump, D. (eds.) Graph Transformation - 10th International Conference, ICGT 2017, Held as Part of STAF 2017, Marburg, Germany, July 18-19, 2017, Proceedings. Lecture Notes in Computer Science, vol. 10373, pp. 159–175. Springer (2017), `https://doi.org/10.1007/978-3-319-61470-0_10`

203. mCRL2: Analysing system behaviour. `http://mcrl2.org`

204. Mehlhorn, K., Sanders, P.: Algorithms and Data Structures: The Basic Toolbox. Springer (2008)

205. Mehner, K., Monga, M., Taentzer, G.: Analysis of aspect-oriented model weaving. Transactions on Aspect-Oriented Software Development 5, 235–263 (2009), `http://dx.doi.org/10.1007/978-3-642-02059-9_7`

206. Mehner-Heindl, K., Monga, M., Taentzer, G.: Analysis of aspect-oriented models using graph transformation systems. In: Aspect-Oriented Requirements Engineering, pp. 243–270. Springer (2013), `http://dx.doi.org/10.1007/978-3-642-38640-4_13`

207. Mellor, S.J., Balcer, M.J.: Executable UML: A Foundation for Model-Driven Architecture. Object Technology Series, Addison-Wesley (2002)

208. Mens, T., Taentzer, G., Runge, O.: Analysing refactoring dependencies using graph transformation. Software and System Modeling 6(3), 269–285 (2007)

209. Mens, T., Van Gorp, P.: A taxonomy of model transformation. Electron. Notes Theor. Comput. Sci. 152, 125–142 (Mar 2006), `http://dx.doi.org/10.1016/j.entcs.2005.10.021`

210. Meta-Tools: Marama. `http://wiki.auckland.ac.nz/display/csidst`

211. MetaEdit+: `http://www.metacase.com`

212. Meyer, B.: Object-Oriented Software Construction, 2nd Edition. Prentice-Hall (1997)

213. Minas, M.: Diagram editing with hypergraph parser support. In: Proceedings of the 1997 IEEE Symposium on Visual Languages (VL '97). pp. 230–237. VL '97, IEEE Computer Society, Washington, DC, USA (1997), `http://dl.acm.org/citation.cfm?id=832278.834445`

214. Minas, M.: Hypergraphs as a uniform diagram representation model. In: Theory and Application of Graph Transformations, 6th International Workshop, TAGT'98, Paderborn, Germany, November 16-20, 1998, Selected Papers. Lecture Notes in Computer Science, vol. 1764, pp. 281–295. Springer (1998), `https://doi.org/10.1007/978-3-540-46464-8_20`

215. Mohagheghi, P., Dehlen, V., Neple, T.: Definitions and approaches to model quality in model-based software development - A review of literature. Information & Software Technology 51(12), 1646–1669 (2009), `http://dx.doi.org/10.1016/j.infsof.2009.04.004`

216. de Mol, M., Rensink, A.: On a graph formalism for ordered edges. ECEASST 29 (2010), `http://journal.ub.tu-berlin.de/index.php/eceasst/article/view/417`

217. Molloy, M.K.: On the Integration of Delay and Throughput Measures in Distributed Processing Models. Ph.D. thesis, University of California (1981)
218. Naeem, M., Heckel, R., Orejas, F., Hermann, F.: Incremental service composition based on partial matching of visual contracts. In: Fundamental Approaches to Software Engineering, 13th International Conference, FASE 2010, Held as Part of the Joint European Conferences on Theory and Practice of Software, ETAPS 2010, Paphos, Cyprus, March 20-28, 2010. Proceedings. Lecture Notes in Computer Science, vol. 6013, pp. 123–138. Springer (2010), https://doi.org/10.1007/978-3-642-12029-9_9
219. Nagl, M.: On the relation between graph grammars and graph l-systems. In: Fundamentals of Computation Theory. pp. 142–151. Springer, Berlin, Heidelberg (1977)
220. Nagl, M.: A tutorial and bibliographical survey on graph grammars. In: Graph-Grammars and Their Application to Computer Science and Biology, International Workshop, Bad Honnef, October 30 - November 3, 1978. LNCS, vol. 73, pp. 70–126. Springer (1978)
221. Najumudheen, E.S.F., Mall, R., Samanta, D.: A dependence graph-based test coverage analysis technique for object-oriented programs. In: Proceedings of the 2009 Sixth International Conference on Information Technology: New Generations. pp. 763–768. IEEE Computer Society, Washington, DC, USA (2009), https://doi.org/10.1109/ITNG.2009.284
222. Nassar, N., Kosiol, J., Arendt, T., Taentzer, G.: OCL2AC: Automatic Translation of OCL Constraints to Graph Constraints and Application Conditions for Transformation Rules. In: Lambers and Weber [187], pp. 171–177, https://doi.org/10.1007/978-3-319-92991-0_11
223. Natkin, S.: Les Roseaux de Petri Stochastiques et leur Application a l'Evaluation des Systemes Informatiques. Ph.D. thesis, CNAM Paris (1980)
224. Norris, J.R.: Markov Chains. Cambridge University Press (1997)
225. Nuseibeh, B., Kramer, J., Finkelstein, A.: A framework for expressing the relationships between multiple views in requirements specification. IEEE Trans. Softw. Eng. pp. 760–773 (1994)
226. OCL: Object Constraint Language, Version 2.2, http://www.omg.org/spec/OCL/2.2/
227. Orejas, F.: Symbolic graphs for attributed graph constraints. Journal of Symbolic Computation 46(3), 294–315 (2011), https://doi.org/10.1016/j.jsc.2010.09.009
228. Peng, X., Lu, L.: A new approach for session-based test case generation by ga. In: 2011 IEEE 3rd International Conference on Communication Software and Networks. pp. 91–96 (May 2011)
229. Pennemann, K.H.: Development of Correct Graph Transformation Systems. Ph.D. thesis, Department für Informatik, Universität Oldenburg, Oldenburg (2009), http://formale-sprachen.informatik.uni-oldenburg.de/~skript/fs-pub/diss_pennemann.pdf, Electronic Dissertation
230. Plump, D.: Critical Pairs in Term Graph Rewriting. In: Mathematical Foundations of Computer Science. LNCS, vol. 841, pp. 556–566 (1994)
231. Plump, D.: Termination of graph rewriting is undecidable. Fundamenta Informaticae 33(2), 201–209 (1998)
232. Plump, D.: Term Graph Rewriting. In: Handbook of Graph Grammars and Computing by Graph Transformation, vol. 2: Applications, Languages and Tools, pp. 3–61. World Scientific (1999)

233. Plump, D.: Essentials of term graph rewriting. Electr. Notes Theor. Comput. Sci. 51, 277–289 (2001), https://doi.org/10.1016/S1571-0661(04)80210-X

234. Plump, D.: The Graph Programming Language GP. In: Algebraic Informatics, Third International Conference, CAI 2009, Thessaloniki, Greece, May 19-22, 2009, Proceedings. Lecture Notes in Computer Science, vol. 5725, pp. 99–122. Springer (2009)

235. Plump, D.: Checking graph-transformation systems for confluence. ECEASST 26 (2010), http://journal.ub.tu-berlin.de/index.php/eceasst/article/view/367

236. Plump, D.: Modular termination of graph transformation. In: Heckel, R., Taentzer, G. (eds.) Graph Transformation, Specifications, and Nets - In Memory of Hartmut Ehrig. Lecture Notes in Computer Science, vol. 10800, pp. 231–244. Springer (2018), https://doi.org/10.1007/978-3-319-75396-6_13

237. Priami, C.: Stochastic π-calculus. Computer Journal 38(7), 578–589 (1995)

238. Radke, H.: HR* Graph Conditions Between Counting Monadic Second-Order and Second-Order Graph Formulas. ECEASST 61 (2013), http://journal.ub.tu-berlin.de/eceasst/article/view/831

239. Radke, H., Arendt, T., Becker, J.S., Habel, A., Taentzer, G.: Translating essential OCL invariants to nested graph constraints for generating instances of meta-models. Science of Computer Programming 152, 38–62 (2018), https://doi.org/10.1016/j.scico.2017.08.006

240. Rangel, G.: Behavioral congruences and verification of graph transformation systems with applications to model refactoring. Ph.D. thesis, Berlin Institute of Technology (2008), https://depositonce.tu-berlin.de/handle/11303/2329

241. Rangel, G., Lambers, L., König, B., Ehrig, H., Baldan, P.: Behavior preservation in model refactoring using DPO transformations with borrowed contexts. In: Ehrig, H., Heckel, R., Rozenberg, G., Taentzer, G. (eds.) Graph Transformations, 4th International Conference, ICGT 2008, Leicester, United Kingdom, September 7-13, 2008. Proceedings. LNCS, vol. 5214, pp. 242–256. Springer (2008), http://dx.doi.org/10.1007/978-3-540-87405-8_17

242. Reisig, W.: Understanding Petri Nets: Modeling Techniques, Analysis Methods, Case Studies. Springer (2013)

243. Rekers, J., Schürr, A.: Defining and parsing visual languages with layered graph grammars. Journal of Visual Language Computing 8(1), 27–55 (1997), https://doi.org/10.1006/jvlc.1996.0027

244. Rensink, A.: Representing first-order logic using graphs. In: Graph Transformations, Second International Conference, ICGT 2004, Rome, Italy, September 28 - October 2, 2004, Proceedings. LNCS, vol. 3256, pp. 319–335. Springer (2004)

245. Rensink, A.: Representing first-order logic using graphs. In: Ehrig, H., Engels, G., Parisi-Presicce, F., Rozenberg, G. (eds.) Graph Transformations. pp. 319–335. Springer, Berlin, Heidelberg (2004)

246. Rensink, A.: Explicit state model checking for graph grammars. In: Concurrency, Graphs and Models: Essays Dedicated to Ugo Montanari on the Occasion of His 65th Birthday. Lecture Notes in Computer Science, vol. 5065, pp. 114–132. Springer (2008), https://doi.org/10.1007/978-3-540-68679-8_8

247. Rensink, A., Distefano, D.: Abstract graph transformation. Electronic Notes in Theoretical Computer Science 157(1), 39–59 (2006), http://www.sciencedirect.com/science/article/pii/S1571066106002271, proceedings

of the Third International Workshop on Software Verification and Validation (SVV 2005)

248. Rensink, A., Schmidt, Á., Varró, D.: Model checking graph transformations: A comparison of two approaches. In: Graph Transformations, Second International Conference, ICGT 2004, Rome, Italy, September 28 - October 2, 2004, Proceedings. Lecture Notes in Computer Science, vol. 3256, pp. 226–241. Springer (2004), https://doi.org/10.1007/978-3-540-30203-2_17

249. Reussner, R.H., Goedicke, M., Hasselbring, W., Vogel-Heuser, B., Keim, J., Märtin, L. (eds.): Managed Software Evolution. Springer (2019), https://doi.org/10.1007/978-3-030-13499-0

250. Romero, J.R., Rivera, J.E., Durán, F., Vallecillo, A.: Formal and Tool Support for Model Driven Engineering with Maude. Journal of Object Technology 6(9), 187–207 (Oct 2007), http://www.jot.fm/contents/issue_2007_10/paper10.html, TOOLS EUROPE 2007 — Objects, Models, Components, Patterns

251. Rountev, A., Volgin, O., Reddoch, M.: Static Control-flow Analysis for Reverse Engineering of UML Sequence Diagrams. ACM SIGSOFT Software Engineering Notes 31(1), 96–102 (Sep 2005), http://doi.acm.org/10.1145/1108768.1108816

252. Rozenberg, G. (ed.): Handbook of Graph Grammars and Computing by Graph Transformation.: Vol. 1: Foundations. World Scientific, Singapore (1997)

253. Runge, O., Khan, T.A., Heckel, R.: Test case generation using visual contracts. ECEASST 58 (2013), http://journal.ub.tu-berlin.de/eceasst/article/view/847

254. Schmidt, Á., Varró, D.: CheckVML: A Tool for Model Checking Visual Modeling Languages. In: «UML» 2003 - The Unified Modeling Language, Modeling Languages and Applications, 6th International Conference, San Francisco, CA, USA, October 20-24, 2003, Proceedings. Lecture Notes in Computer Science, vol. 2863, pp. 92–95. Springer (2003), https://doi.org/10.1007/978-3-540-45221-8_8

255. Schmidt, C.: Generierung von Struktureditoren für anspruchsvolle visuelle Sprachen. Ph.D. thesis, Universität Paderborn (2006)

256. Schmidt, C., Kastens, U.: Implementation of visual languages using pattern-based specifications. Softw., Pract. Exper. 33(15), 1471–1505 (2003)

257. Schnelte, M., Güldali, B.: Test Case Generation for Visual Contracts Using AI Planning. In: Fähnrich, K.P., Franczyk, B. (eds.) Informatik 2010: Service Science - Neue Perspektiven für die Informatik, Beiträge der 40. Jahrestagung der Gesellschaft für Informatik e.V. (GI), Band 2, Leipzig, Germany, GI Jahrestagung (2). LNI, vol. 176, pp. 369–374. GI (2010)

258. Schürr, A.: Programmed graph replacement systems. In: Rozenberg [252], pp. 479 – 546

259. Schürr, A., Winter, A., Zündorf, A.: The PROGRES approach: Language and environment. In: Ehrig et al. [77], pp. 487–550

260. Schürr, A.: Specification of graph translators with triple graph grammars. In: Graph-Theoretic Concepts in Computer Science, 20th International Workshop, WG '94, Herrsching, Germany, June 16-18, 1994, Proceedings. Lecture Notes in Computer Science, vol. 903, pp. 151–163. Springer (1994), https://doi.org/10.1007/3-540-59071-4_45

261. Sleep, M.R., Plasmeijer, M.J., van Eekelen, M.C.J.D. (eds.): Term Graph Rewriting: Theory and Practice. Wiley, Chichester, UK (1993)

262. Society, I.C., Bourque, P., Fairley, R.E.: Guide to the Software Engineering Body of Knowledge (SWEBOK(R)): Version 3.0. IEEE Computer Society Press, Los Alamitos, CA, USA, 3rd edn. (2014)
263. Spivey, J.M.: Understanding Z: A Specification Language and Its Formal Semantics. Cambridge University Press, New York, NY, USA (1988)
264. Steinberg, D., Budinsky, F., Patenostro, M., Merks, E.: EMF: Eclipse Modeling Framework, 2nd Edition. Addison-Wesley (2008)
265. Stevens, P.: Bidirectional model transformations in QVT: semantic issues and open questions. In: Model Driven Engineering Languages and Systems, 10th International Conference, MoDELS 2007, Nashville, USA, September 30 - October 5, 2007, Proceedings. Lecture Notes in Computer Science, vol. 4735, pp. 1–15. Springer (2007), https://doi.org/10.1007/978-3-540-75209-7_1
266. Stevens, P.: Bidirectional model transformations in QVT: semantic issues and open questions. Software & Systems Modeling 9(1), 7–20 (2010), https://doi.org/10.1007/s10270-008-0109-9
267. Stevens, P.: Bidirectional transformations in the large. In: 20th ACM/IEEE International Conference on Model Driven Engineering Languages and Systems, MODELS 2017, Austin, TX, USA, September 17-22, 2017. pp. 1–11. IEEE Computer Society (2017), https://doi.org/10.1109/MODELS.2017.8
268. Taentzer, G.: Parallel and distributed graph transformation: Formal description and application to communication-based systems. Berichte aus der Informatik, Shaker (1996)
269. Taentzer, G.: Parallel high-level replacement systems. Theoretical Computer Science 186(1-2), 43–81 (1997)
270. Taentzer, G.: AGG: A graph transformation environment for modeling and validation of software. In: Applications of Graph Transformations with Industrial Relevance, Second International Workshop, AGTIVE 2003, Charlottesville, VA, USA, September 27 - October 1, 2003, Revised Selected and Invited Papers. Lecture Notes in Computer Science, vol. 3062, pp. 446–453. Springer (2003), https://doi.org/10.1007/978-3-540-25959-6_35
271. Taentzer, G.: Instance generation from type graphs with arbitrary multiplicities. ECEASST 47 (2012), http://journal.ub.tu-berlin.de/eceasst/article/view/727
272. Taentzer, G., Carughi, G.T.: A Graph-Based Approach to Transform XML Documents. In: Fundamental Approaches to Software Engineering, 9th International Conference, FASE 2006, Held as Part of the Joint European Conferences on Theory and Practice of Software, ETAPS 2006. LNCS, vol. 3922, pp. 48–62. Springer (2006)
273. Taentzer, G., Golas, U.: Towards local confluence analysis for amalgamated graph transformation. In: Graph Transformation - 8th International Conference, ICGT 2015, Held as Part of STAF 2015, L'Aquila, Italy, July 21-23, 2015. Proceedings. Lecture Notes in Computer Science, vol. 9151, pp. 69–86. Springer (2015), https://doi.org/10.1007/978-3-319-21145-9_5
274. Taentzer, G., Mantz, F., Arendt, T., Lamo, Y.: Customizable model migration schemes for meta-model evolutions with multiplicity changes. In: Model-Driven Engineering Languages and Systems - 16th International Conference, MODELS 2013, Miami, FL, USA, September 29 - October 4, 2013. Proceedings. Lecture Notes in Computer Science, vol. 8107, pp. 254–270. Springer (2013), https://doi.org/10.1007/978-3-642-41533-3_16

275. Taentzer, G., Mantz, F., Lamo, Y.: Co-transformation of graphs and type graphs with application to model co-evolution. In: Graph Transformations - 6th International Conference, ICGT 2012, Bremen, Germany, September 24-29, 2012. Proceedings. Lecture Notes in Computer Science, vol. 7562, pp. 326–340. Springer (2012), https://doi.org/10.1007/978-3-642-33654-6_22

276. Tolvanen, J.P., Rossi, M.: MetaEdit+: Defining and using domain-specific modeling languages and code generators. In: Companion of the 18th Annual ACM SIGPLAN Conference on Object-Oriented Programming, Systems, Languages, and Application, OOPSLA Companion. pp. 92–93. ACM (2003)

277. Tonella, P., Potrich, A.: Reverse Engineering of the Interaction Diagrams from C++ Code. In: Proceedings of the International Conference on Software Maintenance. pp. 159–168. IEEE Computer Society, Washington, DC, USA (2003), http://dl.acm.org/citation.cfm?id=942800.943599

278. Torrini, P., Heckel, R., Ráth, I.: Stochastic simulation of graph transformation systems. In: Rosenblum, D.S., Taentzer, G. (eds.) Fundamental Approaches to Software Engineering, 13th International Conference, FASE 2010, Held as Part of the Joint European Conferences on Theory and Practice of Software, ETAPS 2010, Paphos, Cyprus, March 20-28, 2010. Proceedings. Lecture Notes in Computer Science, vol. 6013, pp. 154–157. Springer (2010), https://doi.org/10.1007/978-3-642-12029-9_11

279. Tveit, M.S.: Meta-model-based Specification of Graphical Languages and Their Representations. Ph.D. thesis, University of Oslo (2010)

280. UML: Unified Modeling Language, http://www.uml.org

281. Utting, M., Pretschner, A., Legeard, B.: A taxonomy of model-based testing approaches. Software Testing, Verification and Reliability 22(5), 297–312 (Aug 2012), http://dx.doi.org/10.1002/stvr.456

282. Varró, D.: Automated formal verification of visual modeling languages by model checking. Software and System Modeling 3(2), 85–113 (2004), https://doi.org/10.1007/s10270-003-0050-x

283. Varró, D., Bergmann, G., Hegedüs, Á., Horváth, Á., Ráth, I., Ujhelyi, Z.: Road to a reactive and incremental model transformation platform: Three generations of the VIATRA framework. Software and System Modeling 15(3), 609–629 (2016), https://doi.org/10.1007/s10270-016-0530-4

284. Varró, D., Varró-Gyapay, S., Ehrig, H., Prange, U., Taentzer, G.: Termination Analysis of Model Transformations by Petri Nets. In: Graph Transformations, Third International Conference, ICGT 2006, Natal, Rio Grande do Norte, Brazil, September 17-23, 2006, Proceedings. LNCS, vol. 4178, pp. 260–274. Springer (2006)

285. ViaTra: https://www.eclipse.org/viatra/

286. W3C OWL Working Group: Web Ontology Language (OWL). W3C Note, W3C (2009), https://www.w3.org/OWL/

287. Weidmann, N., Anjorin, A., Fritsche, L., Varró, G., Schürr, A., Leblebici, E.: Incremental bidirectional model transformation with emoflon: : Ibex. In: Proceedings of the 8th International Workshop on Bidirectional Transformations co-located with the Philadelphia Logic Week, Bx@PLW 2019, Philadelphia, PA, USA, June 4, 2019. CEUR Workshop Proceedings, vol. 2355, pp. 45–55. CEUR-WS.org (2019), http://ceur-ws.org/Vol-2355/paper4.pdf

288. Wende, C., Thieme, N., Zschaler, S.: A role-based approach towards modular language engineering. In: Software Language Engineering, Second International

Conference, SLE 2009, Denver, CO, USA, October 5-6, 2009, Revised Selected Papers. Lecture Notes in Computer Science, vol. 5969, pp. 254–273. Springer (2010)

289. Winter, A., Kullbach, B., Riediger, V.: An Overview of the GXL Graph Exchange Language. In: Revised Lectures on Software Visualization, International Seminar. pp. 324–336. Springer, London, UK (2002), `http://dl.acm.org/citation.cfm?id=647382.724795`

290. WSDL: Web Services Description Language, Version 2.0. `http://www.w3.org/TR/wsdl20`

291. Xtext: Language Development Framework. `http://www.eclipse.org/Xtext/`

292. Xu, Z., Ke, Y., Wang, Y., Cheng, H., Cheng, J.: A model-based approach to attributed graph clustering. In: Proceedings of the 2012 ACM SIGMOD International Conference on Management of Data. pp. 505–516. ACM (2012), `http://doi.acm.org/10.1145/2213836.2213894`

293. Yazdi, H.S., Pietsch, P., Kehrer, T., Kelter, U.: Synthesizing realistic test models. Computer Science - Research and Development 30(3-4), 231–253 (2015), `http://dx.doi.org/10.1007/s00450-014-0255-y`

294. Zhao, C., Kong, J., Zhang, K.: Program behavior discovery and verification: A graph grammar approach. IEEE Transactions on Software Engineering 36(3), 431–448 (May 2010), `http://dx.doi.org/10.1109/TSE.2010.3`

295. Ziadi, T., da Silva, M.A.A., Hillah, L.M., Ziane, M.: A Fully Dynamic Approach to the Reverse Engineering of UML Sequence Diagrams. In: Proceedings of the 2011 16th IEEE International Conference on Engineering of Complex Computer Systems. pp. 107–116. IEEE Computer Society, Washington, DC, USA (2011), `https://doi.org/10.1109/ICECCS.2011.18`

296. Zündorf, A.: Rigorous Object Oriented Software Development. Habilitation, University of Paderborn (2002)

Index

© Springer Nature Switzerland AG 2020
R. Heckel, G. Taentzer, *Graph Transformation for Software Engineers*,
https://doi.org/10.1007/978-3-030-43916-3

Printed in the United States
by Baker & Taylor Publisher Services